TASCOSA

TASCOSA

Its Life and Gaudy Times

FREDERICK NOLAN

TEXAS TECH UNIVERSITY PRESS

This book is typeset in Plantin. The paper used in this book meets the minimum
requirements of ANSI/NISO Z39.48-1992 (R1997).

Book design and composition by Mark McGarry,
Texas Type & Book Works

The author and Texas Tech University Press
gratefully acknowledge the M. K. Brown Foundation of Pampa, Texas, whose generous
and timely support helped make publication of this book possible.

Library of Congress Cataloging-in-Publication Data
Nolan, Frederick W., 1931–
Tascosa : its life and gaudy times / Frederick Nolan.
p. cm.
Summary: "The ranching boom of the 1880s made the Texas Panhandle town
of Tascosa 'the cowboy capital of the world.' Through it passed many
people, good and bad, who made history in the West. Yet when the large
ranches broke up, Tascosa disappeared as quickly as it had risen"
—Provided by publisher.
Includes bibliographical references and index.
ISBN 13 : 978-1-68283-028-4 (: alk. paper)
ISBN 10 : 1-68283-028-4 (: alk. paper)
1. Tascosa (Tex.)—History. 2. Tascosa (Tex.)—Social life and customs.
3. Ranch life—Texas—Tascosa—History—19th century.
4. Frontier and pioneer life—Texas—Tascosa.
5. Tascosa (Tex.)—Biography. I. Title.
F394.T17N65 2007
976.4'824—dc22   2006037486

07 08 09 10 11 12 13 14 15 / 9 8 7 6 5 4 3 2 1

Texas Tech University Press
Box 41037
Lubbock, Texas 79409-1037 USA
800.832.4042
ttup@ttu.edu
www.ttup.ttu.edu

Dedicated to
J. Evetts Haley
without whose untiring research
this story could never have been told
and to
Evetts Haley, Jr.,
who saved it for us.

CONTENTS

ACKNOWLEDGMENTS

Mr. Hemingway once said writing is a lonely business, but many of us grassroots historians often find the opposite is true—that because of what we are writing, and as we write it, we are regularly and happily in touch with a whole address-book-full of new correspondents, fellow writers, archivists, genealogists, and researchers—and loneliness is the least of our problems. At the end of the task, however, comes the day when the writer realizes how deeply he is indebted to all the friends from whom he asked favors, of all the historians from whom he solicited information, all the archives he pestered and the libraries he raided, the small-town museums whose staff he stressed out with his questions, the amateur photographers who went to so much trouble to try to provide him with pictures of pictures, and so many others . . . Well, that day is here, and it is now not only my duty but my very great pleasure to be able to publicly and (I hope) comprehensively thank everyone who helped me put together the story that lies between the covers of this book. Gentlemen, ladies, friends, colleagues, I thank you. I think I can confidently and authoritatively say that I could never have done it without you.

Wayne Ahr, College Station, TX
Bob Alexander, Maypearl, TX
Dulcinea R. Almager, Panhandle-Plains Historical Museum, Canyon, TX
Kenneth R. Bailey, West Virginia Historical Society, Charleston, WV
Debbie Baxter, Montgomery County Clerk's Office, Mount Ida, AR
Bob Boze Bell, Cave Creek, AZ
The late Alice Blakestad, Hondo, NM
Charlotte Killen Borden, Leighton, AL
James Bradshaw, Haley History Center, Midland, TX
Jennifer Sherwood Braswell, Macon, GA
Donaly Brice, Texas State Archives, Austin, TX
Max Brown, Saint Jo, TX
Quincy Brown, Potter County District Clerk's Office, Amarillo, TX
Don Bullis, Rio Rancho, NM
Betty L. Bustos, Panhandle-Plains Historical Museum, Canyon, TX
Jean Carefoot, Texas State Library & Archives Commission, Austin, TX
Kenneth S. Carlson, State Archives Division, Providence, RI

ACKNOWLEDGMENTS

Wanda Carnell, Fort Sumner, NM

Kathy Carter, Fayette County Heritage Museum & Archive, Flatonia, TX

Karl Clifford, Lubbock, TX

Jeanette Coaly, Hollis, OK

Lois Cochran, Records Coordinator, Cleburne, TX

Billy Charles Cummings, Enid, OK

Sharon Cunningham, Union City, TN

David Dary, Norman, OK

Robert G. DeArment, Sylvania, OH

Carolyn DeBus, Fredericksburg, TX

Jan Devereaux, Maypearl, TX

James H. Earle, College Station, TX

Conley L. Edwards, State Archivist, Library of Virginia, Richmond, VA

Harold L. Edwards, Bakersfield, CA

Brenda Lincke Fisseler, Hallettsville, TX

Elvis Fleming, Roswell, NM

Crystal Flores, Potter County District Clerk's Office, Amarillo, TX

Marsha Field Foster, Plano, TX

Craig Fouts, San Diego, CA

Elizabeth E. Freeman, Del City, OK

Miles Gilbert, Jr., Show Low, AZ

Drew Gomber, Lincoln, NM

Jim Gordon, Glorieta, NM.

Len Gratteri, Hillsboro, OR

Rob Groman, Amarillo Public Library, Amarillo, TX

Becky Groneman, Oldham County and District Clerk, Vega, TX

Evetts Haley, Jr., Midland, TX

Sherman Harriman, Cal Farley's Boys Ranch, Tascosa, TX

Carl Hallberg, Wyoming State Archives, Cheyenne, WY

James R. Hewitt, Roseburg, OR

Frank Hilton, Brownwood, TX

Chuck Hornung, Odessa, TX

Melissa Horton, Garland County Clerk's Office, Hot Springs, AR

Jed Howard, Southeastern New Mexico Historical Society, Carlsbad, NM

Sandra Jaramillo, State Records Center and Archives, Santa Fe, NM

David Johnson, Zionsville, OH

Sherri Jones, Wheeler County District Clerk, Wheeler, TX

Janelle Kerr, Coryell Museum, Gatesville, TX

Harold Kilmer, Clovis, NM

Bob Kingston, Oregon Historical Society, Portland, OR

Dan and Eileen Larson, Denver, CO

Kim Layton, Donley County Clerk's Office, Clarendon, TX

Sammie Townsend Lee, Dallas Public Library, Dallas, TX

Lucille A. Martinez, State Records Center & Archives, Santa Fe, NM

Dennis McCown, Austin, TX

Robert G. McCubbin, Santa Fe, NM

Pat McDaniel, Haley History Center, Midland, TX

Alicia McDonald, Fayette County Heritage Museum and Archive, Flatonia, TX

Diane McElwaine, Ford County District Clerk's Office, Dodge City, KS

Leon C. Metz, El Paso, TX

Alan Miller, St. Jo, TX

Karen Mills, Lincoln County Clerk's Office, Carrizozo, NM

Elizabeth Murray, London, England

Roger Myers, Larned, KS

Dr. Morgan Nelson, Roswell, NM

Jane R. Newton, Forsyth, GA

Lt. Col. Phillip G. Nickell, Las Cruces, NM

Dr. Michael Olson, NM Highlands University, Las Vegas, NM

Nicky Olson, XIT Museum, Dalhart, TX

Roy M. Rutherford, Claude, TX

Arthur Olivas, Museum of New Mexico, Santa Fe, NM

Janelle Osborn, San Diego, CA

Chuck Parsons, Luling, TX

Carlian Massingill Pittman, Hamilton, TX

Lanita Rasak, Corona, NM

Joe Reck, Armstrong County and District Clerk, Claude, TX

Joyce Rein, Farmington, NM

Rachel Roberts, Dallas County Historical Society, Dallas, TX

Nancy Robertson, Raton, NM

Melissa Salazar, State Records Center & Archives, Santa Fe, NM

Nancy Samuelson, Sacramento, CA

Donald F. Schofield, Amarillo, TX

Janice Scott, Kansas Heritage Centre, Dodge City, KS

William B. Secrest, Fresno, CA

Jim Sherer, Kansas Heritage Center, Dodge City, KS

Dan Slagle, Clay County District Clerk, Henrietta, TX

Gregory Scott Smith, Coronado State Monument, NM

Rod Smith, Albuquerque, NM

Zoe Smith, Tulia, TX

Frank Sprague, Hamilton, TX

Jennifer Spurrier, Texas Tech. University Library, Lubbock, TX

Jamie Steinhauser, Arnim Archives and Museum, Flatonia, TX

Karen and John Tanner, Fallbrook, CA

Susan Taylor, Probate Judge, Camilla, GA

Greg Thomas, Amarillo Public Library, Amarillo, TX

Fay Vargas, Donley District and County Clerk, Clarendon, TX

Evelyn Waterscheid, Cooke County Clerk, Gainesville, TX

Lisa H. Watson, Wichita County Archives, Wichita Falls, TX

Elreeta Weathers, Hamilton, TX

Dave Webb, Kansas Heritage Center, Dodge City, KS

Freida Wells, Sedan, KS

Alan Westby, Alta Loma, CA

Michael E. Winter, Beebe, AR

Caroline Woodburn, Potter County District Clerk's Office, Amarillo, TX

Sharon Wright, River Valley Pioneer Museum, Canadian, TX

INTRODUCTION

TASCOSA: YESTERDAY, TODAY

I T WAS ALWAYS a cruel land.
"Not a tree, shrub, or any other object, either animate or inanimate, relieved the dreary monotony of the prospect; it was a vast, illimitable expanse of desert prairie . . . in other words, the Great Zahara of North America," wrote Randolph B. Marcy in 1840. "It is a region almost as vast and trackless as the ocean—a land where no man, either savage or civilized, permanently abides; it spreads forth into a treeless, desolate waste of uninhabited solitude, which always has been, and must continue, uninhabited forever; even the savages dare not venture to cross it except at two or three places, where they know water can be found."

Of all the regions of Texas to be settled, this "Great Sahara," the vast stretch of land called the Panhandle, was the last. From the time of the earliest Paleo-Indians, through the sixteenth century, when Coronado and Juan de Oñate first explored it, to the nineteenth, when the first Anglo-Americans belatedly discovered it, as revolutions and wars ravaged the civilized world, as kingdoms and empires rose and fell, nothing moved across it but its in-digenous wildlife and a few daring hunters. Until as recently as 1870 it was largely a desolate wilderness supporting hardly any human life at all; it was and to a great extent remains—especially in Oldham County—bleak and underpopulated, with a topography that discourages all but the most determined exploration and wayward weather that seems sometimes spitefully extreme. Drought is now, and has always been, a constant threat and a continuing influence upon its history.

It always was a cruel land. In many ways it still is.

"Imagine yourself . . . standing in a plain to which your eye can see no bounds," wrote trapper Albert Pike. "Not a tree, nor a bush, not a tall weed lifts its head above the barren grandeur of the desert; not a stone is to be seen on its hard beaten surface; no undulation, no abruptness, no break to relieve the monotony . . . its still, unmoved, calm, stern, almost self-confident grandeur, its strange power of deception, its want of echo and in fine, its power of throwing a man back upon himself and giving him a feeling of lone helplessness, strangely mingled at the same time with a feeling of liberty and freedom from restraint."

In this landscape the upward tilt of the Great Plains toward the Rocky Mountains is clearly visible: from maybe sixteen hundred feet above sea level in Childress County on the southeast corner the land rises sharply to forty-six hundred feet in Dallam County at the opposite, northwest corner. Apart from Amarillo and one or two other places with no-nonsense names like Hereford or Canyon or Pampa, most of its settlements boast little more than a couple of small stores, a motel, a coffee shop, and a gas station—just enough to take care of the needs of local residents and the occasional visitor. Here and there side roads still marked "FM"—the old highway code for "farm to market"—serve the principal industry of the area. Family, work, duty, and honor are things valued here; people work hard, not just on the land but also for church and school. Practical and reliable is preferred to showy and new; you can't impress these folks with your shiny fifty-thousand-dollar Lexus when they have machinery sitting in a shed outside that cost three quarters of a million dollars and gets used maybe three times a year.

Tourist attractions are few and far between in the Panhandle: apart from the mighty "Texas" extravaganza staged each summer in Palo Duro Canyon, the American Quarter Horse Heritage Center at Amarillo, or the bizarre audacity of Stanley Marsh's Cadillac Ranch, there is not a great deal to see, unless you want to watch some visitor trying to put away a four-pound steak in one sitting. In fact, there's a tired old joke that goes: What's the most popular tourist activity in Amarillo? . . . Leaving. Perhaps that's why, despite the innate friendliness and open-handed gen-

erosity of the locals (who smilingly tell you the Panhandle deer season is all year round—so long as you drive a car), comparatively few people come to the Panhandle for fun. Every twenty miles you travel is pretty much like the twenty miles you just left behind. Perhaps to some extent these facts account for why, slowly but inexorably, the population of the region—like the Great Plains country in general—is steadily falling. Old-timers will tell you it's because folks today, particularly the younger ones, no longer have the same commitment to the land and the lonely, arduous lifestyle their forebears had.

Yet, only a few generations ago hundreds of thousands of cattle dotted these empty hills and rolling plains, and fortunes were made and lost by foreign investors in the so-called beef bonanza. Escadrilles of cowboys worked from sunup to sundown, "from can-see to can't-see," on the huge ranches that had spread across the rich grassy expanses of the unpopulated plains: the LS, the LX, the LIT, the XIT, the Rocking Chair, the Frying Pan, and the Turkey Track among them. Hundreds more supplied their daily needs—mailmen and freighters, storekeepers and saloon owners, blacksmiths, undertakers, barbers, and outfitters.

And at the heart of it all, from the time the first cattlemen drove in their herds in the fall of 1876, was the adobe village that called itself the "cowboy capital of the Panhandle"—Tascosa.

It was never big; at its largest it probably had fifty buildings of one kind or another, a population of maybe three hundred souls. Yet at that apogee a quarter of a million dollars' worth of business was done annually along its single dusty street, and if it did not have its man for breakfast daily, it saw in its brief few decades of existence as gory a procession of violence and sudden death as many a town twice its size and infinitely better known.

Telling its story, however, is not easy. During its early years Tascosa was like an island lost in the middle of an unexplored ocean. Very little of what went on there was reported elsewhere or documented on the spot. Until 1881 it had no law officers, no courts, no formal government; it was a decade old before it got a newspaper. When the county seat was transferred to Vega in 1915, many of its records were burned. As a result, although the recollections of some of its early residents had been lovingly harvested and carefully transcribed, its place in history has been largely ignored.

Today, even though some road maps still show it, there is no Tascosa. There are signs, of course, and memorial plaques, and state markers that tell you where it used to be; but of Tascosa itself hardly more than a memory remains. Indeed, Oldham County, once the thriving heart of the Panhandle, today has only a couple of minor towns worth the name. In all its fifteen hundred square miles there are scarcely more than two thousand residents, half of them in Vega, the county seat. North of U.S. 40 and up State Highway 385 about twenty featureless miles is the handsome road bridge that crosses the Canadian River. As you approach it, off to the right above the sheltering old cottonwood trees can be seen a water tower and the white spire of a church that looks as if it ought to be in New England rather than these dusty Texas plains. Straddling what was once a cattle trail that straggled

Tascosa today: an aerial photo. Boot Hill is in the center foreground.
(Photograph by Brent N. Clifford)

———— ✺ ————

Tascosa today: Boys Ranch chapel.
(Author's photograph)

through Tascosa and on north to Dodge City is a concrete gateway that leads now into Cal Farley's Boys Ranch. Founded in 1939 and built of solid Colorado stone, the complex stands adjacent to the site of the old cow town, its modern buildings providing a home and a learning environment for underprivileged young people from throughout the United States.

Near the entrance, a modern pavilion with a coffee shop sells souvenirs—T-shirts, baseball caps, Boys Ranch memorabilia—and welcomes visitors. Give or take a yard or three, it stands about where on a moonlit night in 1886 four men died and two more were badly wounded in a blazing gunfight on the main street of the old town. On the north side of the wide boulevard that runs east past the church and into the settlement is the old stone Tascosa courthouse, built in 1884, and in front of it stands the endearing statue of Boys Ranch

founder Cal Farley that marks his grave and that of his wife, Mimi, who died within a month of her husband in 1967. Today the courthouse is home to a small museum created in the year Farley died, which features a somehow very touching collection of children's toys, farm tools, and furniture as well as some old photographs and a model of the old town. It is the only original Tascosa building—apart from the little wooden schoolhouse built much later out in back of it—that has survived.

East of all these, along a hummocky stretch of unmade track that used once to be part of the main trail to Dodge City, is the now overgrown cemetery laid out by New Mexican sheepherder Casimero Romero soon after his arrival in the area. A quarter of a mile or so west of the old courthouse, between the modern highway and the "town," lies another cemetery, the so-called Boot Hill. Unlike the Romero plot, this one is meticulously maintained, the names on its grave markers pristine in black and white for the benefit of those very few visitors who might know anything at all about the men who are buried there.

And that's it.

Tascosa is gone, dissolved, and blown away by the rains and winds of history. It is not even a ghost town. Almost everything that took place there has largely been forgotten, and tourists find few memorials to what was, in the words of a grizzled old Texas Ranger who had seen more than a few of them firsthand, "the hardest place on the frontier." Nothing remains of what was once a busy, thriving frontier settlement with business and residential buildings scattered over a six-block site, centered around the "plaza" at the junction of Main and Spring Streets in the "upper" end of town. But when the railroads passed it by in favor of a junction at what would become Amarillo, Tascosa was dealt an economic blow from which it never recovered. Within a few short years the *Tascosa Pioneer* had ceased publication, and two years later, after a devastating flood, the town was in ruins, already well on the way to its final demise and disappearance. The transfer of the county seat to Vega in 1915 was the coup de grâce. With its body fenced in and its heart torn out, Tascosa no longer had any reason to live.

The story of the rise and fall of Tascosa not only shadows the early boom-and-bust beginnings of the range cattle industry but is also in many ways a paradigm of the "outlaw" era of the Old West. About the time the town was getting its first growth, banditry was at high tide: the Jesse James gang was being shot to pieces at Northfield, Minnesota; Wild Bill Hickok was being assassinated at Deadwood, in Dakota Territory; the boy who would become Billy

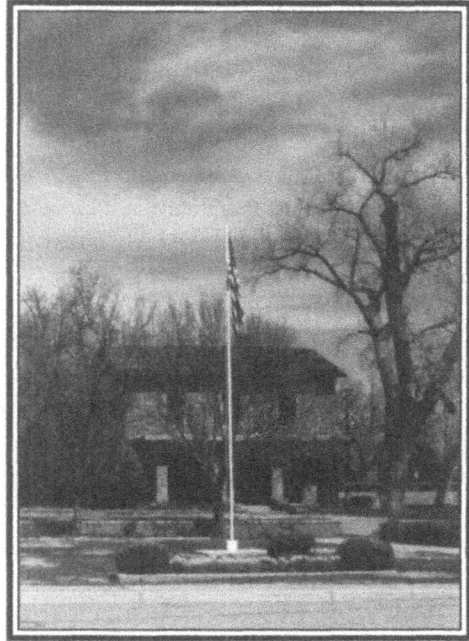

Tascosa today: the old courthouse, now the museum. (Author's photograph)

the Kid was killing his first man in Arizona Territory; and Sam Bass and his gang were taking sixty thousand dollars off a Union Pacific train at Big Springs, Nebraska. Yet, before the turn of the century, just three decades later, the town was dying, and so was the era of the long riders, outridden not only by the development and reach of the telephone, the telegraph, and photography but also by a citizenry that would no longer tolerate their lawlessness. Another decade later, both had disappeared, and the first Western movies were being made, history already turning into legend.

Visitors do come to Tascosa, but not to see the old cow town: they come to visit Cal Farleys Boy's Ranch, its pristine church spire and solid community buildings more reminiscent of a university campus than the site of a Texas hell town. Comparatively few of these visitors evince much interest in Tascosa's tumultuous half-century history. Those who do visit the site of the old town can see what there is to see in less than an hour, and in all probability most of them leave not knowing much more than they did when they arrived.

Yet, beneath their wheels as they drive away is a phantom street along which walked as amazing a collection of characters as could be found anywhere in the West: schemers and dreamers, bandits and gunfighters, cattle barons and storekeepers, tinhorn gamblers and hell-raising cowpunchers, warmhearted whores and cold-blooded killers, big men looking to make a fortune and little men looking to build a home, thrown together for a moment in time in a place that blossomed and died as if in a dream. Each of them played a part, large or small, noble or otherwise, in the brief life and gaudy times of Tascosa, Texas. It's time their story was properly told.

TASCOSA

⌇
Chapter 1
⌇

1875-1876

LAST BUFFALO, FIRST SHEEP

THE HISTORY of the life and gaudy times of Tascosa and the men and women who settled there might quite easily begin by offering tales of Francisco Vásquez de Coronado and Juan de Oñate y Salazar, those first adventurous explorers of the Llano Estacado, or of the civilian expeditions led by Josiah Gregg and William Bent or the U.S. Army explorers like Abert and Long who dubbed the endless plains "the Great American Desert." It could equally easily commence by demonstrating that a significant factor in the settlement of the area was the arrival of guileful Mexican traders who followed the trace of the early explorers in order to exchange goods with the Comanches in the years following the Civil War and who brought back to New Mexico reports of the open grasslands that lay waiting to be claimed.

Most of those early explorations, however, were simply that and no more. There was never any intention on the part of any of those early travelers to settle the country; indeed, most of them did not consider it fit to live in. Even had they done so, the complete domination of the area by Comanches, Kiowas, and Cheyennes was more than sufficient cause to deter even the hardiest would-be settler.

It was only with the coming of the buffalo hunters that "civilization"—and a pretty paltry version of it at that—crept warily into the Panhandle. They, and the merchants and factors who supplied their needs, were the first white men to venture into West Texas and the Panhandle, first to risk the fiery resistance of the Native American tribes whose hunting grounds they were invading. In their wake would come entrepreneurs and exploiters, desperadoes and daydreamers, every one of them a man with his eyes on what he thought was the main chance. And with the possible exception of the quite remarkable Charles Goodnight, no main chancer ever put a larger and more permanent mark upon the land than Wisconsin-born William McDole Lee.

The son of Portage, Wisconsin, farmer and later boardinghouse keeper Perry Lee and his wife, Esther, "Mac" Lee had left home a year or so after the 1860 death of his father and found work as a driver for Wells, Fargo in Kansas. After serving as a quartermaster in Sherman's army during the Civil War, he remained with the Department of the Missouri, supervising wagon transportation between the command's frontier outposts. On December 10, 1869, twenty-eight-year-old "Mac" Lee arrived at Camp Supply, established the preceding year in the northwestern corner of Indian Territory. His aims were to negotiate for and get—by hook or by crook, it might be fair to say—the exclusive right to trade for buffalo robes with the three thousand and more Cheyenne and Arapaho living on the nearby reservation and to provide supplies for the officers and men manning the military post. Having won this concession, he next sought to open a sutler's store, only to find himself in competition with Fort Lyon, Colorado, post sutler and Indian trader Albert Eugene Reynolds, an equally successful business-

man who had come to negotiate for the same rights. Rather than compete, they agreed to form a partnership, and thus the mighty trading firm of Lee & Reynolds was born.[1]

At this juncture there were no buffalo hunters on the West Texas plains other than the Indians, who twice yearly left the reservation to embark upon the chase. Lee & Reynolds soon set up a system by which it received buffalo robes (the Indians themselves ate all the meat they killed) in exchange for "services" the U.S. Army and the Indian Agency could not or would not provide. Short-haired summer buffalo hides were nearly always used for leather; the richly furred ones reaped in winter were the "robes" so prized on the East Coast or in Europe for fur coats, carpets, coach blankets, and much else. This trade was for a year or so a significant, although by no means major, part of the Lee & Reynolds operation . . . until fate took a hand.

In 1870 British leather manufacturers who had been experimenting with buffalo hides were sufficiently encouraged by the results to issue an order to Fort Leavenworth fur trader W. C. Lobenstein for five hundred "flint" hides. He in turn commissioned Indian traders Charles Rath and Charley Myers to fill the order. When its quartermasters found the equipment made from these hides so much superior to that made from domestic leather, contracts were issued for large quantities by the British Army. Coincident with this, tanners in Pennsylvania who had been working on hides sent east by buffalo hunter J. Wright Mooar also found a way to convert them to leather and ordered two thousand more, kick-starting the slaughter that in a few short years would render the buffalo virtually extinct.[2]

William McDole "Alphabet" Lee. (Courtesy of Ruth Sutton-Doland and Donald F. Schofield)

———— ✺ ————

Buffalo hunters' camp in the Panhandle: hides staked out,
tongues hanging from racks to air-dry. (Courtesy of the Texas State Library
and Archives Commission [Ref. 1/112-6])

In the winter of 1871 an extraordinary phenomenon occurred near Fort Dodge, Kansas. During heavy blizzards thousands and thousands of buffalo drifted into the area, and plainsmen—both experienced hunters and raw beginners—hurried there to track, kill, and skin them (apart from the hides, only tongues, hams, and humps were saved). It was estimated that during this one winter hunt, something over seventy thousand animals were killed, resulting in the virtual disappearance of the buffalo from the Kansas plains. As a direct consequence, hunters were forced to search ever farther afield—deeper, that is to say, into Indian country—to locate the herds. The older hands were able to do so successfully; those less well informed or outfitted fell on hard times.

Experienced hunters such as Billy Dixon or the brothers Josiah Wright and John Wesley Mooar, who had their own well-armed and self-sufficient outfits, ranged south across the Arkansas River, over the Cimarron, and into the Texas Panhandle looking for prey. Two hundred miles south of Dodge City, near an old trading post called Adobe Walls, established some thirty years earlier by the Bent brothers and their partner Ceran St. Vrain and scene of a November 1864 battle between the Comanches and Col. Kit Carson's volunteers, the hunters found what J. Wright Mooar poetically described as "a mobile sea of living buffalo."[3]

Toward the end of March 1874, when the hunters got back to Dodge City, their news encouraged other hunters to believe

[3]

that this might well be the time to risk the first full-scale invasion of Comancheria, as the Comanches' homeland was known. Others, however, pointed out the "well-known fact" that the Medicine Lodge Treaty of 1868 barred white men from incursions into the Indian hunting grounds south of the Arkansas. Actually, it did not: no such clause had ever been incorporated into the treaty, nor had Texas ever placed any of its public lands in the hands of the U.S. government, but the hunters were unaware of that. Accordingly, a delegation was sent to seek guidance from the commanding officer at Fort Dodge. "Major," said spokesman J. Wright Mooar, "if we cross into Texas, what will be the government's attitude toward us?" "Boys," the officer replied, "if I were a buffalo hunter, I would hunt buffalo where buffalo are!"[4]

With that the hunt was on; but the remote location of the herd presented the hide merchants with a headache. The farther away from Dodge City the hunters roamed, the more expensive became the task of freighting the hides back there. This, in an economy still severely depressed by the Panic of 1873, was a consummation devoutly to be avoided, so Charles Rath, who had moved to Dodge City and formed a mercantile partnership with local tycoon Robert M. Wright (as had his competitor Alexander Charles "Charley" Myers and a British partner Frederick J. Leonard) decided to open a trading post at Adobe Walls to outfit hunting expeditions and to buy and ship hides and meat back to Dodge.

Myers and Leonard got there first. In March 1874 their caravan of wagons—said to have been loaded with fifty thousand dollars' worth of merchandise—moved out of Dodge heading south for the old Adobe Walls site on the Canadian River—not fifty miles west of the border of the Cheyenne and Arapaho reservation. There, a stockade corral was erected, in the northeast corner of which Myers and Leonard built a log store and in the opposite corner a sod-walled and -roofed mess hall. South of the corral Tom O'Keefe put up a picket blacksmith shop; about fifty yards south of the store, Jim Hanrahan built a sod house saloon. The following month Charles Rath came in and put up his own branch store fifty yards south of Hanrahan's, with an eating house managed by Bill Olds and his wife, Hannah, at its western end. Rath's investment in goods and stock was said to be on the order of twenty thousand dollars.[5]

The reaction of Lee and Reynolds to these developments is not recorded, but they must have given serious thought to how they might most effectively neutralize so serious a threat to their monopoly. Then, at that very moment in April, Kansas horse thieves led by "Hurricane Bill" Martin ran off forty-three ponies owned by Cheyenne leader Little Robe.

The Kiowas, Comanches, and southern Cheyennes were already in a fractious mood, frustrated by being confined on reservations where they were easy prey for white horse thieves and whiskey peddlers, angered even more by the profligacy of the buffalo hunters, who were slaughtering "their" animals and leaving the carcasses to rot on the prairie. Hurricane Bill's raid was one insult too many, and they retaliated: a war party led by Little Robe's son Sitting Medicine pursued the rustlers into Kansas and in the process carried out a raid on Sun City in which Sitting Medicine was wounded.[6]

In June 1874, their thirst for revenge further inflamed by these events, a conference of Comanches led by Quanah Parker, Cheyennes led by Stone Calf, and Kiowas led by Lone Wolf assembled at Elk Creek on the north fork of the Red River, where they drank rotgut whiskey and talked of war.[7]

The flames were fanned by a Comanche shaman called Isa-tai (the name is translated in various polite forms such as "Coyote Droppings," but in blunt Comanche it was said to translate most nearly to "Wolf Shit"), who convinced the assembled leaders that "the only way for them to become the great and powerful nation they once were, was to go to war." If they wore his medicine paint, he assured them, they would find the buffalo hunters asleep in their camp and the white men's bullets would not harm them. It was enough; Quanah and the other leaders decided to burn out every white outpost south of the Kansas line, beginning with an attack on Adobe Walls.[8]

Word of their plans soon reached Lee, and it was decided that a warning should be sent to Charlie Rath. The two employees carrying the message—Jordan McAllister and scout Amos Chapman—were instructed also to check the buffalo hunters' corrals down there for stolen stock. When they reached Adobe Walls they made inquiries but—hardly surprisingly—elicited no information. Nor did the hunters evince much concern about the possibility of an Indian attack; they were far more interested in their rich harvest of hides. According to McAllister, it was a hide pile ten feet high and almost a hundred yards long.[9]

Here the matter of Lee's duplicity (Reynolds, busy with mining interests in Colorado, played no part in these events) merits close examination. His business centered on his exclusive trade in buffalo hides, and the hunters' camp was a clear threat to that monopoly. Although the Indi-

ans would probably have attacked Adobe Walls anyway, the likelihood that Lee deliberately accelerated events by suggesting to his Indian friends—one of whom was Quanah—that their stolen horses might well be found in the buffalo hunters' encampment simply cannot be ignored.[10]

At dawn on Saturday, June 27, the Indians attacked the Adobe Walls settlement, and in the battle that ensued, four white men and an unknown number of warriors were killed. "The battle lasted about three hours," Fred Leonard wrote later to his partner Myers.

> Ike Shadler [Shiedler] and [his] Brother [Jacob], Billy Tyler and Mr. Olds were killed. The latter shot himself accidentally. . . . About 25 or 30 Indians were killed—we found 11. . . . We were taken completely by surprise. Our men behaved like heroes. If the Indians had come one hour later, we would have all been killed, as [Billy] Dixon and Hanrahan and their men would have started out on a hunt, leaving the place with only 17 men and only half-armed. . . . We had 150 Indians around our place at one time. Their intention was to take the place and the hunters as they came in. All the men are of the opinion that the Indians are waiting for reinforcements and then give us another battle, but we are fixed for them.[11]

Darkness brought relief. With Quanah wounded, and discouraged by the firepower of the buffalo guns and the failure of Isa-tai's predictions, the Indians withdrew. Next day there were further brief exchanges of long-distance fire; in spite of the presence of the Indians, two wagons got in safely, one driven by George Bellfield, a former soldier, and another by the English buffalo hunter brothers Jim and

Bob Cator. As darkness fell, Henry Lease and another man (encouraged, it's said, by an offer of $125 if they took the job) volunteered to ride to Dodge for help.

The following morning another party of Indians appeared on a ridge away off to the east. Using a Sharp's "Big Fifty," Billy Dixon shot one of them out of the saddle—the range was later measured accurately as 1,538 yards, slightly less than a mile. Lucky shot it may have been, but what must have looked to the Indians like almost supernatural marksmanship convinced them that their medicine was bad, and they pulled back, although not yet entirely abandoning their intention to drive out the hunters. Sporadic raids and fighting continued, and before the end of the year the settlement was abandoned. The war the Indians had begun spread across the plains, with buffalo hunters everywhere—for by now they were, literally, everywhere—prime targets.[12]

This outbreak brought to an end the U.S. government's attempts to pacify the Indians peaceably. Military intervention was now mounted on a scale the Indians had never experienced and could never combat. The strategy was brutally simple: five columns under the overall command of Gen. Nelson A. Miles would converge more or less simultaneously on the upper reaches of the Red River, encircling the area in which the Indians were thought to be concentrated. Their quarry would be given no time to rest or hunt; their villages when found were to be immediately destroyed. No matter which direction they took, they were to be constantly pursued and harassed—even on their own reservations—until they were worn out or starved out or both.

From Fort Union, New Mexico, Maj. William Redwood Price—fresh from com-

bating a murderous outbreak of civil disturbances known as the Horrell War in Lincoln County—would lead four troops of 8th Cavalry east across the Panhandle. From Fort Sill, Indian Territory, Lt. Col. John Wynn Davidson would march westward at the head of six troops of his 10th Cavalry and three companies of 11th Infantry. At Fort Concho, Col. Ranald Slidell Mackenzie and his crack 4th Cavalry would march north supported by five companies of 10th Infantry. Lt. Col. George Pearson Buell would lead more than two hundred fifty officers and men of the 9th and 10th Cavalries and the 11th Infantry westward out of Fort Richardson, Texas, to fill in the area between Davidson and Mackenzie. Miles's own command, consisting of two battalions of the 6th Cavalry—one led by Maj. James Biddle, the

Ranald Slidell Mackenzie.
(National Archives)

other by Maj. Charles E. Compton (who a few years later would feature briefly in the saga of Billy the Kid)—and four companies of the 5th Infantry, would march south from Fort Dodge to complete the encirclement. What became known as the Red River War had begun.[13]

On August 22 troops of Davidson's command had a severe fight with a band of Comanches and Kiowas who had taken refuge among the "friendlies" at the Wichita Agency. Eight days later, Miles's column confronted some four to six hundred Cheyennes in Palo Duro Canyon and in a five-hour running fight drove them out of the canyon, forcing them to burn their village.[14]

Beginning on September 9 at Whitefish Canyon on the Washita River, a sustained attack led by Satanta of the Kiowas upon Miles's supply wagons lasted five days. During this same time frame there was another fight nearby, the Battle of Buffalo Wallow, in which two scouts and four enlisted men were surrounded by over a hundred Kiowas and Comanches and pinned down in a daylong fight. One soldier was killed and four of the defenders wounded before the Indians scattered on the approach of the column led by Maj. William Redwood Price.

As the weather turned colder and wetter, many of the dissidents, among them the bands led by Satanta, Big Tree, and Woman's Heart, lost their appetite for war and returned to the agency. But the Kwahadi Comanches led by Quanah Parker, the Kiowas under Maman-ti and Lone Wolf, and some of the Cheyennes again took refuge in Palo Duro Canyon, pitching their tipis along a two- to three-mile stretch of the Prairie Dog Town Fork of the Red River. Just before dawn on September 27, Mackenzie made a daring all-out attack on the sleeping Indian village, from which the hostiles fled in panic, allowing the soldiers to capture their entire horse herd, some 1,400 head in all. Mackenzie destroyed everything the Indians had abandoned—more than one hundred lodges, food, buffalo robes, weapons, ammunition, and anything else his troopers could find. That done, he gave orders for the extermination of most of the Indian horse herd, a total of some 1,048 animals; never in the history of Indian warfare had there been such ruthless attrition.[15]

But it worked. Although no one knew it then, this Second Battle of Palo Duro Canyon was the turning point of the Red River War, which Gen. Philip H. Sheridan would later describe as "the most successful of any Indian campaign in this country since its settlement by the whites."[16] Apart from a series of relatively minor winter skirmishes, Mackenzie's victory effectively ended Indian resistance on the southern plains.

Without horses they were unable to fight or hunt. Deprived of their homes and food, the Indians had nowhere to hide. Early in March 1875, the southern Cheyennes under Stone Calf surrendered; in June Quanah came in. Many of the ringleaders in the uprising were deported to Fort Marion, Florida.[17] The barrier to white settlement was gone, the way opened for hunters to complete their extermination of the buffalo, for sheepmen and then cattlemen to claim for their own use the vast grasslands of the Llano Estacado.

The first settlement sprang up when Nelson Miles detailed his force to establish two base camps, one in the Panhandle. The task of locating the latter fell to Pennsylvania-born Maj. James Biddle of the 6th Cavalry. Richard "Uncle Dick" Bussell was one of the buffalo hunters who happened to be there when the column arrived on May 18, 1875: "We rushed up on to a little knoll where we could get a view of the flat which lay on the other side. We saw about a hundred wagons and teams and about four hundred soldiers. They had put up a number of tents and were putting up more. They had lumber for the officers' houses, food and grain. We went up and talked to the soldiers and teamsters. Lee-Reynolds were the main sutler men at the time. . . . [T]hey opened up a saloon there in less than half an hour, I reckon, after they landed."[18]

The campsite Biddle had chosen was on a low plateau overlooking Sweetwater Creek, twenty-seven miles west of the 100th meridian, and was provisioned and garrisoned by officers and men of the 5th Infantry and 6th Cavalry. Construction of permanent facilities began in July. Stables, storehouses, and the guardhouse were built with cottonwood posts, adobe, and thatch available locally, but for the more substantial barracks and officers' quarters lumber had to be freighted in by wagon from Dodge City, 196 miles to the north.

This permanent military presence threw the Panhandle open to civilian settlement, and it was not long in coming. First to arrive were New Mexico sheepmen, not a few of them former *comancheros* familiar with the area, others who had heard about the lush grasslands and the plentiful springs along the Canadian River, perfect grazing country for sheep and free now to any man who cared to claim it.

In the spring of 1875, or perhaps even earlier, Jesús Maria Trujillo from San Miguel County in New Mexico led an expedition of immigrants into the Panhandle and settled on the south bank of the Canadian River across from the mouth of Cheyenne Creek. There he, his wife, their

Richard "Uncle Dick" Bussell.
(Courtesy of the Panhandle-Plains Historical Museum, Canyon, Texas)

four sons and three daughters, and five or six other families built the *plazita* that bore his name, a scattering of small houses and a hundred-foot-square rock corral with walls five feet high. Soon after this, Taos *pastores* Justo and Ventura Borrego led another group of families to the Canadian Valley and established a *plazita* of rock and adobe houses originally named Ventura, although most locals called it Borrego plaza.[19]

On February 21, 1876, about a hundred miles to the east, the army settlement known as Camp Cantonment was formally renamed Fort Elliott, honoring Maj. Joel H. Elliott, 7th Cavalry, killed in action during Custer's destruction of Black Kettle's village on the Washita on November 27,

1868. Here and throughout the entire area surrounding it, Lee & Reynolds—which by now had become one of the largest commercial undertakings in the Southwest—held a virtual monopoly for the supply of "food, feed, fuel, medicines, posts, all sorts of necessities. . . . Their contracts were more than all their competitors combined, and applied to [Forts] Supply, Sill and El Reno, besides Elliott," which had now been made the headquarters.[20]

Soon more buffalo hunters, their safety guaranteed by the presence of the soldiers, homed in on the area, stacking hides out on the prairie to dry. Word of the new settlement below the fort, which went by the name of Hidetown, soon spread. Freighters followed, picking up business from the hunters, hauling the hides up the trail blazed from Adobe Walls to Dodge City by merchant Charles Edward "Dirty Face" Jones and his partner, Joe Plummer.

The first permanent building at Hidetown was a rock house built by Henry Fleming on the north bank of Sweetwater Creek opposite the site of the original tent city. Fleming, who had been one of the first settlers, ran a saloon with a billiard table freighted in from Dodge; other saloonkeepers were William H. Weed, W. L. R. Dickerson, and Joe Mason. Charlie Sing, veteran Oriental launderer to the buffalo hunters of Rath City and Fort Griffin, opened up for business. Gambler and gunfighter Billy Thompson ran a dance hall. Will Weed went to Dodge City and hauled back timber with which he erected a general store and lumberyard, Hidetown's first wooden building. A former army mess sergeant, Mark Huselby, created a truck farm that supplied vegetables for the soldiers' mess hall and later brought in dairy cattle to provide milk. Former Fort Leavenworth teamster Tom O'Laughlin and his wife,

Ellen, who had come down from Dodge City with the military unit that built Fort Elliott, set up an eating house on a piece of land about halfway between the post and Hidetown. Ellen was the first white woman ever to come to the Panhandle; her son Miles was the first white child born there.[21]

In November 1876 a new group of sheepmen arrived on the Canadian, this time from Mora County in New Mexico. One of the largest parties to emigrate to the Panhandle so far, they were led by thirty-seven-year-old Casimero Romero, a former *comanchero* who owned a three-hundred-acre farm near La Junta, New Mexico, one of the largest in that area. Living with him there in 1870 were Salomé Garcia, twenty-four; an adopted niece, Maria Piedád Romero; and a fourteen-year-old Indian servant, Maria Rita. At that time Romero owned five horses, twenty-two mules and asses, twenty-five milch cows, twenty working oxen, fifty-four other cattle, nine pigs, and twenty-eight hundred sheep worth well over six thousand dollars, and he had that year reaped an annual crop of 278 bushels of spring wheat and 375 bushels of Indian corn.

In 1876, now forty-three, Romero packed all his possessions into a flotilla of twelve huge ox-drawn prairie schooners and set out along the old *comanchero* trails he knew so well, bringing with him supplies sufficient for a year's subsistence. Herded along with the caravan were some three thousand sheep plus all his horses and cattle. These, one old resident observed, were "the real Spanish people who were white as any American . . . who pride themselves on their pure Spanish blood, unmixed with Indian and Negro like the 'greaser' Mexicans, [like] old Don Casimero, whose family were all blue-eyed and fair."

Casimero Romero home at Tascosa. (Courtesy of the Amarillo Public Library)

Besides Romero; his wife, Salomé; their five-year-old son, José Ynocencia, affectionately known as "Chencho"; and Romero's adopted niece, Piedád, now twelve, there were about a dozen employees in the wagon train, some of whom brought their wives. Other Mora County families who accompanied the Romeros included those of Agapito Sandoval, with fifteen hundred sheep, and Henry Kimball, a former soldier and Fort Union blacksmith who had lived in Mora County and Las Vegas. He knew the country well, having served under Kit Carson and hunted buffalo along the Canadian in 1874.

Eugenio Romero, another of Casimero's brothers, left the main party and followed the Rita Blanca north to a westerly flowing creek called Punta de Agua, settling on a spot near where the town of Romero, named for him, now stands.

Casimero Romero continued east along the Canadian. "I remember how my father and five or six other men rode horseback up and down the river on both sides inspecting sites for the homes of the different families," Chencho Romero said. "So far as I know no other people lived along the Canadian when we came, and we saw no evidence that anyone had lived there before us."[22]

After some weeks Romero finally decided to settle near a spring-fed creek on land north of the Canadian River. The wagons in which he and his fellow *pastores* had traveled were used to form a circular enclave, with brush piled beneath and between them to form a windbreak. They wintered in this "settlement" while the men scouted for a permanent location, and when one was found, they worked for almost a year building an adobe house that was completed in 1877. This location—which its owner described as *atascosa,* or "boggy"—became the center of a thriving Mexican American sheep-raising community, its only white inhabitants blacksmith Henry Kimball and his wife, Mary.

Agapito Sandoval, his wife, two sons, and two daughters settled on Corsinio Creek, about eight miles below the Romero settlement. Kimball and his wife built a house a short distance downstream. Later, Theodore "Teddy" Briggs, his wife, Ynesa, and a daughter, Perfillia, settled about six miles west of Romero. In 1878 Mariano Montoya, Miguel and José Tafoya—the latter only a few years earlier one of the wealthiest and best known of the *comancheros*—located with their families on the Punta de Agua where it joins the Rita Blanca. Henry Kimball later relocated on the Rita Blanca above the Montoyas and Tafoyas.

Other *plazitas* were built up and down the valley of the Canadian and its tributaries. Salinas, where about twenty-five families lived, was on the New Mexico line near a large saline lake from which salt was hauled and sold; it grew into a fairly big (and very tough) settlement with a racetrack and dance hall. About five miles east of Salinas, former *cibolero* Juan Chavez picked out a spot on the south side of the Canadian that later took his name and built a half dozen houses and a chapel. "The Mexicans had sheep and cattle there," Jim East said, "and used to hunt buffalo down in the Panhandle and trade with the Indians for stolen stock." Other settlements and *plazitas* included Juan Domingo, Ortega, Tecolote, and Valdez.

By this time, thousands of sheep were grazing on the prairie, guarded from prowling wolves and coyotes by armed *peones* and dogs that drove them at night into the sturdy rock corrals that had been built to protect them. At that time the Canadian was a narrow, deep stream, no more than twenty feet wide, running with cold, clear water. Its banks were lined with plum bushes, and the whole valley was covered with tall grass. Fish were abundant in the river, wild fruit everywhere on the trees, game plentiful on the plains and in the canyons—even the occasional buffalo, although by that time most of them were gone. At each *plazita* there would be a *baile* on Saturday nights, parties and games on feast days, an occasional visit from a traveling priest, who would conduct baptisms and marriages and say prayers for the living and the dead.

Life in these *plazitas* was as timeless, as imbued with the *mañana* spirit, as it had been on the high plains of New Mexico. Their inhabitants "led a quiet, placid existence, nothing to bother them except possibly a band of marauding Apache Indians. They had few wants, which were easily supplied from their gardens, flocks and wild game consisting of buffalo, two varieties of deer (white tails in the sand hills and large black tails in the canyons), turkey, prairie chicken and quail. The small streams abounded in sun perch while the finest channel cat fish were found in the Canadian."[23]

Sadly, though, this idyllic way of life was not to continue. About 1877 the first non-Hispanic sheepmen began to graze their flocks eastward into the Canadian Valley. These belonged to the New Zealand Sheep Company, established in that country in 1860 by two Englishmen, Edwin Godwin-Austen and A. B. Ledgard, and a Scot, James Campbell. Poor results in New Zealand had brought them first to California, where they bought sheep and trailed them to a ranch near Liberty, New Mexico, then to a wide-open town that had sprung up just outside the government-set five-mile "prohibition" zone encircling Fort Bascom.[24]

Even bigger changes were in the making. At about the time Casimero Romero decided to move into the Panhandle country, a tough, ambitious rancher in Colorado was looking with covetous eyes at the same wide, empty—and most important, free—grasslands. Charles Goodnight was already something of a legend; no other single man would have a greater influence on the Texas cattle trade in general, and the Panhandle ranching industry in particular, than he.

Born in Macupin County, Illinois, on March 5, 1836, Goodnight had come to Texas with his family when he was nine years old, walking or riding a white-faced mare every yard of the eight hundred miles from his hometown to Waco. At age eleven he quit school and went to work. He rode as a jockey for a racing outfit in Port Sullivan, did a stint as a teamster, and, when he was twenty, began herding cattle on shares. Serving as a Texas Ranger throughout the Civil War, he built up a matchless knowledge of the topography of his adopted state, and when the war was over, he conceived the idea of driving cattle—virtually worthless in Texas—north to market. He knew that in New Mexico, Colorado, and even Wyoming there were Indian reservations and army posts desperate for beef and willing to pay well for it. All he had to do was get the beef there.

In 1866 Goodnight teamed up with an experienced trail driver named Oliver Loving, and together, driving a herd of Texas cattle, they blazed a trail through the heart of Comanche country from Fort Belknap in North Texas to Fort Sumner, New Mexico. In the years that followed, hundreds of

Charles Goodnight as a young man. (Courtesy of the Haley Memorial Library, Midland, Texas)

thousands of cattle would follow the Goodnight-Loving trace and other trails blazed later as cattle drives became the financial salvation of postwar Texas.

In 1870 Goodnight married Mary Ann "Molly" Dyer, the sister of his trail boss, and relocated with her and her younger orphaned brothers at Pueblo, Colorado, where he had invested in a substantial cattle range. He irrigated the land, planted orchards, raised cattle, and invested heavily in city lots, on which he built a bank, an opera house, a meatpacking house, and business buildings. When the 1873 crash and the financial slump that followed wiped him out, he packed his wife off to relatives in California and looked around for a new place to start. That place, he decided, would be the Panhandle.[25]

Chapter 2

HENRY HOYT

EL MEDICO COLORADO

READING his autobiography it quickly becomes clear that for Henry Hoyt some of the best years of his life were the youthful ones he spent "cowboying," and of those years, the brief period he spent in Tascosa was the most exciting. Dodging bullets in Hogtown saloons, rowdying with Jim Kenedy, meeting Billy the Kid, striking up friendships with Charlie Siringo and Jim East that would last another fifty years—how could a red-blooded, red-headed twenty-three-year-old medical student from Minnesota have found the whole experience anything but irresistible?

Henry Franklin Hoyt was the oldest son of Lorenzo Hoyt, born in Richland County, Ohio, on February 21, 1828, and Sarah Philadelphia Terrell, born in Virginia on August 30, 1832. His parents owned a farm near the village of Rose in Ramsey County, Minnesota, to which territory they had emigrated from Illinois in 1848, settling first near Saint Paul, whose population at that time was less than one thousand souls. Henry was born there on January 30, 1854. Later there would be a brother, George, and two sisters.[1]

Flirting with the idea of becoming a civil engineer, Henry accompanied the 1873 David Stanley Yellowstone expedition into "perfectly wild country" to survey the boundary line between the United States and Canada. Returning to Saint Paul in December of that year, Hoyt, encouraged by his uncle Dr. John Henry Murphy, hailed in one history as "the Nestor of the medical profession of Minnesota," decided to become a doctor, beginning his training with a year under Murphy's tutelage before entering Church Hospital (later Saint Luke's) in 1875 as an intern, followed by a year of medical studies at Rush Medical College.

In 1876, following the James-Younger gang's disastrous September 7 attempt to rob the bank at Northfield, Minnesota, Hoyt's mentor, Dr. Murphy, it would appear illicitly obtained the unclaimed body of one of the dead raiders, Samuel Wells, alias Charlie Pitts, and had it embalmed and preserved. When Hoyt returned home from Rush College in March 1877, Murphy turned the remains over to him to make ready for dissection. Following what was then standard medical practice (bleach the bones under water for a year or so),

Henry F. Hoyt. (Author's Collection)

Hoyt packed them into a shoe box together with a few rocks, sank them in a local lake, and then forgot having done so. During the winter of 1878, a local hunter found Hoyt's shoe box lodged in the ice of the frozen lake. When a human skull was found inside it, a murder inquiry was launched. Fortunately for all concerned, Dr. Murphy was able to clear the matter up and later "presented [the bones] to a young physician in Chicago." What happened to them thereafter remains a mystery.[2]

Shortly after returning to Saint Paul, Hoyt decided not to complete the required second year of his medical education and instead headed west for Dakota Territory, where, three years earlier, gold had been discovered. By 1876 the territory's population had more than doubled, with some twenty thousand souls clustered in and

around the new mining towns of Custer and Deadwood. "Deadwood was classed as the liveliest mining town in the country," Hoyt said, "so I selected that for my adventure."

He got there early in May and on arrival checked in at Vandaniker and McHugh's IXL (pronounced "I excel") Hotel & Restaurant, a two-story frame house with "rooms" divided only by canvas partitions. Deadwood had "only one street, built along the gulch, Main Street, in fact as well as in name, and although the hour was late, it was swarming with humanity. Saloons, gambling and dance halls on both sides of the street were in full blast. All in all it was a wonderful sight for a tenderfoot."[3]

When he let it be known he intended to hang out his shingle, the news was quickly picked up by Deadwood's newspaper, the *Black Hills Daily Times*, which announced in its May 12, 1877, issue that "H. F. Hoyt came in last evening by way of Bismark [*sic*]. He intends having a medicine talk soon. Is now at the IXL." Too late to have met Wild Bill Hickok, killed in Deadwood's Saloon No. 10 on August 2 of the preceding year, Hoyt had already become an inveterate people collector, as if anticipating that he would need them for his autobiography later. One of the people he claimed to have met at Deadwood was the notorious lady gambler "Madame Moustache," but that seems unlikely; in 1877 Eleanore Dumont, to give the Madame her real name, was running a brothel in Eureka, Nevada. Two years later she was dead.

Hoyt also claimed to have seen Martha "Calamity Jane" Cannary in Deadwood dressed in a soldier's uniform, riding down Main Street "at a full gallop. She had a Colt's .45 in each hand, and both were in action, the bullets flying in every direction, while the rider emitted a good imitation of an Indian war-whoop." Well, maybe she did at that.[4]

For all the excitement, however, Deadwood's dubious charms palled pretty quickly; or perhaps it was the lack of patients (and therefore income). Hoyt now teamed up with a young mining engineer named Bailey, and they tried their hands at prospecting. Having no luck at all, Hoyt in early September returned briefly to Deadwood, where, "seized with an attack of wanderlust," he packed his bags and joined up with two "Germans" and "an American bachelor, a Civil War veteran" named Hugh B. McCune, heading for New Mexico. They made their way to Cheyenne and thence via Denver to Santa Fe, where they parted company with the Germans. McCune, who was suffering from "a cow complex and he had it bad," heard around town that John Chisum, the so-called Cattle King of New Mexico, was letting out cattle on shares to reliable men, and McCune decided to ride down the Pecos and look him up. Still hoping to run across a promising location where he could set up as a doctor, Hoyt went along.

"There was game in abundance throughout this journey," Hoyt wrote, "and as we had both become first-class camp cooks, we lived like epicures." Skirting Anton Chico, where everyone had smallpox, they forded the Pecos and headed down the east side of the river toward Fort Sumner.

North of the settlement they came to a wide avenue bordered by majestic cottonwood trees that led for several miles to the post through orchards of peach and apri-

Maxwell family home at Fort Sumner, New Mexico, 1883. Billy the Kid was killed in the corner room nearest the camera. (Courtesy of Robert G. McCubbin)

[15]

cot trees and vineyards bearing Mission grapes, planted during the post–Civil War years when the old fort had guarded a concentration camp holding some eight thousand Navajos and Mescalero Apaches. In 1870 the buildings and other appurtenances had been purchased by Lucien B. Maxwell, who made his home there until his death in 1875; his widow, Doña Luz, and her family were still living there when Hoyt arrived.

During their stopover, Hoyt was asked to render medical assistance to a young man he remembered as William Maxwell, "the eldest son of the family [whom he found] dying with a severe case of malignant smallpox for which nothing could be done." In fact, the eldest son of the Maxwell family was Peter, then twenty-nine. "William" was a half-Cheyenne adopted by Maxwell and known to the family as Julian; he was just twenty when he died.

Later, Hoyt claimed to have met most of the people living in the vicinity of the old fort, "one of the most interesting being a very beautiful señorita, Lolita by name, who was about fifteen and as bright and charming as she was beautiful." She was not called Lolita, of course, but because later in his book he would name her as Billy the Kid's sweetheart, Hoyt was probably advised by his publisher—as was Walter Noble Burns, whose *Saga of Billy the Kid* had been published a couple of years earlier—that he could not use her real name. In 1929 Paulita Maxwell was still alive and might be litigious.[5]

Leaving Fort Sumner, Hoyt and his companion, McCune, pushed on down the Pecos in their covered wagon toward the Chisum ranch at South Springs. On the way they ran into the rancher and some of his men rounding up cattle. They camped

that night with the cowboys, who told them "many bloody tales and hairbreadth escapes," although perhaps not, as Hoyt claimed, about Billy the Kid, the "leader of the Chisum fighting men," because in November 1877 the Kid was a relatively unknown newcomer to New Mexico. More probably the cowboys were just having fun with the credulous tenderfeet.

Chisum was unwell, and Hoyt prescribed for him. "It seems I made a hit with him, as he seemed to think a good deal of me," he recalled. It transpired the rancher was not and never had been letting out cattle on shares (in fact, Chisum had sold his entire operation to Hunter & Evans of Kansas City in November 1875), so "Mac" was out of luck. When Hoyt mentioned he was looking for a good spot

Paulita Maxwell, Henry Hoyt's "Señorita Lolita." (Courtesy of the Colorado Historical Society [ID no. F803]. All rights reserved)

to set up a medical practice, Chisum pointed northeast. "Doc," he said, "over yonder is the Panhandle of Texas, a big country, full of people, an epidemic of smallpox, and no doctor. There's the place you're looking for."

Was Chisum serious? He surely knew the Panhandle was anything but "full of people" and that Tascosa, then the only settlement in the Panhandle west of Fort Elliott, was mostly populated by Hispanic sheepherders and a few white settlers. Nevertheless, Hoyt and McCune decided to take a look at this new country. They got there without incident, but after a halt at James Campbell's sheep ranch on Rita Blanca Creek north of Tascosa, McCune took the wagon and headed north for his home in Iowa. Shortly thereafter, Hoyt was summoned to Tascosa to take care of Casimero Romero's fifteen-year-old niece and foster daughter, Piedád, the "Belle of the Panhandle," who was sick with smallpox.[6]

The particularly virulent summer smallpox epidemic of 1877 that decimated the population of New Mexico and Arizona and that was raging during Henry Hoyt's first visit to Tascosa seems to have been accepted very philosophically in the Panhandle. Jim East recalled that

they used to have a good many dances over at Borrego Plaza . . . and invited the cowboys. I went over to a dance one night and we danced until about twelve o'clock. I noticed a pallet of sheep skins and blankets over in a corner with a sick child on them [and] an old Mexican woman go over and give it some tea a time or two. Finally [LIT wagon boss] Dudley Pannell got curious to see what the trouble was. He went over and pulled the blanket back and the kid was rotten with smallpox. He said: "Well, it's no use to go home now. We had just as well dance until morning."

Tascosa, Hoyt discovered,

consisted of two stores, a blacksmith shop and some Mexican houses on a plaza, which was about a hundred yards across. . . . Howard & McMasters store was one of the buildings and I had an office in it. Pedro Romero lived in an adobe house on the east side of the plaza, which was the only one there. On the south

———— ⌀ ————

John Simpson Chisum.
(Courtesy of the Historical Society
for Southeast New Mexico, Roswell)

side was Henry Kimball's blacksmith shop and on the west side Ike Rinehart's store. Lizzie and Irwin were his two children.

There was a little Mexican plaza on the south side of the river about a mile down. I used to have a good many patients down there. All had the smallpox and once in a while one got shot or cut up. A bunch of Mexicans lived there and they had some *bailes*. Only three American women lived in the country west of Fort Elliott . . . Mrs. [Molly] Goodnight, Mrs. Tom [Mary] Bugbee and Lizzie Rinehart.

Casimero Romero was the wealthiest Mexican in the Panhandle. He lived at Tascosa, had a big haciendo [*sic*] and did most of the freighting into the Panhandle. He ran several mule trains and had a bunch of peons. He had a good many horses but I don't know about him having any cattle. . . . The Mexicans used to call me "El Medico Colorado" because I was redheaded and was a doctor.[7]

When he got to the Romero home, Hoyt found Piedád "a most loathsome object," covered with smallpox pustules and frantic from the intolerable itching. Having no medicines, he invented a remedy using what was available—coating her body with a paste concocted from the ingredients of gunpowder: charcoal, saltpeter, and sulfur. It had the desired effect: much to the relief of her foster mother, Doña Salomé, Piedád not only recovered but a few weeks later made her debut in Panhandle society at a Christmas *baile* given by the Romeros at their hacienda. Hoyt was the guest of honor at this function, and James Kenedy, a son of one of the major cattle kings of Texas currently wintering a herd of about two thousand head on the Cheyenne, was also present.

The two young men—Kenedy was twenty-three—became close friends. With "his athletic physique, dark hair and eyes," Jim Kenedy was "about the handsomest bachelor in the Panhandle," Hoyt said. The contrast between his own pale skin and red hair and Kenedy's swarthy complexion and jet-black locks led to their being known locally as the "roulette twins"—red and black. Throughout the spring of 1878 Kenedy and Doña Salomé taught Hoyt Spanish, a very useful skill in a town where all the girls were Hispanic. He even managed to persuade Lizzie Rinehart to give him guitar lessons—his way of getting closer to the only unmarried Anglo girl in the Panhandle.[8]

In the summer of 1878 "Spike" Kenedy took his cattle up the trail to Dodge, where he—albeit unintentionally—shot dead a dance hall singer named Dora Hand. Trying to get back to Tascosa and safety from the Kansas law, he was headed off by a posse led by Bat Masterson and was so seriously wounded it was believed he could not live. He survived, however, not only to be acquitted of the charges laid against him in the matter of the Dora Hand murder but also, following a gruesome operation, to return to Texas, where he married and had a young son.[9]

Despite the departure of Kenedy, Hoyt's "adventures" continued with a lucky escape when two locals, a fellow named Bronco Jack who worked for blacksmith Henry Kimball and another man Hoyt names only as Benito, got into a dispute over cards. Hoyt was standing in the doorway of the Howard & McMasters store when Benito came after Bronco Jack with a Bowie knife. Hoyt warned Bronco Jack of the danger with a whistle; Jack came out of the smithy and started shooting. The bullet went through Benito's body and, missing Hoyt's head by inches, buried itself in the back wall of the store.

As the two men wrestled, Jack fired five more shots, then Benito staggered to a side door and collapsed on the ground. Hoyt ran across the street and asked Jack if he was hurt. "Hell, no," Jack said, "but I put six bullets through that greaser, all right. You had better look after *him*." The wounded man was carried into Pedro Romero's house, where it was discovered that his only injury was a minor flesh wound; all Bronco Jack's other bullets had gone through a buggy standing nearby.

Meanwhile, word spread that Benito was dead, and in the Mexican quarter bad blood came to a boil. In no time at all, an angry armed mob stormed into the upper town, apparently intent on slaughtering every white man in it. Hoyt managed to quiet things down by getting the two combatants to shake hands, but even as they did, a "villainous-looking Mexican, full of whiskey, pulled his gun and fired point-blank at Jack's back." Fortunately for Jack, a cowboy standing nearby had seen the shot coming and, drawing his own gun, whacked the would-be assassin over the head and laid him out, deflecting the shot, which passed under Bronco Jack's elbow, between Hoyt's legs, and into the bed. Clearly, young Henry Hoyt's guardian angel wanted him to have a lot more fun before it was time to cash in his chips, and Henry didn't let his guardian angel down.[10]

Pretty soon, however, he concluded that John Chisum's information about the Panhandle being full of people had been a vast overstatement—at that time there were probably no more than five hundred souls in the whole area—and once the smallpox epidemic receded, apart from sewing up the scalps of such occasional casualties as Benito, there was no future for him doctor-ing in Tascosa. To keep body and soul together—and maybe to do a little more "adventuring" as well—Hoyt signed up as a cowboy on the LX ranch. Its superintendent was W. C. "Bill" Moore, who at that time had about fifty men working for him, a good many of them what Hoyt called "refugees," men wanted by the law elsewhere and hiding behind an alias.

He thought highly of Moore, "one of the best *vaqueros* I ever saw." During roundups, he said, Moore would sit back and watch some wild and exceptionally unruly steer baffle every cowboy who was trying to rope it for branding. After all had failed, "Bill would put spurs to his mount and dash in. And I never saw him miss."

Hoyt was lucky enough also to strike up a friendship with Charlie Siringo, senior foreman of the LX, who taught him some of the "tricks of the trade." After a stint cutting posts and making corrals, he was assigned to line-riding duties with a fellow named "Latigo Jim." If the name was an alias Hoyt never found out, because Jim seems never to have vouchsafed any information about himself. The two of them were assigned to a line shack on Bonita Creek, and each daily rode line, one ten miles east and the other ten miles west of the cabin. Twice during their tour LX cattle drifted south before severe northers and had to be stopped if possible or recovered if not, although heading them off was dangerous work.[11]

For most of 1878 Hoyt worked for the LXs, as they were called, the hard, unrelenting drudgery of his chosen calling occasionally leavened by such events as meeting rustler William Nickel (Nicholson), who went by the name of "Slap Jack Bill, Pride of the Panhandle,"[12] or visiting Charles and Molly Goodnight at their Palo Duro ranch. Sometimes recovering "drift

Charles Goodnight's "Old Home Ranch" in Palo Duro Canyon.
(Courtesy of the Haley Memorial Library, Midland, Texas)

cattle" from as far south as the headwaters of the Brazos and Concho Rivers, other times hunting wolves, once being "marooned" on the empty plains for thirty days, Hoyt "adventured" until the fall round·up was over, by which time he had stashed away enough money to quit cow-boying. Pretty soon he was again comfortably ensconced in rooms at the Howard & McMasters store, "pending the passing of some party with which I might travel to New Mexico, where I had decided to locate." However, a few more adventures awaited him before that would happen.

Chapter 3

1876-1877

THE COMING OF THE LONGHORNS

IN THE FALL of 1875 Charles Goodnight brought down his first herd of about sixteen hundred head from Colorado and wintered it on the Alamocitas, a creek running north into the Canadian River west of Tascosa, while he and his trail boss, Leigh Dyer, scouted for a permanent ranch location. The fiercely independent Goodnight directed his search well away from the settlements, heading for the heart of the Panhandle and the exact mix he wanted of grass, water, shelter, and space. "Even in this year, 1875," wrote his biographer, "the *Texas Rural Register and Immigrants' Handbook* advised the world that it was improbable that the Staked Plains could 'ever be adapted to the wants of men,' adding that this was 'the only uninhabitable portion of Texas.' But Goodnight recalled its miles of unbroken buffalo turf, its rich grama grasses, and its scattered waterings. Besides, he never read guide-books, and hence moved with confidence."[1]

Goodnight had been told about a vast gorge that cut the Staked Plains in half and was confident it would make a wonderful site for a ranch. He found it southeast of

present-day Amarillo: the Palo Duro Canyon, its escarpments providing safety and shelter in winter, surrounded by empty miles of well-watered grassland on which his cattle could range freely the rest of the year. It was late in October 1876 when his guide—a *comanchero* named Nicolas Martinez, who ran sheep south of what would become Tascosa—led them to the rim of the canyon, which they could not see until they were almost at its edge. Reaching it, the chuck wagon team got spooked and stampeded down into the canyon with the terrified cook screaming to Goodnight's men to stop it. "Hell, let 'em run!" the cowboys whooped. "You never saw a prettier place!"

It was no simple task to get the cattle down to the floor of the canyon: they "moved slowly, in single file, down that ancient trace. . . . The cowboys took the wagon to pieces and packed it down the seven-hundred-foot wall on the backs of the very conservative chuck-wagon mules, and supplies of provisions and corn were transported in the same way. . . . After two days the portage was done."

On the floor of the canyon they came

upon a sizable herd of grazing buffalo; riding ahead of the cattle, Goodnight, Leigh Dyer, and Englishman James T. Hughes, son of the man who wrote *Tom Brown's Schooldays,* pushed the animals ahead of them, "an awesome experience in a wild, strange land that Goodnight never forgot. By taking their Sharp-shooters and knocking up the red dust beside them, they stampeded those animals that grazed high on the cañon sides down to join those in the drive. . . . By the time they dropped the wild herd, Goodnight estimated they were driving ten thousand buffaloes."

With the buffalo gone, Goodnight picked out a large open area on the south side of the canyon where a stream ran from a spring in the caprock and paced out space for the corrals, smokehouse, and living quarters that would eventually become the famous Home ranch. He had no neighbors: "A hundred miles [north] toward Kansas, Jim Cator had a buffalo camp on the North Palo Duro; about a hundred miles to the east and a little north, Fort Elliott was staked out on the Sweetwater. Fort Griffin lay a much longer journey southeast; and the nearest settlements in New Mexico, Kansas and Colorado were from two to two hundred and fifty miles away.' [2]

One of the first things Goodnight had done on his arrival in the Panhandle was to make a pact with *mayordomo* Casimero Romero: if the *pastores* kept their sheep out of the Palo Duro to the east, he would in turn guarantee to keep his cattle out of their pastures to the west along the river. Although Goodnight always observed his part of the agreement, a growing influx of cattlemen, each as anxious to take advantage of the free range as he, would soon shift the balance of power, forcing the *pastores* to abandon their *plazitas* and rapidly

bringing sheep raising in the Panhandle to an end.

Around the same time Goodnight moved into the Palo Duro, although quite independently of him, Thomas Sherman Bugbee brought his wife, Mary Catherine, two small children, trail hands, and eighteen hundred head of cattle down from Dodge City in October 1876, losing most of their possessions when a wagon broke loose as they were crossing the flood-swollen Cimarron. Worse still, half of the herd was lost in the same surging current. Despite these setbacks Bugbee soldiered on, and when he reached the Panhandle he set up his Quarter Circle T ranch on what became known as Bugbee Creek, on the north side of the Canadian just inside Hutchinson County.

Not that it was much of a ranch to begin with: the family lived in a dugout with a buffalo hide for a door, and Bugbee and his riders used six-guns to stampede the buffalo off their range. To the south Goodnight and his cowboys solved the same problem by maintaining a line that they rode daily, turning back anywhere from a thousand to fifteen hundred buffalo in order to preserve the grass for their cattle.[3]

Legend aside, however, Goodnight and Bugbee were not the first cattlemen in the Panhandle; that distinction probably belongs to Kentucky-born A. G. "Jim" Springer, a former Santa Fe trail freighter turned buffalo hunter turned Dodge City ranchman, who in the spring of 1875 built, a few miles north of Fort Elliott on the Camp Supply trail, a rambling, multiroom dugout so heavily fortified the buffalo hunters called it Fort Sitting Bull. By September 1877 Springer was "fully embarked in the stock business" and running on the adjacent plains a herd of seven or eight hundred cattle wearing his AGS brand. With the help of a "fine, peaceable and quiet" young Texan named Tom Leadbetter, he also operated an eating house, food store, and makeshift hotel that later became a stage stop called Boggy Station. The gambling bar attached to it was very popular with black troopers from Fort Elliott, who were not welcome in the saloons nearer home.

"Springer's Ranche," according to a correspondent of the *Dodge City Times,* was in "an excellent agricultural section of country, and it does not take much of a prophet to foretell that this whole valley down to the Indian Territory line will be thickly settled up. Mr. Springer is permanently located here, and keeps constantly on hand an assortment of all kinds of supplies necessary for the inner man as well as accommodations for stock—hay, forage, stabling, &c."

The following February, Springer, who had unsuccessfully offered it for rent or lease throughout the preceding year, underlined his intention to make his new home a permanent one by putting his 165-acre farm south of the river near Dodge City up for sale through Wright, Beverly & Co. On it stood a "good frame house, one and a half story, 18 x 50 feet, 5 rooms, good well, stable & corral" which would be sold "very cheap."

By now Springer's had become a welcome stopover for travelers and ranchers moving between the Panhandle and Dodge City. But on Sunday, November 17, 1878, Springer—who had become postmaster just a month earlier—got into an argument over cards with a black sergeant of the army paymaster's escort, drew a revolver, and hit the soldier over the head with it, then fired a shot that grazed the top of the soldier's head. As the other soldiers in the building ran out to get their guns, four men were seen approaching on horseback, prompting the paymaster, Maj. Josiah Adams Broadhead, to suspect a robbery attempt. He ordered his men to fall into line and fire if the men approached, and somehow a volley was fired into the house; when the gunsmoke cleared, Springer and his helper, Tom Leadbetter, were dead and three soldiers wounded.

An inquest held the following week established that Leadbetter had been trying to stop Springer from shooting at the soldiers when he was killed, but it came to no conclusion as to how the shooting had begun except to exonerate the soldiers who had "acted purely in self-defense." An officer from Fort Elliott, Lt. Thomas M. Wenie, 19th Infantry, took possession of the deceased man's effects—about twelve thousand dollars' worth of cattle, one thousand dollars in cash, railroad bonds, and other valuables—until the following month, when Springer's brother and two other relatives came out from the East, disinterred Springer's body to take it back to Delaware, and sold the place to cattlemen John F. Tuttle and Frank Chapman of Hemphill County. In spite of several changes of ownership that followed, the place was known as Springer's ranch for many years.[4]

In 1877 yet another unlikely cattleman arrived in the Canadian Valley. John George Adair, born March 3, 1823, at Rathdair in Ireland of Scotch-Irish descent, had originally been trained to enter the diplomatic service but instead decided in 1866 to set up a brokerage firm in New York. In 1869 he married a widow, Cornelia Wadsworth Ritchie, with whom in 1874 he embarked on a buffalo hunt, during which he managed to shoot his horse in the top of the head and almost killed himself. Enamored of western life, he moved his base of operations to Denver in 1875 and decided to get into the cattle business. Everyone he talked to advised him that the best man he could go in with was Charles Goodnight, so in May 1877 Adair and his wife accompanied Goodnight and his wife, Molly, to Trinidad, outfitted for a trip to the Palo Duro, and reached it May 15 after an adventurous trek of twelve days, two of them without water.

Although during his two-week visit some of Adair's autocratic mannerisms made him less than popular with the ranch hands—and with the Goodnights—the terms of the proposed partnership were thrashed out. On June 18, 1877, Goodnight and Adair signed a five-year agreement under the terms of which Adair would provide finance and Goodnight would supply the foundation herd and run the ranch, receiving a salary of twenty-five hundred dollars a year plus operating expenses. On termination of the agreement Adair's investment, with 10 percent interest, was to be repaid in full and the ranch properties divided one-third to Goodnight and two-thirds to Adair. Heavily weighted in favor of the financier, it seems on paper to have been a surprising deal for as successful a cattleman as Goodnight to have made, but he knew what he was doing. "I did not mind it," he said, "because I knew I had a fortune made."[5]

As the Goodnight ranch (rechristened the JA, Adair's initials) "entered upon a period of expansion, intensive organization, and remarkable growth in range and in herd," a further wave of new men was moving into the Panhandle. One of them, Connecticut-born Ellsworth Torrey, was forty-six years of age when he obtained the backing of a Boston bank and decided to try his hand at ranching. With his two sons,

Charley and William, he built a substantial stone house with a large living room, three bedrooms, a dining hall, and a kitchen, freighting in fine furniture and carpets from the East before bringing out his wife, Anna, a "refined gentlewoman" from Massachusetts. By September 1879 he would have eight thousand head of cattle on his range.[6]

During the summer of '77, Mississippi-born Maj. George Washington Littlefield of Austin, Texas, sent a herd of about thirty-five hundred cattle up the Chisholm Trail to Dodge City. Finding prices ruinously low, Littlefield's nephew and trail boss, Phelps White, having heard reports of the good grazing in the Panhandle, headed the herd south and set up temporary headquarters about three miles west of Tascosa. When spring failed to improve prices, Littlefield decided to establish a ranch in the Canadian Valley and appropriated a range that stretched some fifteen miles on both sides of the river from Cheyenne Creek on the west to John Ray Creek (as it would later be called) on the east, its headquarters three miles from Tascosa. A little later Littlefield bought the well-watered site four miles south of the town originally pre-empted by Henry Kimball, erecting a substantial stone and adobe house, stables, corrals, and branding pens. Charles S. "Bill" McCarty took charge of the ranch, with Dudley Pannell, Bob Roberson, and Bud Wilkinson as wagon bosses, and thus the LIT was born.[7]

Also in 1877, millionaire Boston shoemaker-turned-cattleman David T. Beals and his partner, the prim, devout W. H. "Deacon" Bates, established their LX brand on Pitcher Creek about twenty miles north of what is now Amarillo. The youngest child of Thomas and Ruth (Faxon) Beals, David Thomas Beals was

George Washington Littlefield, 1870s. (Courtesy
of the Haley Memorial Library, Midland, Texas)

David T. Beals, owner of the LX ranch.
(Courtesy of the Haley Memorial Library,
Midland, Texas)

born on March 8, 1832, in North Abington, Massachusetts; his father was a boot
and shoe manufacturer. After a public
school education, and a brief spell at the
New Hampshire Academy, Beals went to
work for a Boston merchant as a clerk but
then returned home to learn the family
business. Commencing in 1859, he established boot and shoe businesses first in
Missouri, then in the mining camps of
Colorado, Idaho, Montana, and Utah.

In 1873 he sold those enterprises and
entered a partnership to establish a ranch
near Granada, Colorado. In 1877, with
ranges there becoming increasingly
crowded, he organized the Beals Cattle
Company in Dodge City and sent an employee, John Ray, to scout a site for a Panhandle ranch. Ray found what he was look-

ing for near a buffalo hunter's supply camp
operated by a man named Pitcher. When
Ray's enthusiastic report reached him,
Beals formed a partnership with Bates,
Henry J. Rosencrans, and Erskine Clement
(Beals's son-in-law). He then drove a small
herd to the Panhandle to establish what became the LX ranch. Unlike those crowding
in to grab "free grass," over the succeeding
twenty-six months, Beals bought land and
more land both north and south of the
Canadian River—8,320 acres on November 12, 1881; 41,920 acres on January 16,
1882; 9,600 acres on March 18, 1882;
19,485 acres on March 27, 1883; and a
final 20,920 acres on February 11, 1884.
Among the herders who came in with the
LX were Ray, Charlie Siringo, Owlhead
Johnson, Jack Ryan, and Bill Allen.[8]

Other cattlemen, smaller and less well known, came in too. "On the south side of Oldham County a man by the name of [Jim] Mitchell, married to a Mexican woman, was located in a canyon which is still named for him. He had both cattle and horses. He was there before 1877, as Dr. Henry Hoyt treated his family for the smallpox. . . . In 1877 Goodrich & Beeman had a small ranch on Pisco Creek, about four miles east of Tascosa."[9]

Another cowboy who got his first sight of Tascosa in 1877 was Illinois-born James Henry East, then every bit of twenty-three years of age. East's people had originally come from England to Georgia about 1784. His grandfather, Henry East, born in that state, emigrated to Nashville and fought under Andrew Jackson, "Old Hickory," in the War of 1812 as a member of Cheatham's 2nd Regiment of Tennessee Militia, and in 1817 he moved to Kaskaskia, Illinois Territory, where he traded for furs with the Indians.

Henry East and his wife, Elizabeth, a South Carolinian, had eight children. The seventh of these was Archibald Eben East, born about 1830 in Kaskaskia. In 1849 he married Nancy Coulter; there were nine children of this union, the second of whom was Jim—James Henry, to give him his full name—born August 30, 1853. His older sister was Amanda; the other siblings were William (Henry), John, Robert, Sarah, Margaret, Elizabeth (Minnie), and Lillie.

In 1870, at the age of sixteen, Jim East decided to go to Texas. "I got the idea into my head by reading an account of the life of Davy Crockett and of the fall of the Alamo," he said. "I had read a smattering of Texas history and wanted to see the place where those men lost their lives." No doubt financed by his fond father, Jim took a steamboat down the river to New Or-

leans and another to Corpus Christi, then traveled overland to San Antonio. "That did not satisfy me and I went on to the open country," he said. "Then I went on into Old Mexico as I had always wanted to see what was on the other side of the hill."

His first job was working for San Jacinto veteran Capt. John F. Tom on the Santa Gertrudis ranch at Seguin. He would be a trail hand for ten years, driving cattle to Louisiana, Old Mexico, Dodge City, and Ogallala, in the process maturing from a raw kid into a top hand. In 1877, while bringing a herd up the trail for King

Jim East (seated right) and friends, Tascosa, ca.1884: Lon Jenkins (seated left), Bill Gatlin (standing left), and Frying Pan cowboy Arthur Childs (standing right). (Courtesy of the Amarillo Public Library)

& Kenedy, he quit the herd at Rock Crossing on the Cimarron and headed back to Tascosa. "It was a rollicky sort of a place," he said. It would soon get a whole lot rollickier.[10]

Perhaps understandably, documentary records for this period of Tascosa's history are sparse, but there is plenty of evidence to suggest it wasn't so much rollicky as downright dangerous, as evidenced by the fate of the Casner brothers, who also came to the Canadian River valley in January 1877. Iowa-born Bill Casner, fifty-two, and his brother Dan, born in Missouri and now forty, were two of the fourteen offspring of Henry and Jincy Jane (Fields) Casner, a restless couple who had married in Iowa in 1822, moved to Missouri, and then in 1852 emigrated on to Oregon. After a family rift, Bill, Dan, and brother John, fifty-five, headed for the California goldfields, where they made their pile. Bill and Dan decided to invest some of their new-found wealth in a herd of about a thousand sheep, which they drove overland to the Panhandle. John and his son Lewis, twenty-six, elected to go prospecting in the area around Silver City, New Mexico.[11]

By the time Bill and Dan Casner drove their flock into the Canadian Valley, guided by an unnamed Navajo boy who knew the country, word had already reached the *plazitas* scattered along the river not only of their arrival, but also of the large sum in gold coins—said to have been more than five thousand dollars—they were rumored to be carrying. At this point fact and legend collide so violently that mere truth becomes a by-product. A number of accounts—each relying heavily on one particularly unreliable original source—suggest one of the men particularly inter-

ested in the Casner gold was a six foot four, blue-eyed bandit and badman named Sostenes l'Archevêque.

It has been claimed l'Archevêque was a grandson of the French-born adventurer Juan de l'Archevêque, who came to America with René Robert Cavelier, Sieur de La Salle, and went into hiding after participating in the 1687 plot to assassinate him. Reappearing in New Mexico in 1696, l'Archevêque married and became a property owner in Santa Fe. He was killed on August 13, 1720, when an exploring party of which he was a member was ambushed by Pawnee Indians in Kansas. L'Archevêque left two legitimate and two illegitimate children; one of the latter, his son Miguel, founded the l'Archibêque family, which was still flourishing in recent times.[12]

According to legend, following the murder of his father by an American at Sapello, New Mexico, Sostenes l'Archevêque—then a child—swore he would kill every *gringo* that he met, and by the time he was finally run out of New Mexico in 1876, he had killed twenty-three Americans. And legend is what it seems to be; no standard history of New Mexico so much as mentions his name, nor has any documentary evidence of what would have been a notably murderous career, even by New Mexico standards, ever been produced. Likewise, there is little or nothing about him or the Casner murders in the extensive oral annals of Tascosa left by the likes of Marion Armstrong, John Arnot, Jim East, Garrett "Kid" Dobbs, and Lucius Dills.

Yet there he is, considerably larger than life, ready and more than willing to kill a couple more *gringos*, especially *gringos* carrying five thousand dollars in gold. The only thing apparently restraining him was the fact that his brother-in-law Nicolas "Colas" Martinez, Charles Goodnight's onetime guide and acknowledged "boss of the Canadian River country," had promised Goodnight that if Sostenes ever tried to revive his hobby of murdering *Americanos,* he would take care of the matter personally.[13]

Tellingly, Goodnight made no mention of either this or l'Archevêque in his memoirs. Perhaps he concluded, as might we, that if l'Archevêque did not exist, it became necessary to invent him: there were doubtless other bandits on the Staked Plains more than ready to murder for that much gold and more than happy to have a mythical bandit upon whom to foist their crimes.

One of these, English-born Philip Joseph Goodfellow, engaged with a crooked assistant quartermaster at Fort Elliott named Charles T. Witherell in the time-honored pastime of selling stolen government property, is said to have precipitated matters by suggesting that should Sostenes (or—more believably—some other local bandits) happen to steal them, he would be happy to buy the Casner sheep flock. Thus provided with a double motive for murder, the story goes, l'Archevêque wasted no time in carrying it out. On or about January 20, 1877, accompanied by a youngster named Ysabel Gurules, he rode into the Casner camp. Discovering that one of the brothers and their Navajo guide were absent, l'Archevêque unhesitatingly shot the one present dead. Shortly thereafter the second brother rode in, and l'Archevêque shot him down. Then, while he was ransacking the camp looking for the gold, the Navajo guide rode in. When it transpired that other than the location of a few coins he did not know where the gold was, l'Archevêque killed him too.[14]

Lt. AQM Charles Tripler Witherell, 19th Infantry (detail from a group photograph). (National Archives)

When Ysabel Gurules reached the Borregos *plazita* and told his father Felix what Sostenes had done, Colas Martinez convinced the community elders that his brother-in-law was a liability; they agreed, and a trap was prepared. When l'Archevêque arrived at Borregos driving the Casner sheep, he was lured to a room in the Gurules adobe, where he was stabbed and shot to death by Colas Martinez, Felix Gurules, and Miguel Garcia. The sheep were then rounded up and (in one version) handed over to Charles Goodnight's trail boss, Leigh Dyer.[15]

At this juncture the plot thickens so densely as to suggest there is not just one scenario but several in play. About the end of March 1877, John and Lewis Casner, having learned of the murder of John's brothers—which earliest reports indicated had been carried out by a man named "Sorty," who was a friend of Colas Martinez—arrived in the Panhandle from Silver City, bringing with them ex–Quantrill raider Edward Berry, Cimarron badman John Bottom, and two others known only as H. Harrison and Bell. Initially, it appears, the Casners had suspected Bottom of having been implicated in the murders because he was apparently in the Borregos area at the time and seems also to have been connected with the Goodfellow-Witherell racket. Bottom not only managed to allay their suspicions but also implicated the Englishman, Philip "Joe" Goodfellow (referred to in some accounts of these events as "Goodanuf" or "Goodenuff").[16]

The Casner party now rode to the home of Colas Martinez and called him outside, where each put a bullet into him; they were restrained from killing the women and children present only by the intervention of a man appositely named Chancy Buman. Later still, the Casners killed Felix Gurules, Agapito Nolan, and someone named only as Florentine. They then moved on to Tascosa, where they robbed Casimero Romero of a gun and some field glasses and announced they were planning to kill on sight George Black, John Tean, José Samora, two other Americans, and Goodfellow. Why, they did not say, but it is instructive to note they were not looking for, nor as far as can be ascertained did they ever mention, Sostenes l'Archevêque.[17]

To further complicate matters, while seeking strayed cattle, Hunter & Evans employee Frank McNab, along with one Frank Hall, alias Tipton, claimed to have stumbled upon the camp of the two dead Casner brothers and found some gold coins hidden in a sheepskin purse, one of

which McNab used to buy supplies at a trading post. Accusations and counteraccusations flew back and forth, and the involvement of Sostenes l'Archevêque in the murders—if indeed he ever was involved—was quickly forgotten. In a front-page story the *Dodge City Times* named Harrison as the murderer of the Casners, while another page carried the story that Harrison was in town "hunting for Tipton, alias Frank Hall, Frank McNab and George Black, who are charged with the murder of the Casner brothers in the Pan Handle." Handsome rewards, it said, had been promised by the surviving Casners for "any information that will assist them to avenge the death of their brothers."

Frank McNab and his buddies looked like prime suspects. While scouting for strayed cattle that same winter they had come upon some Mexicans driving a small herd, killed them, burned their wagons, and sold the cattle in Colorado. In a letter to the *Dodge City Times,* McNab intimated that Goodnight's trail boss, Leigh Dyer, "who entertained the most bitter feelings of animosity" toward the Casners, had said "he would kill the damn sonsofbitches of sheep men if they did not move away from there."[18]

Harrison, it was reported, was "also on the trail of young Robert White, alias Wiry Jack, alias Kit Carson's nephew," one of four men who had "committed a murder for gold in Arizona some months ago." After escaping from custody he "fled to the wilds of the Pan Handle of Texas, where the party again committed the atrocious crime of murder for gold." Mixed up in all this was the matter of stolen government property hidden at ranches near Fort Elliott; newspaper reports hinted that Casner sidekick Bottom was involved in this racket with Goodfellow and Lt. Witherell. What followed—perhaps inevitably—was the removal from the gene pool of John Bottom in "one of the most atrocious and cold-blooded murders ever recorded in the annals of this country."

Goodfellow, who had a ranch on the Canadian, had been accused of complicity in the Casner murders, said the *Dodge City Times,* and "the recent premeditated murder and robbery which he committed upon the person of Mr. Bottom in front of the victim's dwelling in the presence of his family and several other witnesses, proves him to be amply capable of killing the Casner brothers for their gold and sheep, which latter were found in his possession."[19]

When John and Lewis Casner came looking for Goodfellow at his ranch and found the place deserted, they decided to move in and await his return. Having somehow gotten word they were waiting for him, Goodfellow bypassed his spread and instead headed for Fort Elliott. There he informed the commanding officer he knew where some stolen government property was hidden and offered to lead a military detail to it. Escorted by scout T. M. McFadden and a squad of six soldiers commanded by none other than Lt. Charles T. Witherell, Goodfellow led the party toward the Adobe Walls area. On April 15, after they pitched camp near the mouth of the Río Bonito, Witherell and Goodfellow left after sundown and were gone all night. The following morning Goodfellow returned alone, carrying an order from Lt. Witherell instructing scout McFadden and three enlisted men to accompany him—dressed, it is said, in a military blouse and cap—on a foray down the Canadian.

After questioning several sheepherders at ranches along the way, the squad arrived at the Bottom ranch, where they found an old Mexican woman, a man named Strong, and Bottom himself. Goodfellow rode across to him. "Are you John Bottom?" he demanded.

"That's my name," Bottom said.

"This is one of the men!" Goodfellow shouted to the soldiers. "You fellows, have you got the handcuffs?" Informed no one had brought handcuffs, Goodfellow leveled his rifle and shot Bottom from a distance of five feet, setting his clothing alight. Bottom gasped, "Joe, for God's sake don't shoot anymore!" but Goodfellow shot him a second time anyway. When the party returned in due course to Fort Elliott on April 21, his claim that he had killed Bottom in self-defense was overruled, and Goodfellow was confined in the guardhouse.[20]

On May 7 Clay County judge William B. Plemons issued a warrant at Henrietta, Texas, for the arrest of Philip J. Goodfellow for the murder of Bottom, appointing Edward Berry—himself a member of the Casner "hunting" party—to serve it. Eleven days later Goodfellow was released from the Fort Elliott guardhouse into Berry's custody. The following day, accompanied by a noncommissioned officer and a teamster driving the wagon, Berry left for Henrietta with his prisoner. That night, May 18, ten or twelve men rode into their camp and took Goodfellow from them at gunpoint, leaving one man to guard Berry and his companions. About three quarters of an hour later they returned, picked up the guard, and rode off. Next morning Berry and his escort found Goodfellow's body hanging from a tree on the riverbank.[21]

All this sounds very much like a classic case of *los muertos no hablan,* and in all probability was just that. It is not too difficult to concoct a scenario in which either

Harrison or Witherell (or both) send Bottom to Borregos to hire some Mexican hit men to kill the Casners for either their sheep or their gold (or both). The thieves fall out, with predictable results, and the surviving Casners take care of the rest. Whatever the facts may be, the intensity went out of the situation when the Casners expressed themselves satisfied by Frank McNab's protestations of innocence in the matter of the murder of their brothers and withdrew the reward they had put on his head.[22]

Harrison's sidekick, Lt. Charles T. Witherell, and his commanding officer, Capt. Charles W. Hotsenpiller, 19th Infantry, were both later court-martialed, although their "punishment" was risible. The surviving Casners moved to Donley County, where they operated a sheep ranch for a short while, relocating in 1881 to Haskell County. Around the turn of the century both were jailed on a charge of murder but were subsequently freed.[23]

There have been numerous attempts to make some kind of historical sense of all the foregoing events, none of which has ever satisfactorily explained them. Was there ever such a person as Sostenes l'Archevêque? If there was, why is there no documentary record of his existence? Exactly how were Colas Martinez and his fellow sheepmen on the Canadian involved in the Casner murders? Did John and Lewis Casner's search for the killers get in the way of the military racket being operated by Goodfellow and Witherell and by so doing trigger all these killings? All are possibilities, but which is true it is unlikely we shall ever know.

Chapter 4

CHARLES EMORY

SQUIRREL-EYE CHARLIE

AFTER Dodge City, the other great center of the buffalo hide trade was Fort Griffin, some four hundred miles southeast, with its appended roaring hell town, "The Flat," catering to the needs of both the hide hunters and the cowboys taking herds up the Western and Chisholm Trails. Here, many who would later figure notably in the histories of Mobeetie and Tascosa learned the business of survival— among them men as different in ambition and temperament as attorney James N. "Honest Jim" Browning, Texas Ranger G. W. "Cap" Arrington, gunfighter-killer John Selman, and buffalo hunters Pat Garrett and John W. Poe.

Also on the Fort Griffin scene was Charles Emory, a fifteen-year-old kid they called "Squirrel-Eye." He first appears in the historical record in 1875, working as a skinner for a buffalo hunting outfit owned by John B. "Arkansas Jack" Greathouse. On some earlier occasion badly clawed by a mountain lion in the state from which he took his nickname, Greathouse, described as a "bootlegger" and well known around the fort, was a man of property; he owned not only a hunting outfit (which could cost

"Squirrel-Eye" Charlie Emory, real name Charles Arnim. (Courtesy of the E.A. Arnim Archives and Museum, La Grange, Texas)

a considerable sum of money) but also a ranch on the Salt Fork of the Brazos.[1]

Early in April 1875 another hunter, John Cook, crossed an Indian travois trail in the breaks of the Brazos River and decided to head for Arkansas Jack's camp, where he found Charlie Emory, George Cornett, and two other men playing draw poker.[2]

If, as Cook avers, "Squirrel-Eye" was working for Greathouse during the 1874–75 hunting season, it is probably safe to assume he was in 1877 when he became a member of the July–August 1877 Nolan expedition, or, as it was known by the buffalo hunters, "The Forlorn Hope." He was lucky to come out of it alive.

In 1876 Charles Rath and Robert Wright had formed a partnership with Lee & Reynolds and set up their mercantile establishment at "Hidetown" below Fort El-

John R. Cook, 1907. (Author's Collection)

liott. But when the buffalo moved even farther south, the hunters and their suppliers perforce followed them. In December Charles Rath's wagon train, John Russell's fifty wagons, and those of some eighty hunters, all outfitted by Rath in Kansas or at Adobe Walls, headed south to locate Camp Reynolds, or Rath City, about fourteen miles west of what is now Hamlin, Texas. And very soon after that "the saloon operators, the dance hall outfits with about forty women, and ne'er do wells also came."[3]

Rath City consisted of six sod buildings huddled together beside the trail to Fort Griffin. On the west side of the road were George Aiken's saloon and Fleming's saloon and dance hall. On the other side were Charlie Sing's laundry and the big Reynolds, Rath & Co. trading post managed by Rath's business manager Harvey West (another future player in the Billy the Kid saga). Although it was little more than a primitive hide-buying outpost, it was well frequented and before long had its own "Boot Hill."[4]

At about the same time, freighter W. H. "Pete" Snyder set up a store on Deep Creek, not far from the present-day town named for him in Scurry County. It became a new and thriving hide-buying center, as did another built at the head of the Clear Fork of the Brazos by McKaney & Hamburg. "The hunt is the largest ever known," ran a story in the fall of 1876. "Countless thousands of buffalo cover the prairies. Ten thousand hides are now on the way to the railroad, and thousands await transportation to Fort Worth."[5]

Rath City soon became a target for raiding Comanches. On February 27, 1877, they attacked Bill Devins's camp about forty-five miles west of Rath City and killed Marshall Sewell at his own camp

Charles Rath. (Courtesy of the Kansas
Heritage Center, Dodge City, Kansas)

nearby. A punitive expedition estimated at
between forty-five and sixty strong left
Rath City on March 4 with food, ammunition, and guns furnished by Harvey West.
In sum, there were "four or five wagons
loaded with camp supplies and corn for
over sixty horses and mules; something
over thirty men mounted and three or four
on each wagon; also a full fifty-gallon barrel of whiskey."[6]

According to W. Skelton Glenn, the
leader of the party was "Big Hank" Campbell, with Jim Harvey second in command;
other accounts name Joe Freed and
"Limpy Jim" Smith as lieutenants. Their
guide and scout was José Piedád Tafoya,
the former *comanchero* who had been "persuaded" to guide Mackenzie into Palo
Duro Canyon in 1874. They pursued the
Comanches for sixteen days and finally

caught up with them at Yellow House
Canyon (near present-day Lubbock) on
March 18 only to find themselves seriously
outnumbered: some three hundred Comanches had teamed up with a band of
maybe a hundred Mescalero Apaches and
were spoiling for a fight. In the encounter
that followed, Devins, Tafoya, and some
others were wounded, Joe Jackson so seriously that two months later he died in the
Fort Griffin hospital; in desperation the
hunters fired the grass, and the Indians either retreated or gave up, leaving the party
to limp back to the Reynolds, Rath & Co.
store, where they arrived March 27.[7]

On or about the night of May 1 (the
dates and the sequence of events vary from
source to source) Comanches raided the
Reynolds, Rath & Co. store, running off
twenty-five of the hunters' horses. The following day "Squirrel-Eye," John Cook,
Louis Keyes, Hi Bickerdyke, Joe Freed, Jim
Harvey, and George Cornett came in with
the news that Indians had plundered John
Sharp's camp near the Double Mountains,
badly wounding him. Taking Charlie Rath's
buggy, they brought Sharp in. After he was
taken to the post hospital at Fort Griffin,
the hunters decided things had gone too
far; it was time to teach the Comanches
a lesson.[8]

Over the next month or so a new "war
party" consisting of about forty men was
formed, with Jim Harvey again in command and including "Big Beans," Bill
Belden, Bill Benson, Hi Bickerdyke,
Mickey Carr, John R. Cook, George Cornett, B. F. Daniels, "Spotted Jack" Dean,
"Squirrel-Eye" Charlie Emory, Harry Forrest, "Whiskey Jim" Greathouse, "Hurricane" Lee Grimes, "Six-shooter Bill" Hill-
man, Frank Hinton, Tom Hogler, George
Holmes, Louis Keyes, M. N. "Wild Bill"
Kress, Jack Matthias, "Mexican Joe," Bill

Buffalo hides awaiting shipment at Dodge City. Charles Rath is seated at right.
It was claimed there were forty thousand hides in the pile shown and seventy to eighty
thousand in the yard. (Courtesy of the Kansas Heritage Center, Dodge City, Kansas)

Milligan, Bill Nay, Doc Neil, Ed O'Byrne, Paten (interpreter), Sol Rees, "Scorpion Jack," "Slap Jack Bill," "Hog" Jim Smith, "Limpy Jim" Smith, "Smokey Hill" Thompson, Alfred Waite, Luther Whaley, and Dick Wilkinson.[9]

About July 1 some twenty-six of the men from the war party set off in pursuit, but found no Comanches, although one account suggests they encountered a party of twelve *comancheros* on the Las Linguas and wiped them out.[10] On July 20 they ran into a sixty-man cavalry detachment led by Capt. Nicholas Nolan, 10th Cavalry; it was agreed Captain Nolan and forty of the soldiers would join the pursuit. Six days later, while they were camped at Double Lakes, in present-day Lynn County, their guide, Tafoya, sent word that he had sighted forty

Indians near Laguna Rica, about fifteen miles to the northwest. The combined force set off after them, but at Nigger Hill, near Lingo, New Mexico, west of present-day Lubbock, the trail was lost. And so, the pursuers discovered, were they. They were also out of water. The hunters tried to direct Nolan and his men to water, but he insisted on heading back for Double Lakes; it was a bad call.[11]

The hunters headed northeast, making it to Silver Lake that night; a couple of days later a few of them—it had become pretty much every man for himself now—reached Yellow House Canyon, filling canteens to take back to their comrades on the plains. John Cook was one of them; as he was leaving, Sol Rees and Jim Foley arrived. According to Cook, "They told me to hurry to Louie Keyes, George Cornett and Squirrel-eye, that they had given up the struggle [to get to water]. I hurried ahead and about a mile and half from there I met John Mathias afoot. I offered him water. He said: 'No, I know where the water is. Go on; hurry to the other boys; Carr has wandered off. You get to Keyes, Cornett and Emery [sic] first. They are east of the route, about two and one-half miles back.' Hurrying on a half-mile, I met the rest, except for the three or four alluded to. I left three canteens of water with them. They said: 'Burn the earth, Cook, to reach Keyes, Cornett and Squirrel-eye. You will see their horses, two of them, by going this way,' they pointing out the course."

Soon he was beside them.

They were lying down, side by side . . . on their backs, facing the east. They had written their names and had them fastened to their saddles. . . . Each man had his face covered with a towel. Charles Emery's horse had been killed and its blood drank by the three men. . . . [Cornett's] eyes were closed, apparently in death. Then I . . . saturated one of the towels and began rubbing their faces alternately.

Squirrel-eye was in the middle and was the first to respond. Dried blood was on their lips and mustaches. Their lower jaws had dropped. Louie's tongue was swollen and protruding. . . . They were all in a comatose condition. The first murmur came from Emery; it was only a mutter. . . . I began to talk loudly to them. I said anything and everything I thought would arouse them. . . . I dashed water in their faces and on their chests. I raised Keyes up to a sitting position, but his head dropped to one side, and I began to think he was a "goner," sure.

Just then Emery raised himself up of his own accord and said, "Where am I?" I placed Keyes back into a reclining position and, holding the canteen to Emery's mouth, said "Squirrel-eye, *drink!* There is lots of water; we must hurry." I talked loudly. At the first swallow he clutched the canteen with both hands, and would have drained it of all the water had I allowed him to do so. His consciousness came to him when I said, "Now, help me with the other boys."

Just then, Sol Rees arrived, having refreshed himself at the water hole. Sam Carr was still missing, and Rees exhorted Cook to try to find him. After locating Carr some three miles away and taking him to the water hole in Yellow House Canyon, Cook went back with three canteens of water to bring in Emory, Keyes, Cornett, and Rees. He located them by firing the cavalry carbine and watching for Rees's return shots. It was now near dark, and a thunderstorm was approaching from the southwest. They found their way back to the Yellow House by collecting and firing "soap balls" (the tops of the yucca plant, which flare up when touched by flame) to see where they were going. Finally, everyone was back together at the water hole at Casas Amarillas except Bill Benson, who had opted to stay with Nolan's column. He remained with Nolan only a short time; when he was unable to convince Nolan to turn toward the Yellow House, Benson left, arriving at Punta del Agua (Lubbock Lake), where the other hunters found him. He had been without water for ninety-six hours (Nolan's column went without for only eighty-six).[12]

The early spring of 1878 saw the last great slaughter of the buffalo; more than a million hides had been taken during the preceding fall and winter. As summer approached, many of the men who had made their living in or from the hide trade found other ways and other places to support themselves—Robert Wright, Billy Dixon, Charlie Rath, Pat Garrett, John Poe, Jim Greathouse, Harvey West, and Bat Masterson among them. John B. "Arkansas Jack" Greathouse was another: in 1880 he turned up in Tascosa giving his occupation as "gambler."

After a brief stay at his family's home in Flatonia, "Squirrel-Eye" Charlie headed west again. Perhaps, like his erstwhile boss, he picked up some skill with cards and—knowing he had kin there—gravitated to Tascosa, where he took up the profession of gambler. But if he was hoping for a quiet life after his misadventures on the buffalo range, he was in for serious disappointment.[13]

---
crb

Chapter 5

crb

1878

BILLY THE KID HITS TOWN

IN TRADITIONAL accounts Tascosa's metamorphosis from sleepy *plazita* to frontier cow town began in the spring of 1877 when George Julius "Jules" Howard, a merchant and trader from Colfax County, New Mexico, arrived with his partner Isaiah Rinehart. In fact, both Howard and Rinehart paid taxes in Colfax County in 1877, and the latter at least was still in New Mexico in 1878; perhaps, then, Howard arrived first, and Rinehart joined him later.

Other than that he was born in Kentucky about 1839, little is known about Howard; but Rinehart, who had been a close personal friend of Lucien B. Maxwell, was a former sheriff of Colfax County, New Mexico. Appointed March 8, 1876, to complete the term of incumbent Orson K. Crittenden, who had been removed from office, his timing could hardly have been worse.

On March 24, 1876, Texas-born David Crockett—distant relative of the famous frontiersman, former felon turned squatter rancher, and well-known troublemaker—together with his foreman, Augustus "Gus" Heffernon, and another local

named Henry Goodman, shot and killed three black soldiers of the 9th Cavalry outside the Saint James Hotel in Cimarron, apparently because the troopers had the

crb

Isaiah Rinehart and his wife, Sarah.
(Courtesy of Chuck Hornung)

temerity to enter a white man's saloon. At the September term of court in Taos, Crockett was fined one hundred dollars, a slap on the wrist for "carrying arms." Having gotten away with murder, he and Heffernon began "treeing" the town (also known as "hoorawing": making the civilians seek shelter by climbing trees) on a regular basis, riding their horses into stores and saloons and firing their guns into the ceilings, forcing citizens into bars at gunpoint, and making them buy drinks for everyone. Rinehart, as sheriff, seems to have been powerless to restrain them; in fact, one tale has it that Crockett forced him to consume drink after drink until he became helplessly drunk.

Late in September, Crockett and Heffernon again hoorawed the town for two days, letting Rinehart know that if he interfered they would put him down like a hydrophobic dog. That was a threat too far: Saturday evening, September 30, Rinehart deputized his friend, sometime partner, and local rancher Joseph Holbrook and John McCulloch, postmaster and owner of the National Hotel. Arming themselves with shotguns, the trio hid near Schwenk's saloon and waited until Crockett and Heffernon got ready to leave.

As the two men approached, Holbrook stepped out and demanded they surrender, but they grabbed their guns, whereupon the three lawmen simultaneously opened fire. The riders galloped off toward the Cimarron River, where the lawmen found Crockett's horse standing on the bank, its rider stone dead in the saddle. Heffernon, slightly wounded, had kept going but gave himself up a few days later; he escaped from the Cimarron jail with little difficulty on the night of October 31. The following year Rinehart, Holbrook, and McCulloch were arraigned at Taos on murder charges, but they were later acquitted by a jury. Shortly thereafter, it was

Cimarron: scene of the shooting of Crockett and Heffernon as it is today. The building that was Schwenk's Gambling Hall is on the extreme right. (Author's photograph)

alleged, Rinehart (a former school commissioner) absconded with one thousand dollars belonging to the county school fund and went to Texas.[1]

Prior to his arrival in Atascosa, as it was then known, and suggesting that his departure for Texas had not been entirely unplanned, Rinehart had paid $61.50 for an option on forty-one acres of land south of the town's single street. On this, about a quarter of a mile west of Casimero Romero's home, he and Jules Howard built a two-room adobe general store selling whiskey, ammunition, drugs, medicines, and food supplies. Their business association was to be but a brief one, however; within the year Rinehart bought Howard out.[2]

Early in the summer of 1878, James Edward McMasters, Pennsylvania-born son of Quaker parents, who had come to Colorado the year after the Civil War and been a bookkeeper for Lucien B. Maxwell at Cimarron, arrived in Atascosa with a wagonload of dry goods. Deciding it would be as good a place as any to do business, he formed a partnership with Jules Howard, and they opened a store opposite Rinehart's.

Big, burly "Jim Mac," about thirty-seven years old at that time, soon became active in putting Atascosa officially on the map. An application for a post office was filed with the U.S. Post Office Department in Washington, which rejected it on the grounds that an identically named Texas town already existed. A second application was made with the initial A amputated, and on June 24, 1878, Tascosa's post office was established with Jules Howard as its first postmaster.

Soon

a weekly mail Star Route was established between Mobeetie, at Fort Elliott, and Las Vegas, New Mexico, and later on another one between Tascosa and Dodge City, Kansas. On the Tascosa-Mobeetie route a post office was established at the LX ranch and named "Wheeler." This was the first post office in Potter County. Prior to the establishing of the route, any mail taken out of the country or brought in [went to, or] came from, Dodge City, Kansas, 275 miles away by freight wagon or by Old Dad Barnes, a cowboy who collected the letters at the various ranches and took them to Dodge City at fifty cents each and bringing the return mail at the same price.

The mail coach, according to Molly Russell, "was a buckboard that could carry three passengers. A Mr. ["Dad"] Barnes and a Mr. [Cape] Willingham were early operators of this line, it changed hands often."[3]

"Scotty" Wilson, who had quit the LE and taken up residence in Tascosa, con-

James McMasters. (Courtesy of the Haley Memorial Library, Midland, Texas)

tracted to carry mail weekly between Tascosa and Liberty, New Mexico, five miles from Fort Bascom. "One night after arriving at Liberty he got intoxicated, crawled under a billiard table and went to sleep. John Dinan, the proprietor, had also got on a spree and commenced firing his six-shooter in the saloon; one bullet, ricocheting, struck Scotty a slanting shot on top of his head and plowed around under the skin knocking him out. When he recovered consciousness he hitched up his team and started back to Tascosa without the mail. As soon as he arrived there he sent in his resignation as mail carrier—also swore off drinking and did not touch intoxicants again for twenty years."[4]

Mail contracting in this unmapped environment—a sort of government-funded Pony Express—lent itself beautifully to fraud, and fraud ineluctably followed. The Star Route established on September 4, 1879, between Fort Elliott (Mobeetie) and Las Vegas—part of Star Route No. 30,034 from Vinita, Indian Territory, to Las Vegas, a total distance of 725 miles—was operated by a company at whose head was Arkansas senator Stephen W. Dorsey, a man who had already encountered "serious legal difficulties" over his involvement in allegedly fraudulent railroad construction bonds. This firm had contracted with the U.S. government for Star Routes over a number of southwestern states; when its activities were investigated by the Post Office Department, it was found to have been receiving payment for deliveries to and between "towns" and "cities" that simply did not exist.

One of these fictitious places was the "large town" of Wheeler, actually a post office at the LX ranch kept by Billy the Kid's onetime sidekick Josiah G. "Doc" Scurlock. Another was "Silver City," purportedly having a population of ten thousand souls located at Leahy Creek, where a traveler would have found Scotty Wilson keeping the stage station, his only companion a woman "of extremely dark hue." In 1881 Dorsey was indicted for conspiracy to defraud the government but was acquitted in a celebrated trial; insiders said paying off his defense lawyer Bob Ingersoll cost him one-third of his Triangle Dot ranch near Springer, New Mexico.[5]

As already noted, documentary records for this period of Tascosa's history are sparse, but there is plenty of testimony to suggest it was already a dangerous place. One undated document, anonymously compiled, lists twenty burials said to have been made in Tascosa's cemetery in the year 1878; predictably, it contains many errors. According to Ella Sheets McDonald, a daughter of Jesse Sheets, who lived in the town in the mid-1880s, there were twenty-eight bodies in the cemetery, among them a woman and two babies, a man named "Big Jim" Benson killed by lightning, and Johnny Page, an alleged suicide. Of most of the others, however, little or nothing is known.[6]

That a list of nearly twenty anonymous men who all died inside one year might not be entirely the product of someone's lively imagination, however, is confirmed by Jim East. "During the four years I was at Tascosa as sheriff and during the two years before when Cape Willingham was sheriff [that is, 1880–86] there were twenty-six men killed. Judge McMasters and I counted them up one time and that was his tally." More recent research has come closer to identifying the occupants and locations of all the graves in Boot Hill. With the correct dates of their deaths (where known) appended, they are as follows:

1. Jesse Sheets (1886), exhumed in 1928 and reburied at Roswell, New Mexico.
2. John Leverton (1887), was not buried in Boot Hill
3. Ed King (1886)
4. Frank Valley (1886)
5. Fred Chilton (1886)
6. Fred Leigh (1881)
7. Bob Russell (1880)
8. The Dutchman, killed by Catfish Kid [Pete Fulton] (1887)
9. Bacilio Sanches, killed by a horse (1886)
10. Frank Norwood [Bill Gibson] (1882)
11. John Maley (1883)
12. Ruben Juice
13. Apple Axe—Cook's Helper
14. Bill Smith
15. Overton Bounds
16. Ralph Ledbetter
17. Jim Jones
18. Bill Klimm
19. Carl Yowell
20. Bob Luker
21. Unknown adult female
22 & 23. Unknown (two infants), died of smallpox
24. Hugh Dickey
25. George Findley
26. Ed Morgan
27. Bobby Hughes[7]

As we have seen, events in "Tuscosa" went largely unreported in the newspapers of its nearest neighbor, Dodge City. During 1877 and 1878 the *Dodge City Times* cataloged a number of Panhandle shootings, fatal and otherwise, but as indicated

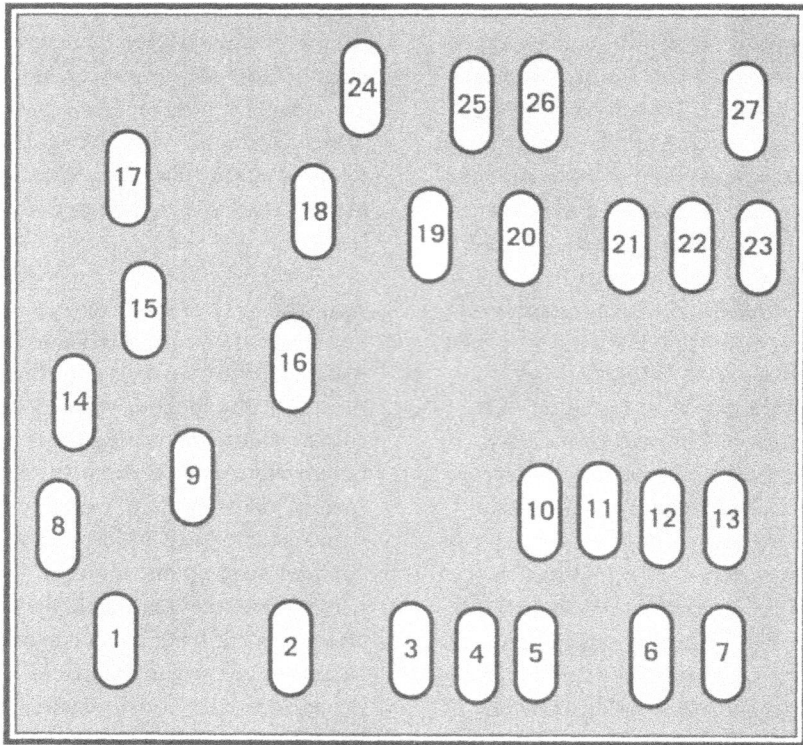

in the following roster, mainly compiled from reports in that newspaper, none of them—with the exception of the notorious Casner killings—were near Tascosa.

Panhandle Shootings/Killings

1877

January 27 William and Daniel Casner killed [by Sostenes l'Archevêque?].

Date unknown Sostenes l'Archevêque killed [?] by Nicolas Martinez, Miguel Garcia, and Felix Gurules.

April 13 Philip J. Goodfellow kills John Bottom.

May 6 Buffalo hunter Tom Lumpkins killed at Double Mountains by another hunter, "Limpy" Smith.

May 18 "Vigilantes" hang Goodfellow.

May 19 Nicolas Martinez et al. killed by Casners.

August 11 "A few days ago" Bill Gibbs, Lee & Reynolds trainmaster, shot "Mexican Joe" Camps [both recovered].

October 27 Capt. Wirt Davis, 4th Cavalry, hangs horse thieves Chummy Jones, Charley Morrow, and "three others."

December 29 Theodore Tesch killed by saloonkeeper Frenchy Manson at Fort Elliott.

1878

January 13 Saloonkeeper Joe Mason shot Ed Ryan at Sweetwater.

March 2 One Brockleman murdered at Palo Duro by Charles Ray [Pony Diehl?].

April 6 One Gibbs shot [and presumably killed] by George Thomas at Camp Supply.

May 25 "Old Bradley" killed between Fort Elliott and Sweetwater by one Hart.

June 22 James Mann killed by Frederick Blackwell [Blakeman?] at Fort Elliott on June 7.

1879

March 22 Private Johnson killed Private Graves, both of Co. "A" 10th Cavalry.

July 5 Three men from Barbour County and another from Iowa went into Indian Territory to buy cattle; four men rode into their camp, killing two and wounding a third.

August 14 J. S. Wheeler beaten to death by J. N. Morris, both Lee & Reynolds teamsters. Wheeler had slapped Morris the night before in a dispute.[8]

It is self-evident that for every incident that got into the newspapers, there were probably one or more that did not, such as the murder said to have been committed at Tascosa in the fall of 1878 by Henry Stevens, a former LX rider who was laid off by W. C. Moore. Stevens let it be known he wanted to kill Moore, but instead when "one of old man Trujillo's boys . . . got to drinking and making some slighting remarks about Texans . . . Stevens shot him dead."[9]

The difficulties inherent in compiling a more reliable rendering of the early-day casualties are highlighted by the sad saga of "the Right Honorable George" related to a reporter at the cemetery in 1936 by an "old Settler":

That was the name the boys gave him, not knowing any other . . . a real nice fellow, as I remember. . . . [T]he fact that he got a good big bundle of mail every month from jolly old England gave rise to the belief that maybe he was the wayward boy out of one of the best families back there and was just laying out until matters had a chance to quiet down and blow over some at home. . . .

Most accounts of [how] Sir George was taken from our midst varied at the time, but I had a chance to know that Billy the Kid, who was a snake if I ever saw one, mistook Mobeetie Mollie's motherly attentions to the Englishman for a horse of another color with consequences which were right regrettable.

Yes, Mollie, she was laid out the same night in the same way. She's down there on the side of that draw away from the hill. I reckon that was a kind of concession to the proprietors. Of course she was dead, but then you didn't know Mobeetie Mollie.

Could the subject of this dolorous tale perhaps have been George Findley? It's possible, of course, but the inference that Billy the Kid killed him can hardly be called evidence. The same is true of another Tascosan casualty described by the same storyteller, who "stroked his flowing silver-white mustache reminiscently" as he related the tale of "the Colonel," who during the Civil War had taken "right hasty leave of his command in the thick of one of the best battles."

Many's the night I have sat at the Colonel's table and lost a whole month's pay, which was only about fifteen dollars for a cowhand in those days. None of the boys ever regretted losing to that fellow though. He was so pleasant and always allowed the customers to owe him, which we always did. He was mighty fond of music and I remember well when things were quiet at the tables he would take down his old fiddle and sit out on the portico and play almost until sun-up.

One night a bunch of high rolling hands from the Fryin' Pan came to town with money to burn and a thirst in proportion and ended up in the Colonel's game. . . . The eyes of one of these young

hotheads was a little quicker under the influence of liquor or else his temper was a little bit shorter than usual with the result that the game broke up in a shower of lead. I have been told since that the old boy never made a move towards the drawer where he kept his weapon, but when they got him he just slumped forward in his chair and said "Thank God."

"The whole town turned out for the buryin', which took place right over there by the gate," said the ancient, spinning the story of the trial of the killer, presided over by Judge Willis, at which a lone juryman held out for hanging when the other eleven were for acquittal. This impasse was finally broken when someone told the holdout there was a high-stakes poker game going on across the street, at which point "the exponent of grim justice" addressed his fellow jurymen with the words, "Well, gents, I personally never let pleasure interfere with business, so we'll let this——off." Whereupon, it says here, the trial was concluded. Although, as we shall see, the anecdote may have some basis in fact, these "recollections" sound more like one of those tall tales for which Texas was (and still is) so famous.[10]

Something similar might be said of many of the other stories recounted about Billy the Kid's sojourn in Tascosa in 1878, which lasted by some accounts a matter of weeks in the fall, by others as long as six months. That he and his *compañeros* were actually there is not in doubt, but as with everything else we know about the Kid, such facts as there were have become colored in the recollections of those who knew him—or claimed they knew him—by "knowledge" acquired much later.

Billy the Kid's life was little more to history than a candle in the wind, yet his is a mightily resilient legend. Where he was born and when (believed to have been about 1859), the name—or even nationality—of his father, where he lived as a child, all these are still a mystery, and much of what we do know is fatally flawed by the overlay of more than a century of myth. What can be stated with reasonable confidence is that his real name was probably Henry McCarty, that he had a brother (or perhaps half brother) named Joseph, that the family lived briefly in Wichita in the early 1870s, and that his mother, Catherine McCarty, married a peripatetic mining prospector named William Henry Harrison Antrim in Santa Fe in 1873 prior to moving to Silver City, where she died eighteen months later.

Henry McCarty—Henry Antrim as he was known in Silver City—fell among thieves following his mother's death and, when he was jailed for petty larceny, skinned out of the Silver City jail and turned to making his living with cards and horse theft in Arizona. In the fall of 1877, after he killed a bullying blacksmith in a deadfall on the fringes of Fort Grant, he drifted back into New Mexico's Lincoln County to steal some more horses with a gang of bravos led by Jesse Evans and known as "The Boys." After what may have been a short, sharp shock of jail time for his sins, the Kid signed on as a cowboy for English rancher John Tunstall.

The Englishman and his lawyer-adviser Alexander McSween (with the financial support of cattle baron John Chisum, who had his own agenda for wanting them to succeed) had for a year been building up a challenge to the existing mercantile monopoly of L. G. Murphy & Co. Known throughout the territory as "The House," Murphy and his fiery-tempered young protégé, James Dolan, ran Lincoln

County—a fiefdom that measured some 170 miles from north to south, 150 from east to west, roughly equal in size to Murphy's native Ireland—the way they wanted, using muscle or the law as the situation required. They owned the local sheriff, maintained a profitable relationship as whiskey supplier and loan shark to the military, offered unlimited credit and subsistence to well-known rustler gangs (like "The Boys") who stole cattle to order for them, and for well over a decade ruthlessly appropriated most of the government money emanating from the Mescalero Apache In-

Billy the Kid: the famous ferrotype believed
to be the only authentic picture.
(Author's collection)

[45]

dian Agency at nearby Fort Stanton. When Tunstall's challenge became too powerful to ignore, the law was manipulated to put him out of business. When that didn't work, he was murdered; his death on February 18, 1878, marked the onset of what became known as the Lincoln County War.

The Kid (he would not be called Billy the Kid until the end of the last full year of his life, long after his sojourn in Tascosa) was going by the name of William H. Bonney. During the internecine guerrilla warfare of the six months following Tunstall's death, he metamorphosed from drifter to undisputed leader of the Tunstall-McSween faction, participating in a series of escalatingly bloody shootouts that included the All Fool's Day assassination of Sheriff William Brady and one of his deputies and ended with the famous "Five-Day Battle" in Lincoln, July 14–19, 1878, which climaxed with the burning of Alexander McSween's house and the death of the lawyer and at least four others.[11]

Following "the Big Killing," as it was called, and his failure to get himself included in the amnesty offered by New Mexico governor Lew Wallace, the Kid turned to rustling full time. On September 5, 1878, he and his gang—all that was left of the group who called themselves "Regulators'—raided a ranch near Lincoln, driving off fifteen fine horses and 150 head of cattle, which the gang drove over to the Panhandle.[12] By the time they got there, they were driving a sizable remuda of horses, its numbers probably swollen by animals appropriated when they were at Puerto de Luna; the idea of stealing horses from horse thieves—of which breed much of that little town's population consisted—probably appealed to the Kid's often perverse sense of humor. About forty miles east of old Fort Bascom, the Kid and his

men caught up with the Chisum outfit. Concerned for the safety of his family and the cattle they had charge of in New Mexico for Hunter & Evans of Kansas City, John Chisum—who was in the East—had instructed his brother James to move their herds out of the Pecos Valley, to which some of the worst border scum of the Southwest had flocked in the aftermath of the Lincoln County War. "Regulators come up with us at Red River Springs on the 25 Sept 1878," Sallie Chisum noted in her diary.[13]

"Jim Chisum had cattle on the Canadian in the summer of 1878," said Garrett H. "Kid" Dobbs, who was working then for Scotsman James Campbell. "Chisum and his daughter were at the camp which was above Tascosa. Charlie Neebow [Nebo] was Chisum's wagon boss in the Panhandle and he had with him among others Johnny Newell, Bill Hutch, Tom O'Phillard [O'Folliard], Tom Pickett, Henry Brown. . . . [John] Chisum came out there in the winter of 1878."[14]

Soon after this, the Kid and his men rode down to Tascosa. On the way they encountered Henry Hoyt, the young doctor "adventuring" in the West and in the process "sowing a good crop of wild oats," as one contemporary put it. The Kid told him they would be bringing down a herd of horses to sell and invited Hoyt to spread the word when he got into town.[15]

When the cowmen heard that the Kid and his men were coming in, they called on him to meet them. Their spokesman, LIT wagon boss C. S. "Bill" McCarty—one can almost see the Kid's impish grin when he learned the name of the man he was talking to—asked him what his business was. The Kid answered frankly; cattlemen were always short of horses, so he had brought some over to sell. McCarty, "a

Texas raised man [who] knew how to handle men, any amount of men [and] never carried a gun," told him they wanted no trouble, and Billy gave his word there would be none. That settled, he and his men pitched camp south of town where Tascosa Creek emptied into the Canadian. "Billy stayed in Tascosa and put his horses on the head of Plum or Tascosa Creek," Dobbs said.

All of the men in the Lincoln County War came out with him or Chisum. One of them [Fred Waite] said he had a good home over in the Cherokee Nation and he was going home while he could. . . . One of Chisum's men was killed in Salinas Plaza. They had a dance there and there was a saloon north of the dance hall. This fellow got on his horse and started down town, loping his horse and hollering a time or two. He came around the dance hall and three Mexicans grabbed their Bill Dukes [belle-duques, a type of knife] or Bowie knives and cut him all to pieces. . . . I think his name was Al Westover. Nine white men were killed at Salinas Plaza before they [the Mexicans] lost a man.[16]

George Littlefield's nephew J. Phelps White was also in Tascosa at the time. "Billy the Kid . . . had what he called a race horse with him," he recalled.

He hadn't been there an hour when he matched a race with old man Rinehart's horse "Spider." He was a race horse and we knew it. We didn't mean to beat him so badly but when we found out it was Billy the Kid we thought that we'd better beat him good so there would be no squabble. They agreed on a short race and we were not to have starter judges. Fred Waite, a Kid man, and I were judges on the finish.

So the Kid and [C.S.] McCarty went down just to see they got off all right. Everybody could see at the finish that the Kid's horse was badly beat, but Fred Waite claimed a foul. He said his horse came out six or eight feet ahead. I replied "If Spider didn't beat him fifty feet, then he didn't beat him fifty inches." The Kid came loping up about this time and we explained the matter to him, Fred contending for the foul and then saying that their horse was beat only a few feet. But the Kid said "Give it up, Fred, we're beat." We had all bet some money as well as some horses on the race. The Kid and his outfit stayed around there about six months but never made any trouble.[17]

Not everyone was so tolerant of the newcomers. When the Kid and Henry Brown rode out to the LX ranch looking to sell horses, ranch superintendent William C. Moore, who himself had a past that was nothing to boast about, made no secret of the fact that he considered the Kid and his men nothing but a bunch of horse thieves who ought to be run out of town. That was a bad mistake, Kid Dobbs said.

The Kid and some of his men came over to the LX ranch . . . stayed all night at the LX, ate breakfast and unhobbled their horses, saddled and tied out their riding horses. Billy called to Moore who was inside the house and said "I want to see you outside, Mr. Moore." He had his gun in his hand and so did [Henry] Brown. "I want to know what you know about my horse stealing," he asked the ranch manager. The yellow showed up in Moore in a hurry and he made a stand that he had not done any talking. Billy the Kid said, "Mr. Moore, I know you are quite a man in these parts and that what you say goes with a lot of people, but if I hear any more of your talk I'll shoot you half in two."[18]

It would appear that even though he knew he was a horse thief, the Kid was averse to being called one. And that wasn't all he was touchy about: on another occasion Ellsworth Torrey, who ranched northwest of Tascosa, is said to have become annoyed because his cook fed the Kid and his men when they stopped off at the ranch. "A big fellow 65 or 70 years of age who wore a leather jacket, dressed like a pioneer scout, was a great poker player [who] would play poker 36 hours at a stretch,"[19] Torrey, a former New England sea captain who was still "awfully green on the country and on the cattle business," unwisely remarked that the Kid and his band

weren't fit to associate with decent people or to eat with them. [So] Billy took four of his men and came to Torrey's house at

noon one day. He asked for horse feed for his horses and dinner for his men. The horses were fed and dinner was prepared. Torrey tried to feed Billy and his men first, but Billy insisted on the family eating with them.

After dinner he called Mr. Torrey outside and said, "Now, Mr. Torrey, do you feel disgraced in any way by our having eaten and associated with your family as you have been saying?" Torrey of course vigorously denied saying any such thing. Billy continued, "You are quite an old man, Mr. Torrey, for this country and you are doing pretty well. You have considerable property about and you can think what you like about me and my men, but don't talk. If you do, I'll shoot that blue streak across your belly in pieces."[20]

Exactly how long the Kid and his pals remained in Tascosa is uncertain, but during their stay they "mingled freely" with

Ellsworth Torrey ranch, Alamocitas, later LS ranch headquarters.
(Courtesy of the Amarillo Public Library)

the Tascosans, "sold and traded horses with anyone so inclined, varying their business dealings with drinking, gambling, horse racing and target shooting."[21] A number of the locals recalled the Kid taking part in shooting matches for a dollar or sometimes five dollars a shot with blacksmith Henry Kimball, a noted sharpshooter; the story is also told of another occasion when the Kid and former Dodge City lawman Bat Masterson were beaten to the money in a shooting match by silver-tongued local lawyer Temple Houston, son of the Texas hero. So good was Houston's shooting that the Kid chose not to compete further; he "pushed through the crowd . . . held up his hands for silence and asked in his mild and quiet manner, '¿Quien puede haserio mejor?'"

This fractured Spanish grammar was probably the work of the narrator rather than the Kid, but the intention is clear: Who, he was asking, could do better than that? At the same time he was showing what a good loser he was. Whether he ever said—or did—anything of the kind is entirely another matter: the Kid was killed in 1881, a year before Temple Houston ever set foot in Tascosa.[22]

Billy wasn't just a shootist, Henry Hoyt recorded, he was "an expert at most western sports, with the exception of drinking." He described the Kid as a handsome youth with "a smooth face, wavy brown hair, an athletic and symmetrical figure, and clear blue eyes that could look one through and through. Unless angry, he always seemed to have a pleasant expression with a ready smile. . . . He spoke Spanish like a native, and although only a beardless boy, was nevertheless a natural leader of men."

Beardless boy or not, Billy ruled his gang "with a rod of iron," Hoyt related. Hoyt went on to tell a hard-to-believe tale

of how one day, while John Middleton was "drinking heavily at the Howard & Mc-Masters store and began to get ugly," the Kid came in, called him a "damned idiot," and ordered him to "light out for camp. Middleton, his eyes flashing, replied, 'Billy, you'd never talk that way to me if we were alone.'" When the Kid put his hand on his gun and invited Middleton to step out behind the store where they *would* be alone, "Middleton's face turned an ashen color, his lower lip dropped, and with a sickly grin he stuttered out, 'Aw, Billy, come off [it], can't you take a joke?' 'You bet I can,' said Billy, 'but this is no joke. You heard me. Git for camp and git quick.'" And Middleton "shuffled out the door like a whipped dog."[23]

Was this the bravo the Kid's old boss John Tunstall had once characterized as "the most desperate-looking man I ever set eyes on"?[24] It's hard to believe, but Hoyt had no real reason to make it up; perhaps, then, there is some truth to the story that Middleton was never the same after being severely wounded in an April 1878 gunfight during the Lincoln County War.

One night they all attended the weekly *baile* at Pedro Romero's house, seemingly observing the unwritten law that no weapons be carried. During the proceedings, Hoyt and the Kid stepped outside for some air, and Hoyt challenged Billy to a footrace back to the dance hall. Billy, going lickety-split, tripped in the doorway and fell headlong in the center of the dance floor. "Quicker than a flash, his prostrate body was surrounded by his four pals, back to back, with a Colt's forty-five in each hand, cocked and ready for business." How or where they had concealed the guns, Hoyt said, was a mystery, as was (and still is) the matter of who they were so anxious to defend Billy from. Anyway, the result of this escapade was that in spite of their contrition, they were thereafter barred from all future dances.[25]

Yet another addition to the legends surrounding the Kid's stay in Tascosa was added by "Frenchy" McCormick, former Mobeetie saloon girl and wife of gambler and livery stable owner Mickey McCormick, who described a scene she claimed to have witnessed in one of the saloons during the Kid's visit. Charlie Bowdre got drunk, then

> leaped on top of the bar with a six shooter in each hand and he sang a song . . .

> *I can take the toughest bronco in the wild*
> *and woolly west*
> *I can ride him I can break him let him do*
> *his level best*
> *I can handle any cattle ever wore a coat of*
> *hair*
> *And I've had a lively tussle with a tarnel*
> *grizzly bear*
> *I can rope and throw the longhorn of the*
> *wildest Texas brand*
> *And in Indian disagreements I can play a*
> *leading hand*
> *Come a ti yi youpy youpy ya youpy ya*
> *Come a ti yi youpy youpy ya*

There was a whole string of verses on that same order with the "Come a ti yi youpa" chorus after every one. We didn't think anything of that in those days. We were used to seeing drunken men and they'd swing their hats and pull their guns and shoot and play tough. It's a wonder more weren't killed.[26]

Alas, Frenchy didn't arrive in Tascosa until 1880, by which time the Kid and his *compañeros* were long gone.

"Another diversion," Henry Hoyt recalled, "was draw poker, which all indulged in. Some time previously I had won a very pretty ladies' gold watch which Billy admired and wished to purchase. In a previous talk he had told me about his romance with a little New Mexican beauty, none other than Senorita Lolita whom I had met at Fort Sumner on the Pecos River, and suspecting he wanted the watch for her, I made him a present of it, which pleased him very much."[27]

Hoyt was being coy with good reason: the "Senorita Lolita" he had met in Fort Sumner, the lady he claimed the Kid was romancing, was of course Paulita Maxwell, still alive and, as noted earlier, still capable of filing a libel suit at the time Hoyt published his book. The matter of whether in fact the Kid was sparking Maxwell's sister as early as the fall of 1878, although not impossible, is open to serious doubt: Paulita would at that time have been only fourteen years old—a veritable Lolita indeed. It should also be heavily emphasized that despite Hoyt's inferences, Paulita Maxwell was no "señorita" but only one-quarter Mexican (her mother was of French-Canadian and Mexican descent while her father was of French-Irish ancestry). By the standards then applying, she would surely have been far too young for her wealthy and aristocratic family to permit, let alone encourage, someone as notorious as the Kid to pay her court.

Late in October 1878, just before Hoyt left Tascosa, the Kid rode into town and made the doctor a present of "Dandy Dick," the best horse in his remuda, an Arabian sorrel branded BB on the left hip. When Hoyt, who was already planning to leave Tascosa, pointed out that he would be taking the horse into New Mexico, the Kid quickly scribbled out a "bill of sale" (in reality just a piece of paper to protect Hoyt from being accused of horse theft) and had it witnessed by the proprietors at the Howard & McMasters store. Many years later Hoyt learned "Dandy Dick" was the horse Sheriff William Brady had ridden from his Bonito farm into Lincoln on April 1, 1878, the day he was killed.[28]

After wintering in Tascosa, the Kid and his old Lincoln County gang broke up for good; with newer, rougher accomplices, he would be a thorn in the side of the Panhandle for a year or two more before steps were taken to put him out of business for good.

Chapter 6

JIM KENEDY

"HE WAS A WILD ONE."

ANOTHER early arrival in Tascosa whose brief, but not uneventful, stay there has been largely overlooked was Henry Hoyt's pal Jim Kenedy, who in 1877 brought a herd of about two thousand head of his father's cattle up to the Canadian Valley and turned them loose adjacent to the Torrey ranch on land occupied later by the LX ranch.

Born on February 22, 1855, James W. Kenedy was the son of Mifflin Kenedy (1818–1895), former steamboat operator, pioneer Texan, and owner of the quarter-million-acre Laureles ranch near Corpus Christi. On April 16, 1852, Mifflin Kenedy married Petra Vela de Vidal, the widow of Col. Luis Vidal of Mier, Mexico, at Brownsville. Among the numerous children from her first marriage was Adrian J. Vidal (1840–1865) who famously "served both the blue and the gray, deserted from both armies, joined a third [the Juaristas] and was shot by a fourth [the French] in 1865."[1]

The Kenedys were a large and wealthy family: the 1860 census for Cameron County, Texas, shows steamboat captain Mifflin Kenedy, born at Dowington, Penn-

sylvania, June 8, 1818, owner of fifty thousand dollars' worth of real estate and the same amount in personal estate.

During that same census year Kenedy became joint owner, with Capt. Richard King, of the Santa Gertrudis ranch in Nueces County. Also listed in the census are six children from his wife's first marriage—Louisa, eighteen; Rosa, sixteen; Adrian, fifteen; Concepcion, thirteen; and Vicenta, eleven—and six from her second—Thomas, seven; James, five; John G. (born at Brownsville April 22, 1856, and for some reason listed in this census as Gregorio), four; Salomé, three; and William, one.

In addition there is an E. J. Kenedy, possibly Mifflin Kenedy's brother, listed as a clerk, and six Mexican-born house servants ranging in age from eleven to fifty-four, indicating that it was a substantial household, as befitted a man of such great wealth. Mifflin Kenedy was one of the first Texas ranchers to enclose his land; in 1869 he encircled Laureles with thirty-six miles of smooth wire fence. By the mid-1870s he had become one of the largest cattle ranchers in Texas: in 1877 his son John, now twenty-one, took a herd of eighteen thousand head branded with Kenedy's Laurel Leaf up the trail, and in 1878 a further fifteen thousand head of Kenedy longhorns went up the trail to Dodge.[2]

Jim Kenedy, always known by the nickname "Spike"—perhaps because he was as wild and as stubborn as a bull buffalo calf, which in those days was also called a "spike"—first went up the trail in 1872, when he was only seventeen. He almost immediately acquired a reputation for violent behavior in an incident that arose out of a confrontation during a card game in Nick Lentz's saloon in Ellsworth, Kansas, when Kenedy, "a swarthy complexioned young man with coal black eyes," cast aspersions on the way cattleman "Print" Olive was dealing the cards. Given a verbal lashing that he had no choice but to sit and take—Olive was armed and he was not—Kenedy stamped out of the saloon promising "there would be another day." And there was.

Later that same Saturday, July 27, 1872, Olive was "seated at a table playing cards in the Ellsworth Billiard Saloon." About six o'clock

Kennedy [*sic*] came into the room, went behind the bar and taking a revolver walked up in front of Olive and fired at him, telling him to "pass in his checks." Olive threw up his hands exclaiming "don't shoot." The second, third and fourth shot took effect, one entering the groin and making a bad wound, one in the thigh and one in the hand.

Olive could not fire, although he was armed, but some one, it seems uncertain who, fired at Kennedy, hitting him in the hip, making only a flesh wound. The difficulty arose from a game of cards in the forenoon, Kennedy accusing Olive of un-

fair dealing. Olive replied in language that professionals cannot bear. The affair made considerable excitement. The wounded were taken into custody and cared for. Drs. Duck and Fox extracted the bullet from Olive and a piece of his gold chain which was shot into the wound. It was feared that Olive would not survive, but the skill of the doctors saved him. Kennedy was removed to South Main Street and put under the guard of three policemen, but by the aid of friends he escaped during the night from the window and has not been heard from.[3]

Although wounded, Kenedy wasted no time returning to the safety of Texas and seems to have kept a very low profile until November 3, 1875, when he joined the command of Capt. Leander H. McNelly as a private in the Texas Rangers, re-created

Isom Prentice "Print" Olive.
(Courtesy of Leon C. Metz)

the preceding year. During Kenedy's service, McNelly's unit spent a brief period in DeWitt County in an unsuccessful attempt to bring the Sutton-Taylor feud to an end and was also sent to the Rio Grande to halt, or at least reduce, both cross-border raiding and cattle theft by Mexican bandits on the one hand and retaliatory raids by American settlers into Mexico on the other. If Kenedy played any significant role in these events, no record of it has survived. He served out his year with the unit and received an honorable discharge on April 26, 1876. What his duties were and how good a Ranger he was is not known; none of McNelly's records mention him by name.[4]

He was twenty-two years old when he arrived at Tascosa; almost immediately he struck up a strong friendship with Henry Hoyt. "He was a wild one," Hoyt said, "so his father put him in charge of two thousand head of cattle with a complete outfit and sent him from the home ranch in southern Texas to the Panhandle with the hope of making a man of him." In another account, Kenedy's father "gave him eighteen hundred head of three-year-old cows and bulls. He cut them out for him at Dodge and he drifted them down from there behind us and wintered them above Cheyenne Creek, camping on the river. But he got to acting bad, gambling and whoring around." "That's about all there was to him," another said, adding in then-typically racist contempt, "Didn't have none of his old Daddy. His Mother was Mexican, you know."[5]

Predictably Hoyt didn't mention the bad acting, the gambling, or the whoring around any more than he mentioned his later involvement with the vigilantes in Las Vegas. In his book Kenedy conducted himself "in an exemplary manner, became

very popular, and his father's expectations seemed about to be fulfilled." Not hardly; that summer of 1878, Kenedy rounded up his cattle, drove them up the trail to Dodge City, and sold them. Other accounts suggest he sold out to Ellsworth Torrey and infer he went to Dodge City only to blow the proceeds. Once in Dodge City, "unable to withstand the temptations of the underworld there, he 'stepped out' and was brought home with a shoulder and one arm shot all to pieces."[6]

In this very guarded version of events, Hoyt not only chose to be economical with the facts but also avoided mentioning the reason for or the manner in which Kenedy had received his injuries, although the circumstances were so notorious he cannot have been unaware of them. Everything indicates that either immediately or soon after he reached Dodge City, Kenedy went looking for trouble. On July 29, 1878, he was arrested for carrying a firearm by none other than Assistant Marshal Wyatt Earp. A couple of weeks later, on August 17, he was again arrested, this time on a charge of being disorderly, by City Marshal Charles "Senator" Bassett. Kenedy reacted to this harassment by accosting Dodge City mayor James "Dog" Kelley in the latter's Alhambra Saloon and telling him exactly what he thought of Dodge and its lawmen. When Kelley brusquely told him to either straighten up or face even tougher sanctions, Kenedy got into a fight with the burly saloonkeeper in which he was soundly thrashed and then kicked out into the street.[7]

To Kenedy, such comprehensive humiliation by a man he doubtless considered a stupid Kansas cow town saloonkeeper was an unbearable affront. Fired with plans for revenge, Kenedy took the train to Kansas City, where he bought himself a fast horse.

Some weeks later he returned to Dodge, and around four o'clock in the morning of October 4 he rode around to Mayor Kelley's cabin. Reaching it, he fired four shots, two in the air then two through the front door into the room where he believed Kelley to be sleeping. But Kelley, who had become ill shortly after their altercation, was in the hospital and had rented the two-room shack to his mistress, Fannie Keenan, also known as Dora Hand, a popular dance hall singer who entertained at the Alhambra. One bullet "passed through the door, several thicknesses of bed clothing on the bed in the front room occupied by a female lodger [Fannie Garretson, a singer at the Comique Theatre]; through the plastered partition wall and the bed clothing on the second bed, and striking Fannie Keenan on the right side, under the arm, killing her instantly."[8]

Confident that he had probably killed Kelley, Kenedy stopped off for a drink at the only saloon that was open; on the approach of Assistant Marshal Earp, he took off on horseback. It was not until two o'clock that afternoon that a posse remarkable in its constitution—Wyatt Earp, Bat Masterson, Charlie Bassett, and Bill Tilghman were said to be among its members—set out in pursuit. Despite the delay and a heavy storm, they managed to get ahead of their quarry and spread out to wait for him on a ranch near Meade City, about thirty-five miles south of Dodge. Late in the afternoon of Saturday, October 5, Kenedy appeared, coming to a halt a few hundred yards away from the waiting lawmen. "Seeing that he would approach no nearer, the officers thrice commanded Kennedy to throw up his hands. He raised his arm as though to strike his horse with the quirt he held in his hand, when several shots were fired by the officers, one shot striking

James "Dog" Kelley, mayor of Dodge City.
(Courtesy of the Kansas Heritage Center, Dodge City, Kansas)

[55]

Fannie Keenan, a.k.a. Dora Hand. (Courtesy of
the Kansas Heritage Center, Dodge City)

morse and self-hatred crossed his face.
Then, seeing the Sharp's Big Fifty in Bat
[Masterson]'s hand, he snapped 'You
damn son-of-a-bitch. You ought to have
made a better shot than you did!' 'Well,'
replied Bat in astonishment, 'you damn'
murdering son-of-a-bitch, I did the best I
could!'"[10]

A story went around among the cattlemen in both Dodge City and Tascosa that
when Kenedy was brought in to Dodge by
the posse, "they put him in a room over
Wright & Beverly's store. He stood in with
the doctor, who reported every day that he
was going to die, but the truth was that he
was getting well, and having plenty of
money, pretty soon he escaped. He stood
in with the Santa Fe railroad people, and
when he got so he could travel, the train
pulled in and stopped the Pullman right in
front of the store. The depot was a quarter
of a mile away, and the officers were
guarding it, as they had a suspicion he
might try to leave. They put him on the
train and it pulled through without stopping at the depot."[11]

Not so. Weak and feverish from his
wound and loss of blood, Kenedy remained
in his room at the Dodge House until October 29, by which time he had recovered
enough to attend an examination in the
sheriff's office before Judge Rufus G. Cook.
No record of the trial seems to have been
kept, nor were there any witnesses. Whatever the proceedings (and we may assume
they were properly conducted, since Judge
Cook had a long and honorable record as a
magistrate), Kenedy was acquitted, probably because of insufficient evidence. Whereupon he was, as a local newspaper angrily
observed, "free to go on his way rejoicing
whenever he gets ready."[12]

If there was any rejoicing, it would be
later rather than sooner. On December 9,

Kennedy in the left shoulder, making a
dangerous wound; three shots struck the
horse, killing him instantly. Kennedy was
armed with a carbine, two revolvers and a
knife. He was brought in Sunday and
placed in jail, where he is receiving medical
treatment, though he lies in a low and criti-
cal condition."[9]

In Assistant Marshal Wyatt Earp's account of the capture, Kenedy's first words
at the time of his arrest were about the success of his murderous attack on the
mayor's cabin. "'Did I get that bastard
Kelley?' he demanded to know. 'No, but
you killed somebody else,' Wyatt told him.
'Dora Hand was asleep in Kelley's bed.'
The wounded man seemed stunned for a
moment. A look of seemingly genuine re-

Mifflin Kenedy arrived in Dodge, and the following day had his son transferred to the military hospital at Fort Dodge. A week later, in a long and difficult operation, local physician Thomas L. McCarty, assistant U.S. Army surgeon William Scott Tremaine of Fort Dodge, and surgeon Maj. Blencowe Eardley Fryer of Fort Leavenworth (the latter summoned to Dodge by Mifflin Kenedy especially for this purpose) removed some four or five inches of shattered bone from Jim Kenedy's right arm near the elbow. Although the patient lost a great deal of blood, the operation was successful, but in the process the arm itself was rendered useless. Throughout the ordeal Kenedy "showed remarkable fortitude and nerve and said afterward that he would not die from the effects of the operation."[13]

In that, at least, he was right. One chronicler of the saga of Dodge City suggested Kenedy later learned to reuse his crippled arm "well enough to shoot a man or two after his acquittal. But before long he met another who was faster on the draw." In November 1880 a wildly inaccurate report in the *Caldwell Commercial* claimed that Kenedy had killed Wyatt Earp at Sand Creek. Yet another source claimed (without attribution) that Kenedy shot "a drunken troublemaker at the entrance to the harness room of the La Parra [ranch] eight months before his death and had a

murder indictment hanging over him when he died of typhoid." Henry Hoyt was nearer the truth when he observed that Kenedy "never recovered from these wounds, although I think he lived for a year or two."[14]

In fact, when he had recuperated from the operation on his arm, Jim Kenedy returned to Corpus Christi, where he seems to have quieted down considerably. In due course he became "the trusted manager of his father's large ranch and cattle business," and in 1882 he married Corina Balli, "a stepdaughter [sister-in-law] of [John] McAllen's [and Salome Balli Young, owners of the Santa Anita ranch in Hidalgo County], for whom the town in the [Rio Grande] Valley is named."[15] Their union produced a son, George Mifflin Kenedy. Not long after the boy's birth, on Monday, December 29, 1884, James Kenedy died of tuberculosis. The funeral, the largest ever attended in the city up to that time, was held the following day at 3:00 p.m., and the body was buried in the Corpus Christi Catholic Cemetery.[16]

If anyone in Tascosa gave much of a damn that Jim Kenedy was dead, it doesn't show. There was no mention of his passing (or that of his mother, Doña Petra, less than three months later) in the *Tascosa Pioneer* nor in any of the recollections of most of the old-timers who knew him then. Those men had no use for wasters.

Chapter 7

1879-1880

GROWING PAINS

SUDDEN DEATHS notwithstanding, Tascosa continued to flourish, largely thanks to the patronage of the surrounding ranches. Trade picked up. New settlers were coming in. In February 1879 Henry Russell; his wife, Zypha; their three sons, Charley, Claude, and Clyde; and daughter, Mary Ada, known as Molly, en route from Groesbeck, in Limestone County near Waco, to Tiptonville, near Watrous, New Mexico, broke their long journey by stopping over at Tascosa. They were a family well used to moving; Russell, forty-three, was a New Yorker who had married an Illinois girl and settled first in Indiana, where his son Charley was born in 1860. They stayed somewhat longer at Morley in Mecosta County, Michigan, where Molly was born in 1863 and Claude in 1875. That same year, Henry Russell bought some scrip for land near Fort Concho, and the whole family, including Russell's parents, came by train to Dallas, but conditions at San Angelo were so primitive "the elderly couple got lonesome and feared the open country so they went to Houston County to visit a friend from Michigan." From there Henry and Zypha moved to Groes-

beck, arriving December 6, 1875; Clyde was born there the following year.

Their trek across Texas was no pleasure trip. "Got along all right until we hit a snowstorm on the Plains," Molly recounted laconically nearly sixty years later. "We got lost and things looked mighty blue for a while. We burned our feed boxes and everything else we could get our hands on, trying to keep from freezing. The first place we found that was inhabited, we stopped. That was Tascosa."

Molly, then sixteen, recorded that the arrival of the Russell family boosted the town's population (seventeen) by one-third. It is probably characteristic of racial attitudes at that time that, consciously or otherwise, she blithely excluded the town's Mexican citizens from that census. "I was the only girl in ten counties," she recalled. "I didn't go with the young men because I couldn't be going with one and then another and I didn't want to hurt anybody's feelings."

On the north side of the street was a three-room adobe building. The corner room housed the Howard & McMasters store; Howard slept in the connecting room east of the store, and McMasters's living quarters were in the rear room. "At the west end of the street," Molly continued, "was a small residence where an old woman and two children lived. Next was the Rinehart store in a three-room adobe. The east room was the store and the other two rooms were home to Mr. Rinehart and two assistants. Kimball's blacksmith shop fronted the street with living room behind the shop."

The Howard & McMasters store was on the north side of the street; McMasters lived alone, but Howard had a Mexican housekeeper, Martina Romero, who, Molly said, later married Henry Kimball. The "old woman" was in fact a Mrs. Jamerison, whose husband ran sheep and was usually away from home; the family left Tascosa soon after the Russells arrived, and she never heard of them again. Rinehart and his fifteen-year-old son Irwin lived in back of their store, which was on the south side of the street, as was the pokey little adobe where Charley Cummings and another man were operating a small restaurant. Visiting it gave Henry Russell an idea. Abandoning his plan to settle in New Mexico, he bought out Cummings and his partner and set up residence and business in their two-room adobe; for now, running the hash house, his longer-term plan was to open a hotel, work on which was begun the following April.[1]

Also in the spring of 1879 another newcomer to town, wealthy Big Spring businessman John D. Cone, sought to buy a site on Main Street to open a store. Finding neither McMasters nor Rinehart sympathetic to competition, Cone negotiated with Casimero Romero for the purchase of a lot a quarter of a mile east of town where there were some old buildings in which

Henry and Zypha (Briggs) Russell. (Courtesy of the Amarillo Public Library)

Scotty Wilson had kept hogs. There, Cone and his brother Will erected what would eventually become a combination store, saloon, and hotel, "a long adobe building consisting of a large double room and a large store room with a large horse corral behind so they could take care of the freight teams."

They opened for business in May, the single room stocked with a full supply of general merchandise and groceries. Later there would be a row of rooms, built Mexican fashion, on the opposite side of the street from the store; in one of them was a restaurant. This rag-tag collection of buildings was at first known as East Tascosa or Lower Town, "but in time the only name it had was 'Hogtown' and it certainly was a very appropriate name for it. This was the wild part of town, and the officers paid very little attention to what went on, outside of murder."[2]

The Marion Armstrong and Cape Willingham families, who arrived in East Tascosa on August 10, 1879, soon found out how true that was. Cape and Mary Willingham had three children: Drew, who was five; Homer, two; and Ada, a babe in arms. Armstrong and his wife, California, who had emigrated west from Wise County the preceding October, had two sons: Tom, four; and one-year-old Melvin. Only a day or two before their arrival a herd of Texas cattle passed through town en route to California, and the cowboys "went to an old Mexican's down where the LIT ranch now stands and began to shoot up the place. The old man picked up his gun and killed two of [them]. . . . A few days following this fight, a row came up in Cone and Edward's [sic] store between a white man by the name of Stroud and a Mexican. Stroud was killed instantly and the Mexican lived only a few days."

Behind this collision was some dirty dealing by Cone's recently acquired partner, Shelton Edwards, who had bought some sheep in Colorado and given a note in part payment; the holder of the note sent his son down to collect. "Tom [Henry], who was an outlaw, told me that Edwards had offered [him] $300 to kill the young man and Tom said 'He would do it, but he didn't believe Edwards would give him the money.' It appears Stroud took up the offer, but didn't live to collect, anyway."[3]

Late in life Molly Russell, who remembered the name as "Stout," said he was killed in a card game in the Edwards "hotel" in lower Tascosa, where some buffalo hunters had been playing poker all night. Stout, or Stroud, whose real name was Louis Keyes, was "killed by a Mexican who in turn was killed by a cowboy by the name of Bill Yandell [perhaps Randall? see ch. 7, n. 4] who . . . shot between Keyes arm as the Mexican pulled his gun." Buffalo hunter Keyes was a half-blood Cherokee who had been one of the "Forlorn Hope" posse, "a pretty good, decent sort of fellow when he was sober. When he got drunk he was as mean as the devil. The Indian would crop out of him, that was all." Such racist assumptions were commonplace then.[4]

Cone's (allegedly) murderous partner Edwards was from New York and was an accomplished crook and forger.

One time he got a requisition from the government of New Mexico to the Governor of Texas for an old man living on North Fork of Red River, somewhere east of Clarendon. He had a bunch of sheep. Edwards sold the sheep, bought a freight outfit consisting of . . . eighteen head [of oxen] and six wagons, and drove them to Las Vegas, NM. [There] he left the old man in a room and told

**Las Vegas, New Mexico: the famous "Hanging Windmill" in the old town plaza.
(Courtesy of the Museum of New Mexico [Negative no. 14386])**

him not to leave [or] he would have him locked up. . . . The old man remained in that room three days. . . . [Finally] he ventured [outside] and found his outfit was gone. Not only his outfit, but Edwards and all had vanished, and Edwards was never heard of any more. . . . The old man came back by Tascosa and . . . stated that the papers were a forgery, that Edwards had forged them, and the poor old man was broke. [Edwards] sold out to Cone and left the country. John Cone and [his brother] Will Cone ran the business and made money, too. [Later] an old man named [Dolores] Duran bought into the business.

Another party—albeit only passing through—arrived in July en route to

Leadville, Colorado. It consisted of Dallas attorney N. B. Laughlin (later an associate justice of the New Mexico Supreme Court); N. J. Fish and G. W. Irving, two Harvard boys adventuring in Texas; and a former Texas Ranger named James W. Bell. At Tascosa they learned of the new gold strikes in New Mexico and changed their plans accordingly. Thus, Bell wound up in White Oaks, became a sometime deputy sheriff, and was killed by Billy the Kid during his famous Lincoln jailbreak on April 28, 1881.[5]

The first mention to the outside world of the existence of the Panhandle's newest town appeared in the *Dodge City Times* on February 28, 1878, following a visit by Ike

Rinehart. "Tuscosa," as editor Nicholas B. Klaine misspelled it, was "a new town surrounded by the finest stock country in the world. . . . There is no danger of Indian depredation or thieves as it is beyond the heart of the Indian hunting grounds and strong men have entire control. There is room for millions of cattle and as soon as its advantages are well known it will be rapidly filled."

If Klaine truly believed there were no thieves in the Tascosa area, he was sadly misinformed, and some of that "room" he had been talking about was already being rapidly taken up. During the course of the next year or so, Hank Creswell located the CC Bar ranch about twenty-five miles east of Adobe Walls, John T. Lytle and A. Conkle established what would become the Rocking Chair ranch, while Charles Goodnight's trail boss, Leigh Dyer, and his brother Walter staked out territory for their T-Anchor brand in Randall and Deaf Smith Counties.

As the ranches and cattle proliferated, ranchers encountered new problems. On the unfenced plains, cattle "drifted" many, many miles from their home ranges, especially during winter weather, and by spring animals from many different ranches would be found spread out over an area the size of an eastern state.

As a by-product of this peculiarity of the cattle business, from 1878 on new, cooperative methods of working were put into effect; as soon as the weather broke in the springtime, and again before it turned in the fall, roundups were organized, with riders from all the ranches combining their efforts to drive all the cattle on their land to an agreed roundup ground. There perhaps as many as forty or fifty outfits, each represented by up to twenty cowhands, "cut out" of the massed herd any animals bear-

ing their brands and drove them back to their home ranges. After they were branded, the cows and steers would be separated, with the steers being driven to market and the cows turned loose to breed. During these roundups the little town they were already calling Tascosa would be full of cowboys with money in their pockets, looking for a good time, be it at the bar, at the gambling tables, in the cribs south of town, or more probably all three.

In 1878 English-born brothers James Hamilton and Arthur L. "Bob" Cator, established their Diamond C ranch in Hansford County. Sons of Capt. J. A. "Bertie" Cator, a distinguished British naval officer, Jim and Bob had arrived in Dodge City in 1871. The following year they began hunting buffalo, and when the boom was over they preempted the land along North Palo Duro Creek on which their hunting camp "Zulu Stockade" (so named because the brothers deemed the country like the homeland of the South African Zulus) had stood and turned to raising cattle.

The same year, Tom W. and J. N. Morrison registered the Doll Baby brand in Donley County, while over on Moore Creek in Hutchinson County Richard E. McNalty (the name appears in a wide variety of spellings that include McNulty and MacAnulty) came in with a Colorado herd branded Turkey Track. Another new arrival, this time from Fort Elliott, was the man whose ambitions would probably more than any other influence the development—and finally, the demise—of Tascosa: sutler, trader, freighter, eponymous partner in Lee & Reynolds, the biggest mercantile establishment in the West, self-made millionaire, and entrepreneur William McDole Lee.

Six feet four or five inches in height, with piercing blue eyes, Lee was at once autocratic and abrupt, charming and understanding. "I always liked him," Marion Armstrong said. "He was not only conscientious in the business of friendship and loyalty . . . but he took good care of his employees, feeding them well and paying them good wages." Not everyone agreed; Jesse Jenkins, who as we shall see had more reasons than most for disliking the man, said, "Lee was an awful overbearing man; had money and felt that everybody ought to bow to him." Love him or loathe him, Lee would become a major fact of life in Tascosa.[6]

At this time fifty-four Texas counties, including all those in the Panhandle, were, and had been since 1876, under the jurisdiction of Clay County, whose county seat, Henrietta, was four hundred miles southeast of Tascosa. Citizens who wished or needed to do business with the state courts had perforce to go there to conduct it; those having dealings with the federal government had to travel all the way to Austin. None of those counties could become "organized," that is, self-governing, until they could produce a petition for organization from 150 qualified male voters. Although it had tried twice, Tascosa had not quite been able to do so, but at the town of Sweetwater, built near Fort Elliott in the fall of 1878 a mile or so southwest of the original Hidetown site, an organizational meeting was held to press for self-government. This proposal pleased the mercantile firm of Lee & Reynolds in the form of "Mac" Lee not at all. As the largest commercial undertaking in the region, the firm had a vested interest in continuing to pay as few taxes as possible, as they had been doing since the military post and the buffalo hunters' camp were established in 1875. They mounted "a strong and bitter opposition . . . against the wishes of the people in the

matter," reported the *Ford County Globe*. In spite of Lee's efforts, the petition was accepted by the Clay County commissioners, and on April 12, 1879, the citizens went to the polls, "beat the Post Traders . . . and elected nearly all the ticket." Former buffalo hunter and Dodge City beer garden proprietor Emanuel Dubbs, presently hunting deer, turkey, ducks, and prairie chickens to sell to the military at Fort Elliott, was elected judge; Henry Fleming became sheriff; and Andrew D. "Frosty" Tomb, county clerk. Wheeler County had become the first self-governing entity in the Texas Panhandle.[7]

Divining (correctly) that the advent of new government in the Panhandle would greatly affect the fortunes of the Lee & Reynolds partnership, Lee looked around

Emanuel Dubbs, the Panhandle's first judge. (Courtesy of the Panhandle-Plains Historical Museum, Canyon, Texas)

for another way to make money. The *Dodge City Times* may well have provided the answer:

The Henrietta *Journal* gives some figures relating to the herds of cattle in that part of Texas known as the Pan Handle. The principal cattlemen and their herds are D. T. Beale & Co., 30,000 head; Capt. Goodnight, 12,500; Cresswell, 10,000; Torrey, 8,000; Littlefield, 8,000; McNulty, 6,000; Baker, 4,000; Karrick, 4,000; Bugby, 3,000; Snowden, 3,000; Pollard, 3,000; Coleman, 3,000; Dickinson, 1,200. There are also several small herds of from 100 to 1,000 head. This makes a total of 120,000 head. Of these about 15,000 beeves will be shipped during the season, though some estimate that 22,000 will be ready for the market. It is fair to calculate that the increase this year from the present herds will average not less than 50 per cent of the entire number. This will give 60,000 calves; the number that will stop this season from the Texas drive will be about 30,000 head, and from Colorado about 20,000 head. This will leave in the Pan Handle for next year's round-ups about 208,000 head and yet this does not begin to fill up the country, as it is estimated it will hold a million head. The cost of keeping cattle per year is about $1.50 a head, or $1,500 per thousand; 4 men with 12 to 16 head of horses will tend to a herd of about 1,500 head. The profits are about as follows: Beeves per head cost $15, running $1.50, sell at $22, with a profit of 32 per cent. Profit on cows costing $13.50 per head, cost of running $1.50, or $15; increase of calves, 75 per cent, worth $5 per head, net profit 23 per cent. On a mixed herd the beeves sold will pay expenses, and the increase will double itself in three years. A discount is made on a mixed herd of ten per cent for losses. The profit of a mixed herd is about twenty per cent. A large herd is more profitable than small ones.[8]

On December 17, 1879, Lee & Reynolds purchased nearly thirty thousand acres of prairie in Hartley and Oldham Counties, a transaction that marked both the beginning of the LE ranch and the beginning of the end of the partnership. The first cattle venture undertaken by Lee and Reynolds had been the LR ranch, established near Camp Supply in 1876. By 1879 Lee's cattle purchases had built up into so sizable a herd that he was ordered by the military to remove them from the Camp Supply reservation, and he decided to relocate them to the Panhandle under the supervision of his long-time employee, Ed McAllister, one of the men who had carried the warning to Adobe Walls, now working as a wagonmaster with "Lee an' Runnels," as the firm was known on the plains.

Born on a farm in Martinsville, Indiana, on March 17, 1846, Jordan Edgar McAllister left home at the age of fourteen for Independence, Missouri, found work as a bullwhacker, and spent the next seven years hauling freight on the Santa Fe Trail. Knowledge of the Indian tribes acquired during those years made him invaluable to the military, and in 1867 he scouted for Gen. George A. Custer, participating the following year in the 7th Cavalry's November 27 attack on Black Kettle's village on the Washita. Disgusted with Custer's methods, McAllister signed up with Lee & Reynolds. Apart from a few months when he scouted for Gen. George Crook and took part in the Battle of the Rosebud on June 17, 1876, McAllister served ten years as Lee's faithful and loyal right-hand man.[9]

He trailed Lee's herd from Camp Supply to the former Trujillo *plazita* west of Tascosa, where, in September 1878, a couple of German brothers named Charles and Frank Sperling had taken over the buildings erected by the early *pastores* and set up a store and trading center. Trujillo was a pretty rough place, but it had a post office and even a hotel of sorts. When McAllister sent word to Lee that the surrounding country seemed like a perfect place to establish a ranch, Lee immediately set about purchasing the land in that area.

Marion Armstrong was carrying the mail from Tascosa to Trujillo, a distance of fifty miles, at night and back the next day:

One evening, just as I was starting on my journey, the postmaster handed me a package. . . . It was a gunny sack containing $35,000. As said before, if the Spurling [*sic*] Brothers had received it as such, it would never have reached its destination. . . . I carried it on past Spurling Brothers Post Office [at Trujillo where] I delivered the mail sack but kept the package in my possession. It wasn't yet daylight when I arrived at my station. . . . I hadn't more than got in the cabin until Mr. Lee came in and asked me if I had brought him a package and as my reply was yes, I immediately handed him the precious charge, and with this money Mr. Lee proceeded to pay cash to all the squatters and settlers [from whom] he had agreed to purchase their land, Spurling Brothers as well.[10]

The legend goes that Lee knew only two Spanish words: *dinero* and *vamos*. You took one and/or you did the other; it was that simple. Having purchased their land, in short order Lee ruthlessly began tearing down any buildings the *pastores* had

erected that might still have housed them. Next, having ordered fifty-six hundred cattle from New Mexico for delivery in the spring of 1880, he got in touch with his partner, Albert E. Reynolds, and offered him a half interest in the new spread for seventy-five thousand dollars. When Reynolds agreed, Lee instructed McAllister to start branding the cattle, and the LE ranch was born.[11]

Among those brought in to work the ranch were Steve Conkling, a.k.a. "Steve Nobody," "Uncle Billy" Urion, Jack Lenard, and Alexander "Scotty" Wilson. As his nickname indicates, Scotty—whose name would become inseparably linked with the rise and fall of Tascosa—was born in Scotland, in 1838; his father had emigrated to Canada when Alex was a child. At the age of sixteen he ran away from home, making his way to New Orleans on a flatboat and from there to Fort Leavenworth, Kansas, where he became a government teamster. One of his taller stories—of which he had more than a few—was that he had been in charge of the train that delivered provisions to Custer's command just before the Battle of the Little Big Horn. Scotty claimed that the drivers could hear the firing but did not know the outcome of the fight until they got back to Fort Riley.[12]

In May 1880 the owners of the New Zealand Sheep Company, credited with owning between sixty thousand and one hundred thousand head of sheep, having already divided their holdings, sold their land to Lee & Reynolds and relocated their flocks on Rita Blanca Creek in Hartley County; as soon as they were gone, Lee moved the LE's headquarters from Trujillo to the sheepmen's old rock house on the Alamocitas. Inside a year, over twenty thousand LE cattle were grazing on the range.[13]

Alexander "Scotty" Wilson in the Equity Bar.
(Courtesy of the Haley Memorial Library, Midland, Texas)

It was during this period of change, the story goes, that

a US Marshal, by the name of Johnson, came to Tascosa from Dallas, hunting for revenue and stolen government property. This marshal was backed up by an escort of negro soldiers. He made himself quite conspicuous by doing many things unbecoming an officer of his standing. Many of our citizens were arrested by this marshal, causing them unnecessary annoyance and expense. . . . [H]e arrested the merchants, Cone and Edwards, and took them away from their business without any excuse whatever, and started to Dallas with them, but when he reached Mobeetie . . . a lawyer of some merit got out a Writ of Habeas Corpus, succeeded

in getting their release and they came back home to their business."[14]

The federal officer in charge of this oddly unbalanced foray was a Col. A. B. Norton, U.S. marshal for the Northern District of Texas, appointed the preceding April. He arrived from Dallas with a bagful of blank warrants to arrest Wheeler County residents selling tobacco (and probably liquor) without a license. As well as Cone and Edwards, Norton and his deputy, Walter Johnson (and perhaps another, Timothy Isaiah "Jim" Courtright), also arrested Isaiah Rinehart for "breaking revenue laws" (Rinehart later said "he was accused of selling cartridges and ammunition belonging to the government"), and incarcerated their prisoners in the guardhouse at Fort

Pillars of the Mobeetie community: front (l. to r.): Newt Locke,
Emanuel Dubbs, and J. J. Long; rear (l. to r.): Joe Mason, G. W. "Cap" Arrington,
and Cape Willingham. (Courtesy of Miles Gilbert Jr.)

Elliott. At Mobeetie Norton made more arrests. "One man was arrested because he
bought a government blanket from a soldier, another because he bought a case of
tobacco and gave part of it to each man
who worked for him. . . . He arrested men
right and left until he had 35 in . . . the
Fort guard house."

The plan, according to Mobeetie
deputy sheriff Jim McIntire, was "to arrest
everyone they could on some trumped-up
charge, and take them to Dallas, where
they could be fined, and the marshal and
the deputies would fatten off the fees. They
had all the merchants and county officials
in the country under arrest, except [sa-
loonkeeper] Tom Riley, a deputy sheriff,
and myself. The county was almost depop-
ulated, and it was 150 miles to the nearest
district judge, where a writ of *habeas corpus*
could be secured."

When Emanuel Dubbs, elected county
judge in April (although he had no idea
what the duties of a judge were), went to the
jail, "Edwards said, 'Judge, this thing stinks,
we've been arrested illegally, that Johnson
so-and-so has a bunch of warrants signed
by the Dallas Marshal, and when he arrests
a man he filled in the blank himself. I don't
know much about law, but I do know this
ain't legal. . . . Issue a writ of Habeas
Corpus and have these men brought before
you to investigate the charge.'"

Despite his complete absence of legal
knowledge, Dubbs cobbled together a document and handed it to Sheriff Henry
Fleming for service, then "held his first
session of court. . . . The evidence was
heard, the arrests announced illegal, the
prisoners were released and the Marshal
reprimanded. . . . The townspeople
whooped and sang that night to celebrate

the Judge's success." But they sang a little too soon.

About one o'clock in the morning, Dubbs was awakened by Isaiah Rinehart, who told him that with the cooperation of Capt. Nicholas Nolan, commanding Fort Elliott (the officer involved in the "Forlorn Hope" expedition), Norton and his deputies had rearrested all the Tascosa prisoners, loaded them into ten army wagons, and set out for Dallas with a military escort consisting of Lt. Henry Ossian Flipper, 10th Cavalry (the first black cadet ever to graduate from West Point and at that time the only black officer in the U.S. Army), and ten enlisted men. Rinehart had managed somehow to slip away unnoticed when the wagons got stuck in a creek about five miles east of town and had legged it back to raise the alarm.

Dubbs decided he was going to "save those men from the Marshal if he went to prison for it." Rounding up fifteen men— Sheriff Henry Fleming among them— Dubbs set out after the wagons. When they caught up with them, "intimidating the armed soldiers in the dead of night with buffalo guns, sheer nerve and strong language," they ordered the soldiers to lay down their arms—which they did with alacrity—then marched the whole party back to Sweetwater. There Dubbs charged Norton and his men with "contempt of court," fined each of them one hundred dollars "plus trimmin's" (an extra twenty dollars for court expenses), and sent them packing. But the game was far from over.

As the first full session of court ever to be held in Mobeetie was due to commence, Norton rearrested Dubbs and all the previous arrestees—plus Captain Nolan and Lieutenant Flipper—and this time there was no rescue. They were taken to Dallas and hauled into court, where

(the story continues) Nolan and Flipper were reportedly tried on a charge of interfering with U.S. officers in the course of their duty and each fined one thousand dollars. When Dubbs and the other arrestees finally appeared, however, the grand jury failed to find a true bill and all were discharged. "R. [Isaiah] Rinehart of Tuscosa, Texas, is on his return from Dallas," reported the *Dodge City Times*. "The arrest of parties in the Pan Handle has caused a great deal of indignation; and now the US Marshal and his assistants are catching it."

One account of these events suggests that everyone who had participated in the illegal arrests of the Panhandle men was arrested, and that Johnson, the U.S. deputy marshal, skipped the country and was never heard of again. U.S. Marshal Norton is said to have been fined one hundred dollars on April 3, 1882, but requested a new trial at which, in August 1882, he was acquitted; of his deputies there is no record. There were those who muttered darkly that this whole series of events had been a put-up job, that "certain parties" (in other words, Lee & Reynolds), still smarting over their defeat earlier in the year, had mounted the whole charade in an attempt to demonstrate that Wheeler County was unfit for self-government, whereupon administration would revert to Henrietta, thus nullifying the taxes Wheeler County was about to impose upon the firm.

Flipper himself, perhaps a more reliable witness, told a somewhat different tale. Following the theft of a large quantity of ammunition from the ordnance room at Fort Elliott he was sent with a dozen men to Tascosa, where, during a search of the Howard & McMasters store, he found a small back room "literally covered with the paper packages in which the ammunition comes packed but not a single cartridge." When McMasters could give him no satisfactory explanation, the matter was reported to the U.S. marshal at Fort Worth.

He came up, made an investigation, went to Tascosa and returned with two men, one of them the mail rider. . . . We discovered that the Quartermaster Sergeant, in charge of this property, had been stealing it and selling it to cowboys, sending it up through the country by mail rider. He was sent to the Leavenworth military prison for three years. . . . When the marshal reached Fort Worth with his prisoners, he reported to the U.S. grand jury and both Capt. Nolan and I were indicted for violating the Posse Comitatus act of 1878, which forbade the use of the Army for arresting or holding civilians.

Lawyers in Fort Worth advised the officers not to go to Fort Worth, as the cases would not be called until the following term. In the event, Flipper never attended court; Captain Nolan appeared, pleaded guilty, and was fined one dollar, as was Flipper, in absentia. "So you see," Flipper wrote with heavy irony, "[I have] been a criminal, deep dyed in crime of the most heinous kind."[15]

One unexpected consequence of these events was a shooting at the Salinas *plazita,* which, Jim East recalled, had "a pretty tough lot of Mexicans living there" and "a bad reputation." One of John Chisum's riders, remembered as Al Westover, had been killed at Salinas in 1878 after he tried to ride his horse into a dance hall. It was said that nine white men were killed at the *plazita* before the locals lost a man.[16]

When word reached Salinas about the U.S. marshal who had arrested Edwards and Rinehart for selling whiskey without a license, a man named Chavez, guilty of the same offense, hid the liquor and then skinned out, leaving his friend Pablo Dierro to run the store until Chavez's wife—who was in Las Vegas—got back. When she arrived, however, Dierro refused to let her into the store.

A man named Kincade, who spoke fluent Spanish, persuaded Dierro to hand over the key. Señora Chavez then asked Kincade to help her collect accounts and close out the store, in the course of which Kincade got into an argument with another local, Guadalupe Circenos, then "turned to George Jones who was with the group and said 'No Goddamn Mexican can call me a liar and get away with it.'" A melee ensued as guns were drawn and fired. Kincade was hit, "ran in a circle out in the street, came back and fell face forward with his hands crossed, barely able to murmur, 'Don't let them kill me.'"

The killing of Kincade almost precipitated a little race war. A day or two later something like thirty-five cowboys led by Jack Ryan rode up to Salinas spoiling for a fight.

When they got across the river and to within 400 yards of the plaza, Alicia Vorregos [came out and] told Jack Ryan to stop his men there and he would go to the plaza and talk with [the locals]. The Mexicans had their houses fixed for a fight, double bars on their doors, lookouts on the roofs and barricades against bullets.

"If they kill me, you will know you've got to fight," said Vorregos.

Antonio Mexicano [Mexicana] was the leader of the [men in the] plaza. He was rich and he was the one who was having all the white men killed. He wouldn't let them get one step out of line until he ordered some of his henchmen to knife them or shoot them. He had a big Roman cross tattooed on his forehead.

"You folks can take six men and come in, but don't bring Kid Dobbs with you," said Antonio.

[Kid] Dobbs, just for devilment, offered to go with any six Ryan would select. Ryan . . . said "I think from what I hear you've [already] been in one time too many."

They arrested Antonio Mexicano and his son-in-law, who played the fiddle, and Mrs. Chavez, the woman involved in the argument. None of them but Mrs. Chavez knew anything about the fight.

Five days after the shooting Dobbs (clearly nothing like as smart as he liked to paint himself) went back to Salinas with John McCracken, taking a bottle of whiskey for Señora Chavez. The woman "burst out crying and begged him not to stay: the men in the next room were from Chaves plaza and would try to kill him." He and McCracken left the house and went to the saloon followed by the Mexicans. "John," Dobbs said, "when we get on our horses we had better leave here in a hurry." He mounted, "swung low on the opposite side of the saddle from the Chavez house doorway, and put the spurs to his horse. His six-shooter was in his right hand."[17]

Kincade's body was taken down to the Sperling brothers' place at Trujillo and buried across the creek in front of the store. Later, because he was a Mason and belonged to a lodge in Las Vegas, New Mexico, his body was exhumed and conveyed there to be buried in the Masonic Cemetery. "They didn't fill up the grave after removing the body and someone made the remark that he had always heard it said, that 'If the grave was not filled up after removing a body from it, that some of the bunch that uncovered it would be put in it soon.' A man by the name of Clark, in answer to this remark said 'Damned if he cared.' It wasn't ten days until Clark went over to a sheep camp loaded with whiskey. The sheep herder, a Mexican, got scared and the result was fatal to Clark. Mexicans at that time were afraid of all Texas cowpunchers. . . . At any rate, in less than ten days after the above remark regarding the empty grave was made by Clark, he occupied it."[18]

In spite of all this, what passed for civilization in Tascosa marched bravely on. By the summer of 1879 the town boasted eight English-speaking women: California Armstrong, Mary Willingham, Lizzie Rinehart, Jennie Mays, Mrs. Prevail, Mrs. Cartwright, Zypha Russell, and Molly Russell herself. "We had a Christmas tree at Rinehart's store. We women strung up corn and made cranberry strings until the tree was beautiful. There were nice presents for everyone. Folks said there were at least $500 worth of presents on that tree. We all sang, played blind man's buff, and other games until late at night." It was estimated the community now numbered about 150 souls, many of them of course Mexican.[19]

Whether that included the badmen is not recorded.

Chapter 8

SELMAN AND LONG

THE OUTLAW CONFEDERACY

WHETHER Tascosans liked it or not, the lawless breed were well aware of the fact that the town—and indeed all of Oldham County and the other unorganized counties nearby—had no law enforcement of any kind and that therefore, if they wanted to, they could literally get away with murder. And when the only available honest options were punching cows, bullwhacking for some freighter's outfit, or trying to make a living as a gambler, crime was a real alternative. Many of the rustlers who preyed on the plains ranchers were former hunters or skinners.[1]

Early in September 1879 one gang made off with nineteen head of horses and a few mules belonging to Isaiah Rinehart, who then "collected a few men to follow the thieves. He succeeded in capturing five outlaws as they rode through the Rattlesnake sand hills [but] four men managed to escape." The report clearly implied the "escape" was a necktie party. Later in the year, four (presumably different) horse thieves were captured on the Saline River, twenty miles north of Hays City, with thirty-one horses in their possession

claimed to have been stolen from Oldham County.[2]

Horse thieves were not the only problem. Out there in the unmapped plains there were other kinds of scum, capable of any crime, ready to steal, rape, or kill as the opportunity or the necessity presented itself. One of the worst of them was a forty-year-old native of Arkansas named John Henry Selman, who, even as Molly Russell and her lady friends were enjoying each other's genteel company in Tascosa, was considering ways and means to effect the complete annihilation of the garrison at Fort Elliott and the sacking of the new and thriving little town of Mobeetie.

In the fall of 1878 some thirty of its inhabitants had decided to abandon the old Hidetown site and relocate at a point a mile or so southwest of the fort. First named Sweetwater, it had become Mobeetie in 1879 when the U.S. Post Office Department turned down its application for a post office because the name was already registered. The "new" town, now the county seat of Wheeler County, featured "some queer habitations: one

John Selman with his son, John Jr.
(Courtesy of James H. Earle)

J. J. "Uncle Johnny" Long's private bank, or the Lee & Reynolds store/saloon, or Tom O'Laughlin's Grand Central Hotel, or maybe it was all of these. Then again, if Selman's career to date was anything to go by, maybe he just liked killing people.

Born in Madison County, Arkansas, on November 16, 1839, Selman was the son of an English schoolteacher and farmer. The family—John was the eldest of five children—moved to Texas in 1858, and when his father died, Selman became the family provider. He is said to have joined the Confederate army and deserted in 1863. The family settled near Albany, Texas, and in 1864 Selman became a lieutenant in the state militia. In August 1865 he married Edna de Graffenried, and four years later both his and her families relocated in Colfax County, New Mexico. After a year they returned to the Fort Griffin area, where Selman became a saloonkeeper and did some creative rustling on the side with his partner in crime, Sheriff John Larn. When Larn was lynched early in 1878, Selman fled to New Mexico, leaving his wife to die carrying their fifth child.[4]

In New Mexico, in the smoldering aftermath of the 1878 Lincoln County War, Selman led a band of plunderers and thieves who liked to call themselves "Selman's Scouts" but were widely, and more accurately, known as "The Rustlers." This murderous brotherhood of bandits had coalesced when some of the hard-core toughs who had sided with the Murphy-Dolan faction during the war teamed up with the even more despicable set of bandits riding with Selman and embarked on a three-week spree of theft, murder, and rape the likes of which had never before been seen in the Territory of New Mexico.

The rampage began when a group of Selman's men—Gus Gildea, "Rustling

house, for instance, contains a hotel, restaurant, barbershop, saloon, shoemaker's shop, dance hall and house of ill-fame, all under one roof," while "within a mile of the post were Frenchy's Hotel, Dutchy's Ranch, Perciller Kesiah & Co's Dugout and Trout Water City."[3]

Why Selman should have wanted to wipe the settlement out, history does not reveal. Maybe he was hoping to help himself to the money being generated by the Rath & Hamburg store, said to be turning over more than a hundred thousand dollars a year. Maybe it was the U.S. Army's strongbox at Fort Elliott he was after, or

Bob" Bryant, Reason Goble, Charlie Snow, and Jack Irving among them— stopped off at Fort Stanton to buy a thousand rounds of ammunition. The appalled post commander, Col. N. A. M. Dudley, 9th Cavalry, confiscated the ammunition and ordered the bandits off the post. Not so foolhardy as to take on the military, they instead repaired to Will Hudgens's saloon, where they tried to force the owner to buy the ammunition for them. When he refused, they wrecked the saloon, abused his wife and her sister, and pistol-whipped a man who tried to intervene.

They then set off on the nine-mile ride to Lincoln, intent on looting the Ellis store. Confronted on their arrival by heavily armed men, they amused themselves by smashing down the doors of houses, breaking up furniture and crockery, stripping women of their clothes, and stealing anything that took their fancy.

At La Junta, downriver from Lincoln, they trashed a store and stole some eight hundred dollars' worth of goods before moving on to loot and burn the Frank Coe–Ab Saunders ranch. At Picacho they stole ten or twelve horses, in the process wantonly shooting down three youths who were watching the animals. At another house they shot a fourteen-year-old boy in cold blood, and a few nights later they gang-raped two young women. Asked who they were, one of them replied, "We are devils just come from Hell."[5]

This chronicle of rape and murder triggered an angry reaction from the citizens of Lincoln, who "got after them and run them two days and one night nearly to Seven Rivers, but could not get close enough to kill any of them. We captured all the loose horses they were driving back, [stock] animals and all their Blankets and Provisions." One of the Selman gang

Lincoln, New Mexico, ca. 1900. (Courtesy of Robert G. McCubbin)

[73]

remembered the pursuit as a "long all day fight made by 9 of our men vs. from 25 to 50 or more of the Modocs [a contemptuous name the bandits bestowed on their pursuers] both Americans and Mexicans, and we fought them from near the Fritze ranche [on the lower Bonito] to the Martin Chavez ranch [below Picacho], about 35 miles as near as I can recollect . . . and lost several of our horses but no man. We whipped them good and plenty . . . but though they used Buffalo guns on us they did not press us very close."[6]

With the military constrained by an act of Congress from intervention, and civil law enforcement utterly powerless to confront so large, well-armed, and completely ruthless a gang of bandits, wagonloads of refugee families fled the country. In Santa Fe, Lew Wallace, recently appointed governor of New Mexico, urged President Rutherford B. Hayes to declare martial law. Instead, on October 7, Hayes issued a proclamation exhorting "all good citizens of the United States and especially of the Territory of New Mexico" who had been committing lawless acts to "disperse and return peaceably to their respective abodes on or before noon of the thirteenth day of October."[7]

A month later, Wallace followed the presidential proclamation with one of his own, granting amnesty for crimes committed during the Lincoln County War; amazingly, the anarchy abated. A major factor in this was the fact that Selman's "scouts" had temporarily moved south into the area between Seven Rivers and the Texas Panhandle.

Selman never availed himself of Wallace's amnesty; he had no need of it. His experiences in Fort Griffin and in Lincoln County convinced him that as long as he had enough men of the same murderous stripe as those presently riding with him, very few frontier settlements—even army posts—could raise anything like as well mounted or as well armed a counterforce to oppose them. He now began formulating plans to assemble a bandit fraternity so big, so unstoppable, that it could and would be able to rob and pillage as it pleased and with impunity kill anyone who got in its way.

That this was indeed Selman's intention is confirmed by former Texas Ranger James McIntire, whose camp near Tascosa was visited by a gang "eight or ten in number" headed by "a man whom I knew at Fort Griffin by the name of A. L. Mont, commonly called 'Long John', now going by the name of 'Jim.' He is under indictment in Shackelford County for killing Virgil Hewey [Hervey] and a colored soldier of the 10th [Cavalry] at Fort Griffin."[8]

"Long John," a.k.a. John Long, who had an endless string of aliases, is yet another frontier mystery man; virtually nothing is known of his origins. A former buffalo hunter turned gambler in the Fort Griffin area, he killed Virgil Hervey, brother of storekeeper Julius Hervey there in June 1877. It was probably at Fort Griffin he got to know John Selman, Sheriff John Larn's deputy there at the time. "He was a six-footer, a splendid shot, and coveted the reputation of a 'bad man.' He was a boisterous bully [who] had killed a man at Fort Griffin, Texas, a short time previously, and saved himself from a furious mob by pleading that it was an accident."[9]

He seems to have been something of a Jekyll and Hyde, on the one hand a paid-up member of the loose-knit New Mexico bandit fraternity known as "The Boys" who boasted to Dr. Taylor Ealy that he had helped hang a preacher in Arizona, yet on the other a self-described "Special Indian Agent of Jicarillo [*sic*] Apaches near Fort Stanton." In one instance a craven loud-mouth who called Billy the Kid a son of a bitch in a Fort Sumner *tendejon*, then chickened out when the Kid threatened to "crack his crust," he nonetheless fought fearlessly, even recklessly, for the Murphy-Dolan faction in the Lincoln County troubles and was indicted for the murder of Alexander McSween.

In November 1878 he was one of those who promulgated the notorious affidavits that suggested, none too subtly, that Susan McSween was a whore. In April 1879 Long accepted Governor Wallace's amnesty; he appeared the following month as a witness for the defense at the military court of inquiry that established that the actions of Col. N. A. M. Dudley on July 19, 1878, when McSween's house had been set on fire and the lawyer mercilessly shot down, did not justify Dudley's being tried by court-martial. The evidence Long gave on that occasion challenges with its coherence the proposition that he was just another frontier lout, yet he is also, undeniably, the murderous Fort Griffin buffalo hunter, the Lincoln County horse thief, the Selman gang bandit.[10]

And, if Jim McIntire is to be believed, he was a bank robber. When they rode into McIntire's camp on the Canadian, Long and his bandit pals assumed him to be on the dodge like themselves and

> told me that if I wanted to come to them, to come from Fort Griffin to Devil's river and that there inquire for Buck Smith or Long John and I would be alright. Long John told me that Buck Smith is the alias

now worn by John Silliman [Selman] [and] showed me alias names of men belonging to Silliman's gang on paper. . . . Long John gave me to understand that in the whole crowd there were about one hundred and seventy five men under command of John Silliman, ranging from the Canadian river to Devil's river. Long John had plenty of money and said that 'We—,' then correcting himself said, 'The boys took in a bank the other day in New Mexico and raised about $15,000.00.' . . . He talked about coming down here with the whole party. He made inquiries about the County organization, the number of people here, and the number of troops at the Post at Fort Elliott."[11]

The implication was clear: Selman and his estimated 175-man "army" were contemplating an attack on Sweetwater that, if mounted, would by definition include the destruction of the army post.

After Long and his men left, McIntire made his way to Sweetwater, where fifteen days later he made a sworn statement before Wheeler County attorney Moses Wiley, who immediately wrote to Maj. John B. Jones, commander of the Frontier Battalion of the Texas Rangers, reminding him that under the Posse Comitatus Act troops would not be able to support the civil authorities, and "if [such an attack were] attempted, and skill used, the chances are [it] would be a success, and this success in supplying arms and horses would soon cause their force to swell to such numbers that nothing short of an army could subdue them."

Would the governor's or president's proclamation, if it could be obtained, serve to authorize the military and civil authorities to act conjointly against these outlaws? Wiley wondered. "It is impossible to say where or at what point they will strike, but when as many desperadoes as they have now are banded together for the express purpose of outlawry and depredations, it is probable that they will accomplish something startling. And occupying as they do the interior lines of communications, they can readily concentrate upon any given point of the frontier which makes a circle about them."[12]

Thankfully, Selman's "six gun empire," as one writer called it, failed to materialize. Shortly after these events, he contracted smallpox and almost died; convinced, when he recovered, that his appearance was so altered by the scarring of the disease that no one would recognize him, Selman changed his name to John Tyson, awarded himself the spurious rank of captain, opened a butcher shop in Fort Davis, and eased back into the activities of the criminal fraternity. Much, much later, on August 19, 1895, he killed John Wesley Hardin in El Paso's Acme Saloon; on April 5 of the following year he was himself killed by Deputy U.S. Marshal George Scarborough.[13]

As noted earlier, John Long returned briefly to New Mexico. An eloquent witness at the Dudley court of inquiry on June 12–13, 1879, he was best man at Lincoln County merchant Jimmy Dolan's wedding, further proof that he was anything but your standard frontier ruffian. For well over a century the assertion by Pat Garrett's ghostwriter that Long was killed "at a ranch on the plains by a Mexican named Trujillo" has been considered to be the last word on his demise. As with almost everything else he wrote, however, Upson only got it half right.[14]

Soon after the Dolan wedding, Long returned to the Panhandle, where he made

James Joseph Dolan at the time of his marriage, 1879. (Courtesy of Robert G. McCubbin)

the mistake of getting into a card game at the old sheepherder *plazita* of Trujillo, where the brothers Frank and Charlie Sperling "ran a store in connection with the post office. These boys had the reputation of being a tough outfit, and to all appearances they lived up to their reputation. They were given credit for having killed about five men or having it done."[15]

Long, a [former] buffalo hunter, went . . . from Las Vegas to Tascosa by horseback. He had started back and stopped for the night at Trujillo. He got into a poker game with some Mexicans and won considerable money. The Sperlings gave a Mexican $50 to kill Long. The Mexican who agreed to do the job walked out of the door, opened it enough with his left hand to turn and shoot Long. He closed it until he thought Long was dead and then they dragged him outside to a slope on the hill. Although dying he managed to raise his head, trying to inquire as to what had happened, and seemed to be getting better. Frank Sperling said, "He is a dangerous man. Better shoot him again." The Mexican shot him again. The Mexican left the country and they buried Long nearby.[16]

This would appear to be the definitive statement on the death of John Long, but the mystery of his split frontier personality remains insoluble. There were many men like him on the frontier, and a lot of them ended up the same way, in an unmarked grave on some forgotten stretch of faceless prairie. Like them, he was unmissed and unlamented, but there were plenty more of the same stripe ready and waiting to move into the spot he had just vacated.

Chapter 9

1880

HUNTING BILLY THE KID

A MAJOR development in the establishment of some kind of law and order in Oldham County came in the spring of 1880 when the Panhandle Stockmen's Association was formed on the initiative of Charles Goodnight. During the preceding fall and winter, he and some of the bigger ranchers had begun examining the advisability of organizing in self-protection, and on July 23, 1880, at a formal meeting held in Mobeetie, Goodnight became the association's first president, with H. H. "Hank" Creswell as vice president and an executive committee that consisted of Goodnight, Creswell, Thomas Bugbee (Quarter Circle T), Robert Moody (PO), and John F. Evans (Spade).[1]

"Judge Nelson and I and Creswell and all the prominent people of the Panhandle were leaders in the Association," Goodnight recalled. "I suppose the first organisation had only about 25 or 30 men but it increased to quite a number later. . . . Some of the ranches [such as Lee & Reynolds] never joined us—Bates and Beals of the LX never joined us. They hired every thief in the country."[2]

One of the new association's first steps was to post a reward of $250 for anyone caught rustling cattle belonging to any member. Another of its initiatives was to address the matter of who was buying the cattle New Mexico outlaws such as Billy the Kid and others were stealing in the Panhandle and driving across the line to

———⚬⚬———

Patrick Floyd Garrett, 1881.
(Courtesy of Craig Fouts)

[78]

the new mining camps that were springing up there at White Oaks and Nogal.

In the fall of 1879, after his second attempt to negotiate a pardon through New Mexico governor Lew Wallace had come to nothing, the Kid made old Fort Sumner his base of operations; by the following year he had become a full-time rustler. His methods, like the men who rode with him, were rough and ready. They would steal horses or cattle or both up and down the Pecos Valley and drive them to a ready market in Tascosa. When their money ran out, the Kid and his gang would then steal stock on the wide-open Panhandle range and drive it across into New Mexico for sale, with no questions asked, to the self-styled "King of Tularosa," rancher Pat Coghlan, who had won a contract to supply beef to the Mescalero Apache reservation adjacent to Fort Stanton commencing July 1, 1880. If there were no horses to steal in New Mexico, the Kid and his sidekicks rode over to the Panhandle anyway and stole the big ranches there blind. It is at least possible that Pat Garrett and Barney Mason, both then living in Fort Sumner, accompanied the Kid on some of these raids.[3]

By the fall of 1880 the Kid's depredations had reached such a level that the Stockmen's Association hired a former LX cowboy who called himself Frank Stewart as a range detective, his brief to identify the rustlers and whoever was purchasing the stolen stock and, if possible, recover the cattle. A party was mounted consisting of LX riders Garrett H. "Kid" Dobbs, Lon Chambers, and Lee Hall, plus Charlie Resoner, who was half Cherokee, from the LIT.

At Coghlan's ranch near Tularosa they found LIT hides on the corral, but when

Barney Mason and his family. (Courtesy of Robert G. McCubbin)

they confronted the butcher, former Lincoln County sheriff George Peppin, he told them he had a clean bill of sale for all the cattle in his corral and it was going to take a lot more than verbal notice from them to get him to hand them over. When on top of that someone told the Texans Billy the Kid and his gang were in the area, and if they ran into him he would wipe them out, Stewart decided discretion was the better part of valor and led his men back to the Panhandle.[4]

This made [LX foreman Bill] Moore mad, so he concluded to rig up an outfit of his own and send them over after the cattle, hence he sending out after me [Siringo]. My outfit, after getting it rigged up, consisted of a chuck wagon with four good mules to pull it, a cook and five picked men, named as follows: James East, Lee Hall, Lon Chambers, Cal Pope [Polk] and last but not by any means least "Big Foot" Wallace [a nickname the boys gave to Frank Clifford, not to be confused with the legendary Texas hero]. . . . On starting, Moore gave me these orders: "Stay over there until you get those cattle or bust the LX company. I will keep you supplied in money just as long as they have got a nickel left, that I can get hold of. And when you get the cattle, if you think you can succeed in capturing 'Billy the Kid,' do so. You can hire all the men you need; but don't undertake his capture until you have first secured the cattle."

At Tascosa we met Stuart [Stewart], who had succeeded in raising a little crowd to join us. Mr. [C. S.] McCarty, boss of the LIT ranch, had furnished five men, a cook and chuck wagon; and Torry [Torrey] whose ranch was further up the [Canadian] river, a wagon and two men, while a man named Johnson furnished a man and

a wagon. The LIT outfit was in charge of a fellow by the name of Bob Roberson, whose orders were to get the stolen cattle before trying to capture the Kid, but in the meantime to be governed by Stuart's orders.[5]

"We left the LX ranch, went by Tascosa and got enough grub to last us to the Pecos," Jim East said. "We went right up the [Canadian] River past Sperling's [at Trujillo] where we camped one night, to San Hilario above Fort Bascom and cut across to the Pecos. Charley [Siringo] said 'Now, I'll go on to Las Vegas, buy grub, and you fellows can go straight across to Anton Chico and wait there until I get back. That would save about seventy-five miles driving for us.'"[6]

In Cal Polk's freewheeling account of the trip, Siringo

Charles Siringo, all dressed up, 1907. (Courtesy of the Haley Memorial Library, Midland, Texas)

[80]

started on ahead to Las Vegas with the male carrier to get corn [for the horses]. He told us to go to Antion Cheeko on the Pacos River and there wait untill he came with the corn. We went ahead and got there on Sunday at 12 oclock. Just as we all rode up into town the cathlick church broke and the Mexacans coming out of it. They all stoped and gazed at us, and wondered what was the matter. We all had 2 belts full of cartridges a peace around us and was armed to the teeth with six shooters, Bowie knives, and Winchesters on our saddles.

While we was there Billy the Kid come in town one night and stole 3 good horses from Mexacans. He then rote a letter to Frank Stuart telling us to not come no further, that he did not want to fite us. But if we came to come a shootin. This was strate goods but we had it to face. As you will see later we had all went deeply in debt while we was there and exspected Charley to come with a pocket full of monnie from Las Vagas. But when he come we was broke. He got to gambling up there and lost all the monnie the LX firm started him with and he had to give a check on them for the corn, so we had to give checks here the same way.[7]

Cal Polk's hairy tales of what the posse got up to in Anton Chico have been published elsewhere, as indeed has the story of the pursuit and capture of Billy the Kid. What is interesting is the independent-minded reaction of the Panhandle men to the proposition that they take part in it, as evidenced in another unpublished memoir, *Deep Trails in the West,* dictated to a friend in 1942 by Frank Clifford, the man known to his fellow possemen as "Big Foot" Wallace.

The morning we left Anton Chico, it was snowing. . . . By the time we stopped at

Las Vegas, New Mexico, showing Wagner's Hotel and Samuel Kohn, Jaffa Brothers, and Charles Ilfeld stores. (Courtesy of the Haley Memorial Library, Midland, Texas)

noon, snow was from eight to ten inches deep. . . . Before we could get started again, Pat Garrett, sheriff of Lincoln County, New Mexico, and Frank Stewart, cattle detective for the Canadian Cattle Association, and another man [Barney Mason] rode into camp. Pat told us that the "Kid" was down by Fort Sumner, and had a large bunch of Canadian River cattle that he was aiming to start for Old Mexico with in the morning. This couldn't be true, as nobody could go any distance through a snowstorm like that with a big bunch of cattle, there would be nothing for them to eat. Bob Roberson and Charley Siringo immediately told Pat so. They demeaned him, and didn't mince words either. Pat insisted he was telling it straight, and after a long argument, Bob and Charley agreed to leave it to their men personally to decide who would go with Pat. We split up exactly even, seven went, and seven wouldn't go. I was one who didn't.[8]

Among others who set down their versions of the pursuit of the Kid and his capture at Stinking Springs were Charlie Siringo, Louis "The Animal" Bousman, and Cal Polk; all stick pretty close to Garrett's account. Jim East, however, added telling detail that appears nowhere else.

We crossed to the Piedrenal [Pedernales] Springs [and] rode all day without anything to eat, rode that night and next

Frank Clifford, real name John Menham Wightman, a.k.a. John Francis "Big Foot" Wallace. (Courtesy of Michael E. Winter)

Calvin Warnell Polk. (Courtesy of Jessie Polk McVicker)

day about five o'clock we got to Puerta de Luna on the Pecos. . . . Our party was made up of James East, Lee Hall and Lon Chambers from the LX; and Emory, Bausman and Williams from the LIT.

Garrett got word by a Mexican runner who came up that the Kid and his gang were at Fort Sumner and if we would hurry we might get them. It was forty two miles from Puerta de Luna to Sumner. About dusk we pulled out. It snowed all the way down, and there were about four inches on the ground when we got there just before day. When we left the wagons we had to cut ourselves out of all our bedding except one blanket apiece, as we could not carry more. We had one six-shooter, a Winchester and a blanket apiece. We packed no horses, and we had only the ones we rode. I slept on the one blanket and rode the one horse all that winter.

We got to Sumner a little before daylight and went to Beaver Smith's store. . . .

Garrett asked him when he had seen the boys last. He said that they were there about sundown and that after they had drunk some whiskey and shot up the store they had gone to a vacant house just across the street and he thought they were still there. We slipped across to the house. It was still snowing. There was a little fire flickering in the fireplace and when it flared up a little we could see the form of a man before the fireplace. We thought that the whole bunch was there. Garrett told us to take no chances and to begin shooting when we went in. Garrett kicked the door open and we all jumped in with our Winchesters ready, and it was only [Mike Cosgrove] the mail carrier from Las Vegas. We came mighty near shooting him, not knowing who he was as there was not much light. He said: "My God, don't shoot, boys." And he was scared to death. He said that he did not know anything about the Kid and his gang and he did not want to. . . .

Anton Chico, New Mexico, 1887. (Courtesy of the Haley Memorial Library, Midland, Texas)

[83]

We went over to a long adobe building, the old hospital building of the Fort, and built a fire in the fireplace, rustled a little chuck, and stayed there all day. It snowed all the time. The next night . . . about eleven o'clock they came in. Lon Chambers and Lee Hall had been placed on guard over our horses. I was rolled up in my blanket trying to get a little sleep before going on second guard, and Garrett, Barney Mason, Tom Emory and Bob Williams were playing poker. The Kid's idea was, as he told us after we captured him, to slip in and steal our horses, put us afoot, and then take his time in killing us. A man on foot in that country was almost helpless.

Chambers, who was on guard, heard them coming, slipped up to the door and said: "Get your guns, they are coming." The boys threw down their chips and cards, got their guns, and we all went out. Just then they turned around the end of the hospital building. The only light was from the snow. Garrett hollered at the bunch to throw up their hands, but they jerked their six-shooters and the fight commenced. All of them wheeled and left with the exception of one. Garrett said: "Throw up your hands; we'll shoot you down!" He [the rider] said "Don't shoot any more, Pat; I am dying." His horse jogged right on up to us and it was Tom O'Phalliard, shot through near the heart. We took him inside and laid him down on my blanket. The boys went back to playing poker and I sat down by the fire. O'Phalliard commenced to cuss Garrett.

He said: "God damn you, Garrett; I hope to meet you in Hell."

Pat said: "I would not talk that way, Tom. You are going to die in a few minutes."

He said: "Ah, go to hell, you long-legged sonofabitch." (Pat was six feet, five inches tall.)

The game went on and the blood began running inside Tom. He began groaning and asked me to get him a drink of water. I did. He drank a little, lay back, shuddered and was dead. The poker game went on. It was a thing to get the minds of the men off the fight and keep them from growing morbid. . . .

We lay over that day, got a Mexican to bury Tom O'Phalliard. We got a Mexican to make a box for him. The next day about twelve o'clock a man by the name of Wilcox . . . came in and said: "Boys, the Kid and his bunch had supper at my house and have gone over to that rock house on the Taiban." We started up there and got to this house just before daylight. Garrett took Tom Emory, Lon Chambers, Jim East and Lee Hall and crawled up the arroyo until he was within about thirty feet of the house.[9]

Kid Dobbs takes up the story:

Billy and his men had tied their horses to a vegas [viga] on the south side of the shack. . . . Charley Bowder got up first the next morning before good daylight. He picked up the Kid's Mexican hat by mistake. This was a $200 hat and had more silver on it than any hat I ever saw. Bowder put on this hat and stepped outside. Pat [Garrett] was 50 feet away. One of his men recognised the hat and said "That's Billy." Pat shot Bowder under the heart. Bowder knew it was Pat and said, "Don't shoot any more, Pat, you've got me." Garrett said "Is that you Charley" and he said "yes."

Pat told him to crawl on down where they were and Bowder did. He told Pat he

**Said to be the stone cabin at Stinking Springs
where the Kid was captured. (Courtesy of Gregory Scott Smith)**

didn't blame him for shooting and said he had a will in his pocket he wanted Pat to carry out. Pat told him he would. Bowder lived 40 minutes. He left his horse, saddle and blankets and $118 in cash to the Mexican woman cook in Fort Sumner. She got every bit of it that day, too.[10]

After a while they saw the tie ropes of the horses tethered outside the cabin move and figured the Kid and his men were trying to get the horses inside so they could mount up and come out running. Without compunction Garrett shot one of the horses dead; it fell across the doorway, blocking it. After a while Garrett called to the Kid that he had them surrounded and there was no chance of escape. The Kid told him to go to hell. About sundown, as East recalls,

Billy said they wanted to surrender, but they wanted the condition that we would give him safe conduct to Santa Fe. . . . So Garrett promised them safe conduct through Las Vegas. The Kid and his men came out with their hands up. Barney Mason said: "Kill the S——— B——— he is slippery and may get away." Mason had been one of the Kid's gang at one time, had deserted him and now was afraid of him. He leveled his gun at the Kid and Lee Hall and I threw our guns down on him and said "If you fire a shot we will kill you." Mason lowered his gun.[11]

The possemen and their prisoners spent the night at the Wilcox ranch. Next day, they headed for Fort Sumner, where the prisoners were put in shackles, and from there to Puerto de Luna, arriving in

Alexander Grzelachowski's store at Puerto de Luna.
(Photograph by Lt. Col. Phillip G. Nickell)

time to eat Christmas dinner at the Grzela-chowski store. They reached Las Vegas the following day, December 26, 1880, and a day later the Kid was taken by train to Santa Fe and incarcerated in the county jail on Water Street to await trial.

The Panhandle possemen had done their job: they had captured Billy the Kid and put him where most cattlemen (and a lot of other people) firmly believed he belonged. In March 1881 Billy was taken to La Mesilla, where he was tried for and found guilty of the murder of Sheriff William Brady. The date for his execution was set for Friday, May 13. But the Kid would write one last bloody chapter in the history of the West before Pat Garrett wrote *finis* to his career.[12]

Chapter 10

"POKER TOM" EMORY

RIDING UNDER A CONSUMED NAME

A s Lon Chambers so memorably put it, almost every one of the men in the Panhandle posse was "riding under a consumed name," and "Poker Tom" Emory was no exception. The night Tom O'Folliard was killed at Fort Sumner, he was in a game of poker when Lon Chambers announced riders were coming. As the possemen grabbed their weapons and got ready for a fight, Emory—with what under the circumstances seems like considerable sangfroid—said, "I want to play out my hand," and showed four kings. "You fellows can show when we get back," he said. "This won't take long." Then he picked up his gun and went to join the killing.[1]

According to one contemporary, Tom was "a little scrawny red-headed strawberry roan of a fellow, . . . small, red-faced . . . and weighed about 130 pounds. He changed his name [to Emory] because when he was 14 years old working in a wood camp, he was accused of taking a yoke of oxen. He was a real cowpuncher when he hit Tascosa and a real gambler."[2]

Exactly when he "hit Tascosa" is not recorded, but twenty-six-year-old Emory was already working for the LIT when the Panhandle posse was formed in November 1880 and was one of the half dozen who elected to ride with Pat Garrett. He banged heads with the sheriff-elect soon after the posse reached Puerto de Luna.

It seemed that Pat Garrett had many lady admirers in each plaza. That certain night young slim Tom Emery [*sic*] who was a fine dancer and was getting plenty of attention from the ladies had danced the third set with this fine little señorita and Garrett got jealous and walked up to Tom where he was setting on a bench talking to her. Garrett said, "Kid, you'll have to cut that out, she is mine. *Sabe?*" Tom . . . said "She is mine and if you want to start anything the Pecos River is not between us." I believe the challenge made Garrett think more of him than anyone else in the posse. He showed it in his actions later.

Another story suggests that when Billy the Kid, Billy Wilson, and Dave Rudabaugh surrendered at Stinking Springs and Barney Mason raised his gun to shoot the Kid, it was Tom Emory who "punched Mason in the flank with his pistol and said

[87]

**"Poker Tom" Emory, real name William Arnim.
(Courtesy of Wayne Ahr)**

would you kill a man after you promised to protect him?"

In the days following, as the party trekked north in polar weather to Las Vegas, the Kid let Emory in on the matter of whose cattle he'd been rustling, and from what he said it would appear he was still working off his grudge with "Outlaw Bill" Moore. "You go home and tell your boss Bill McCarty that he is on a cold trail," the Kid said. "You will not find an LIT animal on the Pecos. Can't say the same thing for the LXs. You see, they are new in the business and will have to learn the cattle business."[3]

Pat Garrett chose his two best men to go with him as escort when the time came to take the Kid, Rudabaugh, and Wilson to Santa Fe by train. Tom Emory was one; the other was Jim East, who recalls:

Immediately we got on the train a mob gathered and they would not let the train start. They demanded Dave Rudabaugh as they wanted to hang him for killing the jailer. Garrett told them they were not going to get the prisoners. We shoved up the windows in a car and Tom Emory took one and I another. The Mexican sheriff came in at the door and was demanding the prisoners. Garrett shoved his six-shooter into his belly and that Mexican just fell back out of the coach. . . . Garrett said: "Everybody better get off here, as we are going to have a fight and we don't want anybody to get hurt." Everybody got off the coach except two men who claimed to be prospectors from Montana on their way to White Oaks. . . . They said they did not want to fight but they had paid their fare and did not want to get off. They said they would help us stand off the mob. Garrett told them all right, that he would be grateful.

The turning point of the episode was this: There was a man on the train by the name of J. F. Morley. . . . At that time he was a traveling inspector for the post office department, but had been a railroad engineer. The mob had the engineer and fireman off the train with their guns on them and would not let them pull the train out.[4]

Many years later Morley related his part in these events:

Pat told me he was going to cut the irons off the Boys and let them make a fight for there [*sic*] lives. . . . I told Pat not to do anything until I could see what I could do. I went up to the residence of A. A. Robinson, Chief Engineer for the Santa Fe Railroad, and asked him for a train crew to take the train out. Robinson told me I could have all the rolling stock of the Company but would have to Man it myself, and then after talking with Romero at that time a Member of Congress for the Territory, also with the Alcalda, and each moment things were going worse, I told Pat I would pull the train out myself which I did.[5]

East said,

Just before that three Americans heavily armed came down from the new town. They were friends of ours. They were Jim McIntyre, [saloonkeeper] George Close and a man named George Poindexter, a gambler there. McIntyre had been in the Texas Rangers. They came in behind the mob and that threw it between us and them, and that made the mob take notice. But just then, Morley sneaked into the cab and jerked the throttle open. He was a little excited, I guess, jerked it wide open, and the wheels spun around a few times but took hold and by the time we got to the end of the siding it seemed like we were going a mile a minute, and the Mexicans stood there with their mouths open. The engineer and fireman caught the train as it pulled out."[6]

"And do you remember," Morley added, "that at Glorieta [Pass] on top of the Glorieta mountains we git a lunch for the Prisoners and how Billy the Kid showed us how far down he could bight on a piece of pie, you remember his long squirrel teeth."[7]

After they got to Santa Fe and turned the prisoners over to the sheriff, East and Tom Emory went back to Las Vegas for their horses and then set off for White Oaks, encountering blizzard conditions on

the way. By the time they got to their destination East was snowblind and Emory had frostbitten feet. "We went on to White Oaks through the snow all the way and found Charley Siringo living pat," East said. You can almost hear the disgust in his voice.[8]

Siringo had been altogether unsuccessful in trying to make Pat Coghlan turn over the LX cattle, so the boys were enjoying themselves in their snug berth at White Oaks.

"We was waiting for Spring to come and the snow to melt so we could Round up Pat Coglon's [sic] Rance and get our cattle. . . . A few Days later Charlie Cringo [Siringo] thaught it Best for Part of the out fit to go Back to the Panhandle to save exspences. So Bob Roberson taken one waggon and Part of the Boys . . . started [back to Tascosa] and left Charley there with the Balance of the Boys to gather cattle and Bring them Back as soon as spring opened up."[9]

Perhaps because his role in recovering the stolen cattle from Pat Coghlan fell somewhere short of glorious, Siringo mostly skips this period in his several accounts. The recollections of "Big Foot" Wallace fill in some of the gaps. When it came time for them to collect the stolen cattle and head back with it to the Panhandle, they had to

put up a pretty stiff bluff to keep Coughlin's [sic] men from taking the cattle, but we stood at the corral gate and held it. About ten a.m. our wagon came in sight, and Coughlin's men agreed to let us cut out our cattle. We also cut out the four-year-old steer with the strange brand. They protested against our taking him, but we seemed to have our bluff working and we took it anyway. A short time afterwards we got word that the Chisum round-up was starting, so we packed our war-bags and loaded up our wagon and pulled out for Roswell, New Mexico, where we intended to camp until the round-up was over.[10]

Wallace's recollections pretty much tally with those of Jim East: "The LIT outfit took its wagon back and Charley kept his and then worked through with the Chisum and Coghlin [*sic*] outfits. They wrote me from the [LX] ranch that they wanted me to come back, take a wagon and go down to work through the Pease River country. We left some time in February from White Oaks and got back about the first of March."[11]

Ahead of Wallace, Chambers, Emory, and Siringo lay "a trip of three hundred miles 'by the sun.' Our orders were to bring back all Canadian River cattle that we found, and this, combined with our ignorance of the route, came to be a large order indeed."

By the time they reached the next water, the herd had swollen to twenty-five hundred head. Luck led them to a "grassy lake of rain water. We knew we were off our course, and the other boys did not want to take the cattle any farther, since our grub was also running very low. We had very little coffee, no flour, and still had more than a hundred miles to go."

Scouting ahead, Siringo and Wallace found "signs of an outfit that had pulled out that morning for the Canadian." They caught up with it at the head of Palo Duro Canyon and learned it was heading for the LIT ranch. "We were out of everything but fresh meat," Wallace said. "I would have given a dollar for enough tobacco to roll one cigarette. We got grub from the LIT outfit and a fresh horse apiece, and the next day we took the herd across the Cana-

dian to the LX home ranch and met the roundup there. When we got back . . . they said we had three thousand head of cattle and they swore that we could not have brought them in with no more men than we had. But there we were and we had the cattle to show, so that settled it."[12]

Following his return, Tom Emory "worked for the LIT until they sold out to an English syndicate [the Prairie Land & Cattle Co., which bought the ranch later that year] and he could not get used to their ways, [so] he got in the habit of wintering in Tascosa and trying his luck at gambling." One time, the story goes, it was quiet in town, with "nothing to do for the gamblers; some one bet Tom a $100 or $150 he wouldn't be living in 36 hours. Tom went up on a hill with two Winchesters and a lot of cartridges and defied them. Won the bet, too." Whether he plied his trade exclusively there is not on record, but Emory was in the Dunn & Jenkins saloon at Tascosa along with his brother, Charlie, Len Woodruff, and some others when the famous March 21, 1886, moonlit gunfight took place, although he seems to have avoided either involvement or indictment. Later,

Tom decided he would also go west, after gambling a few years at Las Vegas, and when the rush was on in starting and building up Roswell, he located there, and he often told me his health was so poor that he could not stand the work as a cowhand. [He] was only a shadow of the old original Tom Emery. He said I'm not even fit now to play poker. It seems I can't win. . . . Garrett would pass Tom sometime on the street and tell him he was like an old cow, should you stumbel and fall, careful and don't catch your head under your neck, you might croke."[13]

Emory moved to El Paso, where, believing himself to be dying, he confessed to Pat Garrett that Emory was not his real name and that he was on the run.

One day he sent a messenger with a note to Pat Garrett. He said it seems I'm headed for the last roundup and I want you to get in touch with my brother and I want him to get in touch with Colquit[t] Governor of Texas. I want to go home to die. He said, Pat! I have put one over on you. You have the name of being a great detective and peace officer. Did you know that I was an escaped convict and my right name is Bill Arnold? Garrett had a quick come back and said no, you did not fool me. . . . The result was that in a few days Poker Tom's Brother arrived in El Paso, and taken Tom to Austin, and the Governor said I have no right to pardon an escaped convict. You take him to the Penitentiary have him to register, and a pardon will follow next mail.[14]

The facts are that on May 23, 1876, twenty-two-year-old William Arnim was convicted in the Fayette County District Court of the theft of an ox and sentenced to two years in prison. On entering Huntsville Penitentiary June 9 as Prisoner #5339, he was a slender young man five feet eight and one-half inches tall, with red hair, blue eyes, and a "sandy" complexion. He escaped from custody on March 21, 1877, and headed west, changing his name to Tom Emory.[15] Sometime later his buffalo hunter brother, Charles, joined him in Tascosa, adopting the same alias. Tom also formed a relationship with a widow named Sally Hunnicutt, who had come to Tascosa from Kansas and whose original name was Sarah Daugherty. The daughter of a Texas cattleman, she adopted and kept Emory's name even after the relationship ended.[16]

In May 1896, bearing testimonials filed by R. H. Phelps and L. W. Moore, respectively, the prosecutor and presiding judge who had tried and sentenced him twenty years earlier, a petition for Arnim's pardon was sent to Governor Charles A. Culberson (not Colquitt, as misremembered above). "The reputation of the convict since his escape from the penitentiary has been good," Judge Moore attested, "and he is represented by those who know him as reformed and making a good citizen. There is no family more esteemed than [that] of this man and I respectfully request that you pardon the convict."[17]

Arnim, alias Tom Emory—clearly not on his deathbed (although he may have *thought* he was when he sought the pardon)—surrendered to the authorities at Huntsville on May 9, 1896, and was pardoned on June 16. He was working on the Pat Garrett ranch in Bear Canyon, New Mexico, at the time of Garrett's death in 1908 and seems to have returned to Texas following that event, thereafter living a blameless life. Fayette County and family records show that William Oscar Arnim (Tom Emory), born January 2, 1854, in Moulton, Texas, died on May 26, 1914, and is buried in the Schulenberg town cemetery.[18] Amazingly, it appears no one in the Arnim family to the present day was ever aware of his "other" existence. "Poker Tom" played his cards close to his vest right until the end.

Chapter 11

1880-1882

LAW AND (SOME) ORDER

JIM EAST came up from South Texas in the spring of 1880 with a herd going to Ogallala.

When they got near Dodge I quit them and went to work for the LX's. . . . David T. Beals was the head of the company of Bates and Beal[s]. . . . He had been a shoe manufacturer in South Abbingdon [Abington, Massachusetts] and all the others in the company were shoe men. They brought a lot of Yankees down who had worked in their shoe factory to make cowboys out of them. They worked a lot of them at fifteen dollars a month to learn the cow business . . . and some never earned their salt. They thought they were learning the cow business, though, and would soon be millionaires. Bates stayed in Kansas most of the time, and every cowboy knew him as Deacon, as he was a rather long-faced Englishman.[1]

That same spring Henry Kimball sold his claim south of Tascosa to the LIT and moved his blacksmithing business to Main Street. Around the same time former LX wagon boss Jack Ryan, who had stayed

away from the saloons long enough to save $160, bought a small lot and erected an adobe housing a saloon alongside Rinehart's store.[2] By late summer Tascosa was looking like a regular frontier cow town, where a cowboy on a bender or a gambler whose luck had been a lady could celebrate with fancy food and fancy women.

Out on the range were the big ranches, with cattle scattered across the plains as far as the eye could see. There were lots of smaller spreads too; in the early days, unlike other strongholds of the cattle industry, most of the Panhandle ranchers tolerated smaller men and nesters as long as they were honest. In fact, things pretty soon reached a stage where "the country got to be settled up so bad that it didn't suit old man Turner [an early resident] and he went out to Arizona where he could have a little freedom."[3]

Panhandle residents today might consider "settled up" something of an overstatement: 1880 census figures indicate the total population of Oldham County consisted of only 61 Anglo and 218 Hispanic residents. To the south Potter County had 23 Anglo, 3 Hispanic, and 2 "colored" inhabitants, positively sparse compared to Wheeler County's 468 Anglos (although 296 of those were soldiers at Fort Elliott) plus 8 Hispanic and 36 "colored" residents. In all the Panhandle counties combined there were only some sixteen hundred souls, roughly the population of Dodge City.[4]

Nevertheless, the town's boomers decided it was time Tascosa cast off its civic and legal dependency on Mobeetie, 135 miles away in Wheeler County.

A delegation of men, Jim McMasters, Henry Kimball and Juan Ortega, went to Mobeetie to the Commisioners court in 1880 with a petition from the citizens of Oldham County . . . praying that the county of Oldham might be organized. Juan represented the Mexican element. . . . The [Wheeler] county judge was Emanuel Dubbs, and about noon they thought it was time to adjourn to get dinner or take a drink. . . . They asked Juan what time it was. He had a big, flashy chain and a little Waterbury. He pulled it out, stuck it over so another man could see it, and said: ¿Quien sabe? One of the representative men of Oldham County [and he] could not even tell time.[5]

An election was ordered for December 8, 1880, to select officials and determine whether Upper Tascosa, backed by Howard, Rinehart, McMasters, and Mc-Carty of the LIT, and Lower Tascosa, or "Hogtown," championed by Cone and Edwards, would be Oldham County's new seat. Votes were cast in Tascosa and Trujillo, and the sale of liquor was suspended until the votes (187 were cast) had been counted. Despite the fact that Hogtown's boosters had the superior numerical support of Romero and the Hispanic element,

Upper Tascosa was declared the winner and new county seat, its "courthouse" a four-room adobe, formerly Jack Ryan's saloon.[6]

Once the result was in, the rush to the bar had a tragic aftermath. LIT cowboy Dudley Pannell and a buddy got plastered, firing their guns and whooping it up as they rode out of town. In some accounts Pannell's horse bolted and he was dragged to death, but in what seems a likelier version, the two men got back to the ranch and emptied their six-shooters in the air to liven the place up. Spooked, Pannell's horse started bucking, and somehow Pannell took a bullet in the back of the head. This is to some extent confirmed—although by no means conclusively—by a later newspaper report that stated, "The deceased and another cow boy had been drinking together . . . the day before. Several bullet holes were found in the body of Pannell." He died within a few minutes and was buried next day in the LIT cemetery on the Cheyenne.[7]

Attached to Oldham County for legal purposes were nine other unorganized counties: Castro, Dallam, Deaf Smith, Hartley, Moore, Potter, Randall, Sherman, and Swisher. New officers were elected: "W. H. Woodman had moved up there [from Mobeetie] and he was elected the first District Attorney and C. B. Willingham who had moved up from Goodnight's was elected sheriff."[8]

With a bailiwick of something like sixteen thousand square miles, Tascosa's new sheriff wasn't exactly overpaid: at three hundred dollars a year he got exactly the same amount as the new county clerk, Kentuckian C. B. Vivian. Witty and well educated, popular and accomplished, one-armed Cecil Vivian was something of an enigma; his background was and remains a

Caleb Berg "Cape" Willingham, first sheriff of
Oldham County, ca. 1900. (Author's Collection)

mystery. He was "an inveterate gambler
and played billiards. He played night after
night. They said he never got up from a
poker game a winner in his life. . . . He tells
one fellow that his arm was shot off, and
then he tells another . . . that he got his
hand in the corn grinder. But he was a
bright fellow." Another recalled how Vivian
talked "about England and Ireland and
Germany and France and every goddam
place over there. After he left, they asked
me, 'Where is that man from?' I said, 'I've
known him for twenty years and nobody
knows where he's from. He knows more
about Scotland than I do, and I was born
over there.'" Jesse Jenkins put his finger on
it: Vivian "was one of the biggest liars in
the world."[9]

Prior to his appointment, Willingham
had been a driver on the so-called Light-

ning Express that carried the mail between
Mobeetie and Las Vegas, New Mexico. "In
the winter of 1880–81 [I] was working on
that notorious mail line," Marion Armstrong said. "My [usual] run was from Tascosa to Dixon Creek. On this occasion I
had to go on to Mobeetie, one hundred
and twenty miles without stopping. To an
auto driver that wouldn't sound so bad but
to a man on a condemned pony in zero
weather it meant something, especially
when we had to ride day and night and
when the snow was on the ground we had
nothing to guide us."

The contractor holding the postal fran-
chise was Dodge City resident P. G.
Reynolds (no relation to the sutler-trader),
by all indications a hard-headed and in-
tractable businessman.[10] One time when
Armstrong reported to him at Mobeetie,
Reynolds "began to roar because I was so
far behind time. I told him I had broken
through the ice on the Canadian River on
my way down and had lost one half day
getting out. That only seemed to irritate
him." Armstrong quit on the spot, but before he left he warned Reynolds that "this
part of the road should be staked off so a
man could find his way across it." Despite
the fact that this was one of the most severe winters within recent memory,
Reynolds thought otherwise. As a result,
the next mail carrier, twenty-six-year-old
John Cannington from Georgia, got lost on
the plains during his second trip, and his
feet were so badly frozen they had to be
amputated. The cowboys banded together
to raise two hundred dollars so he could
have artificial feet fitted; Cannington took
the money and started a monte bank.[11]

Next up was Tom Wilson, "a fiddler of
some repute around the dance halls and
saloons of Mobeetie and Tascosa," who
fared little better. Early in February 1881,

Cape Willingham at the reins of the "Lightning Express,"
the mail line that plied between Mobeetie and Las Vegas. (Author's Collection)

driving a two-mule buckboard with two passengers, William Higgins and a man named Davidson, he pulled out from the North Fork station during a snowstorm, heading for Dixon Creek some thirty miles away. At about the halfway mark "they got stuck in a snow bank and the mules struggling in the snow broke the tongue out of the buckboard." Unable to repair it, the three men decided to continue on foot. Since their tracks were already obliterated by snow, they could not return to North Fork, so they decided to try for Dixon Creek, using the wind for a guide. When the wind changed direction, they missed the station completely and were soon completely lost. "They had a Buffalo robe and a tarpolian [sic] with them which was some help at night for one of their group was soon frozen so he could not walk and they put him on one of the mules and carried him up near where Amarillo now stands. But the mules got away that night, so next

morning they had to leave him. He was still alive, so they bid him goodbye, covered him with the buffalo robe and pulled the tarp over him good and told him they would go on and find the camp and return to get him."[12]

"A dispatch from Fort Elliott states that one of the passengers and the stage driver were found forty miles from the road," reported the *Dodge City Times*. "Both men were badly frozen, their feet and legs being hard up to the knees. The passenger's [driver's] name is Thomas Wilson. When found they had been without food four days. The other passenger named William Higgins of New York is still missing. The stage line belongs to P. G. Reynolds of this city. Two mules belonging to him and which were attached to the buckboard were lost. The buckboard and mail bags were found safe."

Amazingly, Wilson survived the ordeal; his companions were not so lucky.

Two of the boys from the LX ranch, Tom Monroe and Jack Daugherty, were out getting wood and saw one of the men, Tom Wilson, wandering around on foot. They got him back and took him to the ranch. Then they went back and took his trail to try and find the others. . . . They found Davidson near it, wandering around. Davidson and Wilson had left one of the men who was with them. He had got sleepy, lay down and they could not get him up. We found the skeleton the next winter. . . . We took Davidson and Wilson to Fort Elliott. They were pretty badly frozen.[13]

The post surgeon, Dr. Daniel Appel (another veteran of the Lincoln County War), amputated Davidson's feet. "Then they discovered that they did not cut them off high enough," Jim East said, "and had to cut his legs off again higher up, and he died on the operating table."[14]

Not troubling to hide his disgust, Marion Armstrong observed, "It would have cost [Reynolds] approximately, say, ten dollars to have staked that section. But he would not be out that much for his men. The laboring man of that day did not have much to say about their comfort, they generally took it as it came. I remember there was no such thing as a slicker or a raincoat among the cowboys."[15]

On February 21, 1881, Henry A. Russell bought a 70-by-140-foot corner lot at Spring and Main Streets for which he paid Howard & McMasters one hundred dollars, and on that site he built the Exchange Hotel. Beds cost fifty cents, as did a meal, a dozen eggs, or a pound of butter. "We had the first board floor in Tascosa," Molly Russell said. "Father freighted the lumber from Dodge City to floor our 14 by 16 dining room. It took him a month to make the

Henry Russell's Hotel. (Courtesy of the Amarillo Public Library)

trip. The lumber alone cost $50." After the board floor was laid, the Russell Hotel became a sort of community center where the English-speaking inhabitants and any cowboys who happened to be in town gathered in the evenings, pushed back the chairs and tables, and danced while Henry Russell played the fiddle.

Social life "was made up mostly of the old fashioned kissing parties and dances during the week days and regular Sunday School in the big lobby of the hotel on Sundays and church preaching services at any time that an itinerant preacher might come along, generally being a Methodist as they seemed to pay most attention to these parts." When dances were arranged, "it was necessary to cover a territory of fifty miles across to find enough young ladies to take part in the quadrilles. It was generally conceded," Molly added with delightfully unconscious snobbery, "there would be no trouble at the dances where the ladies were present even though there was nearly always drinking among the men, however there was no drinking among the ladies who attended these dances, they conducted themselves as ladies should and if there were characters among the women who drank they separated themselves from the better people."

Lena Dobbs concurred: "A drunk wouldn't any more go in a dance of ours than they would fly. Tom Coffee and Kid Dobbs got most of the dances and the young married women did most of the dancing but they were good women. All the women drank California wine, ate sweet crackers and candy. One night Mrs. Willingham wanted more wine for the party [and] Kid played a trick on her. He knew Frank James could take the wire seal off the wine bottle and replace it without anyone knowing. . . . He and some friends

went after the wine and had James take off the seal. Kid and the boys drank some of the wine and refilled the bottle with good whiskey and took [it] to Mrs. Willingham. Later, when Kid wanted to dance with her she said, 'That last bottle of wine went to our heads, Kid, and the others, too.'"[16]

The hotel was such a success that Jack Ryan, whose Equity Bar had prospered, bought the lot next to it and built a bigger, better saloon. Ryan was not his real name, nor was he Irish, as most locals believed, but Italian, and he had a past. Some time after his departure from Tascosa, Henry Hoyt learned "all about Jack and his affair with a comrade soldier at Fort Union—that was why he was in the Panhandle under an 'alias'. [T]here was a lot of 'queer' names amongst Panhandle boys of the days that are past and gone, it was a Mecca for men with a shady past."[17]

It was indeed that, but above all else Tascosa was famous for its gambling. Every saloon, every building, even the livery stable had gaming rooms, with professionals coming into town to play for pots that equaled anything available even in Dodge City. Everyone played, from county judge to cowboy, from merchant to saloon swamper, and Jack Ryan was no exception. On one occasion, he served on a jury that deliberated all night and well into the next morning. The vote was eleven for acquittal and one—Ryan—for conviction. Declaring he would either hang the defendant or hang the jury, Ryan refused to reconsider until his Equity Bar partner, merchant Frank James, tapped on the window of the jury room. "Jack, there's a big game on, a pot of $1800, come on and get in on it." Telling James to get back and keep the game going until he could get there, Ryan turned to his fellow jurors and informed them that while he still believed the defendant was guilty as hell, he allowed his own judgment might be fallible. Within moments a verdict of "not guilty" was returned, and Jack departed post haste to join the game.[18]

> It was a typical western town, wide open and gambling every place. Jack Ryan's place was where they gambled more. Of course, there was *monte* tables and poker down at Jesse Jenkins, too, but that was the hard part of town. Old man Rinehart was there, too. Howard and Rinehart were the first ones that started the store, and then Rinehart evidently sold out to McMasters. . . . I forgot old man [Theodore] Briggs. . . . He had a Mexican wife. I don't know whether she was his wife or not. They were a little bit loose about those marriages. The priest would come down once a year from Las Vegas and marry those couples that was living together, but lots of times they swapped two or three times before [he] could get there.[19]

Some might have been a "little bit loose" about marriage, but Bob Russell wasn't one of them. A former cowboy who ran a saloon, Russell (no relation to the hotel-keeping family) was, by many accounts, one of his own best customers. His wife, the former Lizzie Rinehart, was a bright, outgoing young woman who didn't always maintain as proper a distance as she ought between herself and some of the more handsome cowboys she encountered, and when merchant Jules Howard commented unfavorably on the impropriety of Lizzie's behavior, Bob Russell got his mad up.

One March Monday, having nursed his grievance all weekend, meanwhile tanking up on ninety-proof, Bob determined to "go

Jack Ryan, cowboy turned bartender. (Courtesy of the Haley Memorial Library, Midland, Texas)

jump old Howard out." This was not a wise move, because Howard was ready and waiting with a six-gun in his hand. As Russell weaved in through the door, Howard "told him to lay [his gun] down. Bob threw his six-shooter down on the counter. Then Howard said, 'To show you, Bob, that I don't want to kill you, or take any undue advantage of you, I will meet you half way,' and he threw his gun down too. Bob, being a little too drunk to manage things as he should, made a grab for his gun, but Howard got his first, and that was the last of Bob Russell."

James Harshman, who claimed to have been an eyewitness, told it differently. Russell, he said, got drunk and decided to ride his horse into Howard's store. Howard warned him not to. At about four in the afternoon, Russell rode in anyway, gun in hand. Howard fired four shots. One struck

The Equity Bar. (Courtesy of the Haley Memorial Library, Midland, Texas)

Russell in the chest, one in the head, and a third took off his trigger finger. Russell himself managed only one shot that went into the ceiling. Harshman, Howard, and Russell's wife, Lizzie, nursed the wounded man until he died about eight o'clock that evening. There was no lumber to be had in the town, so a coffin was fashioned from some packing crates Howard had out behind his store. "I was the youngest one there," Harshman said, "and supposed to have fewer sins I suppose so I was delegated to read the burial service. His wife had a small Bible and we buried him on a high bank overlooking the [Canadian] river and covered his grave with a lot of stones so the coyotes could not dig him up."[20]

The place Lizzie had chosen was on a knoll in her father's pasture about a quarter of a mile out of town. Beside it she erected a sturdy post that could clearly be seen from below, so every time Jules Howard stepped outside his door he was reminded of the man he had killed. Thus was Tascosa's Boot Hill cemetery, named after the one in Dodge City, consecrated, if that is the word. According to legend, it was gambler Mickey McCormick who suggested the name, although others remembered it as being Jack Ryan.[21]

By the time Howard was cleared of murder the following August, Tascosa had indeed become Hoyt's "Mecca for men with a shady past" and the random violence they brought with them. Early in September Pat Dudley, who had formerly kept one of the way stations on P. G. Reynolds's mail route, killed a boy who worked in a store at Trujillo—why, history does not record. A Mr. Pratt, superintendent of the mail route, was sleeping in the store when Dudley "managed to steal Pratt's pistol and stepped up behind the boy while he was marking goods, and blew his brains out." Taking Pratt's pistol belt, the killer lit out for New Mexico, leaving in such haste that he dropped the pistol. When it was found and identified, Pratt was arrested, but he was soon released.[22]

Accustomed though everyone was to such killings, it must sometimes have seemed like all the hard men in Texas were moving into Oldham County, and Sheriff Cape Willingham had his work cut out keeping things in line. In May he had hired himself a deputy who got paid twenty dollars a month as constable and town marshal. Henry McCullough "was a holy terror when he landed in Tascosa and became so mean he could not get along with his own kind. He gave one fellow a 'cowpuncher's shampoo,' that is, he beat him over the head with a six shooter, cutting big gashes in his scalp." Then one day "a cowboy gave him a whack with a gun from which he did not recover for three months. He had been found unconscious with one side completely paralyzed. He lost his memory . . . and had to learn to talk all over again. The beating also changed his behavior; he became a respectable citizen and was appointed deputy sheriff."[23]

Records at Vega show McCullough was appointed constable of Precinct One (Tascosa town) in May 1881 and soon thereafter deputy sheriff and town marshal. Around the beginning of September 1881 he was poisoned, probably by his partner, Tobe Fratner (which might account for the paralysis). What business they were in is

not on the record, but "Pratner left immediately afterwards with the partnership funds. McCullough is still dangerously sick and we learn that the grand jury of Oldham county, now in session, will investigate the matter." If it ever did, its findings are no longer on file. Henry McCullough recovered and resumed his duties as a part-time lawman.[24]

Not the least of several other significant arrivals in Tascosa that summer were Jesse Reagan Jenkins and his brother William Alonzo "Lon" Jenkins from Mobeetie, part of a growing number of that town's "demimonde" who had decided the increasing trend toward law and order there—the place even had a newspaper, the *Panhandle*, edited by Asa Shinn Mercer—was not to their taste and moved on. It is very doubtful that the commissioners court that on October 17, 1881, approved the bond of Lon Jenkins and his partner Charles Donnelly as liquor dealers could have realized their arrival—and especially that of Lon's brother, Jesse—would have as profound an effect upon the future of their town as would (although for hugely different reasons) the advent of William McDole Lee.[25]

Things began to change in Tascosa from the moment Jesse Jenkins arrived. Although still in his early twenties, he was tough, ambitious, and ruthless. A shrewd behind-the-scenes manipulator who, as the old saying goes, never let his left hand know what his right hand was doing, he soon gathered around him a hard crew that ran things the way Jenkins wanted them run. He made some money by grubstaking a freighting outfit, operated the down-and-dirty saloon in Hogtown owned by Lon, and, by extending generous credit, good liquor, and girls, encouraged the gamblers, the drinkers, the drifters, and the hard men

Jesse Reagan McDaniels Jenkins in his prime. (Courtesy of Wanda Carnell)

William Alonzo "Lon" Jenkins (detail from photo of Jim East and friends). (Courtesy of the Amarillo Public Library)

to gather there. His specialty was taking care of business; he "ran [the] honky tonk, laid up with Dutch Phoebe [Miller]. Had a row of houses right in front of his saloon, rented them to the girls," as one terse annotation puts it. Pretty soon, Hogtown had become the rendezvous for every tough and badman in the western Panhandle.[26]

Charles Goodnight had no time for Jenkins, who was "in command of all the cut throats in the Panhandle and was operating every kind of a tough bad place of the worst form, wide open," he said. "Tascosa was then the most lawless place on the continent. Willingham was alone and there was no doubt but that each day they planned to kill him. It seems a providential thing that [Texas Ranger Capt. G. W.] Arrington turned up just then with six men."

Providential it might have been; coincidence it was not. In September 1879 Capt. George W. Arrington and his troop had established the first Ranger camp in the Panhandle. From there in January and February 1880 he had led his men on a wide-ranging tour of the Panhandle and eastern New Mexico, backing up the forces of law and order wherever they found themselves. Tascosa was just one of the places they "happened" to be in when needed.

"Of course Willingham made application to Arrington for help," said Goodnight. "Arrington said plainly that he had no orders for any such distribution of his men but said 'Your necessity is so great I will leave you two men,' which he did. Capt. Arrington straightway called on Mr. Jenkins and told him he had left two men to help the Sheriff and said 'If you allow them to be hurt, I'll return with my posse and hang every Damned one of you and won't leave one 'dobe on top of another!' The men remained unharmed and thence some sort of order was established."[27]

When Arrington and his Rangers went back to duty, Henry Brown, a graduate of the Lincoln County school of law, was hired to assist Willingham as town marshal at twenty dollars a month.[28] Willingham needed all the help he could get; many of the cowboys coming into town didn't take any more kindly to the idea of law and order in Tascosa than they did anyplace else.

One such was a thirty-four-year-old Englishman named Fred Leigh, who came up the trail in the early summer of 1881 with the first herd brought to the Panhandle for the LS. "We had just organized Oldham County," said Justice of the Peace Marion Armstrong, "and sorry to say, those cowpunchers from lower Texas

Henry Brown.
(**Courtesy of Robert G. McCubbin**)

seemed to get it into their heads that we weren't entitled to very much respect, if any, [and] when they would get drunk they would make themselves unnecessarily troublesome."[29]

"Troublesome" seems like something of an understatement. One day in late July, Armstrong and Henry Brown (both of whom were also working on the "Lightning Express" mail line) went together by rowboat across the Canadian to feed some horses. On their way back they ran into a group of cowboys—among them Leigh—leaving town. At least one of them, a fellow named something like Cayho (may have been Keogh) had been involved in a saloon brawl, perhaps even a near killing, soon after the Panhandle possemen got back from New Mexico and

got on a Big Spree as our credit was good at old Jack Rynes [Ryan's] Saloon. While there after every thing was full of Red licker. Bob Roberson got up on a center table to make a speach and while he was speaking, some one shuck the table and Down it came. Just at that time a man By the name of Cayho Jumped up and struck at Bob. Then it tuck all the Boys Busy for sometime to keep Bob from Killing Cayho. After every thing got quite, we found our way to camp which was close by and went to Bed.[30]

Hauled before the bench, "Cayho" addressed a stream of abuse at the court and its officers, whereupon Henry Brown laid his six-shooter on a chair and offered to run for it with him, "but his opponent would not accept, and he picked it up and cursed him for a 'white livered ———.' . . . The bawling out had a good effect on the would-be bad cowpunchers . . . so after venting his wrath on Mr. Kaho, [Brown] proceeded to give the Court some conciliatory remarks, saying 'I want to quit having you afraid of these people, for I can shoot as good as any of them.' After the Court finished shaking so it could talk, he thanked Henry very much for his kind offer, and the cowpunchers all left town and peace reigned for some time."[31]

It is hardly surprising, then, that when Leigh and his pals met Brown and Armstrong out in the open and afoot, liquor-fueled hostility boiled up. Somehow, keeping his voice mild and his hands well away from his gun, Brown managed to defuse the situation; after a while the cowboys rode on. Still smarting from the tongue-lashing, Brown and Armstrong reported to Willingham, and it was decided that if and when the cowboys returned, a close watch would be kept on them, Leigh in particular; if trouble arose, an agreed signal would be given.

Needless to say, they came back. On or about August 8, Marion Armstrong "saw the row from start to finish. We had a nice little ditch of water down the street and some ducks were playing in the water and a woman was watching them. Mr. Leigh pulled out his six-shooter and shot one of them. Of course, that had a bad effect. . . . The sheriff was standing around the corner and was soon on the ground and said, 'Mr. Leigh, you will have to give up your gun.' But Mr. Leigh had the drop on the sheriff and said 'You will not get this gun from me unless you take it out of cold hands.'"

No doubt laughing at having yet again faced down the man he considered a pot-gutted nobody who represented the law in Tascosa, Leigh and his pals rode over to the saloon. As they did, Willingham went back into the Howard & McMasters store, got his shotgun, slipped out the back, and

came around the building facing the cowboys. Leigh had dismounted, a cigar in his left hand. Willingham put the shotgun to his shoulder and told Leigh to surrender his gun. Instead Leigh "made a leap on his horse and started to draw his gun, but he didn't get it more than half way out of his scabbard" before Willingham literally blew him out of the saddle. The cowboy was dead when he hit the ground.

As Leigh fell, Henry Brown stepped into view, McMasters and Henry Kimball emerged from the store, and Armstrong and Rinehart appeared across the street. All were armed with Winchesters. Realizing they were whipsawed, Leigh's companions wheeled their horses around and fogged it out of town. Fred Leigh's body was carried into a room adjoining the saloon, where Marion Armstrong held an inquest, with Jack Ryan, Tee Sillman, Jim McMasters, John Dinan, Henry Russell, and T. F. Cable as jurors. The dead man was buried the same day, "the second one that whiskey had sent to Boot Hill."[32]

Armstrong's account puts the blame for Leigh's death squarely on the cowboy himself. Leigh's friends told a somewhat different story. Leigh (a brother-in-law of trail boss Bob Mitchell, who had played a major role in the Horrell-Higgins feud a few years earlier),[33]

had been drinking a little and decided to go back to town. On the way over he saw some tame ducks in a hole of water just before he got to Tascosa. Pulling his gun he shot into the bunch three times. When he rode up to the saloon, Willingham demanded the gun. Leigh told him all right and reached back to get it [and] when he did so, Willingham pulled the trigger and shot him. . . . The man [who told] Bob Fred was killed did not say anything about a woman being scared. . . . He told Bob not to go over there as they might kill him also, so Bob gave him $50 to see and have Fred put away.[34]

Thankfully, not everything that happened in Tascosa was quite so grim. On June 15, 1882, for example, Mary Willingham's sister Jennie Mays was to be married to thirty-four-year old county clerk C. B. Vivian. There was just one small problem: Judge Jim McMasters had never officiated at a wedding before. So the groom hatched up a scheme, inviting McMasters to come to a picnic but not telling him why. "When they got out on the Cheyenne, C. B. called McMasters off [to one side] and told him what he wanted. The Judge swore frightfully. 'Damn it' he said, 'I don't know what to say.' But Vivian had taken a copy of the service along and took it out and read it to him several times. Then they stood under a cottonwood and McMasters started in to perform the service. He forgot several times and each time Vivian prompted him and finally they got through."[35]

At Tascosa, matters legal—whether dealing with marriage or murder—were considerably less than formal. A study of existing records reveals no evidence of a county court being held there prior to 1911. As a result, all cases over which a county court would have had jurisdiction were tried before the justice of the peace. District court met for the first time on May 2, 1881. A grand jury was selected, consisting of foreman John Cone, John Ryan, Theodore Briggs, Marion Armstrong, Henry Russell, and seven Hispanic residents, with Henry Kimball and J. G. "Doc" Scurlock acting as interpreters, and next day Sheriff Willingham summoned it to appear in court. During its first session the grand jury returned one indictment for murder [G. J. Howard], one for aggravated assault, and one for embezzlement and theft. "We are pleased to state that after diligent enquiry we find that there is not so many cases of crime as was expected and can cheerfully say that the condition of the county is good," said foreman Cone's optimistic report.

Because there was no county court, the power vested by default in the justice of the peace was therefore, shall we say, unusual, and after he made the office his own, bartender Scotty Wilson took full advantage of it. Which probably explains the undying tradition that during that first year, Wilson hit upon a foolproof way to supplement his finances, which were constantly depleted by a ruinous gambling habit. When the first book of marriage licenses reached town, he called together all the dance hall girls and

Theodore Briggs.
(Courtesy of the Amarillo Public Library)

[104]

the cowboys and gamblers with whom they were living and informed them they must comply with the new law by purchasing a marriage license and tying the knot.[36]

This tale might be dismissed as legend but for the fact it coincides with an event often overlooked by frontier historians. For some years, reformers had been making a concerted assault on the bastions of polygamy, especially as practiced by the Mormon Church. During the Chester Arthur administration, Senator George F. Edmunds of Vermont took up the cause in Washington and saw it through to become law. The Edmunds Act of 1882 made "unlawful cohabitation" a misdemeanor, thus requiring men and women living together to prove that they were actually married if asked by an officer to do so. More than probably it was this Act of Congress with which Scotty Wilson "encouraged" marriages such as that of Louis Bousman and Sally Cruce.[37]

Over in Wheeler County, Mobeetie had turned into a thriving town—not to say, as some did, hell on wheels. A memoir by Lucius Dills captures its raunchy flavor. "The principal business there was the saloon business," he remembered.

[C. L.] Pendleton had a saloon by the side of Rath's store. . . . Old man Wilkinson had one and then Johnny Long had a saloon. There was a fine looking fellow [named Joe Mason] that had the biggest saloon and gambling house there. It had more tables and more drunks than the rest. Finally there was a fellow named George Berry—they called him the White Elephant—he came in there and started a little saloon right by the side of Dickson's store, a little lean-to. . . . He had a little bar about eight or nine feet long and had a nice back bar and plenty of glasses

[mirrors] for these fellows to see themselves drinking in. You take two saloons and put them by the side of one another and one with glasses behind and the other without, and the one without them will go broke. . . . Berry only had one chair in the house, and that was behind the bar he set in when he didn't have any customers. He didn't have anything but first class liquors. He didn't have any keg beer, but he had beer in bottles and kept it as cool as he could by water under the ground, kind of a well down behind the bar. He kept it at a temperature of about sixty. By George he made money right along. It was next to [as bad as] killing a whore to go into a saloon and take a drink without asking all the bums up to take a drink with you. . . .

There was one dance hall there about a block out of town. There was just one street that run through the town. They put

Lucius Dills (detail from the photo of a group of early Tascosans). (Courtesy of the Haley Memorial Library, Midland, Texas)

[105]

Sam Dyer before the court contesting a case about whether that was a honky tonk or a nice resort. He stammered and they says, "What was going on there?"

He says, "Nothing much."

"What did you see?"

"Oh, fiddling, fucking and dancing." That was right in open court.

There was some professional gamblers there. Dave Light, or something, was the biggest gambler there. One night . . . they were talking about the connubial qualities of the different whores in town, which one they liked the best and . . . a certain married man that was about half-shot pulled out a photograph of his wife and says "There's something that's always ready and can't be beat." By God, this gambler got up and slapped his jaws and kicked him out and says "The idea of you goddam dirty sonofabitch mixing your wife up in a conversation like this!"[38]

As one of his first acts as the new sheriff of this frontier paradise, former Texas Ranger Capt. George W. Arrington made a tour of the establishments noted above by Lucius Dills and forcefully recommended to some of its less, uh, fragrant denizens that it might be in their best interests to move on. He told the con men and the gamblers and the horse and cattle thieves pretty much the same thing. And move on they did—to Tascosa.

Chapter 12

"OUTLAW BILL" MOORE

LOS MUERTOS NO HABLAN

WILLIAM C. MOORE first arrived in the Panhandle shortly after Bates and Beals established the LX ranch in the fall of 1877 and was taken on, no questions asked, even though not a few people knew he was on the run. In this regard it is important here and elsewhere to remember the social convention that existed then. "A ranch man did not ask to see the family tree of a fellow who came along asking for a job. . . . Usually they gave him a horse and told him to get busy. . . . But a ranchman did not put a drifter in charge of his entire business until the man had proved himself by various range tests—skill with a rope, respect for a brand, ability to get along with men, knowledge of the nature of a cow." Also, as another noted historian has observed, "Some outfits preferred men who were on the dodge, because they stuck closer to business, avoided the towns, and were always ready to fight their way out of a difficulty."[1]

Moore quickly proved he had the right stuff and a personality to match, for within a remarkably short time he had worked his way up to the position of ranch manager and soon had the LX running like clock-work. He was "one of the best cowmen ever in the Panhandle. When it came to handling the riata he had no superior and few equals. He was well liked by his men, and esteemed by his neighboring cowmen. He could also handle a gang of cowboys as well as he could handle a riata."[2]

"Handsome, a great worker, a natural leader, Moore had one distinctive physical feature, a cast in his left eye. . . . He usually kept that eye half closed, and always wore his hat on the left side of his head with the brim pulled down; but even so, you couldn't miss seeing the cast." Most who knew him considered him to be one of the top cattle handlers in the Panhandle "and laughed or winked at the charges that he was too free with a branding iron. All agreed that he was a remarkable roper and rider. Moore was striking in appearance. Men used to say that if a person saw him once he would know him the next time, anywhere. . . . He had drive and power, and swept men off their feet. Even men who disapproved of his standards seemed to like him." Jesse Jenkins, always a tight man with a compliment, said, "Moore had such a hold on his men he

William C. "Outlaw Bill" Moore.
(Courtesy of the Haley Memorial Library,
Midland, Texas)

could make them jump over a 100 foot bank."[3]

Two years passed, during which Moore earned the respect of everyone around him, although there were those who remarked that he wasn't too particular about the men he hired—particularly for that first 1878 roundup—or the fact that they were making pretty free with his employer's cattle. Then one day "a curious incident occurred. A party of six men appeared on the range, well armed, outfitted with a chuck wagon, hack and saddle horses. They told nobody their business, but late one evening they pulled up close to the LX wagon and camped. The next morning over half of Moore's cowhands were missing. The rumor had got about that the strangers were Texas Rangers in

disguise, and those cowhands figured that the next state would be healthier for them! Actually the strangers were surveyors laying out a new mail route."[4]

How much truth there is in the accusations leveled against Moore is as difficult to decide as it is to establish how many men he had working for him. When Cape Willingham came up from Goodnight's ranch to investigate cattle theft at the LX, quite a few of the men Moore had hired "drifted"; after Willingham left to work on the "Lightning Express," things reverted to the way they had been.

The 1880 census for Potter County shows "Wm. More," age thirty, raising cattle, birthplace Missouri, father born in Kentucky, mother in Pennsylvania. Below his name are those of twenty "servants," all "herding cows." Of these, Jim East guardedly remarked, "There may have been about two men on the [LX] ranch who stood in with Moore." John Arnot was more specific: Moore, he said "had four LX cowpunchers in with him on those steals—John Cook, Miller [Mueller] Scott, Bob Thompson and T. Stillman [Sillman]." It is probably safe to assume they joined Moore's team during his final and most profitable year. "While working for the LX," Arnot said, "Moore started a brand of his own and proceeded to brand all of those stray cattle he could find."[5]

Unknown to his employers, Moore had an interest in a ranch near Adobe Walls run by Billy Anderson, a friend of Moore's from California, and operated under the Scissors brand. In partnership with James Huff Wright he had yet another ranch, the Circle H, "at the head of Cold water [Creek] in Sherman County," which in those days bordered "No-Man's-Land," a strip of territory between Kansas and Texas not yet claimed (as it would later be) by Oklahoma. This brand was registered at the end of 1879 by the brothers Melville Bond and James Huff Wright. How they and Anderson became partners is uncertain, but since a year later Moore married Jennie Wright, a niece of the brothers, a connection can certainly be presumed.

Next, Moore "bought a bunch of cattle at Adobe Walls, the Circle H's, from a man named Anderson. He kept these on Coldwater Creek, north of the LX's, threw in with them another bunch branded Double H, and built up a herd. He tended to these cattle by occasionally absenting himself from his work on the LX ranch."[6] And if what his contemporaries said is true, as well as being involved in the wholesale theft of his employers' cattle, Bill Moore had a pretty checkered past.

Most Tascosans believed Moore had "killed his brother in law in California and they run him out of there. He got in with the Swan outfit in Wyoming and he was managing that. Oh, he was an executive. He was fine. But he killed . . . [a black] coachman up there for something. So he had to light out again and he come down here and went to work for the LXs."[7]

Charlie Siringo added a few details: Moore, he said, had killed his brother-in-law (he later corrected that to "father in law") in California and lit out for Cheyenne, Wyoming. There, in 1872, "his talents as a cattleman, and a leader of men were quickly recognized. He became a foreman on both Judge [Joseph M.] Carey's CY Ranch and the huge Swan Land & Cattle Company. Judge Carey and Alex[ander H.] Swan each served as president of the Wyoming Stock Growers Association, an organization that admitted Moore to membership on 5 April 1875." About two years later Moore "shot and killed his Negro coachman, and made his

Alexander Hamilton Swan. (Courtesy of the Wyoming State Archives, Department of State Parks and Cultural Resources)

get away from the law officers in Wyoming, landing at the LX Ranch on a broken down pony."[8]

This story, like so many Siringo told, contains more hearsay than fact. In the alleged killing of a brother-in-law (or father-in-law) in California, for example, no location, no victim's name, no date is given, rendering confirmation of the allegation almost impossible. The nearest probability, gleaned from scant details available in contemporary newspapers, would appear to be a shooting that occurred at Smith's Ferry, about halfway between Fresno City and Visalia, California, on Thursday, March 30, 1871, when a twenty-two-year-old stock raiser named Clempson Moore (the name is also given as Clampson, Clemmons, and Clemens) shot—but did not kill—his wife's stepfather, thirty-four-year-old farmer Clayborne Wright.

Wright, a former schoolteacher, said by

some to be a "very disagreeable man," had married the widow of James Smith, original owner of the river facility, a hotel, and twenty-five acres of land on which it stood, and then expropriated the estate of his wife's former husband, treating it as his own. However, his wife's daughter Harriet, who a year or so earlier had married local stock raiser Clempson Moore, decided to lay claim to her one-third of the property; learning Wright was presently shearing the family sheep herd, she gave her husband a written order to take possession of her share of the wool.

When Moore presented his wife's demand, Wright pretty much told him to go to hell, whereupon "Moore told Wright he guessed he would attend to his wife's business and drew out a revolver and was going to beat Wright over the head with it. Wright got hold of Moore, then Moore began shooting."

Other accounts of what happened next—including Clayborne Wright's own—differ on minor points, but all agree Moore shot Wright through the body, the bullet entering through his left lung and ranging down to his lower spine. Borrowing a horse from his wife's brother, Ham Smith, Moore skinned out, abandoning his wife and daughter. He was never heard from again, although "it was reported that [he] was afterwards elected to the Office of Sheriff at Cheyenne, Wyoming."⁹

Well, a live stepfather-in-law isn't exactly a dead brother-in-law, but allowing for the way anecdotal history is transmitted, it might be said to be near enough. But are the Moore of this story and William C. Moore the same man? Although the account above links him (as does Siringo) with Cheyenne, Wyoming, such other facts as can be unearthed hardly provide a definitive answer. In the 1870 census Clempson

Moore, twenty-three, is a stock raiser, born in California, and his seventeen-year-old wife, Harriet, is listed as a homemaker, born in Missouri. This—not to mention a missing finger said to have been shot off during his struggle with Clayborne Wright, which no recollection of Moore in Texas includes—raises serious doubts that this can be "our" William C. Moore, because he has the wrong birthplace. Of course, Moore may have had his own reasons for claiming he was a Californian, rather than Missouri-born. Records are not history: they only indicate where history may be found.¹⁰

What, then, about the later alleged killing of the coachman in Wyoming? Again, the record is inconclusive. There was, of course, a Swan Land & Cattle Company near Cheyenne, run by the charismatic Alexander Hamilton Swan (1833–1905), but it was not incorporated until 1883, so there is no way Moore can have worked there. Possibly, then, it was the Swan Brothers Cattle Company, established in 1873; unfortunately, such documentation of its activities as may have existed seems to have disappeared. What is certain is that no William C. Moore is listed in the criminal records of the district court of Laramie County between 1870 and 1880.

The CY ranch operated by Judge (later Senator) Joseph M. Carey, a former president of the Wyoming Stock Growers Association, was located in Carbon County near what is now Casper, Wyoming, but a search of that county's criminal dockets proved likewise inconclusive, nor is the name of Moore to be found anywhere in the records of the Wyoming Stock Growers Association. All of this suggests either the accusations leveled at Moore were spurious, or if he ever spent any time in Wyoming he was using another name.¹¹

Giving Moore the benefit of the historical doubt with respect to his alleged crimes in California and Wyoming does not, however, acquit him of the ones he is accused of in the Panhandle; indeed, there seems little doubt that as soon as the watchful Willingham was gone, Moore took on as LX hands a number of known rustlers and with their assistance began stealing wholesale from his employers, in the process setting an example followed by every cattle thief in the Panhandle region. With a half million cattle wandering free across the unfenced plains, the pickings were rich and easy, and by the time Jim East went to work for the LX in 1880, the "boys" were helping themselves without compunction. "All the time Moore was doing this he was posing as taking a strong stand against cattle stealing. He made quite a bit of talking about the men who stole, saying they ought to be strung up, but this was part of his game."[12]

The setup was achingly simple. "Billy [Anderson] came in [at the Scissors ranch] on Adobe Walls down there and when [Moore]'d steal them he'd turn them over to Billy." Anderson would then presumably slap either a Scissors or a Circle H brand on the cattle and that would be that. As we have seen, Moore and the Wright brothers registered the Circle H brand on December 31, 1879. The very same day, Moore also registered the brand MC, which would appear to have been used on cattle held on the ranch he ran with Melville Bond Wright in Potter County—M for Mel, C for . . . Clempson?[13]

"There was a bunch of boys there on the [LX] ranch who did not approve of Moore's action," Jim East (who was one of them) said, adding with touching honesty, "I do not claim that we were higher morally." It was for voicing this disap-

proval, he claimed, that he, Lon Chambers, Charlie Siringo, and Cal Polk were sent to the Pecos with the Panhandle posse; Moore wanted them well out of the way because "they would not help [him] steal."[14]

It's difficult, however, to marry the allegations of large-scale rustling leveled against him with the available statistics on the ranches in which Moore had an interest. To begin with, they were hardly major undertakings: the Potter County ranch, for example, "reported 24 horses, 25 milk cows and 575 head of cattle valued at $7,000. In 1879 they sold 42 head, lost 15 head strayed or stolen, had a calf increase of 140, and purchased 210 head. According to the population schedules, Moore lived in Potter County and Mel Wright lived in Hutchinson County." The inference to be drawn from these figures would seem to be that if Moore was indeed rustling, he was doing it on a relatively small, albeit profitable, scale. Or, perhaps more likely, since taxes were paid on the number of head declared by the owner, the books were being well and truly cooked.[15]

On May 2, 1881, Moore paid Billy Anderson $1,778.75 for three parcels of land totaling 1,423 acres in Hutchinson County; work was begun on an imposing log and stone residence, which was completed in September of that year.[16] Three months later, Moore left the LX. Jim East and some others said he was fired because he was stealing, but there does not appear to be any formal record of this having happened, and it seems highly unlikely that had they identified Moore as a thief, the starchy Bates and the upright Beals would not have filed charges against him.

Just seventeen days after leaving the LX, Moore married Jennie F. Wright, the daughter of Dr. Thomas Jefferson and

Anna (Renick) Wright and a recent graduate in "Scientific Didactics" at her parents' home in Warrensburg, Missouri. The *Dodge City Times* noted their presence in that city. "Mr. Moore has a lot of cattle for shipment," it reported. "He has just finished a magnificent residence in the Panhandle." "Magnificent" might have been slightly overstating things; the house consisted of four rooms, two built of stone instead of adobe and two more of logs. For the time and the place, however, it was well furnished: that December, Jennie's parents shipped a Cottrell & Rand piano and a new Home sewing machine to the Panhandle ranch.[17]

By this time money—big money from foreign investors attracted by the "beef bonanza"—was coming into the Panhandle. In July 1881 the Prairie Land & Cattle Co. bought R. E. McNalty's ranch and cattle for one hundred thousand dollars and later in the year gobbled up Littlefield's LIT. Glidden and Sanborn established the Frying Pan, and W. M. D. Lee, after splitting with his old partner, A. E. Reynolds, teamed up with Kansas City financier Lucien B. Scott to create the LS ranch. On January 19, 1882, Moore sold his Potter County land to Augustus H. Johnson, general manager of the Hansford Land and Cattle Company; the sum involved was seventy-five thousand dollars.[18] It must have been about that time Jim East ran into Moore in Dodge City. "We were sitting there in Dodge playing faro bank and he made a pretty good winning. He slipped me three or four twenty dollar gold pieces. I told him I did not want it, as I had money. He said he wanted me to . . . go and work for him in New Mexico, that I was acquainted with the lower country [i.e., Mexico] and . . . he wanted me to go to Governor Terraza's ranch in Chihuahua,

buy steers and put them on the trail." But East, who was on his way home to see his mother, turned the offer down.[19]

By June 1882 Moore was back in Dodge, "returning from New Mexico, where he had bought a lot of cattle and established a ranch 40 miles south east of Socorro." In fact, he was on his way to Warrensburg, where, on June 17, his wife Jennie gave birth to a daughter, Anna Mary. Nor had he established a ranch, although that may well have been what he said; what he had actually done was to promise to purchase from John P. Casey and Henry M. Atkinson a one-third interest in the American Valley Cattle Co., a planned ranch empire of epic proportions in Socorro County on the western edge of New Mexico Territory.[20]

John P. Casey was something of a rolling stone who had tried farming, working for the railroad, prospecting in the Black Hills, and even the law. He had reconnoitered the country the preceding year and concluded it was an ideal environment for raising cattle. In the spring of 1881 he drove a herd into the area, south of what is now Quemado, and arranged for surveys of townships so that land entries could be filed on those sections containing water, in this case two along Largo Creek. But he had no intention of doing this legitimately: by effecting a partnership with Henry M. Atkinson, surveyor general of the territory, who provided Casey with plats of the area long before they were filed for public use in the Santa Fe land office, Casey was able to identify and preemptively file upon only that land that had water.

Their longer-term plan was to by this means gain control of vast portions of grazing land and then sell the whole package to Eastern investors. Their agent was to be Gen. John Alexander Logan, veteran of the U.S.-Mexican and Civil Wars, former U.S. senator from Illinois, and a would-be presidential candidate, the connection made by Logan's close friend Stephen B. Elkins, to whom they were introduced by Santa Fe attorney Thomas B. Catron.[21]

When it became clear that to realize their plans Casey would have to drum up some serious capital in the East, they looked around for someone to take charge of the American Valley property. Casey must have considered Bill Moore as a gift from God, and in September Moore's purchase of a one-third interest in the ranch was clinched. Using homestead and preemption entries in the names of employees, Casey and his associates took control of their first stretch of land on both sides of Largo Creek.

With Atkinson again manipulating the survey plats, they next filed uncontested claims on six more springs, thereby acquiring water rights that increased their landholdings to an area almost forty miles square. Seeking to extend still further, Casey took a few men and rode south to Gallo Spring, where young French immigrant Alexis Grossetete and his partner Robert Elsinger had staked out a homestead; when the two young men declined even to discuss selling their claim, Casey left in an angry mood.

Putting that matter on temporary hold, the trio concluded that by filing on another thirty-five hundred acres of land with water on it, they would effectively control more than three million acres of prime grazing land. Not surprisingly, at this point Thomas B. Catron demanded to be let in on the deal at a favorable price; reluctant to take anyone else on board, thus diluting their profit, Casey and Atkinson stalled, agreeing that if Catron persisted, Atkinson would tell him Casey was against it.

Toward the end of 1882 a Judge Holderman, representing the Saint Louis National Stockyards, came out to inspect the American Valley ranch and offered $425,000 for it, half in cash, half in stock. Atkinson decided to see if he could do better in Chicago, and Casey headed for Washington to consult with General Logan. When he got there he found awaiting him a letter from Saint Louis parties who proposed the creation of a joint stock company for which they would put up $800,000 with a $100,000 down payment. Logan, greatly excited by such big numbers, suggested they should go to Chicago to see if they could do even better. By the time they joined Atkinson there in April 1883, however, all hell had broken loose in the American Valley.[22]

In Casey's absence Bill Moore had again hired men whose *curricula vitae* were at best dubious. Of course, this might simply have been pragmatism, because at that time the entire lower half of the Territory of New Mexico was literally infested with rustlers, bandits, and other thugs who stole as they pleased and thumbed their noses at the law. Among the most prominent of them was Las Cruces badman John Kinney, a graduate of the Lincoln County War who, with his right-hand man Doroteo Saenz, had command of a band of upwards of forty men. Another gang stealing on a major scale in Socorro County was led by D. L. Gilmore, ironically a former employee of the Casey & Moore ranch.

To combat the thieves, in September 1882 Casey formed and became captain of Company C, 1st Regiment, New Mexico Volunteer Militia, with Moore as his first lieutenant, ranch employee Daniel H. McAllister as first sergeant, and Casey's brother James as sergeant. In December a detachment from this largely Hispanic company ran down the Gilmore gang near Kingston, killing several of them and recovering cattle stolen from the American Valley ranch. It was a minor victory amid many defeats, for despite the deployment of several other companies of militia led by Capt. Albert J. Fountain and Capt. Eugene Van Patten of La Mesilla and Lt. Charles F. Bull of Las Cruces, the rustling continued to escalate. By January 1883 the Rio Grande Valley area between Socorro and Chihuahua, Mexico, was being cleaned out by the rustlers at the rate of ten thousand cattle a month.[23]

At the end of April 1883 Doña Ana deputy sheriff and deputy U.S. marshal Jim McIntire—the same Jim McIntire who had been invited to join the Selman gang in 1879—telegraphed Casey that he was pursuing D. L. Gilmore's band of rustlers. Moore joined the pursuit with members of Company C, 1st Militia, while another detachment of the company left Fort Wingate on the same mission, obviously aiming to catch the thieves in a pincer movement, but the sortie appears to have been unsuccessful. Shortly after this, McIntire and another well-known gunfighter, Jim Courtright, were signed on by Moore.

On May 5 Casey and Moore arrived in Albuquerque to meet a high-powered party that included General Logan; Surveyor General Henry Atkinson; U.S. Marshal Alexander L. Morrison Sr.; famed Indian fighter Captain Henry Ware Lawton, 4th Cavalry, now acting assistant adjutant general of the District of New Mexico; Chicago politician C. C. Campbell; and William H. Patton, who seems also to have had a financial interest in the Casey-Moore operation. Reporters were told the visitors were planning to inspect the American Valley ranch, in which it was believed Logan was intending to invest once he was as-

sured the rustler problem was solved.

While Casey organized transportation, Moore gathered together a party that included Jim McIntire and Jim Courtright, both deputized as U.S. marshals by Morrison, plus Casey's brother James, ranch foreman Daniel H. McAllister, and Mueller Scott, and this group went on to the ranch on Largo Creek ahead of the main contingent. A week later, word reached Albuquerque that on May 6, 1883, Alexis Grossetete and Robert Elsinger, the two young homesteaders who had refused to sell their claim, had been murdered.[24]

The slayings appeared to have been carried out in particularly cold-blooded fashion: Elsinger was found lying facedown with four bullets in his back, and Grossetete—married only nine days previ-

Jim Courtright.
(Courtesy of Robert G. McCubbin)

ously—had been shot twice from such close range that there were powder burns on the back of his head. Rumors that the killings had been the work of "a large cattle corporation trying to secure all the water rights in the area" quickly began to circulate.[25]

The Logan party returned to Albuquerque on May 16; the following day, Casey, Moore, and U.S. Marshal Morrison came in with a squad of militiamen escorting a number of prisoners, including Henry Andrews (Adams), John H. Blair, Jerome "the Kid" Brandon (alias Barney Brandos), D. L. Gilmore, Frank Hogan, Charles F. Jewett, Kit Joy, John W. Sullivan, and some other men arrested on charges not connected with events in the American Valley.[26]

On May 25, on the basis of testimony rendered by twenty-six-year-old Daniel H. McAllister, a grand jury in Albuquerque handed down indictments against William C. Moore, James Casey, Mueller Scott, Jim Courtright, and Jim McIntire for the murder of Grossetete and Elsinger. McAllister—himself charged with eight counts of rustling—testified he had been a member of the party that killed the two nesters but that he had not seen the actual killings. Led by Moore, he said, this group—which included Jim Casey, C. J. Jewett, Mueller Scott, Frank Hoagland, Jack Haines, and "Indian Hank"—had left the ranch on May 4 to "hunt rustlers."

When they reached the Gallo Creek ranch, Scott and Casey were sent down to "see where the boys were." They found only two women there, who told them Grossetete and Elsinger had left in a wagon; the party pursued and "arrested" them. After they had gone a short distance with their prisoners, McAllister said, Moore ordered him and Casey to ride up to the top of a nearby hill. As he reached

its summit he heard shots; he could no longer see Casey. He returned to the group to find Casey with them. There was no sign of either Grossetete or Elsinger. "Well," he said to Moore, "I suppose you have opened the ball." Moore angrily replied, "God damn you, don't you ever mention anything that has taken place today. Forget it." Then Moore (or Casey) said, "We had better bind everyone in the crowd." They stopped, and each man was required to swear on oath "that if I reveal anything that has transpired today, may all of you kill me."

Jim Casey and Mueller Scott were arrested immediately and jailed without bond. Officers sent to arrest Courtright and McIntire obtained Courtright's surrender and left him in the charge of a deputy sheriff while they headed for Kingston to get McIntire. Somehow Courtright got word to McIntire; when the lawmen got to Kingston, he was gone, and by the time they returned to Lake Valley, so was Courtright. Moore, it was learned, had hastily sold his cattle and fled. Tony Neis of the Rocky Mountain Detective Agency trailed him to Las Vegas, where Moore and a companion, said to have been his father-in-law, bought two horses (paying for them with bad checks) and hit out for points unknown.

After three trials in which each jury failed to agree—because, gossip had it, jurors had been bribed each time—James Casey and Scott were released. Governor Lionel Sheldon posted rewards of five hundred dollars each for Courtright, McIntire, and Moore. Courtright was arrested in Fort Worth in October 1884 but escaped from custody. McIntire returned to Albuquerque and stood trial, when the indictment against him was quashed. A second indictment was handed down against him by a Socorro County grand jury in December 1885, but when no witnesses could be found against him, he was released on five thousand dollars' bond.[27]

And "Outlaw Bill"? He is said to have gone to Kansas City, where he bounced a couple more checks. John P. Casey claimed to have later received papers from Moore, who was in Montana. Another story has it that Moore, calling himself "Johnny Ward," worked for a while on a ranch near Alma, New Mexico, but disappeared into Canada when Charlie Siringo arrived unannounced. Siringo himself claimed to have encountered Moore in Juneau, Alaska, about 1895; later, he claimed, Moore opened a saloon and was killed in a drunken brawl there.[28]

Maybe it's true. Or maybe, as some others hinted, "Outlaw Bill" simply knew too much and somebody planted him where he could do no harm. *Los muertos no hablan.*

Chapter 13

1882

THE BEEF BONANZA

As SEPARATED from the rest of the world as the inhabitants of some remote island in the South Pacific, Tascosans were as yet largely unaware of changes in the making that would not only affect the future of their town but also completely revolutionize the cattle industry. One of the most important of these was the arrival in the Panhandle of barbed wire.

In 1881 Joseph F. Glidden, more-or-less inventor and manufacturer of the hated (at first) barbed wire, and his agent, Henry B. Sanborn, purchased 143 sections (91,520 acres) in Potter and Randall Counties, which, by including alternate sections of state land set aside for public school financing, they effectively increased to 250,000 acres.[1] The Frying Pan ranch, as the spread became known, had its headquarters at Las Tecovas Spring, about five miles north of the present town of Bushland.

At that time there was not a single fence in the entire Panhandle—in fact, cowboys could and did boast of having driven herds north through the country "without opening a single gate." To demonstrate the advantages of his invention, Glidden decided to erect a four-strand fence around his range, using wire twice as heavy as anything then being made—120 miles of it in all. To oversee the operation, which would cost forty thousand dollars, he and Sanborn hired a young New Yorker named Warren W. Wetzel, who had come to Texas for his health. It was an enormous undertaking that involved freighting eighty thousand pounds of wire from Dodge City at a cost of $2.50 per hundred pounds and cutting cedar posts in the Palo Duro Canyon and on Sierrita de la Cruz (somehow transformed in cowboy-speak to "Sweetly Croose") and hauling them into position with wagons pulled by ox teams.

"They were the first people to enclose and were very unpopular with the cowboys [because now] any cotton picker could come up and punch cattle then and the wages would go down." Another curious social side effect was that when Frying Pan employees came to town, "they could not get the dance-hall girls to dance with them. Society, you see, was graded in Tascosa. It must have been about the lowest level for them to have been fence builders. Those girls had heard the old cowboys talking

[117]

about them and they would not have a thing to do with boys from that ranch."[2]

Living first in a leaky tent and then a dugout while he supervised the building of the Frying Pan's ranch headquarters, Wetzel and his nineteen-year-old wife, Kate—the only woman in Potter County—lived about as rough as it was possible to live. Later, completed and whitewashed, the nine-room ranch building was known as "The White House." Wetzel stayed on as the Frying Pan's superintendent/bookkeeper; later still, he would serve as an Oldham County commissioner; meanwhile, his wife mothered the cowboys. "She mended for them, sewed for them, nursed them when they were ill, and even gave up her comfortable bed for a boy injured in a fall, she and Mr. Wetsel [sic] sleeping on the floor."

The *Dodge City Times* noted these developments in a prescient news item. "Some weeks ago 80,000 pounds of wire was shipped to the Pan Handle, assigned to Sanborn and Warner. C. Goodnight some months ago received 60,000 pounds of wire. Can't you read the future of the stock business?"[3]

Charles Goodnight certainly could: he had already erected a sixty-mile drift fence "from the edge of the Plains, near the Armstrong County line, along the divide between Salt Fork and Mulberry, to Coleman and Dyer's Shoe Bar range on the east. When connected with the Shoe Bar fence, which ran east by south to near the site of Memphis, it was a hundred miles long. . . . Despite its excessive cost, the prejudice against it, the troubles it caused, and the revolution it wrought in the life of the West, 'bobbed' wire had come to stay."[4]

In 1882 other big cattle outfits also built drift fences. Drifting was a common winter phenomenon: during severe weather, cattle "drifted" ahead of the wind, seeking shelter. Over the winter stock from as far north as Nebraska would move slowly southward, mingling with the Panhandle cattle, which moved along with them, even sometimes—hard as it may be to believe—as far south as the Rio Grande. The complexity of rounding up, cutting out from local herds, and restoring these animals to their rightful owners added an enormous cost in time, energy, and money to the twice-yearly roundups; the cowmen believed the drift fence would render that expense obsolete.

When it was finally built, however, the fence—which ran east almost two hundred miles from the New Mexico line to the Canadian breaks—turned out to be as much a problem as the ranchers hoped it would be a solution. In warm weather when the barrier prevented cattle from getting to water, the cowboys had to cut the wire to let them through; in severe winter conditions storm-driven cattle piled up against the fence and froze to death, piled so high that later arrivals used their bodies as a ramp to cross the fence and continue south.[5]

Increasingly unhappy in his arrangement with Reynolds, "Mac" Lee had reestablished his acquaintance with wealthy Leavenworth banker and mine owner Lucien Scott, owner since 1880 of 35,250 acres of land in Oldham and Hartley Counties. Lee now decided to make the LE brand his and Scott's at a stroke—and at a bargain price, to boot. Confident that Reynolds would not be able to raise the money, he wired Reynolds in Denver to come down to the ranch and met him with what was effectively an ultimatum: that Reynolds either buy him out or sell his 50 percent holding to him. To Lee's surprise, Reynolds asked how long he had to make up his mind.

"Take as long as you like," Lee told him.

"Ten days will be enough," Reynolds replied, and it was.

On his return to Denver he persuaded John M. Bond of the Alliance Trust, a large Scottish investment firm, to take an interest. They went together to New York, secured financing, set up the Reynolds Land & Cattle Company, and paid off the astonished Lee. Reynolds took over the western half of the former LE range, the ranch headquarters at Trujillo, the brand, and all the cattle; like it or lump it, Lee took the eastern quadrant for the new LS ranch and with it his range boss, Jordan McAllister.

The long, profitable partnership of Lee & Reynolds, the name a byword throughout Texas and the Indian Territory, was over; an LE cowboy recorded the bitter argument that marked its passing: "They was just standing there talking peaceful like, and all of a sudden they was both on the prod. It looked like Reynolds was going to kill Lee, so I pulled my freight in a hurry! Turned out to be one helluva cuss fight, but it sure ended Lee's time with the LE."[6]

One account claims that "records at Vega show that for the LE ranch the Reynolds brothers paid $70,000 on July 1 of that year [1881], $17,520 on August 1, a further $25,000 on November 1, and continuing payments of similar amounts until the total, $187,500 was paid." Another, citing the actual records, indicates the deal was a more realistic "payment of $75,000 and other promissory notes totalling an additional $187,000."[7]

To run the ranch, Reynolds and his brother brought down a longtime employee, bullwhacker George W. "Monchy" Russell, "an ex-Quantrill man from Kentucky" who apparently came by his nickname by insisting on being called

Albert E. Reynolds. (Courtesy of the Colorado Historical Society [ID no. F36921].

Lucien Scott. (Author's Collection)

"Monchure" (*Monsieur*). A "nice old man, a big man with humped shoulders, [who] always loved his diamonds and his gold watch," he was also a sucker for a card game. "He tried not to gamble. Sometimes he would come to town and would walk on the far side of the street so as to keep away from the gambling dens, but the boys were too smart for him. They would set a table out on the sidewalk as a decoy and pretty soon Monchy was into a game. . . . He would lose $500 to $600 every trip he made to town."[8]

Concluding (correctly) that free grass would soon be a thing of the past, Lee and Scott now embarked on an ambitious—*ruthless* might be a better word—campaign of land buying. Lee already owned 25,000 acres in eastern Oldham County purchased in March 1881, plus his 15,000-acre share of the LE. Although with Scott's holdings this gave the LS a total of 75,000 acres, Scott purchased further land near Liberty, New Mexico, to insure range and water rights in the territory.

Among the freighters hauling supplies to the ranch from Tascosa and then out to the line camps was an old-timer everyone called Uncle Billy Urion, who remained an employee of the LS for so long he began to believe he owned it. One day, they say, a stranger passing through town asked him how to get to Endee, New Mexico.

"You just start out and ride up the north side of the Canadian River west, 'til you come to where the Trujillo creek is on the south side of the river. Cross over there and follow the creek, angling a little bit off to the southwest, and you'll hit Endee."

"What about landmarks?" asked the stranger. "Can you describe a few I can go by, so I won't get lost?"

"Hell, man, you don't need landmarks!" Uncle Bill barked. "Endee's only about a

hundred miles from here. You can't get lost, you'll be in LS pasture all the way!"

It just never occurred to Uncle Billy that the LS pasture was only a little smaller than the state of Connecticut.[9]

"Mac" Lee's next priority was to get rid of the few sheepmen still living in the valley and applied his *dinero/vamos* technique so effectively that by 1884 nearly all the remaining *plazitas* along the Canadian were deserted, and many had been razed. The day of the *pastores* in the Panhandle was over.[10] Yet further change lay ahead as refrigeration techniques already widely used on railroads were adapted for use in seagoing vessels and it became possible for the first time to export American beef in quantity.

By 1875, substantial exports of "dead meat," as it was called, were competing in England with the superior, but more expensive, domestic variety. Within eighteen months these exports increased from 134,000 to 8,400,000 pounds and in 1877 almost six fold, to more than 49,000,000 pounds. That same year, live cattle were also shipped successfully across the Atlantic; in 1878, 50,000,000 pounds of dressed beef and 136,000 head of live cattle were exported. In just nine months in 1879, the value of beef exported from New York alone was $3,913,770 and of live cattle a further $2,765,127. By this time the trade had become so profitable that British—and particularly Scottish—meat raisers were taking a keen interest in the American cattle trade.[11]

In 1877 reporter James MacDonald of *The Scotsman* had visited Texas to investigate the dead meat business, and the following year he produced a book with the considerably less than beguiling title *Food from the Far West, or, American Agriculture with Special Reference to the Beef Production* and *Importation of Dead Meat from America to Great Britain.* Surprisingly, it aroused so much interest a parliamentary commission, chaired by the Duke of Richmond and Gordon, was set up to investigate investment in the American cattle industry. After spending several months in the United States, the two parliamentarians who conducted the investigation produced a report that suggested investment in the range cattle industry could be expected to yield annual profits of 33 percent, whereupon interest of investors became a positive fever of excitement not only in England but also—spurred there by similar books and reports—the eastern cities of America.[12]

Once the amazing British romance with the cattle industry began, an almost unbelievable flood of money—much of it English but even more from Scotland—poured into America. In the ten years beginning with 1880 seventy-five companies would be organized in Britain for investment in cattle, land, and mortgages. The first of these, the Prairie Cattle Company, was founded in late 1880 by the Edinburgh-based Scottish American Mortgage Company. In short order the company bought the Hall brothers' Cross L ranch in Colfax County, New Mexico, and the Jones brothers' JJ spread near Las Animas, Colorado, and in July of the following year—even though he owned not an acre of the land he was ranching on—George W. Littlefield's LIT headquarters building east of Tascosa, plus 14,000 head of cattle and 250 saddle horses for $250,000, consolidating their purchases into a huge syndicated organization with herds in the region numbering 150,000 head. They also tried to purchase Bugbee's Quarter Circle T, but Bugbee's wife persuaded him to hold out for a better offer.[13]

As general ("range") manager of the LIT, the Prairie Cattle Company appointed thirty-eight-year-old Augustus H. "Gus" Johnson, a former livestock agent for the Santa Fe Railroad who had been general manager of the Turkey Track. When on July 3, 1882, Johnson was killed by lightning near Cimarron, Kansas, he was succeeded by Willard R. Green, who in three years brought a large number of smaller ranches into the Prairie fold, not always "by the book." "More and more lands in southern Colorado and northern New Mexico were acquired, and if reports and records are to be trusted," a contemporary alleged, "hundreds of choice quarter sections bordering the water courses of New Mexico were acquired fraudulently from the government."[14]

Investors in Scotland, cashing in dividends of 20 percent, could not have cared less; news of their good fortune, and hugely optimistic books such as Brisbin's *The Beef Bonanza, or, How to Get Rich on the Plains,* published in 1881, spurred yet more excitement and investment. In January 1883 the London *Times* noted:

The Prairie Cattle Company, with its headquarters in Edinburgh, under the more immediate supervision of Messrs. Underwood and Clark, of Kansas City, and placed in admirable working order by the late Mr. Johnson have bought up plains from far-scattered settlers and graze their herds, which now number 200,000, over an area commencing in New Mexico, about fifty miles south from Trinidad, running 120 miles east, and taking in the north fork and tributaries of the Canadian river and, with the recent purchase of Mr. Creswell's herd, going on to the south Canadian. The Kansas City Cattle Company, in the Cherokee Indian territory, although only recently started, have upwards of 10,000 head, on which they pay to the Indian agent a poll-tax of 20c for young cattle and 40c for steers. The Land and Cattle Company of Dundee started into Beaver Creek, near Camp Supply, last spring, bought 10,000 head of Texans and grades from Cox at $23 and $24, and have since taken over a herd of 10,000 from Berry. The Dominion Cattle Company recently took over the whole of Dr. [James Monroe "Doc"] Day's good brand, well known throughout the western portion of "No-Man's-Land." . . . A purchase of 700,000 acres, chiefly of railroad lands in alternate sections, has just been concluded in Carson, Gray and Mitchison counties, Texas, for $1.65c [per acre] by the Francklyn Land and Cattle Company, which has been chartered in New York, with a capital of $2,000,000. Mr. B. Groome of Kentucky is now in the Panhandle, superintending the purchase of the stock cattle and the fencing of the range.[15]

Groom, "a man of great ability and tireless energy . . . although he was seventy years of age," had already, on February 10, 1882, leased from the New York & Texas Land Company a huge swathe of land, 529,920 acres in all. Four months later Groom assigned this lease to Charles G. Francklyn, New York capitalist son-in-law of E. G. Cunard, owner of the famous steamship line, who helped finance the venture. This transaction resulted in the formation of the Francklyn Land & Cattle Company.[16]

It is estimated that in 1882 alone some £6 million (then $30 million, now perhaps $200 million–300 million) was invested in Texas by British cattle companies, among them the Matador Land & Cattle Com-

pany (headquartered in Dundee), the Hansford Land & Cattle Co. (which gobbled up McNalty's Turkey Track for $100,000 and paid Tom Bugbee $350,000 for the Quarter Circle T, twice what he had been offered a year earlier), the Cedar Valley Cattle Co., the Wyoming Cattle Co., the Cattle Ranche Co., and the Rocking Chair Ranche.

The Rocking Chair Ranche Ltd. was registered in the City of London on March 20, 1883, with headquarters at 9 New Square, Lincoln's Inn (hub of the legal profession), and capitalized at £150,000 ($750,000). Among its shareholders were three Peers of the Realm, a baronet, two members of Parliament, and several high-ranking army officers as well as Jacob John Drew and Earl Winfield Spencer, "ranchemen" of Kansas City, and John Clay.

The brand itself had originally been used by Noah Ellis in South Texas during the Civil War; it came to the Panhandle in 1879 when John and Wiley Dickerson established a ranch at the foot of a range of mesas that eventually took the same name. In 1881 Conkle and Lytle of Kansas City acquired the brand, and on February 17, 1882, they purchased from the New York & Texas Land Company the 235 sections of land on which they were squatting. Two months later they sold out to Drew and Spencer for $355,000, and shortly thereafter Drew, an Englishman, sold the property to the Rocking Chair Ranche Company.[17]

John Drew became general manager and Archibald Marjoribanks (pronounced "Marshbanks"), youngest brother of the Second Baron Tweedsmouth, was appointed assistant manager and bookkeeper. The first herd of "Rockers" went up the trail to Dodge in the fall of 1883, but it soon became apparent that the new owners knew nothing about cattle and had little interest in learning. When the titled owners referred to their employees as "cow servants," the hired hands responded insultingly by renaming the place "Nobility Ranch." Treating the place like a feudal estate "long, tall, green and gawky" Archie, as the cowboys called Marjoribanks, spent most of his time hunting to hounds, drinking, and gambling away his fifteen hundred dollars' annual salary in Mobeetie. Although to begin with the ranch produced satisfactory profits, the Rocking Chair was a disaster in the making.

Then in the spring of 1883 the London *Times* announced the biggest conglomerate of them all. "A syndicate, formed in London, have made a contract for the purchase of 3,000,000 of acres of land in Northern Texas known as the 'Capitol Reservation' for $10,000,000. The sellers are a Chicago company who got the land one year ago from the Texas legislature—on condition of building a State Capitol at Austin—for $1,500,000. The London syndicate will make full payment on April 15th."[18]

This consortium was to become the Capitol Freehold Land and Investment Company, Ltd., formally incorporated on June 25, 1885, with a capital of £3 million ($15 million) in £10 ($50) shares. Headquartered at 139 Cannon Street in the city of London, its chairman was the Marquess of Tweeddale and its American managing directors were John and Charles Farwell.

At its first general meeting on October 2, 1885, Tweeddale painted a rosy picture for his cheering shareholders:

It is estimated that the current fixed charges for the year, when the issue of £400,000 is completed, will be as follows: The interest on £400,000 of debentures issued for purchase of cattle, say £20,000 ($100,000); the interest on £87,740 of debentures for land at 5 per cent £4,387; total £24,387 ($121,935). To which add wages of stockkeepers and general expenses, estimated at the extreme £24,000, or a total liability for the year ending December 31, 1886, of £48,387 ($241,935); the increase of value in the herd of say, 115,000 cattle (usually estimated at £1 per head) at 18 shillings ($4.50) each will give, say £103,500 ($517,500); add 20,000 calves at £1.10s ($5.50) each, £30,000 ($150,000); and it gives increased value in one year, £133,500 and leaves a clear net profit overall of more than £85,000 ($425,000), with the property only about one third stocked.

Once the ranch was fully stocked, he continued, the extra costs involved would only be about £30,000 ($150,000), whereas the increase would be £375,000 ($1,875,000), producing "over £400,000 ($2,000,000) net profit to shareholders" and "the future of this company would in all probability be such as no one present . . . would venture to state."

Thus, on the wings of such wildly optimistic speculation, was born the enormous XIT ranch, two hundred miles long, sometimes fifty wide, with a brand that, actually designed to prevent alteration, spawned the legend it was shorthand for the ten counties in the Texas Panhandle over which its enormous herds ranged.[19]

Small wonder, then, that with promises like these, and overheated newspaper reports such as the following item from the London *Times,* speculators were clamoring to invest.

A striking instance of the profitable nature of the ranching business is furnished by the brothers Hartwell, who went [to Texas] from Bloomington, Illinois, in the fall of 1875. The aggregate of their worldly possessions amounted to $48,000. This sum they invested in 4500 cattle. Now they are the owners of 60,000 head, and are worth at least $1,500,000. The largest ranch in the State is that of Mr. Charles Goodnight, at the head of Red River. He began buying land only four years ago and now he controls 700,000 acres. To enclose his landed possessions, 250 miles of fencing are required. . . . The Matador Cattle Company's ranch is another immense property, which was recently sold to a company of Scotch capitalists for $1,250,000.[20]

Nor was the speculation confined to the Panhandle. In November 1882, for the sum of $2,553,825, the Swan Land & Cattle Company, Ltd. (a British limited liability company), bought out three Wyoming corporations. As a part of the transaction Alexander Hamilton Swan was employed as general manager at the astronomical salary of $10,000 a year (a top range foreman earned $50 a month). To clinch the sale, he is said to have shown the investors tally books purporting to show 89,167 cattle on the range. Much later Swan slyly observed, "In our business we are often compelled to do certain things which, to the inexperienced, seem a little crooked." The following year, 1884, the company purchased from the Union Pacific 550,000 acres for $2,300,000, giving it control over 3.25 million acres. It owned so many brands that it had to publish a brand book to enable its foremen to identify them. The home ranch in Chugwater was connected to headquarters in Cheyenne by a telephone line that cost £1,000 ($5,000) to install. Additionally, the company maintained its own hotel in Cheyenne for visitors.[21]

Such huge financial investments meant that within a very short time cattle ranching—and by definition cowboying—underwent radical change. No longer the domain of one man—a Goodnight, say, or a Bugbee or a Creswell—the ranches became businesses, often owned by absentee corporations and syndicates looking for fat dividends, managed by men employed more for their financial acumen than their ability to "tally" a herd, who frowned on the old free-and-easy open range traditions and insisted on industry-agreed pay scales and scheduled working hours. Even more contentiously, the new administrators declared taboo the old tradition that permitted cowboys to slap their brand on any mavericks they encountered and build up a little herd of their own.

The cowboys, needless to say, not only strongly objected but refused to obey. The more the syndicates tried to enforce them, the greater became the resistance, and rustling, always a problem in the Panhandle, became pandemic. Little men stole from the big men; trail herds passing through gathered up strays and mavericks; even the bigger ranchers often appropriated unbranded stock if their route took them across someone else's range. As one cowboy slyly observed, "It was an awful good trail driver that didn't land at Dodge City or out there with more cattle than he started with." To counter this casual theft, the Stockmen's Association would later initiate the practice of stationing "brand inspectors" at the primary cattle markets: Dodge City, Caldwell, Kansas City, Saint Louis, and the rest. "In the first years of this practice," John Arnot said, "it was not uncommon for inspectors to cut back as illegally shipped one-fourth of a herd."[22]

Needless to say, brand inspectors were less than popular. One of them was "a Mr. Plummer, an elderly, quiet gentleman, who on one occasion cut 25 per cent out of a sixteen-car shipment made from the Cherokee Strip by a large man of fine physique. Naturally the shipper made a strenuous kick; but Plummer held the cattle and the rightful owner got the proceeds of sales. The shipper on meeting Plummer later proceeded to beat him up, injuring him so seriously that he had to retire for some months, and we sent Tom Martindale . . . to succeed him; and Tom went there with instructions to go armed and to shoot to kill if attacked."[23]

Were it not for his nickname, one might believe the "large man of fine physique" was "Deacon" Bates, who, Jim East said, "once drove a herd [north] himself. In driving through someone else's range, the range cattle are hard to keep out of a herd and a lot of these got into his. Someone who had it in for the LXs went to Mobeetie and maliciously filed an indictment against him."[24]

This incident took place during the summer of 1883, when a cattle inspector at Caldwell, Kansas (Mr. Plummer, perhaps), cut as strays nearly a quarter of a herd of LX cattle. Cattle detectives from the Stockmen's Association quickly established that Bates had trailed a herd into the Cherokee Outlet, picking up strays along the way and, after fattening them in the spring, shipping them to Caldwell. Further investigation revealed that seventy-two more head with Panhandle brands had been unloaded and driven across the river into East Saint Louis, Illinois. Justifiably angered, the Panhandle ranchers swore out warrants against Bates, only to find he had

skinned out for Boston. Temple Houston handed the papers to Sheriff Arrington and said, "Cap, go get him. We can't let that rich sonofabitch get away with this!"

In Massachusetts, however, Arrington discovered rounding up rich sons of bitches wasn't quite that easy: to make an arrest he needed extradition papers signed by Governor Benjamin Butler, and when he tried to get to Butler, Bates's political cronies and legal advisers did everything they could to hamper him. Finally Arrington bulled his way into Butler's office. The governor read the charges and smiled: Bates, it transpired, was an old personal and political enemy. "Well," he mused, "the Deacon finally got himself into hot water," and without further ado he signed the papers.

"Arrington thanked him and hurried Bates toward the Panhandle, changing trains frequently in a zigzag course to avoid losing him through *habeas corpus* and other legal dodges already set in motion by the rich man's lawyers." A few days later, to use his favorite laconic expression, Arrington "calaboosed him."

Bates's hearing was set for November, but before he appeared Temple Houston resigned to run for the Texas Senate and Lucius Dills was appointed district attorney to complete his term. When Bates paid the Panhandle owners for their cattle and Dills entered a motion that there was no longer evidence to sustain any allegation in the indictment, and that the ranchers would "exonerate" the defendant, Judge Willis dismissed the case.[25]

In spite of, or perhaps even encouraged by high-profile cases such as this, the rustling went on; even when the thieves were identified and arrested, it was almost impossible to secure a conviction. "More often than otherwise the grand jury personnel included men whose interests

Judge Frank Willis. (Courtesy of the Panhandle-Plains Historical Museum, Canyon, Texas)

demanded they forestall such inquiry. So many men were doing 'some branding on their own' a jury list might be made up of half of them." In addition, "The country was full of perjurers who almost made a business of going from court to court where, with the help of sympathetic jurors, they swore thieves from under convictions in spite of incontrovertible evidence."[26]

"Sympathizing with the lawless element, directing, co-operating with and encouraging it, was a man of unusual craftiness," said Goodnight. This was none other than Jesse Jenkins, using his brother Lon's saloon as a front, manipulating his minions as skillfully as any Mafia godfather. Although he had only been in Tascosa a year or so, he was already "the organizer,

the brains and the manager of a gang whose sole object was 'wholesale' cattle stealing. Jess had every man lined up in his business convinced that any dogie they could slap a brand on was theirs by divine right."[27]

"It seems that Jenkins and his cohorts set out to see that there should be no courts in the Panhandle or, if courts, then no convictions," Goodnight said, citing Jenkins's intervention in the case of John Petrie, good cowhand, likable college graduate, and manager of the RO ranch owned by English brothers Alfred and Vincent Rowe. Early in 1883, Petrie was accused of rustling, but the Rowes kept him on, defying the Stockmen's Association rule that the employment of a known rustler was cause for expulsion. Called on to show cause why they should not be expelled, the Rowes capitulated, and Petrie and four of his men were arrested and taken to Clarendon to stand trial.[28]

In the evening preceding the trial Jesse Jenkins showed up with "two wagons, plenty of whiskey, five or six noted rustlers and perjurers, and two or three bad women, and camped just across the creek from the courthouse." Wasting no time, Jenkins sent Judge Frank Willis a note adorned with a skull and crossbones. The message was brutally plain: convict our man and you're dead. Charles Goodnight stepped in.

"They scared the life out of the old judge. He thought they would kill him. I said: 'I have eighteen men here and we have plenty of guns. You go on and open the court and if they start anything there won't be a man on the hill in five minutes.' I guess they would have broken it up if I had not been there. . . . If they had broken up the court no telling when they would have gotten a court. We could have killed every one of them in five minutes. . . . We had some thieves to try but they swore them out and did not break up the court. We decided we could not convict them so we got them to take an oath to leave the country."

This decidedly new judicial ploy was effected by bringing as many indictments as possible against each defendant, so that if nothing else he would be broken finan-cially. The thieves' attorney, W. H. Wood-man, cut a deal whereby Petrie and the other defendants volunteered to leave the Panhandle providing the charges against them were dropped. The rustlers then signed formal papers agreeing to leave within ten days, never to return. "We got rid of six of them," Goodnight said with considerable satisfaction. But there were plenty more where those had come from.[29]

⌀
Chapter 14
⌀

CAPE WILLINGHAM
"TOUGH, FAIR, AND RESPECTED."

FOR SOMEONE who played so conspicuous a part in the early years of Tascosa and the development of the cattle industry in the Panhandle and New Mexico's Pecos Valley, Cape Willingham, to use the name he is remembered by, remains something of a shadowy figure. In accepted accounts of his life, Caleb Berg Willingham is said to have been born on April 8, 1853, in Georgia, but his family background and the actual location have remained largely unknown until now. Cape's ancestor, Thomas Henry Willingham (in Old English the name means "happy home"), came to South Carolina from Market Rasen, Lincolnshire, England, in 1790 and settled on Sullivan's Island near Charleston, South Carolina, where he pursued the occupation of merchant. One of his thirteen children, William, who died about 1798, had five daughters and six sons, among them Isaac, Cape's father. It is clear from a multitude of documentation recording their history that the Willingham clan was both prosperous and influential.

On May 26, 1839, Isaac Willingham married Louisa Garrett, daughter of Eli and Patience Garrett of Lincoln County, Georgia; she appears to have died a few years later, for on May 31, 1844, Willingham married her sister Martha, and by 1850 he, his wife, and three children had settled in Jasper County in central Georgia, where Isaac owned a plantation. By 1858 they had moved farther south to Monroe County; shortly thereafter, he and his wife (listed as Mary), who was blind, had moved south again, this time to the new town of Camilla, Mitchell County, incorporated in December 1858. There were now six children, two girls and four boys, the youngest being eight-year-old Caleb Berg T. Willingham, on this evidence born in 1850. Such schooling as he got must have been pretty sketchy: "His father went into the army during the Civil War and took Cape with him as his mother was dead," Goodnight said, although Mary Willingham was certainly alive as late as 1860.

Cape was only thirteen [sic] years old and fought through all the war under Gen. [Joseph] Wheeler. His father was captured, shot in the leg, and Cape stayed with him.

His leg got better and they escaped—Cape stole two six shooters from a sleeping guard and together they went into the woods. The worms got into his father's wound but Cape got them out and they stayed until the leg got well and then slipped back into the Federal camp, stole two horses and saddles and joined Lee's army as it was marching south, probably through Georgia. Cape said that they came up to the army at night and he yelled to the soldiers so as not to get shot. "Oh, hell," came back the answer, "It's that Willingham boy," and he said the yell went from one end of the column to the other.[1]

Another account of his life avers that Willingham was born in Monroe County, Georgia, in 1852, and

was only 9 years old at the outbreak of the great Civil War in which his father at once enlisted. Two years later the son joined his father at the front. He was not eligible for enlistment on account of age but was permitted to stay with the command and fought by his father's side until the last year of the war. . . . At Murfreesboro [his father] was severely wounded [and] both were captured, when his father recovered both escaped and returned to the Confederate lines. In the last year of the war [Willingham] enlisted in the 2nd Georgia Cavalry. When hostilities ended he attended school for two years. When his father died, he remained on the plantation during the following year, then he went to work in a grocery store . . . until he was elected city marshal of Camilla, Georgia, which [position] he held until he came to Texas in 1869. Shortly after coming to Texas he hired to a Brown County rancher to break bronchos at a monthly

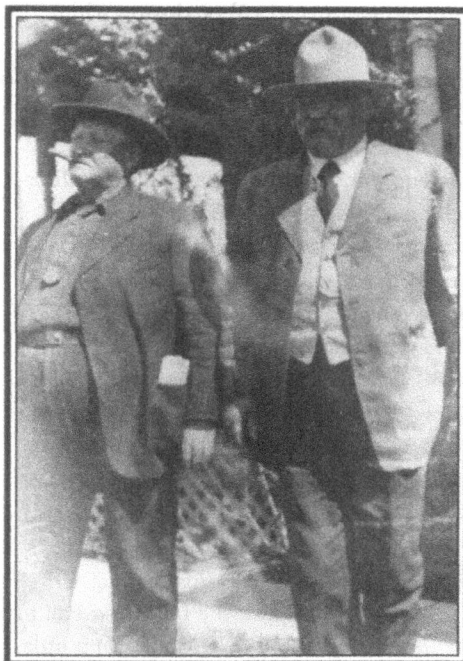

Cape Willingham and Jack Ryan, ca. 1903.
(Courtesy of the Haley Memorial Library,
Midland, Texas)

salary of $20. In the spring of 1873 he went to Colorado with a herd of cattle; after spending a year there he returned to Texas, locating in San Saba County. Returning to Colorado he hired to Charles Goodnight and was in his employ until 1878 when he returned to the Texas Panhandle.

Goodnight's recollections confirm the latter detail: "After the war Cape came up to the San Saba country, got a small herd, drove west to my [Goodnight] trail on the Concho and up it to Colorado and wintered just south of me in the Huerfano [County region]. He began working for me [at the Goodnight Rock Canyon ranch] in

[Pueblo County in 18]75, during which year we drove two big herds from the Pecos to Colorado that I had got from [John] Chisum."[2]

Jesse Jenkins, cryptic and secretive to the end, hinted darkly that "Cape Willingham was a fictitious name . . . and [my] brother [Alonzo] saw him when he was about 18 years old and he had 'C. B. Cox' across his hat band."[3]

Twenty-six years old and married with three children by the time he arrived in Tascosa, Cape had certainly had some remarkable adventures. "I had done some work for Charles Goodnight in New Mexico in [18]75," he said. "He wrote me and wanted me to come into the Panhandle. I worked on the old Goodnight ranch in [18]78 and went back the following Fall to my family. I worked for Goodnight a little over a year and then joined the LXs who employed me to do a little detective work for them in regard to some stolen cattle."[4]

It was doubtless in connection with this "detective work" that Willingham found himself in Dodge City in September 1878 when Charlie Siringo rode in with another cowboy, John Ferris [Farris, later killed by Barney Mason], and found "the first man on the main street was Cape Willingham . . . who gave us our first news of the great Indian outbreak. He told us of the many murders committed by the reds south of Dodge City the day previous—one man was killed at Mead[e] City, and two others near the Crooked Creek store."

Siringo's "great Indian outbreak" was the one led by Dull Knife, who left the reservation at Fort Reno with a band of about three hundred Northern Cheyenne on September 9, 1878, fighting off pursuing cavalry and mounted infantry as they headed north toward their homeland in Montana. On September 16 they killed

mail carrier Washington O'Connor, while another band raided the Chapman & Tuttle ranch about eighteen miles from Dodge. With fewer than twenty soldiers on duty at Fort Dodge, the citizens quickly banded together as volunteers, and when a report came in that the home of Harrison Berry, four miles from the city, had been torched by the Indians, "[a] locomotive loaded with civilians was at once despatched to the scene of conflagration. . . . P. L. Beatty, Chalk Beeson, Wyatt Earp and S. E. Jackson were principals in extinguishing the flames."[5]

Whether Willingham was among the volunteer civilian firefighters is not on record, but it would have been characteristic of him to get involved. It could be it was in Dodge that he got to know Louis Bousman, who claimed to have been there at the time of the outbreak; when Willingham became sheriff of Oldham County, he regularly swore Bousman in as a deputy. He continued working for the LX until the following year, when he "took charge of the US Mail line from Fort Elliott to Las Vegas NM. This line was called the 'Star Route.'" Before this service was established the mail had been carried by military personnel. Among the drivers was former buffalo hunter Dick Bussell, who worked the Dodge City–Fort Elliott run. "It would leave Dodge in the morning and they would eat dinner at Appleton, Kansas, supper at Ashland, Kansas, and ate at midnight at Cimarron. . . . Breakfast was eaten at Fort Supply, dinner at Commission Creek just south of the site of Higgins, supper at the Springer Ranch on the Canadian, and breakfast at Mobeetie. The distance was about 200 miles."[6]

Willingham's "Lightning Express," also operated by P. G. Reynolds, had a schedule of fifty-nine hours for the horseback run from Fort Elliott (Mobeetie) to Fort Bascom, a distance of two hundred miles, with stations at the North Fork of the Red River, Dixon Creek, Bonita Creek, Leahy Creek, Tascosa, Trujillo, Red River Springs, and a place called Huney that doesn't seem to exist anymore. From Fort Bascom to Las Vegas a hack was used. "I worked on the line until November [18]80," Willingham said. "We drove mules and buckboards and changed teams at each station. We very seldom had over two passengers, for there was little travel. We traveled night and day and changed teams at all hours of the night as well as the day. We went double quick time, too."

Kid Dobbs recalled that "every rider had his own string of horses and the station men cooked for us, fed the horses and kept them rested up for us. The station men knew what horse we were to ride next and always had him ready for us to change mounts fast and keep riding." He remembered the mail contractor as a Californian named Austin Barnes,

a good old clever man [who] talked both languages, Mex and English [and] told me if any of the mail was ever lost it would cost him $4000 in bonds and those old broom tail horses wasn't worth a fraction of $4000 so for us to ride them to death, but get the mail through on time. We knew the horses were not worth much so we co-operated in not losing the $4000 for Barnes. . . . It took 59 hours to get mail from Mobeetie to [Fort] Bascom every day and we were told if we ever got behind not to spare horseflesh. . . . If the mail was on time and not too heavy we could make six or seven miles an hour but if we were late we rode our horses for all [they] would stand.

Barnes tried to do away with horses several times to carry passengers by buckboard, but when the river was high they couldn't get across and had to go back to horseback routes.[7]

Just before Willingham quit the "Lightning Express," he may have played a key role in the 1880 power struggle between W. M. D. Lee and A. E. Reynolds and the citizens of Mobeetie, then lobbying for self-government in Wheeler County. From the time Fort Elliott had been established, Lee and Reynolds (with the benign acquiescence of the military) had run the town, the county, and most of the country around it pretty much the way they wanted—which was the way Lee and Reynolds liked it. Because the county was unorganized, the firm paid no taxes, a situation they were equally anxious to maintain. So when the State of Texas sent a contingent of Rangers commanded by Cap Arrington to the Panhandle to report on the advisability of allowing organization, Lee did everything he could to put difficulties in Arrington's way.

"Lee and Reynolds . . . , who handled all the mail that came here, were in opposition to the movement for organization," Arrington said, "and were doing everything in their power to prevent [it], even to holding up letters which they thought might be instrumental in bringing the new condition about. . . . To get my report in, I sent the letter all the way to New Mexico by C. B. Austin, for I knew it would not reach its destination if it had to go through the trading post at Mobeetie." In a more likely account, when he completed his report advocating organization, Arrington sent one of his men to locate Cape Willingham, who took the packet to Las Vegas and "by this roundabout way it finally reached Austin. The county was organized, law was established, and the absolute reign of Lee & Reynolds was ended."

When Oldham County was organized and Willingham became sheriff at Tascosa, he must have known he was taking on a town considered by no less an authority than Arrington himself—and he had seen more than a few—to be "the hardest place on the frontier." Nevertheless, "with a double barrelled shotgun [Willingham] undertook, somewhat successfully, the cultivation of those conventions of settled life the environment had hitherto discouraged." Tough, fair, and respected, he seems to have had no competition for the office of sheriff, and once installed he turned out to be a good one, even if, time and again, he either arrested men for murder only to have the court throw out the case for lack of evidence or was unable to apprehend criminals indicted by the district court because after committing their crimes—a lexicon of lawlessness that ran from illegally branding a colt all the way to bloody murder—the perpetrators simply disappeared into the trackless vastnesses of the Panhandle. Perhaps because of all this Willingham remains one of the least-known law enforcement officers of the Old West, his name missing from most compilations of frontier biography. He might have been better remembered had he served longer, but—and this is of course pure speculation—most of the qualified voters were cowboys, and even though they liked Willingham, their opinions might have been influenced by what at least some of them thought was the unnecessary killing of Fred Leigh. "You had to like [Willingham]. He was irresponsible and would borrow your last dollar and never pay you back. But if he had one, he'd give it to you, if it was his last. He was a good officer. He killed a man [Leigh] there [at Tascosa].

That could have been avoided maybe, but the fellow was going after his gun . . . and you could [hardly] blame Cape for killing him. If Cape had stayed out of sight, which a good officer wouldn't have done, [Leigh's] friends would have . . . gotten him out of the way."[8]

If losing the sheriff's office to Jim East bothered him, Willingham gave little sign of it; at the end of his term of office he moved back to Mobeetie, where he ran the Cattle Exchange saloon for about six months.

While there I received a letter from a man I had never seen, J. M. Coburn, who wanted to know if I would take charge of a big ranch operation. I wrote him that I would if the salary was justifiable. He arranged a meeting with me at Adobe Walls. He stayed in Kansas City and gave me charge of all the business down here. . . .

The name of our company was The Hansford Land & Cattle Co and had been organised by A. H. Johnson. Shortly after the organisation of the company he was killed by lightning on the Cimarron. Mr. Coburn was taken off of a Kansas City bank to be made general manager of the ranch. When the company was organised they bought out the Turkey Track ranch, which was owned by the Snyder brothers, the Quarter Circle T owned by Tom Bugbee and the Double H owned by Moore & Anderson. There were supposed to have been 35,000 cattle in the three brands.

Willingham's summary begs a few facts: Coburn, a Scot who had established himself in Kansas as a banker, was actually the founder of the Hansford Land & Cattle Company, the Scottish syndicate that had bought the Turkey Track in 1882 and added it to the company's holdings in Hutchinson County (which included Bugbee's Quarter Circle T and Anderson's Double H). Following that purchase Coburn was elected secretary, and A. H. "Gus" Johnson general manager of the Hansford. As we have seen, Johnson died in a Kansas lightning storm, whereupon Coburn appointed Tom Coffee range foreman, only to find to his chagrin that Coffee was not only turning a blind eye to the rustling going on at the ranch, but also flatly refused to obey Coburn's orders. There was only one way to solve that problem: hire a man whose orders Coffee would not dare to ignore.

So in 1883 the new Hansford superintendent Willingham "brought his family to [live in] the Quarter Circle T headquarters on Bugbee Creek until he could go to Dodge City for lumber. Near the [old headquarters] rock house he built a home, the first frame house in Hutchinson County. As lumber was eighty five dollars a thousand feet and freight rates were high, this was an expensive residence. Willingham . . . built the house at a distance that ensured quiet and yet was not too far for him to go down and gamble with the boys until midnight when he chose."[9]

In this house two more children—both girls—were born. Each time a child was expected, Cape took Mary to Canadian for medical attention. "Cape would not suffer his wife to go through this ordeal with nothing but the kindly ministrations of a neighbour woman. . . . Other women, looking on, doubtless envied Mrs. Willingham. She had a good home, near other people; she had an indulgent husband—although

Mary Willingham and her children (l. to r.): Ada, Drew, and Homer.
(Courtesy of the Amarillo Public Library)

one of his indulgences was poker; when there were illnesses in the family she always had a doctor. In the eyes of most women, Mrs. Willingham was a lucky woman. . . . Five children, a house, a husband, occasional visitors, kept Mrs. Willingham busy and happy."[10]

Willingham probably knew from the start—for his contemporaries certainly did—that the Hansford outfit's cowboys were stealing the company blind. As one of them noted, "There had been considerable cattle stealing going on in that range, and Willingham had been recommended to the management as one who could and would put an end to such lawlessness, and that recommendation was not misplaced, as it was but a short time until the rustlers left that part of the country."[11]

The new superintendent wrought this small miracle by letting the boys know exactly what he would and wouldn't stand for, and under his supervision the Turkey Track soon began to prosper. Even Tom Coffee, former range boss of the Quarter Circle T, turned over a new leaf; he and his six nephews all stayed to put down roots in the Panhandle, and one, Woodson "Woods" Coffee, later succeeded Willingham as manager. Another noted resident of the Turkey Track was Billy Dixon, he of the famous mile-long shot, who became postmaster when the Adobe Walls post office was established in 1887. Dixon took up some subirrigated school land near ranch headquarters, planted an orchard, and moved onto that site a two-room log house in which Olive King Dixon set up housekeeping after marrying the hero of Adobe Walls in October 1894.[12]

Soon after his appointment, Willingham—representing the Hansford company—was one of the fifty-two ranchers embroiled in the drawn-out and bitterly contested "grass-lease fight," which traced its origins back to the Annexation Resolution of 1845, by which Texas was permitted to retain ownership of its land, the only state in the Union to do so. The state legislature had divided these vast areas into three categories: soldiers' or veterans' grants awarded for service in the U.S.-Mexican War, school and university lands that were to be leased to generate money for building public educational facilities, and finally railroad grants, made to encourage railroad companies to build lines across Texas. In order to prevent one individual or corporation from monopolizing large blocks of land, a checkerboard surveying system was employed so that alternating sections were allotted to schools and railroads. The intent was admirable, but without any facility for policing, or any sanctions against misappropriation, the rules were ignored by cattlemen, who bought up railroad land certificates for piffling amounts—one hundred dollars a section—and turned their stock loose not only on this land but also the intervening school sections. Later, when barbed wire arrived, they blithely fenced thousands of acres whether they owned them or not.

In 1883, however, the legislature passed the Land Board Act, which, among other things, provided for the leasing of land for ranching at eight cents an acre. The ranchers, who had been using the land free, either refused to pay anything or refused to pay more than four cents an acre. Led—of course—by Charles Goodnight, and seeking an equitable settlement, the Panhandle ranchers took their case to the courts in Austin while newspapers lambasted the "cattle kings" for fencing entire counties without paying the state a single cent for using the land.

Surveys soon confirmed that cattlemen were grazing stock on millions of acres in the Panhandle and that school lands were being illegally fenced. In January 1884 District Attorney W. H. Woodman appeared before the grand jury at Clarendon to ask that some fifty ranchers be indicted on charges of illegal enclosure. The jury, of which Goodnight was foreman, found a total of seventy-six true bills against Panhandle ranchers, several of whom were on the jury themselves. At the end of December 1885 Woodman prosecuted the cases before Judge Frank Willis in Austin. He never stood a chance; the jury, consisting almost entirely of cowboys and cattlemen, Goodnight among them, refused to indict a single defendant.

Concluding that Judge Willis had clearly supported the cattlemen, Attorney General John Templeton instigated impeachment proceedings against him; the trial, held at Austin in February 1887, attracted enormous interest, the more so because the cattlemen hired Temple Houston to defend Willis. When Houston won him an acquittal, Willis went home to Mobeetie in triumph. It would be another ten years before the growth of the railroads, the continuing influx of settlers, and the financial setbacks suffered by the ranchers after the Big Die led Goodnight to conclude that "nothing will ruin us that settles the country," and, as he and other ranchers began to sell parts of their holdings, the more equitable distribution of land the state had originally sought came to pass.[13]

For all his involvement in such matters, Willingham never let them interfere with Hansford business. In November 1886, after having charged the Leverton brothers with cattle theft, he served as a deputy on Cap Arrington's posse and participated in the shootout that ensued when they tried to arrest the rustlers. Leverton's widow subsequently filed murder charges against Willingham and Arrington, but both were acquitted. Willingham continued to send herds to the railhead at Dodge City until 1888, but after the arrival of the Panhandle and Santa Fe Railway in Hemphill County, he was able to ship directly from Canadian and Miami. Coburn, happy to leave the day-to-day management of the ranch in Willingham's capable hands, continued to maintain the company office in the Walworth Block in Kansas City and have his residence in that city, but he brought his family to the Panhandle every summer for a visit. By 1890 the Hansford Company owned some 85,000 acres of land and leased an additional 350,000, with an average cattle count of 35,000 head.[14]

In 1893 the Willinghams moved to Canadian so that their five children could go to school there. The same year, Cape

heard of a tract of land down on the Pecos River near Roswell, New Mexico, a part of the John Chisum property then owned by a Kentuckian who longed to sell and go back to his blue-grass country. Willingham needed more range. Nesters were coming in faster and faster and crowding the Turkey Tracks. Cape bought the land with the intention of making it his main ranch later on. . . . The Hutchinson County ranch had gradually been built up until 85,000 acres were owned and 350,000 were leased, while the average cattle count was 35,000 head. More cattle were bought for the Pecos range and for years Cape shuttled from one ranch to the other, looking after both and always keeping "on the go."

With Willingham gone, however, rustling again became a problem at the

Panhandle ranch, and it was one Coburn could not handle. Unable to inspire the same loyalty from his employees that Willingham commanded, Coburn even went so far as to try to bribe Woods Coffee to tell him who was behind the rustling, to which Coffee replied, "I'm blind and deaf and dumb, Mr. Coburn."[15]

In the eyes of one early chronicler of Panhandle history Willingham *was* the Turkey Track, and vice versa. "He did not start it, he did not own it, but he made it . . . by giving his fullest years to it, twenty years in which he did his best—and Cape's best was a forceful quality. [He] was a good cattleman. He knew a cow 'from grass to T-bone.'" But what set him apart was his courage. "Charles Goodnight said that Cape always smiled when he got in a tight place, and any man who knew Cape recognized that under his gentle, easy-going, soft-voiced manner was the elemental type of bravery that does not recognize danger, or, seeing it, ignores it."[16]

Willingham was what in those days they called "a man's man." He ate, drank, and gambled enthusiastically and pursued the opposite sex with considerable zeal. "He loved not only pretty women but also beautiful horses and there was always a string of racehorses wherever Cape was," Goodnight said. "He was a big fat pussy man. . . . My wife always liked him."[17] By 1903, however, with twenty years of service under his belt, Willingham resigned his position as Hansford superintendent and went into business as a cattle commissioner in El Paso; he also did some ranching in Mexico. In later years he described 1903 as the best year of his life, though he did not explain why.[18]

After a decade and a half as a successful cattle dealer and suffering from cardiac asthma and chronic rheumatism, Willingham left El Paso and moved to Arizona, doubtless hoping to benefit from the climate there in his last years. He died at age seventy-three at Ajo, Pima County, Arizona, on January 20, 1925, and was buried in the cemetery there two days later.[19]

1883

THE GREAT COWBOY STRIKE

I T WAS NOT until 1876, when the area was divided into fifty-four counties attached to Jack and Clay, that formal courts governing the Panhandle region came into existence. After the organization of Wheeler County, however, this 10th Judicial District, as it was known, was reduced to twenty-seven counties, which in turn became, on February 15, 1881, the 35th Judicial District of Texas, centered in Mobeetie.

On March 28, Oran M. Roberts, governor of Texas, appointed Indiana-born Frank Willis of Montague County to the office of district judge; for the post of district attorney he chose noted Shackelford County attorney and prosecutor James N. "Honest Jim" Browning. When Browning quit in March 1882 because the job didn't pay enough, he was replaced by eloquent, hard-drinking Brazoria lawyer Temple Houston, son of Texas hero Sam Houston.

In April 1882 Willis and Houston attended the spring term of the Oldham County District Court at Tascosa, where Houston enthusiastically joined in the "pageantry that kept the town in a constant state of expectancy. When a session

of court adjourned, lawyers, clients, and court officials would gather in a saloon and drink at the same bar and engage in a game of poker. . . . Drinking, like gambling, was an integral part of life."

Temple Lea Houston. (Author's Collection)

Lucius Dills, who arrived there in May 1882, was unsparing: "It was a little old one-street dobe town. There was two places: Howard and McMasters owned the townsite. Cone and Edwards had established a store, and Jenkins and Donnelly, a saloon and whore house [where they] assembled all the commercial whores in that region and the cowboys made a periodical visit. At one time, I think, they had ten or twelve. Cone's place [in lower Tascosa] was called Cuntville. Bollicksburg was the name of the [upper] town on the other side. That was euphonious." During his two years in Tascosa Dills claimed to have "assisted in, or looked on at, the burial of nine of the first sixteen men (each with bullets in him) to be planted on Boot Hill."

The first, which he unequivocally labeled "as vile a case of planned murder as has ever come under my knowledge," involved deputy sheriff and town marshal, survivor of poison and loss of memory Henry McCullough, who in July 1882 went down to Hogtown to arrest gambler "Mexican Frank" Largus for a gaming irregularity or perhaps, as Dills phrased it, "trying to keep the 'sensualities' within the realm of lax frontier etiquette."[1]

Largus, "a good gambler, smart and a good dresser" who came from San Antonio, was something of a hard case: he and Kid Dobbs had a run-in at Liberty, Fort Bascom's red-light town, following a drunken spree in which Mexican Frank— who cannot have been much more than nineteen at the time—and a man named Oates shot up a store and threatened to kill its owner.[2]

The confrontation between Largus and McCullough happened "at about eight o'clock on the night of July 18 [actually July 17], 1882, in the billiard room of [the] Jenkins and Donnelly saloon and harlotry

dance hall, which abutted the south end of John W. Cone's general store [in Hogtown]. At the time of the murder the room was well-filled with people . . . and several of the 'Ladies' were sitting on the north edge of the [billiard] table, their legs hanging down, and the victim, coming in the east door, was talking to one of these" when into the room stalked Mexican Frank, who "spoke Spanish with an accent, English with a brogue, and had features and a body odor suggestive of a Sudanic blood infusion. . . . Frank came out of the bar-room, on the south. . . . When turning the corner of the table he fired to McCullar [sic]—not ten feet away—who had grabbed for his pistol, and Frank's shot [hit] his hand, causing the weapon to drop, and entered his body just above the hip bone. McCullar reached down for the pistol and ran out the door, making his way off the road to the Hamlet of Tascosa. It seemed to me . . . that a number of the male visitors present that night were at least not surprised at what happened."[3]

As Dills hurried uptown to inform Sheriff Willingham, Mexican Frank skinned out for the New Mexico line. Mortally wounded, McCullough crawled the agonizing quarter of a mile to the home of Jenny, the dance hall girl with whom he lived; it would take him several days to die. Meantime, after sending Dills to Fort Elliott to put out a telegraphic wanted notice for Largus, Willingham deputized local gambler, occasional jailer, and odd-job man Louis Bousman (who had just the previous day married seriously soiled dove Sally Cruce), told him to "run this thing until I get back," and swung into the saddle. Thanks to his superior knowledge of the country between Tascosa and the New Mexico line, Willingham "managed to get ahead of him [Largus], seen him coming, laid up in a hollow, and caught him as he come by," Bousman said. When the sheriff stepped out in front of him with his double-barreled shotgun cocked, Mexican Frank surrendered without a peep. "Cape was a good man," Bousman added, "but he was fractious though. . . . If a man cussed him who he had arrested, he wanted to beat hell out of him." Maybe Mexican Frank knew that too.[4]

There was no doubt in Dills's mind that the murder "had been fully pre-arranged, even to the roan mare—all saddled and ready for the escape of the honka-tonk hero. . . . The getaway steed was furnished by one of the 'girls' whose [real] name I have forgotten, other than that she was known as Carrie and 'Feather-legs'; and there was but one source whence the killer derived the money which was on his person."[5]

On his return from Fort Elliott five days later, Dills learned McCullough had died and had been buried on Boot Hill and that Frank Largus had been committed to the Oldham County jail without bail. At his trial in September, Largus asked for a continuance on the grounds that he was unable at that time to produce witnesses who would testify the deputy "had told witness that he intended to kill this defendant as soon as he saw him . . . but that the defendant was too quick for him . . . and that the deceased in the same conversation told witness that he was the cause of his own death and by his own rash acts brought his death upon himself."

Unfortunately, these witnesses—one John Collie, a Miss Nick (or Vick) Turner, and George Gamble (Gamel?)—were unavailable, Collie being in Las Vegas, New Mexico, and the other two in Crosby County. Judge Willis refused the application, and the trial proceeded, Temple Houston prosecuting and W. H. Woodman acting for the defense. Two days later, "due to some 'able-bodied' swearings on the part of defense witnesses, and a far from vigorous prosecution, the jury returned a verdict of murder in the second degree."[6]

Sentenced to twenty-two years' imprisonment, Largus was clapped in irons fashioned and fitted—custom-made, you might say—by blacksmith Henry Kimball and sent to the penitentiary at Rusk, arriving there October 26, 1882.[7]

No one was much surprised when it was revealed that the "one source" of the money Mexican Frank had been carrying was Jesse Jenkins's partner, Charles Donnelly, arrested by Cape Willingham as an accomplice to the murder on September 21, too late to be brought to trial before the district court. When the case was heard at

Henry Kimball.
(Courtesy of the Amarillo Public Library)

[139]

the April 1883 term of court, testimony chillingly indicated just how cheaply life could be bought—or ended—in Tascosa: it was alleged Donnelly had given Mexican Frank ten dollars to kill McCullough.

Unfortunately, according to Lucius Dills, elected county judge in the same November election that Jim East became sheriff, "when the case came up for trial the District Attorney [Houston] got drunker than was his custom when coming to Tascosa and the Judge pushed me into the prosecution without a chance to marshal my facts, and he was acquitted."[8]

Justice in Tascosa appears to have been administered in an atmosphere of ongoing pandemonium, as exemplified in the story that immediately prior to the Donnelly trial Judge Willis peremptorily instructed Sheriff East to go out and get 120 venire men and told him he had an hour to do it.

> I said: "Judge, you know how difficult it is to get venire men." But he said "Go out and get them" [so] I went out and herded in every Tom, Dick and Harry, all that were not too drunk to come. I got my 120 men within an hour and never went to any place but the dance halls and saloons. The judge was afraid some of the cowboys would shoot up the courthouse and told me to be sure to disarm them before they came in. My office was next to the courtroom. When the boys came in I said: 'Boys, go in my room and throw your guns off.' I had an old bed in there and every one of the boys had a six-shooter and some had Winchesters besides. I'll tell you, they threw so many belts and guns on that bed that they broke it down. The mattress touched the floor.[9]

And so, freed by a jury of his "peers," Charlie Donnelly went back to his "saloon and harlotry business," no doubt as he left telling the boys who had acquitted him that if they felt like riding over to Hogtown the drinks would be on the house.

And worse lay ahead. In the early fall of 1882, having resigned his commission as a Texas Ranger, Cap Arrington was elected sheriff of Wheeler County and the fourteen counties attached to it, based in Mobeetie. As noted earlier, among the first official engagements of the "iron man of the Panhandle" was a tour of the downtown redlight district, where he let it be known to one and all that the easygoing regime of former sheriff Henry Fleming was about to be replaced by one considerably less forgiving. His tough stance convinced many of the resident gamblers, shills, deadbeats, cardsharps, and bunko steerers it might be smart to seek less restrictive surroundings; before long a sizable party of them drifted west to relocate in Tascosa, together with a contingent of exotically named ladies of the evening, among them Frog Lip Sadie, Rowdy Kate, Panhandle Nan, Slippery Sue, Canadian Lily, Box Car Jane, and a young woman destined, along with her live-in lover, gambler Mickey McCormick, to play a large role in Tascosa's legend: Frenchy McCormick.

The competition for the incomers must have been pretty fierce, because Tascosa already boasted a chorus line—the very nicknames themselves convincing evidence of their complete depersonalization—that included Old Knox, Old Kit, Pissing Jenny, Santa Fe Moll, Carrie "Feather-legs" Gauntz, Rocking Chair Em (Emma Horner), Sally Emory, Mustang May (Harris), Jo Rice, Bronco Bride, and a lady named Wild Bill who later married Charlie Resoner and lived in a dugout near town.

Wild Bill had the kind of morals her

name implied: whenever Jack went to town, a Mexican living nearby would drop in on Wild Bill for a little entertainment. One day, however, Charlie came home unexpectedly and found his wife *in flagrante delicto*. Thinking fast, Wild Bill yelled rape. The miscreant was arrested and tried in Jack Ryan's saloon. The verdict, rendered with due solemnity, was that if the accused had raped Wild Bill he had done so in self-defense. He was released with the warning that if he did it again the court would fine him his chili crop.[10]

Some of the "girls" operated in style: Rocking Chair Emma "had her own wagon and on the side of it she had her brand: a rocking chair and an M." She was "about 28 years old, dark hair and brown eyes, rather tall and a perfect feminine form. . . . She was well educated and showed every mark of good breeding." Santa Fe Moll, who later married Tobe Robinson, was blonde and heavy. Sally Emory was "small, not pretty [but had] lots of sense. Sally didn't like women, occasionally tolerated one chum, but liked men very much. She was Tom Emory's sweetheart and achieved her name that way." Jo Rice was Tom Harris's main squeeze when he was in town. Pissing Jenny was "a little tidbit, slim, poor, not very smart." Billy Jarrett remarked: "Those street girls at Tascosa made fine mothers. Jack Ryan's wife [Elsa Jane Kuney, the former "Pissing Jenny"] was one of them."

As with the members of the gambling fraternity—Lon and Jesse Jenkins, Mickey McCormick, Tom Emory—who regularly paid twenty-five-dollar fines (and costs, which brought the figure up to maybe forty dollars) for "keeping a disorderly house" or "keeping a bank for the purpose of gaming," so the "girls"—Nora "Old" Knox, Kitty Swain, Sallie Henry, and

Phoebe Miller—appear frequently in the legal calendar, repeatedly hauled in for "vagrancy" (not until the mid-1890s would it be recorded as "common prostitution") to plead guilty and pay a five-dollar fine with costs. In fact, so frequent were the arrests that in April 1883 the grand jury requested the court "to instruct the officers of the town that prostitutes shall be kept off the streets and out of public places in day time and shall be kept orderly while out of their own apartments." It is not too difficult to imagine how the prostitutes—who probably numbered most of the members of the grand jury among their clients—reacted to such civic self-righteousness.

Thus Tascosa's saloon girls were both victimized and simultaneously rendered invisible, made an inescapable aspect of frontier town life the presence of which somehow had to be accommodated. That they in turn accepted this status quo—and the deprivation that went with it—underlines how incapable of change it was; frontier communities were largely satisfied to remain ignorant of the payoffs and deals struck between the prostitutes, the saloon owners, and law enforcement, and Tascosa was no exception.

As a result, a sort of compromise came into effect by means of which certain of the town's red-light ladies arranged to be the exclusive companion of this or that cowboy or single man when he was in town, or even on a semipermanent basis. Thus, Jesse Jenkins lived with Phoebe Miller, as did Henry McCullough with Pissing Jenny. Tom Harris liked Rocking Chair Emma Horner, and Bill Gatlin always stayed with Sally Emory, the former Sally Daugherty, who had taken the name of her earlier consort, Tom Emory. If not by any means perfect, such dispensations may have given at least some of the town's prostitutes a sense of self-worth and belonging.

The downside of these arrangements, of course, was that the woman had little choice in the quality of her partner. Generally speaking, it was only the most disreputable frontier males who became the consorts or even husbands of prostitutes, and frequently such arrangements merely formalized a liaison in which the male partner not only tolerated but also encouraged the woman to solicit sex as a means of making money.

In time, a strange symbiosis developed between the "bad" girls and the good. Marion Armstrong's sister Mary Snider "often sewed for the girls of the red light district, but had no further intercourse with them, knew nothing of their lives. They did not come on the streets except during the day to buy the necessary things of life for themselves. Styles which she made for them were conservative for daytime wear. She did not make the clothes they wore in the dance halls. Dresses had long sleeves, high necklines, bustle effects, and voluminous skirts. Petticoats had numerous ruffles and were worn several at a time."[11]

Late in the year 1882 Hogtown again lived up to its murderous reputation. The victim this time was a cowboy going by the name of Bill Gibson, who had

> saved his summer's wages and came to town to enjoy himself for a few days. He drank, danced and dined, spending most of his time in [Jenkins and Donnelly's Hogtown] saloon, and had been making quite a display of his money. Johnny Maley, a bartender in the saloon, coveting the money Gibson had been displaying, was accused of inducing Sally Emory . . . to get Gibson to go to her room . . . and

sleep off his intoxication. In a short time Maley left his work and went over to the cabin. Going to the back window he shot the sleeping man through the head and took his money. There was an official investigation. The facts were plain enough but [there was] no legal proof so the guilty pair escaped punishment—as they thought.

Bill Gibson, real name Frank Norwood, was buried on Boot Hill, and that appeared to be that, but there was more to come. Although no one knew it—he had not even attended the funeral—Gibson's brother, Ed Norwood, worked for the LE. On Friday, March 9, 1883, Norwood rode into Hogtown and proceeded to duplicate his brother's reckless behavior, dancing with Sally Emory, drinking heavily, and making a display of his money. "Finally, acting sleepy, [he] induced Sally to let him occupy her bed—the bed his brother had been slain on. He lay there a long time expecting the bartender to come and rob him, but he failed to show up. Finally Norwood, getting impatient, went back to the dance hall and shot Maley through the heart."[12]

Another version of these events that reached Dodge City via J. S. Jackson, agent for the mail line, added a few details to the bloody tale. Norwood "was drinking some, and with two friends went into the saloon where Mabry [Maley] was behind the bar and said. . . . 'You have poisoned me' and shot him, the ball taking effect near the left nipple. Mabry is probably dead now. The two were thought to be friends and no reason can be assigned for the rash deed. After the shooting, Norwood went back to the upper town where he was arrested. Other facts were probably developed at the examining trial Monday [held on March 12]."[13]

Indeed they were. When the grand jury met, "despite his apparently truthful story, they returned an indictment of murder in the first degree and Norwood was held without bail. Protest was heard from all over the range and friends of Norwood set about trying to solve the problem and bring about what they conceived to be justice." And in due course, they did just that.[14]

But by this time Tascosa—and the Panhandle cattle industry in general—had bigger problems on their plates. In March, just before the spring roundup was scheduled to begin, the cowboys decided to call a strike, their particular animosity directed at the "big five" ranches: the LIT, the T-Anchor, the LE, the LX, and—especially—the LS. It would seem quite a bit of forethought was involved. "In anticipation of this strike the participants had been saving their money," John Arnot said, "and when the big day arrived they drew their wages and departed for their rendezvous on the Alamocitas Creek twenty five miles west of Tascosa. The boys anticipated an easy victory, as round up time was close at hand and that work was bound to go on."[15]

That there was considerable apprehension as to the methods the cowboys might employ is evident in a letter addressed to the governor's office in Austin by the aggressive Jot Gunter of the T-Anchor:

We have advice . . . that the cowboys throughout the Pan Handle have all combined and agreed to strike on April 1st for an increase to Fifty Dollars per month. . . . Should they carry out their programme, they will turn loose upon that country 250 to 500 reckless well armed men and may result in the loss of many lives and much property. We wish Gv. Ire-

land and Adjut. General in the event of trouble to send a force of Rangers to protect the property and lives of the Ranchmen. We do not wish our names to go out as moving on this matter as the cowboys if specially mad at us could ruin us by burning our range.[16]

Unlike the ranch owners, the cowboys felt their demands were fair and reasonable, and by and large they were. Even today, the grounds for their discontent are easy to understand: to begin with, the increase in the value of cattle—not to mention the profits being made by the owners as the "beef bonanza" accelerated—had not brought any corresponding improvement in the earnings of the cowboys who did all the work. Not only did wages remain at about thirty dollars a month for range hands and fifty for wagon bosses, but the cowboy felt he was being steadily reduced to little more than a hired hand with no prospect of self-betterment; new rules forbidding any employee from owning his own place or cattle stuck in the gullets of men long accustomed to slapping their brands on a few mavericks with a view to one day having a ranch of their own. There was even talk among the "big bosses" of firing men for carrying six-shooters or getting drunk. What next?

Proud and independent to a man, the cowboys said the hell with company rules and regulations, and under the leadership of Tom Harris of the LS, Waddy Peacock of the LIT, and Roy Griffin of the LX, they drew up the following ultimatum, signed by everyone in the line camps:[17]

We, the undersigned cowboys of Canadian River, do by these presents agree to bind ourselves into the following obligations, viz:-

First. That we will not work for less than $50 per month, and we farther more agree no one shall work for less than $50 per mo. after 31st Mch.

Second. Good cooks shall also receive $50 per mo.

Third. Anyone running an outfit shall not work for less than $75 per mo.

Anyone violating the above obligations shall suffer the consequences. Those not having funds to pay board after March 31st shall be provided for 30 days at Tascosa.

Signed

Thos. Harris	Jas. Jones
Buc Davis	Roy Griffin
C. M. Hullett	T. D. Holliday
J. W Peacock	A. (or V) F. Martin
C. F. Goddard	J. L. Howard
Harry Ingerton	E. E. Watkins
W. D. (or S) Gaton [Gatlin?]	
J. A. (or S) Morris	C. B. Thompson
B. G. Brown	Jim Miller
G. F. Nickell [Nichols?]	
W. B. Boring	Henry Stafford
Juan A. Gomez	D. W. Peeples
Wm. F. Kerr	John L. Grisson
	[Grissom?]

This bold initiative met with widespread approval and within a short time the number of strikers grew until somewhere between 160 and 200 men were involved. One report put the figure as high as 325, but this seems unlikely. The big ranches responded swiftly and in almost every case negatively. Bob Roberson of the LIT rode out to the strikers' camp and offered to up the rate for cowboys to $35 a month and $65 for wagon bosses; when they refused, the company let the men go and confiscated their horses. The LX held fire, but both the LE and the T-Anchor immediately discharged every striker on their payrolls. For the LS, Jordan McAllister—perhaps seeking a compromise until W. M. D. Lee could get to the Panhandle from Leavenworth—offered $40, but the strikers were in no mood to negotiate.

Tom Harris probably knew a strike would be especially damaging to the LS, but even if he did not, "Mac" Lee certainly did. He had already drawn up plans for a complex cattle drive to Montana involving the merging of two herds, one in New Mexico and the other in eastern Texas; without trail-savvy wagon bosses and riders it would be a disaster. As soon as word reached him, he got on a train to Dodge City and from there made all possible speed to Tascosa, an exhausting thirty-six-hour nonstop marathon that probably did nothing to improve his temper.[18]

At the LS he found a large number of the strikers nearby. He "spoke to them cordial like and went inside," where he "bawled McAlister [sic] out for not paying the men what they demanded and stalling them off for a time. He said he could have got carloads of men later at whatever price was fair or that suited him." In other words, McAllister should have given the men what they wanted, got the herds on the trail, and then fired every one of them as soon as the roundup was over.

The next morning Lee sent word to Harris to come up to the house and talk with him. Harris, instead of going alone, carried along seven or eight men and when about midway from their camp to the house they jerked their six-shooters and fired into the air.

Lee said, "Guess they are trying to bulldoze us, but I'm not afraid of them."

When they came in Lee asked Tom Harris, "Tom, when you went to work here who set the price on your services? Who asked you what pay you wanted to run a wagon for the LS?"

Tom replied, "I priced myself at $75 a month."

"Have you ever asked for a raise? Why didn't you ask for more money if you thought you had to have it and were worth it?"

"I went into this strike to help the other boys, not to help myself, Mr. Lee," replied Tom.

"Tom, you know men and you know the cattle business, and you know what it takes to handle cattle. Do you believe every man here is worth $50 a month?"

This was a particularly telling point, for Harris knew there were "nester kids" working on the ranches, cheap unskilled labor for whose inexperience the owners relied on older, seasoned hands to compensate on the trail. Harris admitted some of the strikers weren't first-class cowhands but said they could soon learn. Lee dismissed the argument and instead offered to pay Harris $100 to keep the wagon and $50 to any man who was worth it. To his eternal credit, Harris "said he could not take it and he would stay with the boys."[19]

Given no option, Lee let him go. Harris was replaced by Jim May; Dunk Cage, Sam Buford, and Tobe Robinson were promoted to run outfits, and Kid Dobbs was hired to handle a fifth wagon. All were paid the demanded amount, but when the roundup was over, wages were immediately cut back to the old rate, take it or leave it. Anyone who protested was fired on the spot.[20]

Meanwhile, newspapers in places as far away as Colorado to the west and Fort Worth to the east had fastened on to the story; most were promanagement and, if

not anticowboy, openly unsupportive of the strike.

This strike assumes a serious phase, for [the cowboys] are armed with Winchester rifles and six-shooters and the lives of all who attempt to work for less than the amount demanded are in great danger. The strikers number about 200, and are located in Tascosa county [sic], near the New Mexico line. They threaten to cut fences and burn ranches if their demands are not acceded to. The novelty of the strike is that the men have struck before work has begun, and the serious feature is that it is in anticipation of the spring work, or the regular annual roundup which can not go on without them.[21]

In a letter to the *Texas Live Stock Journal* dated April 5, Harris denied the cowboys intended "to resort to any violence or unlawful acts to get adequate compensation for their services, but to do so by all fair and legal means in their power." Very well, replied the *Journal:*

If Mr. Harris is in earnest in his statements, and is able to control his followers and keep them from committing unlawful acts, this local strike will soon be settled much more to their satisfaction than it ever can be should they place themselves outside the law. Cowboys have a perfect right to ask for a proper remuneration for their services, they have also the right to leave work in a body, unless satisfied; they assert their manhood in so doing. They may benefit themselves by such combined action, but directly they make threats of damage to property of others, they lay themselves open to suspicion, and the good among them, the law abiding element, are likely to suffer from the acts and words of those who do their best to bring into dispute the interests they are apparently trying to advance.[22]

Just four days later, a Colorado newspaper, apparently unaware of Harris's disclaimer, took another wild, if ill-informed, swipe at the strikers:

The cowboys of Texas are on their muscle and nerve. They demand an increase of pay from $30 to $50 a month. Failing to get it, they propose to burn the ranches, confiscate the cattle and kill the owners in that particular part of the world called the Panhandle, which was recently sold by the state of Texas to a Chicago syndicate and transferred by them to an English company. With the country the English millionaires have bought a hard constituency, as they are in a fair way to find out. An ordinary cowboy is as explosive as a nitroglycerine bomb, and a good deal more dangerous. We shall watch the war with interest, not caring much which side whips or gets whipped.[23]

But there was no war and no real violence, certainly none of the sort allegedly threatened in pieces like these. Some brawls in saloons, and some later—and fatal—confrontations, undoubtedly had their origins in hard feelings engendered by the strike, but during its brief duration there were no physical confrontations between what might have been considered to be "union men" and "management" at all.

Then all at once, it was over. "The cowboy's strike in the Panhandle has been a failure," the *Dodge City Times* reported. "Those of the strikers who could obtain employment have gone to work and others have left the country. We understand that a number of the most prominent and violent ones have been refused work on the range and have been forced to abandon the country to secure employment."[24]

The bare economic facts of life had doomed the strike before it even got started. "Lee stopped feeding them and they could only raise $80 among them for food," Kid Dobbs said. "The cowboys soon scattered out, got work wherever they could until Harris started his ranch on one prong of the Trujillo Creek near [what became] old Endee, New Mexico." Hands who didn't trust the ranchers left the country; others roistered in the saloons and brothels until their money ran out, then left.[25]

Not coincidentally, cattle rustling—in the western Panhandle mostly of LIT and LS stock—became a growth industry. "The cowboys had begun their individual herds by branding strays," John Arnot wrote, "cattle that had drifted from far away ranches into the Panhandle, though the owners themselves followed this practice. In fact, the owners began it. And the cowboys, seeing no evil in running the owners' irons on strays, saw none in running their own." Lucius Dills was not the only one who felt strongly that there was a dark motive behind the strike, that it had been "initiated as a smoke screen to hide an organized design to engage in wholesale stealings from all the cattle companies in the district."[26]

Although Tom Harris shouldered most of the blame, it was in fact Jesse Jenkins who was masterminding the rustling. In spite of this, however, his "sagacity in never letting his name be connected with shady cattle deals amounted to downright genius."

Through Tom Harris, he succeeded in planting about twenty-five men on the LS ranch pay roll, where they would be in a better position to help secure a herd for Tom, and in the final wind-up, for Jess. One of their schemes was to cut a cow's teats off, so the calf could not suck. . . . Then in the fall roundups, these [by now weaned] calves were branded as sleepers. After LS cowboys found about twenty head of cows in this fix, the general man-ager of the LS, J. E. McAllister, through a little scheme of his own, ran the entire gang off the ranch without gunplay. From that time, ill feeling between the LS men and the Jenkins gang grew out of bounds.[27]

And it looked like it was going to get a lot worse.

Chapter 16

TOM HARRIS

"I'M TIRED OF THIS, PUT ME AWAY."

FOR A MAN who made such a memorable—not to say momentous—impact on the cattle industry in the Panhandle, history has been unkind to Tom Harris Because of the dearth of records and newspapers at that time, so little is known about him that this brief outline of his life is offered almost apologetically, and yet it would be grossly unjust to relegate him to little more than a footnote to his times.

In the 1880 census for Hartley County, Texas, he is shown age twenty-two, of Alabaman parentage, working as a "herder" for the LS alongside—rather unexpectedly—former sheep owner, thirty-two-year-old E. C. Godwin-Austen. How long Harris had been in the Panhandle, and where he had been before that, is a matter for guesswork. Jim Gober, who knew him then, called him "a fine specimen of manhood, about 6 feet tall, broad shoulders, and well proportioned from head to foot, light brown hair, blue eyes, and what would be termed a medium blond. He knew no fear and always stood for justice and equity among men. He was about 33 years old when I first met him in 1882."[1]

In 1882, Harris would have in fact been twenty-four years of age, an attractive and dynamic personality who generated intense loyalty but seems to have kept his origins pretty much to himself. CC Bar cowboy Dave Lard, who knew him well, said,

> I don't know where Tom Harris was from. He had been in Colorado. He hatched the strike up. He was the leader. You can say what you please, but Harris was in the right, really. Them companies moved in there [as] cold blooded as a bunch of damned snakes and they wouldn't allow people to have cattle or state land or nothing. Peons, that's what we were. I may get the devil for saying this but I always was in sympathy with them [strikers]. . . . [A] whole bunch of the best cowpunchers and men was in with that outfit and I tell you they was a damned sight better men than some of the cowmen that brought that on.[2]

Thomas B. Harris was born near Hallettsville, Lavaca County, Texas, on January 7, 1857, second child and first son of General Buckner and Permelia Jane (Peeler)

Harris, log-cabin pioneer settlers. "Buck" Harris, as he was known, was born in northern Alabama in 1833; Permelia Jane, the same year in South Carolina. Buck came to Texas when he was about fifteen and settled in the Hallettsville area five or so years later. The Harris children were Sarah A. (Sally), born May 21, 1854; Tom; Catherine A. (Kate), born in 1859; John, born in 1861; Mary L. (Mollie), born in 1863; and Susie F., born July 6, 1871. Both Sally and Susie lived to be centenarians.[3]

At the time of the 1860 census, Sally, Tom, and Kate (just one year old) were enumerated with the five children of a Smith family at the Hallettsville home of laborer L. M. Hoffler; in adjoining properties were B. Harris, twenty-eight, a farmer, and his wife, Louisa, both from Alabama; and an A. Smith, twenty-eight, likewise a farmer and also born in Alabama. It may well be (allowing for the possibility of a census-taker's error with Permelia's name) that Buck Harris, his wife, and farmer Smith were working for Hoffler, and their children were staying at the Hoffler home during the day. If so, it was not for long; Leonard Hoffler enlisted in the Confederate army at Hallettsville on January 1, 1862, and died on the following May 16.[4]

Soon after the outbreak of the war, Buck Harris enlisted in Company B of Maj. John W. Whitfield's Brigade, Texas 4th Cavalry, organized in the fall of 1861 and subsumed early the next year into the Texas 27th Cavalry Regiment, the renowned "Whitfield's Legion." Wounded during the Corinth campaign at Iuka, Mississippi, on September 19, 1862, Harris was captured at Hatchie Bridge and paroled. After he was exchanged he made his way home; there, in November, he joined Company B of Col. William P. Hardeman's Regiment, Gano's Brigade,

Texas 1st Cavalry. He served as a private to the end of the war in Indian Territory and in Arkansas during the Red River Campaign, including the bloody Battle of Jenkins' Ferry near Little Rock on April 30, 1864.[5]

By 1870 Buck Harris was a farmer of sufficient means to have two black girls aged ten and eight living in as servants. The family lived at Rocky Creek about seven miles from Hallettsville, near which a small cemetery plot was set aside for the grave of Permelia, who died in 1873 at the age of forty; it is marked by a simple stone that says, MOTHER HARRIS 1833–73.[6] Some years later, Buck Harris married a twenty-four-year-old Alabama girl; the union appears to have divided the family, for by 1880 Buck and Alice were living alone. There seems to have been a falling-out over land and other property that had been jointly owned by Buck and Permelia, with the father refusing to give the children their inheritance.

In 1880 Tom Harris, "a resident of San Magill [San Miguel] County, New Mexico"; his sisters Kate, now living in Fayette County, and Sally, now Mrs. J. H. Jury; together with younger brother John (and representing Molly and Susie, still minors) brought suit against their father "for partition and division of certain real estate and personal property belonging to the community estate of Permelia Harris, deceased." It was in connection with this suit that Harris—en route to a court hearing in Baylor County—detoured to Hallettsville in March 1886, during which time Jesse Jenkins must have met and proposed to Tom's sister Molly.[7]

Later that month, Harris also appeared in court at Seymour, Baylor County, where he was successfully defended by Jesse's brother, Charles Jenkins, on an allegedly trumped-up charge of horse theft (see chapter 10). He and Jenkins were back at or near Tascosa at the time of the gunfight between the gamblers and the LS men; some accounts even suggest they were involved, although the evidence remains far too flimsy to convict. It is more than probable that Harris accompanied Jesse Jenkins back to Hallettsville and was present on Sunday, May 23, 1886, when his friend and Molly Harris were married by Baptist minister Benjamin F. Miller. Harris and Jenkins either stayed on or returned to Hallettsville not only to oversee the family's case against their father, which was heard before Judge George McCormick at the August 1886 term of Lavaca County District Court, but also to get married himself, as this item in the *Tascosa Pioneer* indicates: "From the *Herald and Planter,* a paper published at Hallet[t]sville, Lavaca county, Texas, copy of which was handed to us by Jesse Jenkins, we discover that Thomas Harris, well known in and about Tascosa, was married at the Baptist church in Fistonia, the county seat of Fayette county, on the Sunday before Thanksgiving. The bride was Miss Clara Paulus."

Like many a newspaper report, the *Herald and Planter* got some of the story right and vital bits of it wrong. There is no such town as Fistonia; the county seat of Fayette County was and still is La Grange; and it was there on November 21, 1886, that Tom Harris and Clara C. Paulus were wed by Baptist minister O. Y. Simpson. The twenty-one-year-old bride was one of the four children of La Grange physician Augustus Paulus, born in Denmark.[8]

When the family's suit against Buck Harris was heard at the February 1887 term of court, Lavaca County commissioners H. H. Russell, M. M. Dillard, and S. J. Dickey were ordered to "proceed to partition and divide said real and personal property as set forth and described in [the attached] decree between the parties." This included several substantial town and farm lots at Hallettsville together with livestock, upon which the three commissioners placed a value of $6,140; after a small loan of $400 was repaid, the plaintiffs (following their marriage Jesse Jenkins had added his name to his wife's in the suit) were awarded property worth $2,870, a sizable sum in those days.[9]

In the spring of 1887 Tom and Clara Harris returned to New Mexico and, one assumes, set up in married life at the Harris ranch on the upper reaches of Trujillo Creek just a few miles west of the Texas line in what was then San Miguel County; on November 5 the *Pioneer* noted they were in town visiting the Jenkinses. The following year Harris decided to move his ranching operation back into Texas along with his neighbors and friends, the Isaacs brothers.

William C. Isaacs, born in Alabama December 4, 1853, arrived in the Panhandle in 1883, with his brothers John and Sam following a year later. The younger Isaacs brothers—born in Bosque County, Texas, in 1864 and 1866, respectively—worked for ranches with leases in the Indian Territory until 1885, when they relocated the Mallalay and Forbes herds to near Endee, New Mexico. Will Isaacs ranched on the Tierra Blanca, south of Tascosa, in 1887. Two years later, Sam moved his employers' cattle to Red Deer Creek, near Canadian. In 1893 Sam and Will Isaacs bought out Mallalay and Forbes at Canadian and formed a ranching partnership on thirty thousand acres that lasted until 1912, when the brothers divided up their assets.[10]

"The spring following the shootout in Tascosa [that is, 1887], Tom Harris, with two Isaacs brothers, moved their cattle to a much better range, some two hundred miles east [from New Mexico], five miles west of the city of Canadian." And then, just when it would have seemed that Tom Harris had everything to live for, he killed himself. "A few months after they were located on the new range, Harris went to Canadian City with wagon and team after ranch supplies. He put his wagon and team in the wagon yard for the night. Next morning Harris was found dead in his camp bed in the bunk house." To some of his contemporaries such an action was not only unaccountable but craven. This was the man who led the cowboy strike, defied the big ranchers, and yet "he killed himself—a man that was supposed to be a desperado and nervy."[11]

According to one historian, Harris "never got over the failure of his venture [the cattle pool syndicate, see chapter 17]. One evening he was found dead in a wagonyard. One hand clutched a note saying 'I'm tired of this, put me away,' and an empty bottle of morphine." A creative explanation, perhaps, but the truth, as recounted by Dave Lard, who ranched near Canadian, is much sadder: "I gave Tom Harris half of my place on Chicken Creek when he moved down there. His wife [Clara] was making my wife's wedding dress when he killed himself in Canadian. . . . He was one of the finest neighbors you ever lived by. Him and I told [toiled?] all the day before hunting a beef on Dry Creek. He had the pock awful bad, when he had married a pretty nice woman. . . . It was in the fall of the year . . . and we was hunting that beef and his old peter had got kind of sore. He was afraid it was coming back and it was bothering him. He had an awful nice woman . . . and he had financial troubles too . . . that was in [18]89 or [18]90."[12]

The grave of Tom Harris at Canadian, Texas. (Photograph by Sharon Wright, River Valley Pioneer Museum, Canadian, Texas)

There is no death certificate, nor any other formal record of Tom Harris's death in Hemphill County other than an entry in the Hemphill Cemetery Book, which indicates that he died (or was found dead) on Friday, December 12, 1890, and was buried in the Edith Ford cemetery at Canadian; his gravestone, however, gives the date as December 16.

Most poignantly of all, the legend on his grave says "Gone but not forgotten." In fact, Tom Harris very soon became and has remained a forgotten man; until now, no one seems to have been interested enough in his life, let alone his death, to try to chronicle it.[13]

Perhaps because they were responsible for bringing by-now legendary lawman Cap

Arrington out of retirement, there is a little more detail available concerning the events in which another of the Isaacs clan—some say a brother, others a cousin of Will and Sam—became embroiled a few years later:

In November 1894 an attempt was made by some desperadoes from the Indian Territory to rob the [Wells, Fargo] express office at Canadian, Texas and in resisting the attack Sheriff Tom McGee was shot and killed, his death was a severe blow to the cause of law and order. In selecting a man to fill the vacant office and bring the murderers to justice, Arrington's name was the first to occur to all. . . . It was but a short time until he had George Isaacs and a man by the name of Harbold [Harbolt] in custody. Isaacs had sold some cattle in Kansas City and converted the proceeds into one dollar bills. He then made them up into a package and expressed to himself at Canadian, but desig-

nated the contents as being twenty five thousand.

The plan was to rob the express office of the package and get paid the supposed twenty five thousand dollars. . . . [Isaacs] was hanging around the depot with one or two more men aiming to get the money before it was put into the safe but when it did not show up they left and returned the next night. The agent on seeing them hanging around again phoned the sheriff to come down as he was afraid that they meant harm and he wanted some protection. Sheriff McGee came to the depot with a heavy overcoat on and buttoned tightly around him. He proceeded to question the men as to their business there, guns were drawn and before McGee could unbutton his coat and get his gun he was shot down and the robbers fled. The money came in that night but was never called for. As soon as Arrington was appointed sheriff and went into the case

Early-day Canadian, Texas. Main Street, about 1910.
The AT&SF railroad depot where McGee was killed is at the bottom of the hill.
(Courtesy of the River Valley Pioneer Museum, Canadian, Texas)

[152]

they opened the package and discovered the attempted deception."[14]

Another account adds important detail:

On the night of November 24, 1894, George Isaacs arrived in [Canadian]. On the same train [were] five packages of money, each purporting to contain $5000, billed by Isaacs at Kansas City to himself at Canadian. In an attempt to steal these packages, Sheriff McGee was murdered. . . . The packages were opened and found to contain in all $500. Isaacs confessed, and upon trial which was held in Vernon in October, 1895, was sentenced to the penitentiary for life, and his sentence has since been affirmed by the Court of Appeals.[15]

Still another version of the robbery suggests there were six men involved, among them Jim Harbolt, Dan McKenzie, and "Tulsa Jack" Blake. George Isaacs is said to have been apprehended, convicted in 1895, and sentenced to life imprisonment at Huntsville. He later escaped and fled to Mexico, then to Arizona, although some sources indicate that he was released. The three men accused of being accomplices—Harbolt, McKenzie, and Tulsa Jack, a member of the Doolin gang—were later apprehended by deputy marshals and returned for trial to Canadian.[16]

Much of this is suspect: Isaacs was certainly tried, but it was not until 1897 that Cap Arrington escorted him to Huntsville Penitentiary. Tulsa Jack [real name William Blake] was killed following a train robbery by the Doolin gang near Dover, Oklahoma, on the night of April 3–4, 1895. A posse led by Chris Madsen pursued the robbers, and Blake was killed in a running gun battle during which the others—among them

"Red Buck" Weightman, "Bitter Creek" Newcombe, and Doolin himself—managed to escape.[17]

Jim Harbolt was

captured at Taluga, Oklahoma, on the 3rd day of February, 1895, which at the time was the rendezvous for all the murderers and thieves in that part of the Territory, and brought back here [to Canadian] and placed in jail. The grand jury found a bill against him, charging him with murder. In August of the same year, and previous to Isaacs' trial, Judge Hurt, upon *habeas corpus* hearing, granted him bail to the amount of $2250, which he gave, Bill and Sam Isaacs, brothers of George, being his bondsmen. At the next term of court, Harbolt failed to appear and his bond was

—ɔⱱɔ—

Thomas T. McGee, sheriff of Hemphill County. (Courtesy of the River Valley Pioneer Museum, Canadian, Texas)

forfeited. Another warrant was issued for his arrest, which was finally effected in the Chicksaw [*sic*] Nation last year. He was then placed in jail in Fort Worth for safe-keeping where he remained until brought here by Sheriff Boyd at the last November term of the district court, when the venue was changed to Donley county, where he was to have been tried on the 8th of February next and while awaiting that time he was retained at the Canadian jail.[18]

About the middle of December 1896 a man named Gilliland spent time in the jail with Harbolt. On his release after the 1897 new year, Gilliland told a local man that Harbolt had hacksaws in his possession; a search was made but no evidence of an escape attempt was found. Shortly there-after, Sheriff Boyd departed for Oklahoma, leaving his deputy, Dick Rathjen, in charge. A few days later, Harbolt broke jail. A five-foot iron bar and a heavy stay chain were found under the prisoner's bunk, and close examination revealed the bars had been sawed apart and the marks filled with soap. There was much speculation about how he had obtained the tools and who helped him escape.[19]

The following Saturday, Will Isaacs went out to fetch coal and heard his name called from the barn; it was Harbolt, starv-ing, sick, and weak and ready to surrender. Harbolt was arrested and taken to Claren-don, where on Monday, February 8, 1897, his trial for the murder of Tom McGee began. The following Friday he was found guilty and sentenced to life imprisonment. He was sent to Fort Worth to be held pending an appeal, and it would appear this was successful, for Harbolt was "freed shortly afterwards . . . but he did not live long. Involved in an argument with a farmer, he was shot and killed."[20]

Pleading not guilty to all charges, thirty-eight-year-old George Isaacs was tried, found guilty, and in November 1896 likewise assessed a life term in the peni-tentiary. After a few years, however, "someone in the Governor's office placed a [forged] pardon for Isaacs amongst some genuine pardons that the governor was signing, thus securing the governor's signature for one for Isaacs[;] the plan worked to perfection and Isaacs was gone and well gone before the deception was discovered and until this day he has not been heard of."[21]

Sam and Will Isaacs turned out consid-erably better. In January 1892 Will mar-ried Canadian's first teacher, Mary Brainard, and the following year he and Sam bought a thirty-thousand-acre ranch and four thousand head of cattle. The fol-lowing year, their brother John, a.k.a. "The T-Anchor Kid," established a ranch east of Canadian. On June 1, 1898, he married Viola Bloom, a Medicine Lodge, Kansas, girl; they would have four chil-dren. In 1906 the three brothers estab-lished the Canadian Building and Loan Association and the Canadian State Bank, with Mary Isaacs's father, Edward H. Brainard, as president. On August 6, 1907, Sam was married to May Louisa Stevens of Kansas City. He was one of the founders of the Panhandle-Plains Museum at Canyon and liberally sup-ported it and the Panhandle-Plains Histor-ical Society. The brothers remained in partnership until 1912, when they divided the property to operate independently. Will died May 18, 1934, and John on October 22, 1937. After leasing his ranch in 1942, Sam passed on, full of years, on September 28 of the following year. They are all well and fondly remembered to this day.[22]

Chapter 17

1884

RUSTLERS VS. RANGERS

FUELED BY a mixture of fierce resentment of the "don't tread on me" variety and the cowboy's natural inclination toward independence, the resistance of the "little men" to the sanctions of the big ranches grew stronger and stronger. So let the county (its judicial face perhaps still red following the almost contemptuous ease with which Ed Norwood had been delivered from the existing jail) announce the building of an imposing new seven-thousand-dollar stone courthouse and jail building in which arrestees would be securely held for trial; they'd have an interesting time putting together a jury that would bring in a guilty verdict. Let Bates and Beals go ahead and sell the LX to the American Pastoral Company of Dundee, Scotland; the "boys" were planning a "pastoral company" of their own that would give them a fair share of the big money being generated by the beef bonanza.[1]

With Jesse Jenkins as their silent financial partner, Tom Harris, Wade Woods, Tom Fitzgerald, and a few others established the Bar WA ranch just over the state line near Liberty, New Mexico, and early in 1884 organized a cattle pool, or syndi-

cate. The plan was simple: working cowboys would be able to buy one-hundred-dollar shares in the syndicate, which would use the pooled money to buy and raise livestock. At the end of five years the syndicate would be dissolved, the cattle sold, and the profit divided up. Among its first investors was Jordan McAllister. Bill Ruth (formerly of the LX but presently based in New Mexico) chipped in two thousand dollars and Jim Gober managed one thousand; many Panhandle cowboys bought smaller shares.[2]

The reaction of the larger ranches to this enterprise was immediate and vigorous: antagonizing the cowboys still further, many threatened to fire any employee misguided enough to invest in the syndicate. When Lee demanded that McAllister withdraw his twenty-five hundred dollars, and McAllister acquiesced, "Harris was terribly sore. . . . In a saloon one morning [he] jerked out a big red bandanna handkerchief, flipped it toward McAlister [*sic*] and said 'Grab one end of that and I'll shoot it out with you, you red-headed sonofabitch!' McAlister kept his nerve and said 'You know, Harris, that I'm not a gun man.

[155]

Tascosa Courthouse, 1884. Left to right: Dr. C. Chepmell, Lucius Dills, O. S. Hitchcock, Howson H. Wallace, C. B. Vivian, Nettie and Jim East, and Isaac P. Ryland. (Courtesy of the Haley Memorial Library, Midland, Texas)

You've got the best of me and there is no sense in my throwing my life away."[3]

Taken in tandem with John Meadows's comments on the LS general manager (see page 156), Harris's reaction could be read as suggesting McAllister was playing both ends against the middle and would explain why, when he later fired LS cowboy Waddy May for investing in the selfsame syndicate, May pulled a gun on McAllister and only the intervention of another LS hand prevented what would surely otherwise have been a killing.[4]

Next, Lee called on the members of the Stockmen's Association to discharge and blacklist any man who owned shares in the syndicate, and soon what the cowboys had seen as a real chance to get themselves a foothold in the ranching business began to fall apart. As investors withdrew, control passed inexorably into the hands of Jesse Jenkins, and before long the syndicate—together with a number of smaller ranchers who had settled on land as neighbors to Harris and had registered "maverick" brands—had abandoned its "cover" and was being referred to as "the System" or, more blatantly, the "Get Even Cattle Company."

"There was an organized bunch of

———— ⌘ ————

**Jordan E. McAllister and family. Jordan's son Earl is on his knee,
daughter May and wife Luanna are standing.
(Courtesy of the Haley Memorial Library, Midland, Texas)**

them," McAllister said, "and Jess Jenkins was president of the outfit. Each maverick a man branded in the organization brand entitled him to five dollars."[5] And anything or anyone who interfered with the operation was dealt with ruthlessly, as in the case of Tascosa's first—and last—Mexican deputy, David Martinez, appointed in March 1884 when the local Mexican community urged Sheriff Jim East to deputize one of their number. "I told them the cowboys would kill him if I did," he said prophetically.

Just one night later, on or about March 23, Eugene Watkins (a signatory of the cowboy strike manifesto) killed Martinez and his brother Guillermo in Jesse Jenkins's old Hogtown saloon (while doubtless retaining an interest, Jesse had moved uptown and, in partnership with W. A. Dunn, had opened a new saloon on the plaza), now operated by thirty-eight-year-old former LIT rider "Captain" W. E. Jenks.

Watkins, said East, "was a boy of good family from South Texas, but a fighter. It was an eternal triangle case. Gene was a

Jim East (right) and his deputy, David Martinez. Dave and his brother Guillermo were shot dead the day after this photo was taken. (Courtesy of the Haley Memorial Library, Midland, Texas)

Eugene Watkins, who shot David Martinez and was himself killed. (James H. East Collection. Courtesy of the Haley Memorial Library, Midland, Texas)

little bit stuck on a Mexican woman and David's brother also liked her. This brother, Guillermo Martinez, met Gene at a dance, and they got to shooting. David broke in and Gene shot him before he could open up, and then Guillermo, but they in turn killed Gene. My deputy, my only Mexican deputy of the Panhandle, did not last long."[6]

East's laundered version of events—many of his contemporaries strongly hinted the sheriff was snugly in Jesse Jenkins s pocket—is contradicted by Kid Dobbs's account. Tom Harris (and by inference Jesse Jenkins) "made the talk he had 57 of the best men in the Panhandle on his tally. . . . If anyone got in the way of

his plan or any other activities Harris would hold a meeting of his men and vote on a man to kill the objectionable person."[7]

One such was Guillermo Martinez, who had charge of the LS remuda. Watkins was "a Harris and Jenkins man," that is, a rustler. "Some of the maverickers and the Harris and Jenkins men would steal LS horses out from the range and ride them while they went about their mavericking."

One time Gene Watkins and another man took two LS horses and rode them to a frazzle. This angered the Mexican very much and he jumped out Gene Watkins and warned him definitely that he would

[158]

report him if it happened again. That caused hard feeling. In town one day they had a squabble and that settled it. That evening Gene Watkins was to work behind the bar in Hogtown. Jess Jenkins was dealing Monte in the northwest corner of the room. Watkins was leaning on the table. Sally Emory was there paying off. Martinez came in and stopped across the table from Watkins, looking at the game. Gene at once brought up the quarrel which the two had agreed to drop and so Martinez said "I'll give you the best I've got." Gene drew on him and fired. The powder burned and blinded the Mexican, but he killed Watkins as he was blinded. Jess Jenkins reached under the table and got a six shooter from a shelf and shot Martinez. . . . [Then] Wade Wood and Bill Fitzgerald went out and shot Jiermo's [Guillermo's] brother in the back five times. He was lying outside drunk. [In my opinion] Watkins had been voted to kill Martinez.

A few nights later, Woods and Tom Harris poured drinks into an old Indian who hung around the saloon and had witnessed the shooting. When he staggered outside and fell down drunk near where someone had been making adobe bricks, they "shot him all to pieces right there in the mud." As Dobbs put it in his spifflicated Spanish: "*Las muertas no hablan.*"[8,9]

The Indian was Pascual Montoya, "an old Navajo [who] was awfully bad when he got drunk. The Comanches captured him when he was a boy and traded him to Mariano Montoya as a slave for thirty head of sheep. . . . He ought not to have been [killed] in the way that he was. Whoever shot him had his six-shooter so close to him that it set his shirt on fire. He was drunk, had stumbled and fell in a hole

where someone had taken out mud to make adobe, and gone to sleep."[10]

In John Arnot's version, Dave Martinez, "hearing the shots, came running into the saloon with his gun in his hand. Just as he got inside the door, an unknown bystander shot him thru the head, he also dying in his tracks." Before the Martinez brothers came to the Panhandle, Arnot added perhaps by way of justification, their father had been shot and killed by some Mexicans near Floresville, in southern Texas, "which caused them to hate all natives from across the Rio Grande."[11]

Somewhat, but not much nearer to the truth, Jim East said, "It was generally supposed that a pretty tough character, a gambler called Fitzgerald, did it." In February 1885, however, the grand jury handed down no fewer than five indictments naming Jesse Jenkins, A. N. Fitzgerald, and J. E. Thompson as the murderers of Guillermo Martinez, and Lee Blackmore and Fitzgerald as the killers of David Martinez; there is no mention of the Indian. Jenkins and Thompson were found not guilty; the other three indictments carry no endorsement, so what final disposition (if any) was made of the case remains unknown. Watkins was buried alongside the unfortunate Dudley Pannell in the LIT plot on Cheyenne Creek, and the Martinez boys were laid to rest in the Romero cemetery. No one was ever brought to justice for their murder.[12]

The "System" was also behind the attempted murder of LS rider John Brophy, who—once again the dates are vague—pursued a gang of New Mexico rustlers who had stolen horses from McAllister's ranch near Endee, New Mexico.[13] Ignoring warnings from his bunkies that the rustlers would shoot him on sight, Brophy pursued the thieves and, ten days later, returned with the horses. "I just tracked till I found 'em, and it was a cinch getting 'em back," he said, and would say no more. Some time later, the rustlers sent Brophy word that when they met again they would kill him.[14]

"Harris and his men voted . . . to kill John Brophy," Kid Dobbs said. "In this case there was a big dance at an old Mexican's ranch at old Liberty. . . . The man selected to kill Brophy suggested they go outside the main dance floor and Brophy was suspicious enough to let the man go first. He was quick to see the man drawing his gun and Brophy threw down on him. Tom Harris . . . grabbed both guns and stepped between the two men, cautioning against any trouble. They would not agree to his suggestions so he said he would just . . . let them shoot it out. He held Brophy's gun longer, turning the other man's hand loose first. The man shot at Brophy and the bullet hit his big heavy watch case and just turned it into a saucer-like shape. The force of the shot knocked Brophy down but he fired and killed the other man as he was going down. [Then] out of a dark place . . . at least four men began shooting at him. . . . One of the bullets struck him in the back, giving him a terrible wound." Dobbs always believed it was Tom Harris who shot Brophy, but again it would appear no arrests were made.[15]

A quite different version of these events came from former Lee & Reynolds bullwhacker Manny Leppard, who told Brophy, "You'll dance with a bullet in your back if you go to that *baile* tonight." Sure enough, "the moment he appeared in the doorway a bullet hit him in the chest. As he toppled out the door a second bullet lodged in a hip. Apparently his assailant had great faith in his marksmanship and believed Brophy to be dead, for he rode away in the night and was never identified."

But Brophy was not dead. "A big silver watch he always carried in his vest pocket had caught the bullet dead center. The impact flattened the watch, drove shreds of clothing into his skin, and left a black and purple bruise twice the size of a saucer exactly over his heart. A Dr. Black came from Las Vegas, New Mexico, removed the bullet from John's hip, pulled the bits of cloth out of his chest, and took him to Las Vegas for additional treatment." When Brophy was able to travel he was brought back in a wagon to the LS, where he was nursed by Mrs. McAllister and the cowboys until his father and a sister arrived from the Dakota Territory and stayed until John no longer needed their care.[16]

Despite these occasional explosions of violence, Tascosa's residents insisted the town was a friendly, desirable place to live; in fact, sometime in 1884 Dr. C. W. Croft went so far as to pen a paean of poetic praise—perhaps *doggerel* would better describe it—to the town, which began: "If as travellers you land on Canadian's strand/ In the region of Tascosa City/ Just stop one and all, and give us a call/ Which you will after reading this ditty." There followed a versified listing of all Tascosa's attractions: Jack Ryan's livery stable, McMasters & Mabry's store:

> *They sell dry goods and notions, medical*
> *lotions*
> *Soaps and perfumes for the hair*
> *Canned goods of all kinds you surely will*
> *find*
> *From a strawberry to a pear*
> *Pickled tongue and pigs feet, potted ham fresh*
> *and sweet*
> *Tomatoes, corn, mushrooms and peas*
> *Lard, bacon and hams and all kinds of jams*
> *Up to that which is made by the bees.*

The Howard & McMasters store, Tascosa, ca. 1885. Left to right: Tobe Robinson with Rocker, "generally conceded to be the best saddle horse in the country"; unidentified man; James McMasters; Frank Valley with Ike Rinehart's race-horse "Spider"; two unidentified men in background; and Isaac P. Ryland standing outside surveyor Seth Mabry's office and the millinery and toy store owned by Charlie Ross and his wife next door. (Courtesy of the Haley Memorial Library, Midland, Texas)

Russell's Exchange Hotel, Tascosa. (Courtesy of the Haley Memorial Library, Midland, Texas)

A group of early Tascosans, ca. 1884. Standing (l. to r.):
W. Seth Mabry, Lucius Dills, L. C. Pierce, and the photographer, Fletcher.
Center row (l. to r.): Silas Hitchcock, Jim McMasters, and Cecil B. Vivian.
Front row (l. to r.): Dr. C. W. Croft, Brack Thomas, and Jim East (defaced; why is not known).
(Courtesy of the Haley Memorial Library, Midland, Texas)

"To the right from the door in house number four" was Henry Russell's Exchange Hotel, then the Dunn & Jenkins saloon and the others run by Lon Jenkins and Tom Emory, Frank James, and Jim East. Blacksmith Henry Kimball got a mention, as did Lugton's boot shop, the law firms of Vivian & Ryland and Wallace & Dills, the Cone & Duran store, and town druggist Dr. Charles Chepmell.[17]

Dr. Chepmell was an Englishman, "a fully credited graduate of a well-known medical college [who] became the proprietor of Tascosa's one and only drug store." The town's other "doctor," C. W. Croft, was "a little Cockney Englishman [who] had served as a nurse in some hospital a sufficient length of time to have, in some degree at least, earned that title. At any rate he came nearer to being a doctor than any other citizen of the village."[18]

The "citizens of the village" set their

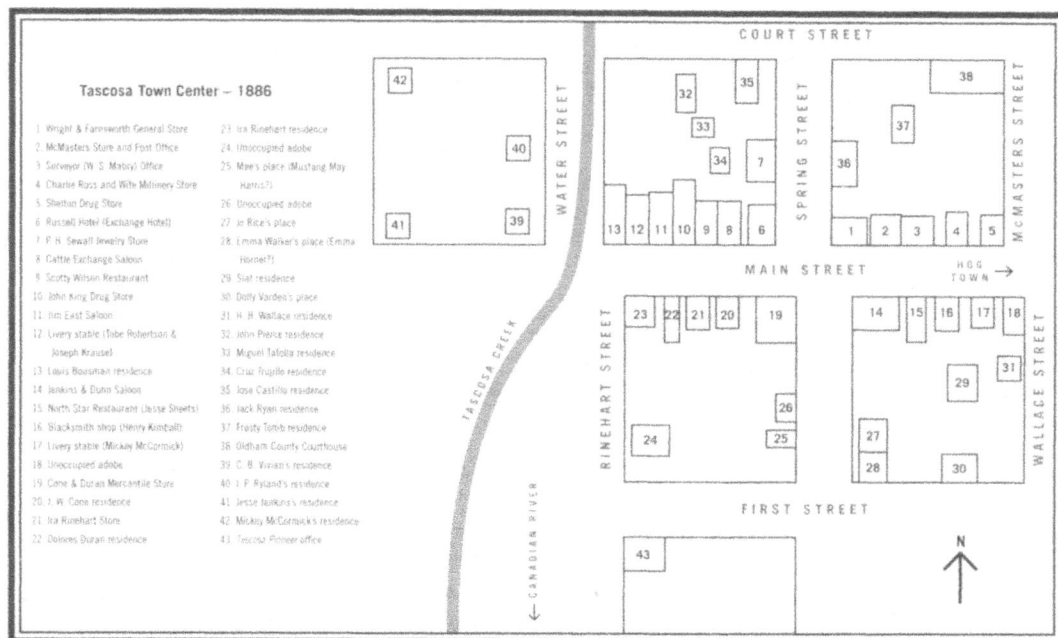

Street plan of Tascosa.
(After the map "Life in Tascosa," in John L. McCarty, *Maverick Town*, p. 191)

own rules, as Isaac P. Ryland (recently arrived from Missouri) discovered when he appeared before Justice of the Peace Scotty Wilson to defend a cowboy accused of raping a young Mexican woman. "They had Mexican witnesses and they talked back and forth, and come about twelve o'clock and Scotty couldn't get heads or tails of it. [He] told Ryland 'I'm tired of this goddamn thing. Jack [Ryan, the interpreter] you tell them copper-colored sons-a-bitches to get out of here or I'll throw them in jail and stay with their wives myself.' [Ryland] said next day 'That beat anything I ever seen or heard.' Ryland cleared his client allright."

JPs, it seems, could do as they pleased in Tascosa. On another occasion Ryland appeared before Henry Russell, who briefly occupied the chair because nobody

else wanted the job. "He was as ignorant as a goddam burro," an old-timer recalled. "There was a fellow stole a horse, and Jim East . . . caught him twenty miles above Tascosa. . . . So they tried him before Russell and he sent him to the pen for ten years. Ryland got up and said 'You can't send a man to the pen for that; I'll appeal the case.' Russell said 'Appeal? Hell, there's no appeal from my court!'"[19]

On high days and holidays, however, everyone minded their manners. "There were days when *all* and *all* was the word," Edwin Godwin-Austen recalled.

Xmas day, July 4th, District court, and the Commissioners Courts, at these convivial meetings we were *all* there, and every one had a time. . . . At the Christmas gathering the boys from the several ranches

[163]

Dr. C. W. Croft (detail from the photo of a group of early Tascosans). (Courtesy of the Haley Memorial Library, Midland, Texas)

would come to town and I have never seen such liberality extended to children as they did to the children of Tascosa. Not many toys in those days but useful articles were placed on the tree for the children, of course candy & fruit, the children were first, last and all the time. Then there was the July 4th celebration and everyone was there, not a picnic for the classes, all were on the same footing and such picnics Oh! Boy! The fried chix [*sic*] the pies the cakes, don't think we were out of the world we were in it, and best of all everyone in the best of humor.[20]

But out on the range, with rustling still a growth industry, the big ranchers were not "in the best of humor" at all. "Mr W. M. D. Lee, we called him 'Alphabet,' was

very arbitrary and wanted to put down what he called cow stealing," East said. "The boys hardly considered mavericking this." Not that the "boys" operating along the borders of the western counties were the only ones doing it; at the Turkey Track, now owned by the Hansford Land & Cattle Company, whose general manager, former Kansas City banker J. M. Coburn, knew little or nothing about the cattle business, cowboys Oscar Thoms, Tom Monroe, and John Cook were burning Cook's SAM brand on "every stray and every big calf they found."[21]

At the English-owned Rocking Chair in the eastern Panhandle—where Texan resentment against the milords of "Nobility Ranch" had grown like a festering sore—practically everyone who worked on the place was mavericking. "Men who had never thought of playing the cattle game in anything but a fair way grew to believe that it was perfectly [all] right to take all they could from the 'high-and-mighties' from across the Atlantic," John Arnot said. "They would 'get theirs' from these stuck-up nothings, declared a number of men from the ranch, and 'get theirs' they did, in clever and devious ways. . . . Men killed cows to maverick the calves, the most flagrant sin of all the cattle ranges. The brand was burned without scruple."

When Coburn brought in Cape Willingham from Mobeetie as range manager at the Turkey Track, Cook and his sidekicks hastily got rid of all their "hot" cattle in Kansas City. Cook found new employment at the LIT; Monroe and Thomas left the country. Another who decided to cut and run was LIT foreman Bob Roberson.

"He was working for the Prairie Cattle Company, but he had [an illegal] brand of his own," Lucius Dills said: "He says, 'Judge, I've got to get out of here. This thing is coming up and it can have but one ending. These boys are going to lose out and nearly all of them in here have helped me. They'll expect me in turn to go around and help them. I can't do them any good, but I can rope myself mighty quick, and the only thing for me to do is get out.' So he sold out his brand of cattle and moved and went to Arizona." It was an open secret that Roberson and Jesse Jenkins were in cahoots.

> Jess handled the Cimarron end of the business. They established a ranch out of the offspring of the LIT cows in there right below Kenton [Oklahoma]. They worked on the LXs and the LITs and the Syndicates but the breeding end of the Syndicates was too far away to work on the calves, so they worked on the steer outfit. So they made an 80 out of that XIT and put OH on the other side. They'd burn them in the winter and take them up in the summer and ship them out in the fall. They'd drive them to Liberal [Kansas] and ship them out. Robertson's [*sic*] right name was Bill Hughes. He got to be very wealthy and died at Clayton [New Mexico].[22]

The departure of a couple of thieves was not the major cleanup Lee was looking for. Now Jot Gunter's idea of bringing in a force of Rangers resurfaced, and after seeking and receiving the blessing of Governor John Ireland, the big ranches—notably the LS—agreed to create and finance a detachment of Rangers to put an end to the rustling. The man chosen to command it was Pat Garrett, with whom the Stockmen's Association had worked so successfully to put Billy the Kid out of business.

Still riding (fairly) high on his reputation as the man who killed Billy the Kid,

Tascosa lawyer Isaac P. Ryland. (Courtesy of the Haley Memorial Library, Midland, Texas)

Garrett was offered five thousand dollars a year if he would lead the "Home Rangers" (they were not, it seems, full-fledged Texas Rangers). "Hank Creswell, probably Tom Bugbee and the LS outfit, Lee-Scott, were the men who paid the Ranger company," Jim East said. "Lee . . . was the instigator of the whole business and was the heaviest payer." To clinch the deal, Jordan McAllister—acting for Lee—threw in a sweetener: if Pat took the job, he would sell him some prize cattle at a quarter of their market value with a promise to buy them back at full price when the job was done.[23]

Far too old a hand to rush into such a situation, Garrett hired John Meadows to make a reconnaissance. What he found out—which was that the big outfits were just as cavalier about branding other people's cattle as were the rustlers—cannot

LS ranch headquarters on the Alamocitas. Some believe this is a group photo of the LS Rangers and that the man on the extreme left is Jordan E. McAllister. If so, could that be Pat Garrett with the dog? (Courtesy of the Panhandle-Plains Historical Museum, Canyon, Texas)

really have come as much of a shock, but apparently it wasn't what Garrett wanted to hear. "You're working for as big a bunch of damn thieves as you're hunting," Meadows told him:

Nope, he couldn't think it. "I don't blame you for not thinking it," I says, "I wouldn't like to either, but I'll convince you of it. You're going to go down on the Canadian with me, and I'll show you something." . . . Me and Pat went down there and I showed him that old fellow McAllister. He was just as crooked as could be. I showed Garrett what I wanted him to see. "Now," he says, "you lay still. Don't you say nair a word. You leave this to me." McAllister, he went away to Cali-

fornia or someplace and was gone quite a little while, and W. M. D. Lee he wrote to Garrett. I read the letter myself. He says, "You break this mess up around Tascosa and I'll give you ten thousand dollars of my own money." . . . I says, "I wouldn't give you two cents for what you're going to get off him," and he never got a dime.[24]

In spite of Meadows's warning, Garrett signed up to lead the Home Rangers and "came over [from New Mexico] in the spring of 1884 and brought with him Barney Mason and George Jones. . . . The Rangers stayed at the LS ranch and it was there that the company was organized out of LS men." Mason ("a damned old no-good trouble maker," according to Jim

East) had worked undercover for Garrett during the pursuit and capture of Billy the Kid. George Jones was "a stinker."[25]

According to a May 19 roster sent by Garrett to W. H. King, attorney general of Texas, he enlisted Mason, Jones, Albert Perry, Ed King, Garrett H. "Kid" Dobbs, M. R. "Charlie" Resoner, and Bill Anderson. Perry, who had been working as a cattle detective, was made first sergeant of the company, which locals quickly and disdainfully dubbed "the LS Rangers." In his covering letter Garrett noted he expected to enlist two more men. One of these would be Alonzo "Lon" Chambers, who had been in the Billy the Kid posse; the other was John Lang. Everything was quiet, he reported. "I do not think there will be any serious trouble."[26]

"The first thing that Garrett did when he got to the LS, got his commissions and his men, was to tell the big companies that he couldn't do anything without papers," said Ranger Kid Dobbs. "[The Rangers] could follow the round-ups, keep trouble down, watch out for burned brands and things of that nature, but legal papers were necessary before they could do any serious work." Because only property owners could serve as grand jurors, "W. M. D. Lee bought up one-half the townsite of Tascosa and gave each of the [LS] men a deed to a lot in Tascosa."

Dobbs knew exactly what Lee was up to. "You boys just wait and you will see," he said. "You don't have that fine a courthouse without a grand jury. There is going to be a grand jury this fall and there will be more [true] bills passed than you ever heard about."

With Garrett around, "Harris and his men knew they had to be careful," Dobbs said. Their unease is nicely caught in a letter from Garrett dated April 28, in which

John Meadows. (Author's Collection)

he asks Governor Ireland to send him "a fugative list as I think it can be used to an advantage here, things are going quietly now the Rustlers are on stand still waiting for developments[;] they seem to think there is something going on that is not to their best interest but I think as yet have not learned just what it is. I expect to let it be generally known by the 15th of May what my business is here, the roundup commences at that time."[27]

The ranchers' next step was to get Governor Ireland to issue a proclamation "to all men to put off their six-shooters and other firearms. Up to that time they had been allowed [to carry guns] on account of the Indians. The proclamation was issued for the whole state and an effort was made to include Winchesters carried on saddles but this could not be put into effect."

Beginning May 1, 1884, Garrett's Rangers "went from wagon to wagon, seeing as many as 200 men in one day. Some of the boys would buck up but Garrett . . . would tell them it was the law and they must comply. . . . Most of the cowpunchers immediately ordered [under]arm holsters or scabbards and kept on carrying their six-shooters." Garrett simply told the boys, " 'Go wrap your gun up in your bedding, and you won't be bothered. But if I catch any one of you with your gun I'm going to pull him.' And that saved another war. . . . They got Pat Garrett just in time to save another Lincoln County War, and Pat he understood it, and he disarmed every doggone one of them."[28]

"Stolen cattle became so numerous along the Canadian River and over the line into New Mexico that it was impossible to track down the altered brands or find out who claimed them," says one account. Jordan McAllister of the LS, newly elected as a county commissioner and no doubt under pressure from Lee, leaned on County Judge Jim McMasters to outlaw what the big ranches declared were "maverick" brands. Notable among these were Tom Harris's T48—a shameless "improvement" of the LS brand—and the notorious Tabletop brand owned by Bill Gatlin and Wade Woods, which could literally obliterate any other brand extant. Any cattle wearing these outlawed brands were to be confiscated by the Rangers and would be considered the property of the county.[29]

On August 22, 1884, County Commissioners Warren Wetzel and Jordan McAllister promulgated an order that "all Mavericks found on the range within the jurisdiction of this county be held as strays

by the owners or lessees of the ranges upon which they are found." On October 16, the court ruled that "a suitable price be taken for all the burnt or maverick cattle now held as strays, said cattle to be driven to market and sold and the proceeds . . . placed in the treasury," such sales to be superintended by Ranger W. D. "Billy" Anderson. County Commissioner "Monchy" Russell was authorized to receive all such proceeds and bank them in Kansas City.[30]

One unlooked-for by-product of these new laws was that some three hundred head of impounded cattle deemed to have been mavericked or sleepered were driven to Springer, New Mexico, where their two herders sold them, pocketed the proceeds, and left for points distant. When others being held on the LS range were turned over to Justice of the Peace (and local butcher) Scotty Wilson to be kept for sale by the county, he butchered the animals and sold the meat. "The boys steal them from the ranches, the County steals them from the boys, and By God, I steal 'em from the County," he said unrepentantly (although he did cancel the county officials' meat bill).[31]

When the grand jury made its report in August, its frustrations were evident: "Witnesses, either from fear or moral perpetude [turpitude] are exceedingly loath to give any information," they complained, "and from this cause our investigations have not been as satisfactory to ourselves as could be desired. Crimes have been committed of the most deplorable nature and all our efforts so far have not proved entirely effectual." Nevertheless, as Dobbs predicted, the grand jury "passed 159 bills, most of them for [cattle] theft of one kind or another. Those were the papers which Garrett had wanted. . . . All he had to do now was to go to work making his arrests."

If Jesse Jenkins and his pals were worried, they gave little sign of it, perhaps because Jenkins was "tipped off from two to four days in advance of any expected trouble in Tascosa," said Kid Dobbs, who named Albert Perry as the informer, because he knew none of the other Rangers would have turned traitor.

Next, "[t]he Rangers got after Jim Strupes [Stroope] and Wade Woods [Bill Gatlin's partner in the Tabletop brand] wanted on complaint of [Tascosa rancher] George Isaacs who came to town and swore out papers against them for mavericking." Stroope stood trial and was cleared. "Red-headed, red-whiskered, tall, heavy-set" Wade Woods broke jail at Mobeetie and lit out; word came back down the trail that he drowned while with a herd in the Black Hills.

In his campaign against the rustlers [Garrett] "always worked with Jim East and his deputies and always gave them a chance to go with them on every raid or trip to arrest anyone." One of these, in February 1885, was the pursuit and capture of two of the more recalcitrant backsliders, Charley Thompson and Bill Gatlin. East and Garrett got word their men were hiding out in a rock house at Red River Springs, just over the state line. Because his father-in-law had built the cabin, Kid Dobbs was appointed scout.

"Garrett told us we would have to wait for a storm so that we could catch all the outlaws holed up in their homes," he said. "Hence we waited until there was a real storm on and we rode 60 miles one night. . . . When we got to the Canadian the ice was solid for six or eight feet from the bank and then was just icy slush. I told Garrett when we topped the hill that the outlaws would see us. He asked how far it was to the place by going up the river. I told him

two and one half miles. He said 'Put the steel to that horse and lead the way.'"

When they got close to the house, Garrett told them to get around to the windowless north side of the cabin, which was built into the side of a hill with the back roof not much more than three or four feet off the ground. As they deployed, guns drawn, they were seen by a fellow named Bob Bassett, who

> started running for the house throwing wood every which way. He yelled as he got inside that Pat Garrett was out there with 150 Rangers. Tom Harris came out of the house and said to Garrett: "What! Are you fellows up here for me again?" Tom had just beat the Rangers in a [court] case a short time before.
> "No, we are not up here for you, but do you have Wade Woods, Charley Thompson and Billy Gatlin in that house?" replied Garrett.
> "Wade Woods isn't in there, but Billy Gatlin and Charley Thompson are . . ." replied Tom Harris.[32]

Garrett called on the men in the house to surrender. Nine men came out with their hands in the air, but not Gatlin. "You fellows ain't gonna get me," he shouted. They learned later that he wouldn't surrender because he thought Jim East had come to arrest him for a murder he had committed elsewhere. After a while a tenth man, Charley Thompson, came out coatless and shivering. Garrett told him he could go get his coat if he promised to come back out again. When he got inside, however, he "got a pistol in his hand, partially opened the door, and told Jim East 'Jim, I told you I was going to give up, but I believe I'll stay with Billy and make a fight of it.' East [told him] it was foolish of him to get killed when he might beat the cow theft charge against him. Finally he got [him] crying and he said, 'Billy, I'm not going to lie to Jim East.' He gave up then and there."

But Gatlin was still inside. "I told Garrett that I had cow-punched with Billy," East said, "and that I did not believe he would kill me if I went in, but if he, Garrett, went in after him, Billy would kill him sure. The door stood about half open [and] I could see the brim of his hat and that he was sitting by the door holding his six-shooter pointing at it."

According to Dobbs,

They worried there all day with Gatlin until Garrett finally got mad and . . . told [Charley Resoner and Ed King] to go up on the roof and start jerking off the roof poles. They pulled off three poles when Bill Gatlin yelled for Jim East.

"I'm right here, Billy," replied Jim.

"You come in here and we will talk five minutes and then one or the other of us will die."

When the door opened Jim East hit it hard and quick with his Winchester pointed at Gatlin. [His deputy Charlie] Pierce was right behind him. [I] was just behind Pierce and the others crowded in so quick it was all over in a minute. Bill Gatlin was standing there with a gun in each hand, one hand crossed over and resting on the other, and both guns pointing at the nipples on Jim East's chest.

Gatlin asked Garrett how many men he had and Garrett told him, nine.

"Suppose I was to take two pistols and cut a road through you on my way to that river bank?" Gatlin said.

"Try it and we will do the best we can to see that you don't," Garrett told him.

Pat Garrett and friends at Tascosa, 1884. Rear (l. to r.): Seth Mabry, Frank James, C. B. Vivian, and Isaac P. Ryland. Front (l. to r.): Jim East, Jim McMasters, and Pat Garrett. (Courtesy of the Amarillo Public Library)

Gatlin turned to Jim East. If he surrendered, he asked, would East promise to protect him if there was any sign of a lynch mob? East replied that if it came to that he would not only give Gatlin back his guns but help him, at which juncture Gatlin surrendered his weapons and they brought him out of the cabin.

"After the arrest they built a fire, cooked some bacon and made coffee," Kid Dobbs said. Surely, as they did, Pat Garrett and Jim East must have experienced a very serious case of déjà vu.[33] "We took them to Tascosa and put a man named Jim Moore to guard them. He was no good but had been elected constable. We had leg irons on them but someone slipped a file in. I always thought it was Jess Jenkins, and they filed them off. We had them in an adobe house and they jumped out of a window and made a run. Moore shot at them but . . . Gatlin got away and later killed a sheriff at Buffalo [Lusk] Wyoming. He was caught, taken to Cheyenne, but broke jail and escaped."[34]

The Gatlin arrest was the last hurrah of Pat Garrett's Rangers, and the unit was disbanded in the spring of 1885. Garrett returned to Las Vegas to head up the Southwest Livestock Detective Agency, a short-lived organization set up by Lee and supported by LS riders to investigate rustling—and rustlers—to the west and north of the Panhandle. By all accounts Garrett was relieved in more senses than one, having come to believe the sole reason he had been hired was to give credibility to an organization whose purpose was not just to harass the rustlers but also, if the opportunity presented itself, to kill them.[35]

John Meadows later discussed the experience with him: "It was a cold day and we was in camp. He was looking right straight in the fire, and he busted out in a big laugh. He says, 'John, damn your crazy soul. You ain't got no sense.' He says, 'You ain't no damn fool either. By God, that's just what I done. I put down a damn nasty little war, and I wasn't even thanked for it, much less paid for it.'"[36]

The former Rangers went back to work for the LS up and down the river and often rode into Tascosa to sample its dubious delights, wearing out a little more of their welcome with every visit. It was claimed they threw their weight around, were arrogant and quarrelsome. They were resented for what they had done, for getting an easy ride from the big ranchers, and perhaps most of all for getting better pay than others doing the same work. "This was always aggravating to the boys who were mavericking," Jim East said. "It made many others, even good men, sympathize with the mavericks and it made the LS outfit very unpopular."[37]

Billy Jarrett, who arrived in Tascosa from Quincy, Illinois, in November 1886, unerringly pointed up the real reason for the enmity. The Rangers, he said, had thrown in with the thieves "and got their share all the while they were [being paid] to break up the stealing. Throw in with one side and whack up [with the other]. [That was what] caused all that trouble."[38]

Chapter 18

BILL GATLIN

BAD CLEAR THROUGH

JUST HOW potentially deadly was the confrontation between Pat Garrett, Jim East, and Bill Gatlin becomes evident when Gatlin's murderous career is examined more closely: Gatlin was one of the breed then prevalent on the West Texas plains who would kill a man to check whether the gun was loaded. Like half the population, he was using a "summer" name because he was wanted—as an accessory to murder—in that embattled center of East Texas feuding, Hamilton County. His real name was Daniel Bogan.

Immediately following the Civil War, two sets of gangs—the "Blue Ridge bunch" and the "River bunch"—vied ruthlessly for control of the county. The Bogan clan—originally from Alabama, where Dan was born in 1860—apparently supported the party led by one Crockett Hendricks, and according to oral tradition in Hamilton, one of the several Bogan brothers was involved, along with David L. Kemp, former John Chisum foreman (and killer) James Highsaw, and a man named Chapman, in the 1880 murder of forty-year-old local cattleman William Snell. Kemp, not yet eighteen, was charged with the murder

but acquitted when Dan Bogan and his four sisters provided him with an alibi. Shortly after this, Frank Cockrill, a deputy under Sheriff Sam Terry, went to arrest another of the Bogan boys (possibly Bill) on a charge of horse theft. "He stepped on to a high porch. Bogan had a pistol on the sewing machine, shot Cockerel [sic] in the hand, and it knocked him off of the high porch, and he fell onto the ground. Bogan then jumped on Cockerel's horse and dashed away, or started to. Cockerel got up, rested his pistol on a tree, took careful aim, and shot Bogan off the horse and killed him."[1]

It was not long before the Bogan clan was again in trouble; this time twenty-one-year-old Dan was at the center of it. On May 1, 1881, local rancher Daniel "Doll" Smith, well liked and recently married, drove into Hamilton for supplies, stopping at the Cropper & Hide meat market on the southeast corner of the square. Bogan and some other locals—among them Dave Kemp, now age nineteen—were in an adjacent saloon drinking. When Smith asked them to move their horses so he could load his goods

Daniel B. Bogan, alias Bill Gatlin,
alias Bill McCoy, alias ? (Courtesy of the
Haley Memorial Library, Midland, Texas)

David P. Kemp.
(Courtesy of the Southeastern New Mexico
Historical Society, Carlsbad)

Bogan refused and cursed Smith, telling him he had no business in that country. Smith again asked the party to move, when Bogan approached the wagon and taking therefrom a chair, brandished it about and threatened to brain Smith. The latter then became angry and descending from his wagon declared that while he desired trouble with no one, and was unacquainted with Bogan, he did not propose to be abused, and that if Bogan wished to fight with him he could, but the weapons should be fists. The desperado made no reply and Smith accused him of cowardice. Bogan then . . . drew a six shooter, but before he could use it Smith knocked the weapon from his hand and proceeded to thrash him.[2]

At this point Dave Kemp jumped down from his horse and hit Smith with his six-

shooter. The gun went off and Smith, not unnaturally assuming Kemp was trying to kill him, grabbed Bogan's gun, still lying where it had fallen. As Smith, who "was about 35 years old and very stout and muscular and weighed about 175 pounds," advanced on Kemp, "a slender stripling of a boy," the latter pulled the trigger four times, but each time the gun misfired.[3]

Now Dan Bogan, grabbing a heavy rock, ran up behind Smith and smashed him over the head. As the rancher reeled, Kemp put a bullet through his heart, killing him almost instantly. Amid all the excitement, Dan Bogan jumped on a horse tethered outside the courthouse and made good his escape, but "Kemp backed into the street almost into the arms of the sheriff [George N. Gentry] who grabbed and shook him, putting him under arrest," an eyewitness recalled. He was marched off to the local hoosegow, and on May 10 both men were charged with murder.[4]

Because of heightened local feeling, a change of venue was granted, and the case was tried with commendable dispatch during the June 1881 term of court at Gatesville in Coryell County. Even as the death sentence was being pronounced, Kemp—convinced he would be lynched as soon as they returned him to jail—"rose up and knocked back the officer next to him, jumped out of an upper window, broke his ankles, but got on a horse and started away. The merchants drew guns and he gave up" and was returned to jail.[5] After an appeal was allowed, he was tried again at Stephenville, Erath County, where a jury

found him guilty of murder in the second degree. On April 3, 1883, he was sentenced to serve twenty-five years in Huntsville Penitentiary.[6]

Dan Bogan had better luck: heading west, he adopted the name Bill Gatlin, turning up later that year in Tascosa accompanied by a trio of hard cases. Marion Armstrong, then operating a rowboat ferry across the Canadian, described their arrival:

I heard a call down there, and . . . found four men, Merida Taylor Crow, Bill Gatlin, John Page and another man whose name I do not remember. When they were all ferried across the river they all, of

Original Coryell County Courthouse, Gatesville, Texas, showing the window from which Kemp jumped. (Courtesy of the Coryell Museum and Historical Center, Gatesville, Texas)

course, went to the town and proceeded to full up on Spirits of Fermenti, with a remarkable degree of success. Of course, under such influence, they began to show their ugly natures. . . . Cape Willingham the sheriff had quite a tussle to get their guns away from them. It was later learned that all of these men were wanted in different parts of the United States, for numerous and various offences, mostly perpetrated in Texas and the Indian Territory.[7]

Gatlin signed on as a rider for the LS and seems to have kept out of trouble for a while, but only for a while; he may well have been a signatory of the manifesto that announced the famous 1883 cowboy strike. Shortly thereafter, the story goes, he and two other cowboys rode their horses in through the front door of a dance hall, then out the back, firing their pistols. When Gatlin and his pals came back around front and made as if to ride in again, the owner of the place bravely barred their way.

"You can't come in here again except over my dead body," he told them.

"That's easy enough," Gatlin said, and shot him dead.[8]

Once again Gatlin appears to have evaded justice by the simple expedient of skinning out, this time signing on with a herd going north via Dodge that was delivered at Deer Trail, Colorado, on September 25, 1883. Returning to the Panhandle the following year, when things had cooled off, Gatlin is said—although it seems an unlikely pursuit for such a bravo—to have operated an eating place in Hogtown for a while and, with backing from Jesse Sheets, to have bought or run a saloon in Upper Tascosa.[9]

What is more certain is that with his partner Wade Woods, Gatlin set up a

rustling operation on the New Mexico side of the state line and, as we have seen, got started on some serious stealing. Since no formal documentation of all these events appears to have survived, it remains unclear whether it was for killing the dance hall owner or for his rustling proclivities that warrants were finally issued for Gatlin's arrest. Not that it matters: within twenty-four hours of his being arrested by Garrett and lodged in the new stone jail at Tascosa, Gatlin escaped and skinned out yet again, this time adopting the new traveling name of William McCoy.

He may have again signed on with a herd going north, or maybe just headed for the far country alone; in Tascosa it was believed he had teamed up with an old Texas buddy named Tom Nichols (now using the alias Tom Hall), who was foreman of the Keeline ranch, near Fort Laramie in Wyoming, said to be run by fugitives and ex-convicts from Texas. In fact, until 1886 when the Fremont, Elkhorn & Missouri Valley Railroad reached Lusk, McCoy worked for Quint Pennick, foreman of Luke Voorhees's LZ ranch at Rawhide Buttes. It may safely be assumed that during his stint there McCoy, as he was then known, continued moonlighting as a rustler, because by the time the rails reached Lusk, he had enough money to open a saloon and livery stable in partnership with John Hogle.[10]

Situated about forty miles north of Fort Laramie at a spot where the Texas Trail crossed the Cheyenne-Deadwood road, Lusk had the usual end-of-track town population mix: miners, Texas cowboys, saloonkeepers, gunfighters, gamblers, pimps, prostitutes, and various other varieties of camp follower.

On October 9, 1886, an individual known as "the Stranger" arrived in town, left his horse in Reddington's livery, and had a few drinks at Johnny Owens's place, where he made the mistake of telling one of the girls he was a horse thief, one of a gang camped near town. The girl passed this information to City Marshal Charles Trumble, who arrested the Stranger and then swore in a posse to round up the gang. When no gang was found, Trumble threatened to hang the Stranger unless he told where his pals were.

When the shaken Stranger confessed the story was a hoax, Johnny Owens persuaded Trumble to release him, and all concurred that by way of apology they should take him on a tour of the town's drinking establishments. At Whitaker's saloon Trumble asked the Stranger if he was friend or enemy and got a somewhat noncommittal answer. Trumble drew a revolver and repeated the question.

"I will have to be a friend to you now," the victim mumbled.

"You damn coward," Trumble rasped. "Are you a friend or not?"

"Do you want the truth?" the Stranger replied. "Well, Charley, I don't like you."

There was only one way such an insult could be expunged; so Trumble shot him dead.[11]

Trumble was immediately arrested and confined in the county jail at Cheyenne to await trial. He was still waiting when another equally senseless murder was committed in Lusk. This time the victim was City Constable Charlie Gunn, and the assassin was Bill McCoy.

Lusk's first deputy sheriff, former Texas cowboy, cattleman, and saloonkeeper Charles S. Gunn, thirty-two, was appointed in November 1886 at a salary of one hundred dollars a month. "Tall,

well built and every inch a man" and "not addicted to a single bad habit,"[12] Gunn enforced the law rather more energetically than the good people of Lusk actually wanted, and they petitioned to have him replaced. The new incumbent, sworn in after the new year, was none other than Johnny Owens. A former scout for Sterling Price during the Civil War, he had been in Wyoming since the mid-1860s, first as a stagecoach driver, trapper, cattleman, and later saloonkeeper-gambler. He came to the job fresh, as it were, from running the notorious Three Mile Hog Ranch near Fort Laramie. The displaced Charlie Gunn stood for the post of constable and was elected.[13]

There was bad blood between Gunn and McCoy, thought to date back to their Texas years, a theory to some extent rein-

Johnny Owens. (Courtesy of the Wyoming State Archives, Department of State Parks and Cultural Resources)

forced by the recollections of a Hamilton County old-timer: "Bogan left the county and went to Arizona and was running a saloon. A little scrubby fellow named Gann . . . went into the saloon and recognized Bogan. For some reason, or no reason, Bogan shot and killed him. He was sentenced to hang but influence got him [out] of it." Substitute Wyoming for Arizona and Gunn for Gann, and it all fits together: Gunn recognized McCoy and let it be known around town that his real name was Dan Bogan, wanted for murder in Texas, where one of his brothers was in jail for horse theft and another had been killed by a sheriff when he resisted arrest for the same crime.[14]

McCoy put the blame for spreading the news about his past on J. K. Calkins, publisher of the *Lusk Herald*. Accompanied by fellow Texan Sterling Ballou, he went to Calkins's favorite watering hole, pulled a gun, and invited any supporter of Calkins —Charlie Gunn, for example—to step up and see what happened. One of the Cleveland brothers, who owned the saloon, came up from behind the bar with a double-barreled shotgun and invited McCoy to take a hike. Anyway, he told McCoy, Gunn was out of town. Backed down but unfazed, McCoy and his pals began riding horses on the sidewalks and threatened to shoot anyone who interfered.

On his return Gunn told McCoy he better not shove any citizens around when he was in town. McCoy told him he'd do whatever the hell he liked, whether Gunn was there or otherwise. To prove the point, he and his pals—named Pennick, Jester, and Braziel—took to shooting off pistols in the early hours of the morning, then denying any involvement when Gunn came running.[15]

On Friday, January 14, 1887, there was a dance in Jim Waters's saloon. Because women partners were scarce, men were issued numbers and admitted onto the floor in order. When McCoy tried to jump the queue, floor manager Jim Waters held him back, and a scuffle ensued. Charlie Gunn stepped in and told McCoy if he was looking for a fight, now would do. Further trouble was—only just—avoided, but the hard feelings persisted.

About nine o'clock the following (Saturday) morning McCoy and two pals, Phil Watson and Jesse Lockwood, went into Waters's saloon. A little while later, Charlie Gunn came in. McCoy was standing at the bar, his revolver held behind his back.

"Charlie," he said, "are you heeled?"

"I'm always heeled," Gunn replied.

"Then turn her loose," McCoy said, and immediately fired, the ball passing entirely through Gunn's body in the region of the abdomen. Gunn fell forward on his hands and knees, his six-shooter dropping from his breast to the floor. He picked it up and commenced to raise slowly to his feet, when McCoy placed his six shooter near Gunn's temple and fired the second shot. The ball passed entirely through his head, lodging under the skin at the rear. McCoy then went out, ran to the rear of [his own] saloon, jumped on a horse and started north-east, waving his six-shooter above his head. Deputy Sheriff Owens was sick, but immediately jumped up and he and John Steffen and one or two others opened fire on the murderer. Out near the jail the horse fell and McCoy was unable to catch him when he got to his feet again. Owens commanded him to "throw [his hands] up" which he did.

Hit in the arm and shoulder by two buckshot balls, McCoy made no attempt to resist as he was taken prisoner. "I guess you've got me, boys," he laughed, "but I sure would like to fight it out with you on even chances."

He was taken before Esq. [H. Roe] Kingman, examined and committed. . . . The jail being still incomplete, there was no alternative left but to guard the prisoner. Mr. Owens stayed up until midnight, when he retired, having been sick ever since his return from Cheyenne. He left six men to guard the prisoner, and had him handcuffed and shackles riveted to his ankles. Owens returned again at 1:15 and found the prisoner asleep. He examined everything in the room to discover if a file was hidden anywhere, but finding none, he retired again after seeing that the shackles were secure. He was awakened at 3:30 and on going to the room where the prisoner had been confined, found the window—which had been securely nailed down—raised and McCoy gone. Between the two visits it had snowed and blowed very hard and no track was left to tell which way the prisoner had gone. Two of the guards, Mr. [Tuck] Jester and Mr. Phenix [Quint Pennick], were arrested on the charge of aiding and abetting the prisoner's escape and bound over to district court under $500 bonds.[16]

Owens must have been really sick, not to say blind and deaf, if he didn't know all six guards were friends of McCoy's (Quint Pennick, for example, had given McCoy sanctuary when he first arrived in Wyoming) and that in between Owens's visits they had even arranged for McCoy's mistress, Emma Riggs, to sleep with him before his escape. A reward of five hundred dollars for his capture was posted, and a description circulated: age about

twenty-four; wearing dark clothing; height about five feet nine inches; weight about 156 pounds; light complexion; scar on the back of the neck caused by a kick from a horse. Sheriff Seth K. Sharpless, who came up to Lusk with four deputies, sent several posses out to scour the area, but no trace of McCoy was found.[17]

A week later, however, the fugitive sent word to Johnny Owens that his wound was infected; he wished to surrender but was afraid of being lynched. As assurance that no such thing would happen, he was met by a protective posse of four men, each armed with two pistols and a shotgun (McCoy was even given a pistol to use in his own self-defense), brought into town, and (in one account) lodged under guard in the back room of Sweeney's saloon. In another, Owens let McCoy "go from saloon to saloon treating all those who were willing to drink with him, having at the same time weapons of defense upon his person, there was not a businessman in town but that thought it was an outrage that the murderer was not locked up in the jail, especially as it had been finished only a day or so before. They had another reason also, as McCoy had made the remark that 'there was a couple more that he wanted to get.'"[18]

On Friday, February 4, 1887, Owens delivered McCoy and Phil Watson (charged with being an accessory) to the county jail in Cheyenne, where, according to the local press, McCoy had a steady stream of visitors, both male and female. Arraigned before Chief Justice McGinnis on June 3 on a charge of murder in the first degree, he pleaded not guilty and his trial was set for June 16.[19]

It was apparent from the heavyweight legal team handling his defense that McCoy either had plenty of money or someone with plenty of money was backing him. W. W. Corlett, dean of the Wyoming bar, led the defense, with John W. Lacey and John A. Riner, two of the best—and most expensive—lawyers in Cheyenne as his backup. They first requested a rescheduling of the trial because of the absence of material witnesses. This was followed by a motion to request a new judge, which was granted; after further deliberation, trial was scheduled for Monday, August 27, Samuel T. Corn, associate chief justice of the 3rd District Court in Evanston, presiding.[20]

The territory had subpoenaed W. T. Cropper, owner of the meat market outside which Doll Smith had been killed, together with Hamilton County sheriff James A. Massie and Judge (later Senator) Charles K. Bell, who had prosecuted in the Dave Kemp trial. Before they even left Hamilton County—*sub judice* be damned—they supplied full and lurid details of McCoy's murderous past to the Wyoming newspapers, which immediately passed them along to an eager public. Seeing these three in court for the first time, McCoy "weakened perceptibly and became very nervous." His unease, it transpired, was not due to fear of extradition to Hamilton County (which was what Bell had in mind) but because he believed Cropper had been deputized to take him back to the Panhandle to answer for the killing of the dance hall proprietor.[21]

On Sunday, August 7, an abortive escape attempt was discovered and scotched by Sheriff Sharpless; since McCoy was one of the ringleaders, it is clear he didn't think much of his chances before a jury, although it is difficult to imagine how the court could be persuaded in the wake of such newspaper coverage that any jury it empaneled could be impartial.

The trial finally went ahead on August 29 before Judge Corn; Walter Stoll, later to become famous for prosecuting Tom Horn, would lead for the state, with U.S. Attorney A. C. Campbell assisting.[22] After two days of defense motions and jury selection, the prosecution presented its case, commencing at 11:00 a.m. and continuing until evening. The following day the defense called its first witnesses, some of whom had already appeared for the prosecution. Late in the afternoon, McCoy took the stand. His testimony was to the effect that Gunn had told him at the dance he could whip him for five dollars, and

> that after the dance Gunn, Waters and others came into his [McCoy's] saloon, got into another spirited wrangle, and before this affair was over the crowd went out of the saloon, after which he heard Waters or Gunn calling him out and through the window saw two revolvers. He started to go out but was held back by Peter Sweeney. . . . [Next morning at Waters's saloon] Gunn came in, having looked through the glass front. McCoy met him and said "good morning, Charlie," to which Gunn replied in a gruff voice and McCoy, convinced Gunn had come to fight him, said, "Are you heeled?" to which question Gunn replied "I am always heeled" and instantly both drew their revolvers "at about the same time" but McCoy got his out first, fired and shot Gunn, who fell to the floor, got up on his knees, picked up his revolver, pointed it at defendant, who fired again and shot Gunn through the head. He then went out of the saloon and being afraid of getting killed, went to his stable, saddled a horse, mounted it without stopping to put on the bridle but was fired at and eventually arrested. He escaped because he was afraid of being lynched.[23]

On Tuesday, September 6, the jury retired and took less than two hours to find McCoy guilty as charged, and he was sentenced to be hanged. The defense immediately filed for a new trial, and McCoy was returned to the county jail.[24] Even while his lawyers were preparing his defense, however, McCoy's friends had decided they were not going to leave him to either hang or rot in jail. Accordingly, "an old friend of Gatlin's & foreman on the Keeline ranch hired a safe blower to commit a petit crime in Cheyenne, so as to be put in jail, in order that he could saw the steel bars of the prison and liberate Gatlin."[25] Unlikely though it sounds, that seems to be exactly what happened. On July 15, after shadowing him for several days, police officer F. C. Van Thomason arrested one James Jones, alias Carr, on suspicion of having stolen a gold watch and other trinkets from the home of one Hattie Hammond Jones failed to produce bond and was consigned to the county jail to await trial.[26]

Within weeks, the pretrial escape attempt already described was attempted, but failed. With the hangman fashioning his noose, as it were, springing McCoy now became a priority. Shortly after 8:00 p.m. on October 4, 1887, Mrs. William Morgan, who lived nearby, saw four men clamber to the ground from the one-story brick building in the rear of the courthouse and then disappear. When the alarm was raised, Sheriff Sharpless hurried to the jail to discover that horse thieves Charles H. LeRoy, William Sterry, "burglar, safe blower and all around crook" James Jones, and—of course—Bill McCoy were missing. They had somehow sawed a hole in the roof of the "escape-proof" metal cage that was their cell, climbed out through the skylight above, and disappeared.[27]

A crowd quickly gathered near the jail, and when Sheriff Sharpless called for possemen, there were so many volunteers not enough horses or firearms could be found; it was nearly eleven o'clock before the posse actually left. Others were organized: one in the Fort Fetterman area; one at Laramie led by Nathaniel K. Boswell, chief of detectives for the Wyoming Stock Growers Association; and another in northern Carbon County led by Boswell's deputy Frank Canton. To what degree they were all motivated by civic duty or the fact that Governor Thomas Moonlight had posted a total of $1,500 in rewards ($500 for Bogan and Jones and $250 each for LeRoy and Sterry, with an extra $500 thrown in for Bogan—dead or alive—by Sheriff Sharpless) is not clear.[28]

In spite of this hue and cry, which even included a company of the 9th Cavalry from Fort Russell, no trace of the escapees was found. On October 8, however, Phil Watson delivered to Judge Lacey a letter in which McCoy commended him and defense counsel John Riner for the able manner in which they had defended him and closed by saying, "I thank you, Judge, but I have concluded to take charge of my own case. Yours respectfully, Bill McCoy."[29]

When information came into County Attorney Stoll's possession that suggested McCoy was hiding out somewhere on the Platte with Tom Hall, alias Tom Nichols, the former Panhandle cowboy who had masterminded his escape, he called in the Pinkerton Detective Agency, which assigned Charlie Siringo to the case. Posing as a fugitive from Texas, Siringo managed to infiltrate the gang and was told by Hall that a professional jailbreaker—probably Jones—had been paid five hundred dollars to get jailed so he could cut McCoy free. After hiding out in the hills until the posses gave up hunting for him, McCoy had left for points south.

In New Mexico, Siringo claimed, McCoy stopped over at the Portales Spring camp of his old Tascosa buddy Len Woodruff, with whom he had been in correspondence. He had with him a twelve-year-old runaway boy from Utah who wanted to go with him to South America, but he killed the youngster, Woodruff said, because he knew too much. Whatever the truth of that tale (and there are numerous holes in it), McCoy/Gatlin/Bogan headed for New Orleans and from there to Buenos Aires.[30]

Although there is little more than circumstantial evidence to support the proposition, he may have returned to the United States about 1890 and headed for newly organized Eddy County, New Mexico, where, according to Dee Harkey (grinding numerous axes of his own), "the majority of the first county officers elected were crooks and criminals, and especially the sheriff," who just happened to be Bogan's old pal Dave Kemp.[31]

Historians are still arguing over whether David Leon Kemp was a badman-killer who had gone straight or a badman-killer who was pretending to go straight.[32] Having earned a conditional governor's pardon in 1887, and following his release from Huntsville Penitentiary, Kemp worked for a while in Nolan and Fisher Counties with his half-brother Walker Bush; during this period, on a trip to Louisiana, he met and on Christmas Eve 1888 married Elizabeth Keene, the daughter of a prominent landowner. In 1889 they settled in boom-town Eddy, New Mexico, where Kemp quickly became a leading figure among the sporting crowd.[33]

In April 1890, having announced his candidacy for sheriff, he sought the restitu-tion of his civil rights, without which he could not run for office; his lawyers submitted two petitions for absolute pardon, and with commendable celerity Texas Governor Ross approved both.[34]

Kemp was elected sheriff of Eddy County in December 1890. His close friend Tom Fennessey served as county clerk. When Walker Bush (reputed to have killed seven men) arrived at Eddy late in 1892, Kemp installed him as chief deputy and chief of police. The Kemp circle was soon being referred to locally as "the courthouse ring."[35]

When his second term as sheriff came to an end in November 1894, and precluded by territorial law from standing again for office, Kemp supported the candidacy of Walker Bush, but John D. Walker was elected. When the following January Bush also lost his bid to become justice of the peace, it was clear the power of Kemp's "courthouse ring" was on the wane.

In October 1895, while working as a cattle detective for the Texas–New Mexico Cattle Raisers Association, James Leslie "Les" Dow arrested Kemp and Bush for rustling a calf; Kemp was discharged the very next day, but Bush was bound over for $750 and only acquitted two weeks later. Tit for tat, Kemp accused Dow of stealing twenty-three of his cattle, but Dow convinced the court that the animals were improperly branded. From then on there was bad blood between the two men.[36]

In 1897 Dow became sheriff of Eddy County, taking office on January 1. Just seventeen days later, as he stood reading a letter outside the Eddy post office, Kemp shot him, inflicting a mortal wound. Kemp and a man named Will Kennon were arrested and charged with murder, but it took eight months for the grand jury to indict them. The trial venue was changed to Roswell in Chaves County, where, in March 1898, Kemp pleaded self-defense and was acquitted; by all accounts almost everyone involved perjured themselves. Judge A. C. Campbell, who had assisted prosecutor Stoll at Bill McCoy's trial in Cheyenne and who attended the Kemp hearing, claimed Kemp told him McCoy had been present throughout the proceedings. "I did him a good turn once," Kemp is alleged to have said, "and I needed his assistance in case I was convicted" (to engineer an escape, presumably). Thinking to collect the outstanding Wyoming reward on McCoy's head, Eddy County sheriff Cicero Stewart asked Campbell if he would identify the fugitive. The learned judge said the only way he would identify Bogan was if he saw him in a coffin and could be absolutely certain he was dead.[37]

It was suggested that perhaps Kemp's pal Will Kennon was Bill McCoy using yet another alias, but it does not seem very likely. McCoy's—or rather, Dan Bogan's—death, whenever and wherever it happened, is, like the man himself, still a mystery. In December 1899 a Wyoming newspaper reported he had been killed by a Mexican near El Paso; in another memoir he was said to have been killed in New Mexico about 1905 when a bucking horse threw him, breaking his neck. In 1931, however, Judge Campbell, who might have been expected to know, claimed Bogan had "married, owned a ranch someplace in Texas, and was branding mavericks and raising Hoover Democrats"; this possible outcome is partially borne out by John Arnot, who believed Bogan became a "well to do cattleman" but places the ranch in western New Mexico.[38]

After a failed attempt to establish a town (modestly christened LaKemp) in Oklahoma, Dave Kemp, who had remarried (for the fourth time), moved the whole settlement a few miles south into Lipscomb County, Texas, where he founded the town of Booker and where he was a sometime deputy sheriff. He died there of a heart attack on January 4, 1935.[39] It would be a pretty safe bet that if anyone on earth knew what happened to Dan Bogan, a.k.a. Bill Gatlin, Bill McCoy, and possibly Will Kennon, it would have been Kemp. But like many another true Texas feudist, David Leon Kemp took his secrets—and they were many—to the grave.

Chapter 19

1886

"ILL MET BY MOONLIGHT"

S PRING OF 1885 saw the Panhandle's largest roundup ever, and Tascosa's saloons and whorehouses welcomed its cowboys with round-the-clock service. "There must have been a hundred men in town every night," John Arnot said.

The six saloons did a "land office" business as there were about twenty wagons engaged in the round-up and they had to be restocked with provisions and corn for the teams, while many of the boys had to replenish their wardrobes. There were outfits from the Arkansas, Cimarron and Beaver Rivers, North Palo Duro on the north; also from New Mexico and the south Plains engaged in this work, besides the local Canadian River ranch outfits. There would be from ten to twenty men with each wagon and each man would have from seven to ten horses assigned to his mount.[1]

Warned to "stay on their own side of the street" in this volatile environment, but reluctant to miss the fun and unwilling to back down from the challenge implicit in the warning, the former Rangers (still on the LS ranch payroll) kept pushing their luck, and pretty soon they were being contemptuously referred to as "barroom gladiators."

On the other side of the Tascosa street were gamblers like "Squirrel-Eye" Charlie Emory and his brother, "Poker Tom" Emory; John Gough, a.k.a. "The Catfish

━━ ⌘ ━━

Charlie Emory (Courtesy of the E. A. Arnim
Archives and Museum, La Grange, Texas)

Louis Philip Bousman, 1934. (Courtesy of the
Haley Memorial Library, Midland, Texas)

of Sheriff Jim East with a shotgun. Dixon had not been the target, East told Dobbs: "You are the man they are after. Tom Harris and his men are out to get you."[2]

Not surprisingly, Louis Bousman, an open supporter of "the System," put the blame for the poison in the atmosphere squarely on the former Rangers. "The trouble would never have developed if [Garrett had stayed on]," he said, "for he wouldn't have stood for their cutting up, raising the devil, and trying to run it over everybody. A few months [after Garrett left] the trouble came on."[3]

"The trouble" seems to have centered around Bousman's pal and Jenkins's henchman Len Woodruff, "a likable young fellow . . . of medium size, with dark brown hair, blue eyes, and the same pleasant smile for everyone." Born in Illinois about 1860, he had been a cowboy for the LIT and the LS and had worked as a mail carrier in Oldham County before becoming a bartender at the Dunn & Jenkins saloon. Len also co-owned a small herd with Theodore Briggs, who "had a little bunch of cattle . . . and they got so they wandered off. He didn't have any horses . . . so he gave Len Woodruff a half interest in that bunch of cattle to look after them for him. Len . . . gathered them in and he might have gathered something else."[4]

It certainly looks that way. In April 1885 Woodruff, granted a change of venue from Oldham County and defended by none other than Charles Jenkins, had been tried in Wheeler County for theft of cattle and acquitted. The fact the Rangers had already nailed him for mavericking would alone have been enough to cause friction, but there was an additional irritant: former Ranger Ed King was currently shacking up with Sally Emory, who'd been Woodruff's main squeeze until he got cozy with her

Kid"; and Louis "The Animal" Bousman —a twenty-eight-year-old gambler who, like Lon Chambers, had been a member of Pat Garrett's posse. Bousman, who often stood in as a part-time jailer and sometimes deputy sheriff in Tascosa, had a particular loathing for the former Rangers, but when it came to a fight, any LS man would do. Kid Dobbs, now running an LS wagon, recorded a couple of occasions when he stood Bousman off after the gambler pulled a gun on LS rider Jack Dixon. Both situations were defused by the arrival

rival, Rocking Chair Em. Local gossips believed Sally persuaded King someone ought to settle Woodruff's hash.[5]

No matter how often his wagon boss, Kid Dobbs, tried to tell him "what the country was like, the danger in it and the foolhardiness of King going to town and getting into trouble," his warnings fell on deaf ears. Just a little later, King was about to ride his horse into the Dunn & Jenkins saloon, but Dobbs talked him out of it. "They then went in to get a drink. Old Man Dunn was in a chair and went behind the bar. Ed King jerked his pistol, saying in his drunken voice, 'Old Man Dunn, if you want to fight, get your gun smoking.'" Somehow disaster was again averted.[6]

In another incident Jim Gober claimed the Catfish Kid tried to maneuver him and a very drunk Harris into the sand hills between Hogtown and Tascosa, where two LS Rangers, Fred Chilton and George Jones, were waiting to kill Harris. Gober "spoiled their aim at Harris, who was running in a circle and returning their fire." After firing some fifteen shots, the Rangers ran out of ammunition and fled as Gober hustled Harris into the shelter of a nearby stable. A few moments later, Jim East and his deputy, L. C. Pierce, arrived on the scene accompanied by three Rangers from Seymour come to arrest Harris for horse theft, a charge, Gober said, cooked up by some LS cowboy, seeking to make a reputation with Lee, who informed the authorities that five (in fact it was ten) horses Harris had bought the preceding fall bore the brand of a ranch near Seymour, Baylor County. Gober made an impassioned speech:

> East, you are the high sheriff of this town and county. You are well aware . . . that it is a long established custom that if a man

Len Woodruff. (Courtesy of the Haley Memorial Library, Midland, Texas)

in your official territory is wanted in some other county or state, the foreign officer calls on you to make the arrest. Now I don't know what these three rangers want with Harris, but I do know that two of the LS Rangers tried to assassinate him a few minutes ago, and Harris has no way of knowing but that these three strangers are on the same mission. Harris has always respected you, your deputies, and the law, as I guarantee he will this morning, but I suggest that you ask these strangers to go back to the courthouse while you and Pierce go to Harris, who will, I promise, peaceably submit to arrest.

As Gober finished speaking, Jesse Jenkins thundered up to the rescue on Harris's horse, riding "Indian style" on the side away from the lawmen, and ran into the stable where Harris had taken cover. When finally East agreed to send the Rangers who were with him back to town, Harris and Jenkins came out of the stable and the sheriff then arrested Harris.[7]

"The three Seymour rangers took Harris, accompanied by Jenkins, back to Seymour," Gober said, "where Jesse had wired his brother [Charles], an able lawyer of Brownwood, to meet them. They made bond for Harris, . . . having thirty days to wait for grand jury action. . . . When the district [U.S.] court convened, the grand jury failed to indict Harris for lack of sufficient evidence, so Jenkins and Harris . . . started back to Tascosa."[8]

Gober's highly charged account of this alleged assassination attempt is not substantiated by any of the other Tascosa memoirists. That the LS men might have tried to kill Harris is believable enough, but that the Catfish Kid—very much in the Jenkins-

Harris camp—would have set him up does not make sense. That the mood of the times was confrontational, however, is not in question, as yet another Kid Dobbs tale further illustrates. Tom Harris sent him a message he had better quit the LS or else. "I'm my own man and I'll work for whoever I damn please," Dobbs told the messenger. "You tell Tom Harris if he wants trouble to name his weapons and the ground he wants to fight on." Two weeks later, Ed King and Dobbs ran into Harris, "who was very friendly and said 'Hello, Kid, how are you?' 'I never felt better nor had less,' Kid Dobbs replied, looking Tom straight in the eye and keeping his hand near his gun. That was the only exchange [between them] and Harris never crossed Kid again."[9]

Clearly, then, the LS men were as ready for trouble as any of the Jenkins-Harris crew, and the one who seems to have gone most particularly out of his way to give

Jim Gober. (Courtesy of James R. Gober)

L. C. "Charlie" Pierce, deputy sheriff (detail from the photo of a group of early Tascosans). (Courtesy of the Haley Memorial Library, Midland, Texas)

offense was Ed King, a former detective for the Stockmen's Association, born and raised in New Mexico's Colfax County. Men who worked with him said he wasn't a badman, "just another cowpuncher, afraid of nothing, loyal to friends and, sober, could hold his own with a six-shooter."[10] But not with liquor, which made him aggressive and reckless.

On one occasion King and Frank Valley (whose family name was actually Vallé) went to a dance at Romero's, where they caught the Catfish Kid and Louis Bousman trying to scare their horses away. The two cowboys "kicked those two men clear down to the Main Street in Hogtown, cussing them for everything they were worth."

In Bousman's version, things went exactly the other way:

King came in and said, "What in the hell did you fellows turn our horses aloose for?"

"I didn't have a damned thing to do with turning your horses aloose," I said. "Listen here, you god-damned sonofabitch, you get your men and get out of town."

He turned to his men and said, "Look out and keep all the dogs out from behind us."

Jess Jenkins was behind the bar, and he pulled his six-shooter out from under the bar and said "Yes, and there may be some more dogs around here."

When King looked around I threw my six-shooter down in his face and cussed him and said, "You god-damned dirty sonofabitch, you get out of here and get your men with you," and they got out of the saloon.

Of course, Bousman was a shameless liar, but in the final analysis it doesn't really

Frank Valley, or properly, Vallé. (Courtesy of the Haley Memorial Library, Midland, Texas)

matter who was telling the truth; what all these incidents demonstrate is the intensity of the antipathy between the two factions.[11]

By now it was early March, when in the Panhandle the annual appearance of parasites known as "heel flies" would drive cattle to distraction by clustering on and biting their heels. Seeking relief, the cattle headed for water; if the refuge proved to be boggy or "quicky"—the banks of the Canadian were notorious for quicksands— the animals would get stuck, chill rapidly, and die or drown. Dragging them out was gut-wrenching work, and every cowboy hated it, but it had to be done, so four-man line camps were set up for "bog riders" who "rode the river" extricating any bogged cattle they came across.

King, Valley, Fred Chilton, and John Lang of the LS were riding the river at

John Lang. (Courtesy of Miles Gilbert, Jr.)

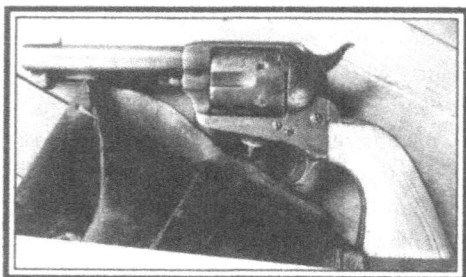

John Lang's Colt SAA,
the gun he used in the fight at Tascosa.
(Photograph by Miles Gilbert Jr.)

Jerry Springs, about four miles west of Tascosa. This meant they could spend an evening in town and get back to camp comfortably by midnight. For a while they did just that, but after weeks of bog riding they decided what they really needed was less work and more rest and recreation.

Perhaps if Jordan McAllister had been around his boys might have stayed out of trouble, but on January 26, 1886, the LS manager had married Luanna McCalister, a friend of his niece he had met in Iowa two years earlier; perhaps understandably the misdeeds of his riders were not his first concern at this time.[12]

So with the fleshpots of Hogtown all too temptingly near, the four men, and King in particular, began spending more time in town than at work. After literally carrying him back to camp on two separate occasions, Kid Dobbs once more implored King "to stay out of town and thus out of trouble. King was a good enough cowman and had been a good ranger in the year they operated, but he didn't get along too well with town people."[13]

For certain—perhaps thanks to Sally Emory's pillow talk—he didn't get along with Len Woodruff, who was tending bar and looking after Jesse Jenkins's interests in the Dunn & Jenkins saloon during the owner's trip to Seymour and Hallettsville with Tom Harris. There was almost a flare-up on Friday, March 19, when King and two other LS men came into town and taunted Woodruff, calling him "Pretty Len" and slapping his face. Outnumbered three to one by men itching to shoot him full of holes, Woodruff had to take it, but that didn't mean he liked it. It's not difficult to imagine him sharing his grievance with his buddies Bousman, Emory, and the Catfish Kid, nor to imagine them deciding that it was time someone taught the "barroom gladiators" a lesson.[14]

The following evening, March 20, 1886, King, Valley, Chilton, and Lang rode in and joined the crowd heading for Hogtown's Saturday night *baile*. John Lang, the only LS man who ever got the chance to tell their side of it, recalled a very drunk

Jesse Sheets and his family. Left to right: Ella, Sarah, Billie,
Martha, Jesse, Henry, and David. Sarah later married Matt Atwood.
(Courtesy of the Amarillo Public Library)

Frank Valley standing on a table singing "Little Nell of Narragansett Bay," egged on by an equally inebriated Fred Chilton. In the early hours of Sunday morning, March 21, they left the dance and rode in bright moonlight to Upper Tascosa.[15]

Accounts of what happened next vary wildly. In one, Valley and Chilton dismounted, handed the reins of their horses to Lang, and went into the Equity Bar as Lang and King turned back east on Main, intending to hitch the horses behind the McMasters store. As they passed the Exchange Hotel, Sally Emory appeared and called out to King, who dismounted. Handing his reins to Lang, King put his arm around Sally's waist and they set off on foot toward her place.[16]

In the Dunn & Jenkins saloon on the plaza were Len Woodruff; Texas-born Charlie Emory; his thirty-one-year-old brother, Poker Tom; twenty-four-year-old John B. "Catfish Kid" Gough; and Louis Bousman. Out in a back room of his adjacent North Star restaurant, Jesse Sheets had settled in for the night to keep an eye on an employee who he thought was robbing him. It was to prove a fateful choice of location.

As King and Sally Emory neared the saloon, someone in the shadows called out something, in response to which King stepped up on the porch. Without warning a gun blazed, and King fell, shot in the face, blood gushing from his mouth. As Sally Emory ran off as fast as her feet could carry her, Len Woodruff came out of the saloon, jammed the barrel of a Winchester against King's neck, and pulled the trigger before retreating inside.

Lang, seeing Woodruff administer this coup de grâce, hastily tied up the horses and ran into the Equity Bar yelling, "Boys, they've killed Ed! Come on!" Chilton and Valley grabbed their guns and with Valley in the lead ran across to the cramped yard behind the Dunn & Jenkins saloon. As Valley charged in, guns blazing, Len Woodruff took two bullets, one through his belly and the other through his groin, and Charlie Emory went down with a chunk shot out of his leg. Woodruff staggered to the rear of the saloon and half fell inside, closing the door. Firing several shots at the door first, Valley pushed it open. A rifle blazed, and Valley fell dead on the doorstep, shot through the left eye.

In almost the same moment, Jesse Sheets opened his back door to see what the shooting was about. As he did, Chilton, who had taken cover in the shadows at the corner of the saloon, shot him, crowing, "I got that sonofabitch Louis Bousman!" A second later, rifle shots from the woodpile cut Chilton down.[17]

Finding himself suddenly the sole and badly outnumbered survivor of the LS quartet, Lang fled up Spring Street pursued by a hail of lead. Now Jim East and his deputy, twenty-nine-year-old former LIT cowhand Charlie Pierce, came running, and as Pierce warily approached the rear of the saloon a man ran out from behind the woodpile. Pierce yelled at him to stop, but when he kept going the deputy loosed off a shot, and the man—it was the Catfish Kid—went down. Thinking he was dying, Pierce left him where he had fallen. He would later discover to his considerable chagrin that the Kid had been play-acting and had not received a scratch.[18]

The foregoing is what might be called a consensus: details vary from account to account. Jim East, for example, remembered:

> Woodruff and Charlie Emory met King right in the open, and the shooting that took place there was the only shooting that was in the open. Woodruff shot King and as he fell he shot Emory, I suppose. At

least there was no one else there to shoot Emory. . . . Lang, an LS man, gave the alarm to Chilton and Valley . . . who were playing poker in the Equity Bar . . . [and] ran out hurriedly. By then Woodruff was in his room. They ran over and found King dead and Lang told [them] that Woodruff had killed him. . . . As the LS men started across the little space between Woodruff's room and the saloon they were cross-fired upon by two men, Louis Bousman and the Cat Fish Kid, a man named Gough. I saw a man running down towards the river and I ran after him. I threw down on him with a *double barreled* shotgun. He threw down his six shooter and up with his hands. I kind of wanted to kill him. It was the Cat Fish Kid."[19]

It has to be said this version sounds no more likely than the earlier one: for one thing, the Kid, who had a crippled right foot and badly deformed toes, couldn't have been much of a runner, although even a man with a crippled foot can move pretty fast if the bullets are flying thick enough. Suffice it to say that, one way or another, the Kid was out of the frame.

Many years later, Louis Bousman went into self-aggrandizing detail about his part in what happened that murderous moonlit night—although how truthfully is another matter. Woodruff, he said, had just closed up the saloon, and he, Woodruff, Charlie Emory, and the Catfish Kid

> were standing out by the hitching rack in front of the saloon . . . [when] King and his men, four of them in all, came from over towards Jim East's saloon on the north side of the street, and King walked up to us and said, "Well, I see you sons-of-bitches are still in town," and the shooting started.

One of them hit Charlie Emory through the arm, and we backed up behind the saloon, and they kept following us up. We went back to a house that Jess Jenkins had behind the saloon, where Len Woodruff slept, and went inside. Ed King rushed us and I shot him with a .45–60 Winchester and blowed his head off. Fred Chilton rushed us, and I blowed his head off too. The others were shooting too, and Lang run like a son-of-a-bitch. Jesse Sheets stuck his head out of the back door of his restaurant . . . and they killed him thinking it was me.[20]

In John Lang's slightly—but only slightly—more trustworthy version (the only one giving the LS point of view), he and King were crossing the street to get their horses from the hitching rack outside the Dunn & Jenkins saloon when Woodruff, Emory, and Bousman stepped from the shadows, their six-guns drawn. "What does this mean, boy?" King rasped and tried to grab Woodruff's gun. As he did Emory shot him in the face; mortally wounded, King managed to fire one shot that severely wounded Woodruff, but not badly enough to prevent his putting another bullet into the Ranger. As King fell, John Lang whirled to see the Catfish Kid aiming a rifle at him from point-blank range. As he went for his gun Gough fired but missed; backing away, Lang emptied his gun and then turned and ran toward the Equity Bar as the Catfish Kid retreated toward the Dunn & Jenkins place.

In the Equity Bar, Chilton and Valley were playing cards; within moments all three of them were back on the street. Chilton ran up to the dead body of Ed King and took it in his arms, rocking it, crying, and shouting. Seeing movement in the darkness, and thinking it to be Louis

Bousman, he raised up and fired. The bullet tore through Jesse Sheets, who died almost instantly. Valley and Lang had meanwhile run to the rear of the saloon. As they came into the open space the door swung open and a fusillade of shots ripped into Valley. Simultaneously shots came from behind the woodpile. Lang turned and fired in the general direction of the hidden shooters, and the shooting ceased. Then, as Fred Chilton came around the corner, tripping over the bleeding body of Frank Valley, another burst was fired and Chilton went down with three bullets in his back and one in his left side.[21]

The gunfight was over.

After a while, townsfolk edged warily onto the street with lanterns "to see who had kicked the lid off Hell." Boss Neff and Sam Dunn had been sleeping in a room in back of the Exchange Hotel when they were awakened by the gunfire; after Justice of the Peace Edwin C. Godwin-Austen had assembled a coroner's jury and viewed the bodies, they "got out and helped carry in the dead. Valley was shot near the nose and lived several hours. Sheets fell at the rear door of his café, shot high up on the forehead. Ed King was shot near his mouth. Fred Chilton was dead, shot through several times." Valley lingered for an hour or more; finally, his feet had to be tied together to keep him from thrashing around as he struggled for breath.[22]

"Pierce took Emory, who laid where he was shot, and me to jail," Louis Bousman said. "Len had been hit by a bullet that struck his watch but turned into his stomach. He walked out to the [Theodore] Briggs place on the Cheyenne two and a half miles from town. It was about day and they caught the Catfish Kid and then went up to Briggs' and got Len and put him in jail. They tried to get the bullet out but never did. Mrs. Sarah Bousman went up and talked to them at the jail, and Len, who was, on the bed, said 'I may die, Sallie, but I got some of the sons-of-bitches.' "[23]

That last line gives the lie to Bousman's vainglorious claim to have killed both King and Valley; if he shot anyone at all it was probably Chilton, and in the back at that (although the Catfish Kid seems a likelier suspect). There seems little doubt that Woodruff killed King, but throughout all the accounts assiduously collected over three decades by Amarillo newspaperman John L. McCarty, grass-roots historian Earl Vandale, and that redoubtable researcher J. Evetts Haley, there are dark hints to the effect that there were other shootists involved and that maybe Jess Jenkins was one of them and Tom Harris another.

Jim Gober fixed as "the night before their arrival" the same Friday that Ed King and his buddies roughed up Len Woodruff in the Dunn & Jenkins saloon, thereby placing both Harris and Jenkins in Tascosa before the gunfight and leaving open forever the question of what part they might have played in it. Jenkins himself (needless to say) claimed he and Harris were "camped some thirty miles from there, enroute to Tascosa from Seymour." Tascosa's first historian, who suspected they had a larger hand in these events than history gave them credit for, said only, "Several did put in a few shots who have never been mentioned as participants." Elsewhere, however, he noted carefully that when he asked if Harris was in the fight, Kid Dobbs replied, "If Harris was in the fight he came in that night. He had a quilted arm scabbard made in 1884 and the officers found it on the foot of that bed the next morning."[24]

"Mackenzie and me went up there," another eyewitness recalled. "Right across the street [from where the fight happened] . . .

they carried these men over and laid them side by next. We went over and [got] a wagon sheet and put it over them. They all had their boots on except Jesse Sheets— four great big men."[25]

Saloonkeeper A. L. "Bud" Turner and former buffalo hunter Tobe Robinson, now working for the LS, were deputized to search for Woodruff and the Catfish Kid. Although no one yet knew it, Woodruff was at the Briggs ranch about a mile and a half out of town. The Catfish Kid later surrendered to East and his deputies.

"H. H. Wallace came to my house at about 2 a.m.," Godwin-Austen recalled:

[He] said Get up quick there are 4 dead and don't know how many wounded. I got up and went down town, things looked threatening [but] the Sheriff . . . appointed many deputies and no further trouble occurred.

All were in jail but Len Woodruff [who had] managed to get as far as Mr. Briggs ranch on the Rica, where he was found by Mr. Pierce . . . badly shot up and did not expect to live. . . . I was sworn in as J. P., a jury summoned and off we went. There were 42 witnesses examined by H. H. Wallace, and as far as I am able to judge, it was the most wonderful court ever held, deputy sheriffs all round armed to the teeth, but everybody else disarmed. Gus Fritchie [Fritsche], bookkeeper at the Wright & Farnsworth store was clerk of the court and to save time he . . . headed all the papers with the names of the several witnesses i.e., so and so being duly sworn deposeth and saieth. &c &c. Now when Louis Bousman . . . was brought to the bar of Justice and told to tell all he knew, he did and a lot more, being a prisoner he should not have been sworn, but told the evidence he gave would be used against him in the trial and then he did not know as much as formally [*sic* formerly] and I had also forgotten some things. When a lawyer for the defense asked me if I had sworn him (Mr Bousman) I could not remember and the evidence was thrown out [because] it was so contradictory, he had made too [many] opposite state-

ments and could not be believed, the trial ended with a hung jury. . . . Mr Woodman was the prosecuting attorney and . . . Mr Charles Jenkins in the defense also Mr Temple Houston.[26]

LS rider Dunk Cage, who had been in town right after the fight and had seen the bodies, nearly killed a horse getting out to

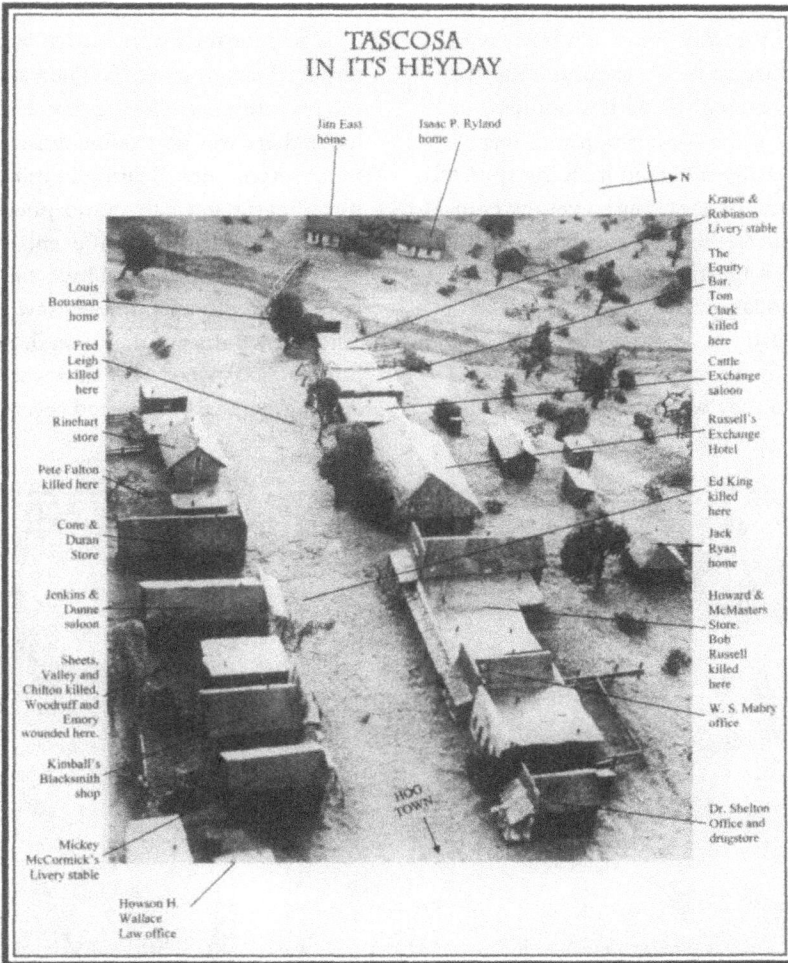

Tascosa in its heyday.
(From the diorama in the Tascosa Museum at Boys Ranch.
Labels added by the author.)

the Alamocitas, arriving there about two in the morning. Jordan McAllister and his wife at once roused the entire outfit and headed for town. When the phalanx of more than fifty LS cowboys rode in, a rumor swept through town that Tobe Robinson, who had gone looking for Woodruff the day before and who would later succeed East as sheriff, had told McAllister that all he had to do was say the word and the boys would hang every member of the opposition and burn every saloon in Tascosa to the ground. That they were angry enough to do it is not hard to believe, but if the proposition was ever voiced, McAllister vetoed it on the spot. "'I don't want to do anything to get the company in bad," he told his men. "If you boys want to do it I'll stay with you in money matters and lawsuits."

This wasn't at all what the boys wanted: they expected McAllister to lead them, since they were thinking about the reputation of the LS outfit. When he backed down, and that is what Dobbs very emphatically said he did, "they gave it up and let it go." A week or so later, when W. M. D. Lee arrived from Dodge City, he endorsed McAllister's decision, concluding that the fight had been a brawl and had not involved the protection of LS property. "If it had," he told his men, "I would spend every dollar I've got to prosecute it."[27]

The four men were buried later that day. Perhaps because East had sagely taken the precaution of closing down all the saloons there was no trouble during the funeral ceremonies. Bearing in mind how extraordinarily tense the atmosphere must have been, his account of events is oddly muted. "My deputy and I were armed and we had no difficulty. I never saw a more orderly crowd than at the funeral. Some of both factions were there and were armed, and if anything had started several would

Jesse Sheets's graves at Tascosa (left) and Roswell (right). (Author's photographs)

have been killed. . . . Of course there was bitter feeling and if anybody had started anything there might have been more killed than the night before."[28]

Horrified that her husband might be interred alongside the men who had killed him, Sarah Sheets insisted his grave be dug for him a little distance from theirs, and that was done. Judge Howson Wallace—the town had no minister—"read the funeral service from the Episcopalian prayer book"; and without so much as a hint as to whether they appreciated the irony, a large crowd—pretty much the entire population of the town—sang "Nearer My God to Thee." A separate service was then conducted for Jesse Sheets.[29]

The sandstone gravestones erected for the men who died "ill met by moonlight" have all but disappeared, but new markers stand in the old Boot Hill cemetery as a monument to one of the West's bloodiest and most controversial gunfights. One of the four graves, however, is empty: the body of Jesse Sheets, archetypal innocent bystander, was exhumed by his family in 1928 and reburied in Roswell's South Park cemetery next to his wife and adjacent to the graves of many early pioneers who had known Pat Garrett and Billy the Kid.[30]

Chapter 20

THE ANIMAL AND THE CATFISH KID
"US FELLOWS HAVE TO STICK TOGETHER."

Louis Philip Bousman, self-proclaimed hero of the great Tascosa gunfight, provided history with several versions of his life story, all of them different, few of the "facts" susceptible to documented confirmation. In one he claimed his father died when he was young, and when he found his mother was to marry again he ran away to Texas, severing all connections with his former life. In another he got somewhere nearer the truth when he claimed he lived in Virginia until he was "a good sized boy and then moved to Missouri, where I lived until after the Civil War. Then I moved to Grayson County, Texas, when I was about fourteen years old. Later I went to Cherokee Nation, close to Fort Gibson, and stayed a number of years. When I was about twenty years old, I moved to . . . Tascosa."[1]

Three years later, however, he told an entirely different—and completely false— tale about coming to Texas with his parents "when I was just a little lad . . . [living] around there until I was about sixteen years old with . . . friends as my people died when I was small. They came to Oklahoma some time in the early days and set-tled around the Osage and Creek Nation. I went back to Texas with some people and settled . . . in Oldham County."[2]

The facts are somewhat different: Lewis P. E. Bousman (the name is given in the census as Bowsman) was born in Kanawha County, Virginia (now West Virginia), on January 4, 1857, the son of Joseph Henry and Anna Mary Bousman. He seems to have had little or no formal education and even late in life could barely write his own name. Farmer Joseph Bousman was the heir of Philip Bousman, a substantial landowner whose will, probated in 1860, listed some twenty slaves as part of the estate, a large number for that part of Virginia. It would appear Joseph and his wife sold their inheritance almost immediately; in 1860 and now thirty, he was farming on 160 acres in Lafayette County, Missouri.[3]

According to his son, when the Civil War began Joe Bousman "joined the Confederate army and served under [Sterling] Price. He served all around over that country and was home every once in a while. Just right after the surrender, we went to Colbert's Ferry, Grayson County, Texas. My father run a grocery store and saloon right there on the banks of the [Red] river, at the old crossing . . . [for] about two years." From there they moved to "Chickasaw country" and later "north to Shell Creek," five miles west of Fort Gibson, Indian Territory, where "about four years later" (that is, 1873–74) Joseph Bousman died, leaving his wife, Anna, with three sons and three daughters. The family moved to the Creek Nation, north of Tulsa, and then moved again, renting a farm "at the Childers Settlement. We raised just corn and oats. We were there several years and sold our cattle by driving them to . . . Parker . . . on the Verdigris River. . . . I stayed on the farm until I was about twenty years old [then] I went up through Wichita and on to Dodge City and hired there to George Littlefield. . . . This was in 1877."

At this point, all Bousman's recollections become vague, perhaps because he had a lot to be vague about. One authority suggests he was a member of Dutch Henry's band of Kansas horse thieves, which might explain why "Lewis Bousman alias Charles Smith" was arrested on May 27, 1879, at Kiowa, Barber County, Kansas, and there identified as Frank Johnson, "a young fellow well known at Kiowa." He was reportedly taken under arrest to Topeka, which indicates that his offense was a serious one, but there is no record of the disposition of the case, which in turn suggests Bousman may have been on the run when he signed up with the LIT. At one point he claims to have married Sarah Cruce at Tascosa when they were both nineteen years old, that is, in 1878; again, the facts are somewhat different.[4]

Sarah Eldora "Sally" Cruce was one-quarter Choctaw. Her father was Tom Cruce, born in Virginia but resident in Lampasas, Texas, when he married Katherine Rutledge, a Choctaw who later

became the notorious prostitute "Indian Kate" at Fort Griffin. Kate and her daughter, "Swayback Mag" (this would appear to have been Sally), take up considerable space in early Shackelford County court records; Kate is said to have had her own adobe brothel, "a known rendezvous for criminals." They were said to have been living with a renegade black man named Cato, but whether he ever actually existed is open to question.[5]

Following tribal custom, Sally married John Bolt when she was thirteen, and they had two children: Hannah Annie, called "Nanke," born September 7, 1873; and Edward Forrest, born the following year. One day while Sally was hanging out washing, Bolt rode out and never returned. In 1880 she was living in Mason County as Sarah Cruse, divorced with one daughter, Nancy ("Nanke"); her son is not listed. She married Louis Philip Bousman in Tascosa on July 19, 1882.[6]

Bousman appears to have met her when he was in the Fort Griffin area "gathering trail cattle on the general roundup that had been lost from Littlefield's herd. One of those trips, in 1882, I bought a hack and brought my girl, who was living at [Fort] Griffin, through to Tascosa. I took her over to Jack Ryan's house until I could get a house and then we married. . . . Henry Kimball, the blacksmith, married us. . . . Mrs. Bousman was a widow with two children when we married, but both of these children are dead. [She] lived at Fort Mason for fourteen years. Her mother was Mrs. Kate Gamble [Gamel]."

Why Bousman lied so much and so often is unclear; maybe it was his nature. Sally was not a widow when he married her. The two children referred to were not dead; Edward lived to June 30, 1922, and Hannah Annie died October 7, 1925. From

Sally's marriage to Bousman there were four further children: Frank James, born April 12, 1886; Kinnie, born 1890; May, born August 4, 1891; and Kate, born 1892.[7]

While it is tempting to speculate that Bousman might have been involved in the Mason County troubles (as were the Gamel brothers, kin to his wife's mother), by the fall of 1880 he was working for the LIT and was one of the "Panhandle posse" that captured Billy the Kid. Following that experience, he made his living as a gambler, odd-job man, and occasional deputy/jail assistant for Sheriffs Cape Willingham and Jim East.

"He was just an old rounder," Harry Ingerton said. "He was as lazy as the dickens and quite a liar, would rather lay around and drink whiskey and let his wife wash [laundry] for a living. He had a quarterbreed Indian wife, a very handsome woman. She washed for them there and brought them something to eat and got water and wood from the creek. He would lay around and sweat poker games and monte games. Most of the time he would lose." John Arnot was more succinct. Bousman, he said, was "about as sorry a man as you could find."[8]

On May 10, 1886, Bousman was arraigned before Judge Frank Willis and pleaded not guilty to murder charges; next day Charlie Emory and John Gough, the Catfish Kid, did likewise. In the case of the *State of Texas* vs. *John Gough* for the murders of Ed King and Frank Valley—and later, those of Bousman and Emory for the murder of King—their attorneys pleaded for a change of venue on the grounds that it would be impossible to assemble an unbiased jury in Oldham County. District Attorney Woodman concurred, and the trials of the three men were scheduled for the first Monday in July 1886 in Clarendon, Donley County.

Such sketchy court records as have survived indicate that although the grand jury (foreman Dunk Cage) had also indicted him to appear before the Oldham County court commencing May 3, 1886, Woodruff was still too ill to be moved (in fact, he was confidently expected to die), so his case was postponed. The records of the commissioners court show sums paid for board and also medical treatment for prisoners Woodruff and Gough.[9]

Charlie Emory's attorneys were Jim Browning and the firm of Scott & (Charles) Jenkins, who also represented Gough. Court records suggest the defense was going to show that although Emory and the Catfish Kid had been present when King was killed, Woodruff had done the actual killing; Bousman was home in bed. Browning also planned to use Gough

James N. "Honest Jim" Browning.
(Courtesy of the Panhandle-Plains Historical
Museum, Canyon, Texas)

as a material witness for the defendant; he would testify that in fact Emory "took no part in [the] difficulty . . . but was himself murderously assaulted and shot down by one John Lang."[10]

On the Fourth of July, as Mobeetie celebrated Independence Day with the Panhandle's first ever barbecue, a very mixed bag of Tascosans set out for Clarendon. Among them were Edwin Godwin-Austen, George Jones, Dr. Shelton, Sam Dunn, Jim East, Charlie Pierce, John Lang—principal witness for the prosecution—and what the *Pioneer* tactfully described as "many more besides," a noisy party that included (for the defense) Jesse and Lon Jenkins, Josie Rice, Sally Bousman, "Rocking Chair Em" Horner, and Nancy Bolt (Bousman). They reached Clarendon July 7, and Jim East handed over their three prisoners to Sheriff Al Gentry.[11]

Determined to see "the boys" got a fair shake, Jim Gober "took up a collection at the LX ranch, then swam the Canadian River when it was out of its banks with waves of sand and water rolling twenty feet high; went to the T-Anchor ranch and took up another collection; from there to the Frying Pan and collected there; then to Tascosa by swimming the river again, and turned over to Jessie [*sic*] Jenkins something over $600 for Woodruff's defense." Like Bill Gatlin in Wyoming, "the boys" had the best lawyers money could buy. In the Panhandle, as in Wyoming, the "System" looked after its own.[12]

On June 24, prior to the opening of the trial, Emory's attorney, Charles Jenkins, asked the court that writs of attachment be issued to enforce the attendance of witnesses Thomas Nolan, George Doty, Dan Coigne, and William Stokes. He expected to prove through the testimony of Nolan, he said, that the killing of King had not been

premeditated (although how he proposed to do so when he must have known that local stonemason Nolan had died following an accident the preceding month, is another matter); through Doty's evidence that prior to the gunfight King had made threats against the lives of the defendant and others; through the testimony of Coigne that Louis Bousman was not present when King was killed, but at home in bed; and through Stokes that the killing of King, if done by the defendant and others charged, was done in self-defense.[13] To everyone's surprise, the State of Texas next announced it would offer no evidence against Bousman, who had agreed to turn state's evidence, that is, to testify against his codefendants in return for a dismissal of the charge of murder against him. The case was abandoned forthwith, *nolle prosequi*.[14]

Next, its having become apparent that the four "vital" witnesses for the defense would not be forthcoming—as already noted, one of them, Tom Nolan, was dead—Jenkins and Browning argued successfully that their clients could not expect a fair trial in Donley County either. Accordingly, on December 27, 1886, District Attorney L. D. Miller granted yet another change of venue, the trial to be held this time in Mobeetie, Wheeler County, during the January 1887 term of court.[15]

On November 10, however, in spite of an earlier assurance by Dr. Shelton that Woodruff would be fit to make the journey, the *Tascosa Pioneer* reported he was still too ill. When the Wheeler County District Court convened, Woodruff was granted bail in the sum of five thousand dollars, and the case was continued to the following April, as were those of Emory and Gough.

At long last in Mobeetie John Lang had his day in court, supported by Lee and

Wheeler County Courthouse and jail, Mobeetie. Bousman, Emory,
and Woodruff (and quite a few others) were tried here.
(Courtesy of the Panhandle-Plains Historical Museum, Canyon, Texas)

Scott and defended by Temple Houston. "My client," Houston thundered, "was *forced* to join the fight in an attempt to apprehend parties who had shot down a friend. He arrived at the back of the saloon only after Jesse Sheets had been slain."[16]

When Bousman took the stand, "the lawyer said: 'Now, Louis, you know that in turning state's evidence, you are lying, etc.' and . . . Bozeman ('who didn't have much sense [but] wasn't afraid of anything') replied; 'Yes, I know, but us fellows have to stick together.' The lawyer said also: 'You know that in return for this lying you are to get your freedom.' Bozeman acknowledged the promise."[17]

When the absence of important witnesses for the state again occasioned a request for postponement, "the trial soon reached the wrangling state. There were several bitter clashes among the prosecution [Woodman and Houston], the defense [Charles Jenkins and L. D. Miller], and Judge Willis. Woodman was charged with carrying a pistol, and he and Miller were fined twenty-five dollars for using abusive language toward, against, and concerning each other, each of them guilty of contempt of court." At the end of it all, two of the cases were thrown out and all three defendants (it is not clear whether Woodruff ever actually appeared) were admitted to bail "because the State had exhausted its right to continue, and processes issued for witnesses had failed to produce them for more than two terms," and "further, the witnesses have left the State and gone to parts unknown." The case was closed; the defendants were released.[18]

Because Wheeler County court records

Cone & Duran store, Tascosa. Jim East is on the right in the doorway.
It would probably be safe to assume Messrs. Duran and Cone are the gentlemen in suits.
(Courtesy of the Haley Memorial Library, Midland, Texas)

for that period have not survived, we will probably never know what evidence—or lack of it—persuaded the court to render that verdict. More than likely it was because "sentiment in the Panhandle was strong against sending a man to the penitentiary who had killed another man in combat. Murder was a different thing. But it was hard to convict for man-slaughter as they would generally plead self-defense."[19]

So the somewhat tarnished "knights of the green baize" walked free. Bousman, having sold out his pals and thereby lost whatever credibility he might formerly have had, moved to Mobeetie, where he worked "about a year" as a stage driver for wagonyard owner Bert Clampitt. Charlie Emory seems to have faded quietly from the scene; he does not appear again in the annals of Tascosa. He later returned to

Fayette County, where he died on March 9, 1895.

The Catfish Kid, however, backslid almost immediately; three months after his acquittal, he was back in front of a judge, this time for allegedly robbing but certainly killing "an inoffensive old man from Springer, New Mex. [who] had sold some property up there and was going to Mobeetie to some friends."[20]

At about two thirty in the morning of June 22, 1887, former cowboy Lige "Dobie" Lynch and James Thurber, stage drivers from Potter County, were making beds for themselves near their wagons in back of the Cone & Duran store when a man came over and asked them if there was any place he could sleep; they told him he could use the corner of the corral. Soon after this, the Catfish Kid appeared, a pistol in his hand. Hearing a noise in the corral, Gough asked what it was, and Thurber said, " I think it is that Dutchman," to which the man responded, "If you want anything out of that Dutchman *you can get it,*" and then they saw him coming toward them. "Hold up!" Lynch said, but the man did not stop. "The Kid then started toward him and throwed his gun in his face" and pushed the Dutchman back. Angry words erupted; as the two frightened freighters ran out of the corral they heard the Dutchman say, "Oh, don't," and then a shot. Crying for help, the Dutchman reeled out into the street and collapsed in front of the store, blood pumping from the subclavian artery, which the Kid's bullet had severed.

Isaiah Rinehart ran out into the street and found the man lying facedown but still alive. He sent his son Irwin to fetch Deputy Sheriff Dave Barker, but by the time Barker got there, the Dutchman was dead. Hurrying to the courthouse, Barker awakened Sheriff Tobe Robinson, and they both returned to the store. Nobody knew who the dead man was or why he had been killed, although word quickly spread that the Catfish Kid had "rolled" the old man for his money and killed him when he woke up during the theft.[21]

Meanwhile, the Catfish Kid had walked to Jesse Jenkins's cabin on the far side of Tascosa Creek, where he told Jenkins he had "struck a fellow and thought he had killed him. . . . He said the fellow was coming to him with a club, said he halted him and he would not stop." Jenkins "told him to go back and see if the man was dead[;] he come back and said he was shot through the shoulder. I said would it not be a good plan to get out, he said no there were two or three men saw the racket and [he] would wish me to go with him to the Sheriff. I came over and found the man

dead and Kid was in the [Dunn & Jenkins] saloon. I told him to give everything up to Mr. Robinson."

When the Catfish Kid handed over his pistol, Robinson checked it and found four cartridges and one empty shell that "looked [as] if it had just been fired." Gough was taken to the jail, where Barker asked him why he had shot the man, who had nothing, meaning they had found no weapon on or near the body. "He might have had a club," the Kid said. "I have a good many enemies in this country and I can't take too many chances."[22]

An inquest was held immediately; the deceased, name unknown, was about twenty-five years old, about five feet eight inches tall, stoutly built with a sandy complexion "and was a German." An examination of the body by Dr. Shelton showed no sign of bruising, as from a blow, and a witness testified that after the shooting the Catfish Kid had told Thurber, "Now you boys lay low about this," or words to that effect.[23] Not that anybody was in any doubt at all about who had killed the man, whose name they later learned was Pete Fulton; Gough was remanded to jail without bail. "The general sentiment is that this Catfish Kid has done enough devilment," Charles Rudolph, editor of the *Tascosa Pioneer*, fulminated, "a hempen lesson is all his case deserves. His kind should be thinned out as soon as possible."[24]

Jim East was on the grand jury that handed down the indictment against the Catfish Kid. Foreman George "Monchy" Russell, a hard-liner whom the boys called "Rain-in-the-Face," told them, " 'Gentlemen of the jury, this thing has gone far enough. We have had a good many murders here. They are getting pretty raw and it is time someone was made to suffer for it. . . . If the petit jury fails to convict this man, we'll take him out and hang him. Every man that will help me in this, rise.' And every mother's son of them got up. Old Rain-in-the-Face did not hold life so seriously when it came to what he thought was his duty."[25]

They need not have worried. Tried at the October term of court, John B. Gough, alias the Catfish Kid, was found guilty, although the jury adjudged the killing murder in the second degree, which meant the Kid escaped the death penalty. Gough, "one of those waifs that probably came from Dodge [who] laid around those saloons and drank whisky and gambled a little, and was just a dead low, hard character," was sentenced to sixteen years' imprisonment.[26]

He entered Rusk prison as Convict 2936 on October 23, 1887. If the records are anything to go by, he was indeed as sorry a specimen as his contemporaries said: born in Illinois, twenty-five years of age, unmarried, five feet five and one-quarter inch tall, and weighing 125 pounds, with a fair complexion, blue eyes, dark brown hair, and a badly crippled right foot. His habits were "intemperate," his education "limited," and he was penniless. He couldn't even hold on to the few cents prisoners were paid for their labor: during his brief incarceration he was twice punished for gambling. In 1888 he was transferred to Huntsville Penitentiary, where he died of tuberculosis ("consumption" as it was called then) on January 28, 1890.[27]

After his short stay in Mobeetie, Louis "The Animal" Bousman dropped out of sight for a while; the family does not appear in the 1900 census of either Texas or Oklahoma. There is some evidence that Bousman was a deputy sheriff at Texline and that they camped for a while near the oil fields in Ardmore and Fleetwood. During that time their teenage son, Frank, died on January 30, 1899. Sally Bousman's version, which does not mention her son, says only that they "came to Oklahoma in the early days [about 1899] and settled close to a little town called Fleetwood. We had four children born to us. My husband was Deputy United States Marshal and Ranger, when we came to Oklahoma. We did some farming and cattle raising, but not very much as he was away from home a great deal of the time."[28]

By 1910 they were living quietly in Waurika, Jefferson County, Oklahoma. In 1934, however, Bousman emerged from obscurity to make a personal appearance at a Wichita Falls cinema in connection with the showing of the Johnny Mack Brown movie *Billy the Kid;* his speckled career came to a close after a brief illness at his home in Waurika on Friday, January 2, 1942. Funeral services were held Sunday afternoon at the Morris Chapel and were conducted by Rev. H. H. Bowles, and Bousman was buried in the Waurika cemetery. To this day, no one knows why they called him "The Animal."[29]

Gutshot Len Woodruff's story had a surprise ending. The tradition in Tascosa was that his

friends [that is, Jesse Jenkins and Theodore Briggs, who put up his bail] furnished [him with] money to go to Dr. Greenway at Hot Springs, Arkansas. Dr. Greenway performed a successful operation and . . . Woodruff stayed at Hot Springs and went to work as a drummer for a hotel, run and owned by an old lady who was very wealthy in property in Hot Springs and in Boston, Mass. . . . In this same year of 1888 [he] and his wealthy landlady married [and in 1889 she] bought him a ranch near Roswell, New

Mexico, and stocked it with registered Hereford cattle. In six months Len died on this ranch. His wife shipped his remains to Hot Springs and gave him an elaborate burial. Six months later she died and was laid to rest by the side of her much younger husband.

It makes for a good story, but it's not what happened. Leonard Albert Woodruff lasted until January 14, 1902, when he died at the Great Northern Hotel in Hot Springs, Arkansas. Like Len, his ranch at what used to be McMillan (now subsumed into the town of Artesia, New Mexico) was on the small side; at the time of his death he owned about 130 head of cattle. His entire estate amounted to less than a thousand dollars. His heir was a son, Lamar Albert Woodruff, "born out of wedlock on or about June 19, 1891." In 1905 Lamar died, and his mother, now Mrs. Wright and living at Hot Springs, petitioned to have Cape Willingham (whose son or brother Harry had purchased Woodruff's cattle) appointed guardian of Lamar's estate, but her request seems not to have been granted, for on November 6, 1905, the remaining money was paid to one Leonia O. Fuller (the signature is unclear) as Lamar's legal guardian. Curiously, the probate clerk in all these proceedings was none other than W. R. "Jake" Owen, veteran of the Lincoln County War and former member of the John Selman gang. The world was a much smaller place back then.[30]

Chapter 21

1886-1890

WHEN TROUBLES COME . . .

THE "great Tascosa gunfight" and subsequent events emphasize yet again the analogy of the town as an island in an unexplored sea. As far as it has been possible to ascertain, this traumatic event did not make the papers in any of the nearest frontier towns, not in Dodge City in Kansas nor in Las Vegas or Springer in New Mexico. Yet, far less dramatic collisions were regularly headlined throughout the American West: so why not the Tascosa fight?

Perhaps because so much of the evidence is hearsay (and all of it conflicting), or perhaps because no "headliners" were involved, it has largely been written off as the drunken brawl Mac Lee deemed it to have been instead of the high-water mark of the war between the corporation ranchers and the "little men" that it actually was. Whatever the reasons, properly argued and researched accounts of the casus belli have only comparatively recently begun to appear. And what they make inescapably clear is that while the "little men" might have won the battle, they had almost certainly lost the war.

For some months after the event, feel-ings ran high in Tascosa. Jim Gober was having a drink in the Dunn & Jenkins saloon when Jim East came in "bareheaded, with an Indian blanket around his shoulders":

> "Do you know what I am going to do with you? [East said] . . . I am going to shoot your brains out and eat them up."
>
> Before he had a chance to draw, I leveled my .45 on him and said, "Your appetite for brains will spoil your future if you aren't careful."
>
> At that moment Pierce, who was East's faithful friend, had trailed East and was behind me and put his gun against the back of my head and said, "Jim, if you kill East, I will have to kill you."
>
> Then I heard a double click still behind Pierce, and Jesse Jenkins's voice rang out, "Off the kid with that gun, or I will blow your head off." I realized in a moment that he was behind East, Pierce, and me.
>
> Jesse had a cap-and-ball shotgun with the barrel sawed off to about eighteen inches long and with a six shooter handle on it. He kept it loaded with two inches of

black powder and fifteen buckshot in each barrel, and if it had gone off, not only Pierce but East and I as well would have been headless. . . . [A]ll was silent for a minute. Then Pierce stepped around me and took East by the arm and led him out of the house, and, fortunately, East left without resistance. It was then that I realized that . . . I was marked as an undesirable by the sheriff as well as W. M. D. Lee.[1]

If he was right, perhaps Gober got the timescale wrong and it happened after East became manager of the LS ranch. Or maybe East was just fighting drunk: he could be "a pretty hard character. He had

plenty of courage and when he was sober, he was very much of a gentleman. The trouble was that while he was in Tascosa he was never sober. He would play Indian and get a blanket to throw over him. The Mexicans used to make a kind of blanket with a hole in the middle [a poncho] and you put it on like kind of a raincoat. He had one of those. [When he was drunk he] was quarrelsome."[2]

But there were no more collisions; angry and resentful though all the men who rode for the LS were, Lee and Scott forbade reprisal and decreed normal ranch work must be resumed as soon as possible. Boss Neff, who joined the LS shortly after the funerals, was one of several replace-

Jim East and his wife, Nettie Bouldin East, ca. 1884.
The hounds were used to hunt and kill lobo wolves. (Courtesy of Hazel M. White)

ments sent out to the Jerry Springs camp until the heel fly season was over.

"April 15th we gathered some 300 saddle horses that were to be the mounts of some 40 riders," Neff recalled. "The 40 men were cut into 4 outfits. Two outfits were to drive two herds of yearlings to Montana (about 3,000 to the herd) while the other two outfits were to remain on the ranch, brand calves and participate in the general roundup. Tobe Robinson and Dunk Cage were the two wagon bosses or foremen on the ranch." About September, he said, with Bud Turner as wagon boss, they "gathered about 2,500 four and five year old steers and drove them to [the railhead at] Lamar, Colorado."[3]

Lee and Scott paid for solid sandstone grave markers to be erected over the graves of King, Valley, and Chilton, each man's name, age, and date of death incised beneath a Texan Lone Star. To McAllister's wife fell the sad duty of writing to their parents and returning their personal effects. In Frank Valley's pocket she was perplexed to find a rabbit's foot. John Lang, still so embittered by the death of his friends that McAllister felt it necessary to keep him on the home ranch, explained that on their way to Tascosa a cottontail had run across the trail in front of them. "Frank shot it and cut off a foot. We asked him if he'd lost his mind, but he started laughing and said, 'Don't you fellows know a rabbit's left hind foot is the luckiest charm in the world? Watch me tonight, boys, I've got my luck in my pocket.'"[4]

If the story is true, Valley had cheered up considerably; a few days earlier, he had given Nettie East photographs of himself and the girl in Saint Louis he was planning to wed, leading Jim East to believe he had a premonition of death. Valley had been born and raised in Saint Louis and educated for

the ministry; his French-born father was an attorney. Ed King, they said, had killed a man somewhere in South Texas before drifting on to Tascosa. Fred Chilton and his brother Sam were from East Texas; Fred was twenty-one years old and was said to have been easily influenced by older men (such as King) whom he admired.[5]

As we have seen, John Lang and the other three accused appeared before Judge Frank J. Willis, presiding over the district court, which sat from May 3 through 12, 1886. When their respective attorneys petitioned for a change of venue, the court concurred, and their trial was set for July 1886 at Clarendon. Except in the case of Lang, however, Willis ruled that bail was out of the question. So until such time as the sheriff delivered them to Donley County sheriff Al Gentry, the prisoners

**Charles H. Jenkins as a young man.
(Courtesy of Wanda Carnell)**

were consigned—with the exception of Woodruff, still being treated by Dr. Shelton at the Briggs house a mile or two from town—to Tascosa's new escape-proof county jail.

Commissioned in June 1884 and built "in a masterly and workmanlike manner" of "Ashter [stone] wall bedded and jointed" by Borders & Cavanaugh of Las Vegas, New Mexico, at a cost estimated at $6,976, the building contained a stone jail and also sheriff's and jailors' rooms. A cement floor was laid in February 1885, and in March Jim McMasters and County Surveyor Seth Mabry were paid $100 for the two town lots on which the building stood. Bousman, Emory, and Gough were its first occupants.[6]

Tascosa was "someplace" now, with an annual cash trade well in excess of a quarter of a million dollars. To the establishments immortalized in Dr. Croft's doggerel

———— ⌒ ————

W. S. Mabry, county surveyor. (Courtesy of the Haley Memorial Library, Midland, Texas)

a couple of years earlier had been added saddle and boot shops, a millinery store, a bakery of sorts, a wagon yard, a livery stable, and even a barber shop with three chairs. And finally, in June 1886, confirmation of its progressiveness arrived in the form of its own newspaper: the *Tascosa Pioneer.*

The *Pioneer* was the brainchild of Charles Francis Rudolph, a twenty-seven-year-old Ohioan who moved to Saint Jo, Montague County, and in 1882 took over the editorship of that town's weekly newspaper, the *St. Jo Gladiator.* Within a couple of years he had turned it into a successful daily, married a local girl, and been blessed with a son. Convinced the railroads that were reaching into the Texas Panhandle would generate new settlement, opportunities, and prosperity there, Rudolph decided to move west and get in on the bonanza; he arrived in Tascosa a week or two after the gunfight.

On Saturday, June 12, he published the first edition of the *Tascosa Pioneer,* its front page a fulsome "Salutatory" promising "to labor for the good of Tascosa, the best town of its size on the continent, and the good of all the Panhandle." A seven-column four-pager, "sent to any post office in the United States at the rate of $2.00 per year, payable in advance," the *Tascosa Pioneer* would "take the future at what it would hold," and, "Father Time will tell the rest."[7]

From the start the paper's columns were in classic small-town style, playing no favorites in noting in its first issue such matters as the visits to town of Frank Mitchell, Warren W. Wetzel, George W. "Monchy" Russell, and Walter de S. Maud, managers respectively of the LIT, Frying Pan, LE, and XIT ranches, or the recent arrival in Tascosa of the Reverend J. T.

Bloodworth, a Methodist minister from Mobeetie who was touring the Panhandle and who conducted several services during his stay.

Rudolph made only two understated references to the recent gunfight. One was to note, "Tascosa had not had a man for breakfast in all the two weeks history of *The Pioneer*. This will be surprising news to a good many people on the outside who thought we kept our streets always running with blood."[8] The second noted that a "good number" of Tascosans would be starting for Clarendon in the course of a week or so, "many as witnesses in the cases against Charles Emory, John Gough and Louis Bousman." It was clear Rudolph was not only shaking hands but also doing his homework.

Throughout the long, hot summer of 1886, the *Pioneer* worked hard to find its place and to express its commitment. Sometimes his headline was a local tragedy, as on July 25, when the Mexican population celebrated *El Dia de Santiago* (misreported by Rudolph as St. Diego's Day),[9] with a street game called *Gallo*, or chicken. First, a rooster was buried in the earth,

> his head only being left above ground, and the young men and boys who wished to participate in this part of the programme were mounted and gathered about ready. Then they dash by, one after another, and as they pass the rooster each man swings himself down from his saddle and reaches for its head. The chicken naturally dodges more or less and renders it no easy matter to catch him. Finally secured, however, by a lucky grab, the body is brought out by a jerk which generally breaks the neck, and the horseman, chicken in hand, dashes away at his best

speed, all the rest giving chase for possession of the rooster. If another overtakes it and wrests it from him, then he leads the race until someone else can take it.

This Sunday, however, it all went wrong. In one race, Bacilio Sanches's horse fell and rolled over on its rider. The horse got up, but Sanchez lay unmoving with blood coming from his mouth and ears. Hurriedly summoned, Dr. Shelton found the boy had a fractured skull and other internal injuries. He was taken to a nearby house and died at about ten o'clock the next morning.[10]

When the story called for it, Rudolph was not afraid to be controversial. Taking what might have been an unwise stand against the big ranchers in general and one in particular, he editorialized angrily about the debacle of the first projected bridge over the Canadian, scheduled to be completed that October but abandoned after threats of enjoinment from "a well understood source of opposition," that is, William McDole Lee.

In March 1886 the commisioners court had accepted a bid from the Kansas City Bridge & Iron Company for the construction of a 1,061-foot bridge across the Canadian River at a cost of $21,990. In May, County Clerk Andrew D. "Frosty" Tomb, recently arrived from Mobeetie, proposed a levy of a road and bridge tax of fifteen cents on each $100 of taxable personal property in Oldham and attached counties; the motion was seconded by Warren Wetzel. Predictably, Commissioners Jordan McAllister and "Monchy" Russell—LS and LE, respectively—voted against. County Judge Henry Kimball cast his deciding vote in the affirmative. Tomb and Wetzel then proposed a levy of twenty-two and one-half cents on the $100 for building the courthouse and jail. Once more McAllister and Russell voted against, and once more Judge Kimball's affirmative vote quashed their protest.

At this juncture attorney Jim Browning, acting on behalf of the big ranchers, presented the county commissioners with a petition of grievance, claiming they had entered the contract to build the bridge without legal authority, that the price agreed was exorbitant, and that the cost would "unnecessarily burden the undersigned and all taxpayers of Oldham County." The signatories were Lee for the LS, Reynolds for the LX, Maud for the Capitol (XIT), and W. J. Todd for the Prairie (LIT), by a very long

chalk the most significant taxpayers in the county.[11]

"Lee came to town," Kid Dobbs recalled, "and said [the bridge] would [not only] hurt the stockmen but hurt them all alike because it would help develop the country and the stockmen would have to leave." Bridges and roads, they contended, and the railways that were bound to follow, would attract a different and unwelcome kind of settler—in other words, "nesters"—and end the era of the open range.[12]

Rudolph's response was uncompromising: "That Tascosa needs the bridge, that Oldham county needs a good, substantial bridge over the Canadian is a proposition

Tascosa Courthouse and jail, ca. 1887. In the doorway is Sheriff Tobe Robinson;
in the adjoining house doorway is the daughter of Andrew "Frosty" Tomb.
(Courtesy of the Amarillo Public Library)

not open to dispute or doubt. . . . It is of course true that the taxation will fall heaviest on those who own most property. That is one of the principles of our form of government and our mode of taxation. That is what the rich man pays for protection of his riches, and what the corporation pays for being a corporation."[13]

Even though in September the commissioners relet the bridge contract to the King Iron Bridge & Manufacturing Company of Columbus, Ohio, at the lower price of $18,000, most of the tax burden still fell on the big ranches. When on top of that the commissioners appointed a panel of surveyors to lay out a "first class road" on the south side of the Canadian, the cost to the LS assessed at $350, Lee instructed attorney Isaac Ryland to give notice of appeal against the commissioners' decision. Meanwhile, he was preoccupied with a problem that made the bridge and road argument pale into insignificance and—for the moment, at least—set aside his anger at Tascosa's refusal to accommodate him and concentrated upon other, longer-term plans.[14]

Over the preceding year or so, as it moved its first stock onto the range, the burgeoning XIT ranch—or more properly the Capitol Syndicate, which ran it for the Capitol Freehold Land & Investment Company—had discovered that the three million acres deeded to it by the Texas legislature was not, as it had expected, one consolidated tract, but many parcels of land scattered across the Panhandle. Slowly and carefully, general manager Abner Taylor had begun trading land with ranches throughout the area in order to consolidate the XIT holdings into one contiguous, manageable tract and contain what would otherwise be an enormous expense for fencing.

He must have been quite a negotiator. On April 5, 1886, Lee signed an agreement by which in exchange for 106,707 acres of the LS in Oldham and Hartley Counties (including Lee's share of the divided LE ranch) Lee & Scott would acquire 71,131 acres to the east of the XIT and south of the Canadian.[15] As a result, not only was the LS reduced to two-thirds its former size, but it also lost access to much of the water Lee had so assiduously bought up in the early days.[16] Early that summer, which from its onset looked like it would be an unusually dry one, the LS branded something like twenty thousand calves, bringing the total number of cattle on its range to forty-five thousand head. Realizing that so large a herd could never survive the following winter with less water and the poor grazing that would inevitably follow the drought, Jordan McAllister urged his employers to move the LS herd west for the rest of the summer, pasturing them on land he had leased near his own ranch in New Mexico, thus conserving grass in the Panhandle. When they declined to accept his managerial judgment, McAllister quit.

It was a significant separation; "Mister Mac" had worked closely with Lee for more than two decades, and the parting was considerably less than friendly. When Lee & Scott hired Jim East to replace him—East's second stint as sheriff of Oldham County was just coming to an end—everyone who knew McAllister felt he had been "sold out." He left immediately for New Mexico, where he terminated his ranching partnership with Kim Ritter and, taking his share in cattle worth about seventy-five thousand dollars, drove them to Colorado, later establishing a ranch at Walsenburg.[17]

The same summer, a long-simmering standoff between the Panhandle "cattle kings" and the State of Texas—the "grass-lease fight"—came to a head.

Attorney General John Templeton indicted some fifty Panhandle cattlemen, including Charles Goodnight, on charges of illegal enclosure, and in the summer of 1886, District Attorney W. H. Woodman haled them into court before Judge Frank Willis at Clarendon in the same session that saw the trials of Charlie Emory and the Catfish Kid. But as we have seen, the trials were a farce; with a jury composed entirely of cowboys and cattlemen, Goodnight and the other defendants were acquitted.[18]

In September, as the fall roundup that had commenced August 25 was completed, news reached Tascosa that the huge Francklyn Land & Cattle Company in Greer and Wheeler Counties had collapsed: "The papers issued by [resident manager] George Tyng who had been sent by the New York creditors of the company to investigate its range affairs, show a very interesting result. Out of fifty-six thousand head, less fourteen thousand sold, which the Mobeetie managers reported as being on their ranges, Mr. Tyng can find about four and a half thousand. The cattle are wasted, scattered, lost, and debts confront a stock-less, broken corporation. Just how far this fearful mismanagement was a swindle, the company themselves cannot even answer." The Francklyn company had failed to pay bonds due amounting to more than two million dollars. In accordance with the original agreement of November 1882, the New York & Texas Land Company swiftly exercised its option "to foreclose, or at their option enter upon the land forthwith and take possession thereof, and sell the same or any portion thereof." When bondholders brought suit in federal court at Dallas, the land was sold and payments foreclosed. In due course the syndi-

cate was reconstituted as the White Deer Lands Trust, and New York capitalists Cornelius C. Cuyler and Frederic de P. Foster took possession of the lands.[19]

In light of these and other developments such as his partner Lucien Scott's decision to "free himself as fast as possible from business cares" by divesting himself of many of his investments, Lee must have even more closely reconsidered his involvement in cattle raising, for very soon afterward he began to explore new horizons.

Rudolph's *Pioneer* continued to chronicle the town's events, trumpeting news of Tascosa's growth, exhorting the city commissioners to get the bridge across the Canadian River built, and noting the results of the November election—J. M. "Tobe" Robinson beating Matt Atwood for the post of sheriff; H. H. Wallace and Seth Mabry unanimously voted in as county judge and county surveyor, respectively; Scotty Wilson for justice of the peace; Dave Barker for constable. On top of that, he constantly banged the drum for what he was confident was the inevitable arrival at Tascosa of the Fort Worth & Denver City Railroad, presently finished to Vernon in Wilbarger County. When that happened, he predicted:

> Much of the beef shipment will be turned in a new direction, the labor of the country will find a new field and thousands of venturous immigrants and home seekers will push promptly for the New West thus opened up. It will be the beginning of a change in business and in the products and in the very landscape of this section, and the result will probably for a while be such a mixture of failures and successes, such a variety of enterprises and under-

takings, such a diversity of interests and speculations as no country has yet experienced. It will be an interesting time to be here the next ten years.[20]

Whether he didn't know or chose to ignore it, an "interesting time" of a totally unforeseen kind was shaping up right under his nose. On November 17 the paper announced the first snow of the season and in doing so yet again emphasized the yawning chasm of its own isolation, for on the more northerly plains stockmen were already witnessing the beginning of what was to be one of the cruelest winters ever to strike the West. On November 16 the temperature over the Rockies had dropped to zero and below, a northwesterly wind pushing six inches of fine snow across the dry ranges; it would continue snowing for a month. Yet even while this was happening, on the ranges outside Tascosa they were still fighting prairie fires such as the one in late October that over three days burned out the whole south pasture of the LX.[21]

On December 1 Tascosa was once again agog with horrified rumor and speculation about another bloody shootout, this time at the ranch of the Leverton brothers, George and John, who had formerly ranched in Hardeman County and ran a few hundred head of cattle on LX land at Evans Canyon, adjacent to the western boundary of the Turkey Track ranch. The details are colored, as always, by the sympathies of the narrators. To the ranchers, especially the LX and the Turkey Track, the Levertons were at worst rustlers and at best nesters, and in either guise unwelcome. To others, what was seen as the killing of John Leverton under the cloak of law looked very much as if the ranchers were victimizing the "little men" again.

The stone ranch house in Evans

Canyon had been built about 1882 by a railroad surveyor named B. C. Evans; the Leverton families, first John and his wife, Mollie, then George W. and his Norwegian-born wife, Cora, moved in during the summer of 1885 with the permission of LX manager John Hollicott, granted on the understanding that they would vacate the property in the fall when the LX would need it as a winter camp. When fall came, however, and the Levertons refused to vacate, claiming the house was built on a school section and was therefore state property, the LX went to court claiming trespass and sued the brothers for five thousand dollars.

Early in the spring of 1887, it was said, two Turkey Track riders met John Leverton, who was driving a calf well inside the ranch boundary. They told him if he turned it loose so it found its way back to its mother, they wouldn't mention the incident. Leverton agreed, and they went on their way. The next morning, it was discovered that the calf had returned and that it was wearing the Leverton brand.

Harry Ingerton was among those who chose not to believe the story. Leverton, he said, "was very hotheaded but not a fool. No one but a rank fool would have, as John was accused of doing, gone back after those two Turkey Track men saw him with that yearling . . . turning it loose to go back to its mother. . . . If he branded that calf he would have taken it on home with him, not turned it loose as evidence against him as he knew they were out to get him."[22]

True or otherwise, Turkey Track ranch superintendent Cape Willingham applied at Mobeetie for a warrant for the arrest of the Levertons on charges of rustling, and it was placed in the hands of newly reelected Wheeler County sheriff Cap Arrington for service. On the last day of November the

George Washington "Cap" Arrington.
(Courtesy of the Panhandle-Plains Historical
Museum, Canyon, Texas)

but he never had a chance, the second he moved Arrington pulled the trigger and filled him full of buckshot. . . . John then staggered thru the partition into George's room and then out at his front door calling for George. . . . He only made a few steps when he fell. By that time old man English the Levertons' stepfather got there and assisted Mrs. Leverton to get John into the house and on his bed. After suffering intense agony for about 12 hours, death ended his pains and he was buried the following day.

By most people this killing was considered a cowardly uncalled for murder. John had heard that they were going to get papers out for his arrest [and] he sent word to Willingham . . . just to send a man after him and he would come in.[23]

In an outraged version of the shooting supplied by Leverton's widow and brother that appeared in Rudolph's *Pioneer,* all six of the posse burst into the house. Arrington asked if this was Leverton,

sheriff deputized a posse consisting of Willingham, Mack Sanford, Rube Hutton, Woods Coffee, and two others and headed upriver.

Early on the morning of Wednesday, December 1, they arrived at the Leverton ranch—a long building divided into two rooms by a rock wall with a door in it, each room also having an outside door. George Leverton had left earlier to hunt a lobo wolf that was killing cattle in the area. John and his wife were preparing breakfast in their portion of the house when the door was pushed open and Arrington stood there with a shotgun leveled. Leverton jumped toward the bedstead on which his six-shooter was hanging,

and upon being answered that it was fired a shot that took effect in the man's arm. Other shots were fired and Leverton fell to the floor and under the edge of the bed. He had no weapon and was in reach of none. But seeing that his murder was inevitable, his wife endeavored to get him out and arm him for something like a defense. He then fired five shots himself; whether any of them took effect or not is not known. . . . Thirteen shots are said by the brother and brother-in-law of Leverton to have struck him. . . . Arrington read the warrant for Leverton's arrest after the man to be arrested was in a dying condition, shot thirteen times!

It was, said Rudolph, deliberate and cold-blooded murder, a "bloody tragedy . . . which is . . . regarded in but one light by all our citizens and that is— horror!" A week later, however, after hearing what the possemen had to say, he became a little more circumspect. Their account was "very different from the story of the surviving Levertons. It is made to appear that John Leverton was a cow thief and a desperado, and that he invited the first shot by jumping for his weapon while two guns were leveled on him."[24]

Kid Dobbs offered the likeliest scenario. Leverton was grinding coffee while sitting on the edge of a bed in which a child was lying. "Willingham opened the door and began firing at Leverton. He shot him up badly but Leverton managed to shoot Willingham in the leg. Leverton tried to crawl out of the house and into a ditch where he would have some chance with the men and Arrington shot him in the back." He believed the big men wanted to be rid of Leverton.[25] Support for this theory appears in Charles Goodnight's characteristically forthright and completely unapologetic account, given many years later. When Willingham and Arrington went into the house

at crack of day Leverton shot at Arrington in his tight rock house but the pistol snapped in Arrington's face. Leverton shot Arrington's necktie off and then shot Arrington through the leg. Leverton threw himself behind the cradle. The shot set the cradle afire and the child in the cradle, now a grown man, still threatens to kill Arrington. As the cradle caught on fire Leverton's wife ran out of the house and held a gun on Cape, who told Arrington to come and take it away from her, which he did. In the excitement Leverton came

out and got away fifty or sixty yards when Arrington shot him. He was an outlaw and a thief.[26]

"If Leverton stole an animal," the *Pioneer* concluded, "he should have been arrested; if he resisted arrest he should have been shot. If, on the contrary, he was murdered without a chance to surrender, the duty of every law-abiding man would be to see that his murderers, if they were ten times sheriffs, were punished to the fullest extent of the law."[27]

Bowing out as gracefully as he could, Rudolph concentrated instead on the good news; after all, 'twas the season to be jolly. There was the usual Christmas tree with wonderful presents for the town's children. There was "a dramatic exhibition" by the Tascosa Minstrel & Dramatic Association. There was a Grand Ball, there were Christmas Day horse races for a purse of four hundred dollars between Lon Jenkins's bay and a black horse owned by George Jones of the Frying Pan and between another Jones horse and a black pony of Jim McIntire's. The Springer Mercantile & Banking Company was opening a store on a lot leased to them by Henry Kimball.

And love was in the air. From Jesse Jenkins came the news that on the Sunday before Thanksgiving 1886, Tom Harris had married Clara Paulus. On December 13 Judge Howson Wallace officiated at the marriage of County Clerk "Frosty" Tomb and Mrs. Julia Crain, and on January 4, 1887, that of Bill Ruth and Flora Rains. On January 19 he performed the same service for LIT manager Frank Mitchell and Miss Georgia Byrum, and he officiated again on January 31 for Alexander "Scotty" Wilson and Mrs. Emeline McAulpin. On February 1 yet another wedding united LS wagon boss Jim May and Mary A. Wilson, the former Molly Russell.[28]

Amazingly, practically no mention of the terrible weather conditions on the ranges farther north—where January 1887 was the coldest month anyone there could remember—appeared in the *Pioneer*. Rudolph noted that a temperature of nine degrees below zero had been recorded on the morning of January 8, but a week later he commented that the winter of 1886–87 would "long be remembered for the remarkable mildness." Yet, only the day before, just 150 miles to the north, the *Dodge City Daily Globe* noted,

> The heavy snow and bitter winds of the past ten days have caused the most serious apprehension among cattlemen as to their probable losses. Up to this time but few have come in from the range country, but within a few miles of here no less than five hundred head have drifted to the river, where they perished in attempting to cross, or drifted up to fences, where they remained until frozen to death. A gentleman from a ranch south of here reports seeing cattle on his way up that were still standing on their feet, frozen to death. The water holes are frozen over, the grass is snowed under, and the weather is cold, with every prospect of more snow.[29]

And it came, with a vengeance on January 28, 1887. For seventy-two hours, howling winds drove nonstop blinding snow into massive drifts across the empty plains, cutting off towns. The temperature dropped to forty below, rendering movement by any form of transportation impossible. Wyoming, Montana, Colorado, western Nebraska, and western Kansas were snowbound and frozen solid and would re-

main so until March. Settlers died of exposure in their flimsy shacks, unable to go outside to find fuel, even had there been any to be found. Cowboys died trying to rescue helpless cattle. And the cattle, the hair worn off their legs to the hocks, began to die in droves. Too weak to stand, they were simply blown over by the tearing wind, or, with their feet anchored in the ice, they froze to unsheltered death like statues. Inevitably, thousands and thousands of survivors began to drift south only to be halted by homesteaders' fences or, in the northern Panhandle, the drift fence. And there they huddled and there they died of hunger and exposure, piled in a ghastly 150-mile-long mountain of dead flesh.

It was not until March, when the prayed-for warm wind known as a "chinook" finally brought a thaw and a tally was made, that

> the real truth was discovered—and then it was only mentioned in a whisper. Bobby Robinson, acute judge of conditions, estimated the loss among through cattle at less than fifty percent. It turned out to be a total loss among this class of cattle and the wintered herds suffered from thirty to sixty percent. . . . It was simply appalling and the cowmen could not realize their position. From Southern Colorado to the Canadian line, from the 100th Meridian almost to the Pacific slope it was a catastrophe which the cowmen of today who did not go through it can never understand. The three great streams of ill-luck, mismanagement and greed met together. In other words, recklessness, want of foresight, and the weather which no man can control.

It was estimated that as much as 80 percent of the cattle on the range in

Wyoming had perished, and other states lost similarly devastating numbers. As John Clay put it, "The big guns toppled over; the small ones had as much chance as a fly in molasses." With their demise would go—not all at once, but sooner rather than later—the extravagant financing, the astonishing indifference to theft and mismanagement, the grandiose ambitions generated by the myths of the "beef bonanza." From that point on, the survivors would be "men with the bark on." And they would run a considerably tighter ship.[30]

If any of this got through to Rudolph— if indeed, he was aware of it—he went on pretty much as he had before, proselytizing for the railroad—any railroad—whose arrival would inevitably transform Tascosa into the Queen City of the Panhandle. "Once Tascosa has railroad facilities, the other concomitants of a large city will rapidly follow," he said on February 23. A week later he noted that the Fort Worth & Denver City (FW & DC) "has its present terminus at Quanah, which is two hundred miles from here. . . . Fifty miles of extension are to be added each month until the Canadian is reached 'at or near Tascosa.' By that calculation . . . the graders will reach this point by the last of June and cars will come in by September."

Then on Saturday, July 30—triumph! "AND THE LITTLE CITY HAS ONLY TO GO ON TO GREATNESS," shouted the *Pioneer:*

The Fort Worth & Denver is located to and through this town, and bright beams the future. . . . Since his return here from below, Mr. McCrickett, the locating engineer, has been giving the route up the river his close attention, evidently satisfied from his first inspection that it was much superior to the Indian creek route in several respects. Our county surveyor, W. S. Mabry, who we may here add has done more for the town in this matter than the town could ever have done for itself, devoted to the work much valuable time and labor, and by his knowledge was able largely to assist in discovering the route now determined upon. . . . Thus Tascosa has so far in her history met with not a single disappointment.[31]

She was about to. Quite apart from the growth of a settlement at an FW&DC graders' camp in Potter County, which Rudolph insisted on dismissing as "Amorillo," Tascosa was about to experience a major setback in its bid to become a railroad town. The brain behind that setback was none other than W. M. D. Lee, who "had always let it be known that he did not wish the settlement and development of the country." The letting of the bridge contract had in particular provoked him to warn the commissioners that if they voted to finance its building—resulting in even higher taxes for the LS—he would build a town within three miles of it that would ruin Tascosa forever. He now set out to do just that.[32]

Chapter 22

JESSE JENKINS

"HE NEVER OWED A DEBT THAT HE DIDN'T PAY."

MASTERMIND, organizer, backup, fixer, and—very probably—killer, Jesse Jenkins was for most of the town's existence not only the unproclaimed "boss" of Tascosa but simultaneously the most successful and brazen of all the hundreds of thieves who preyed upon the cattle corporations of the Panhandle. Feared as much as he was respected, he wound up owning property worth more than a million dollars, with holdings of thousands and thousands of cattle, many of which, he finally admitted, had been acquired by other than honest means.[1]

Jesse Reagan McKenzie Jenkins was the son of Jonathan Eppler (born 1821) and Mahala Rebecca (Bonner) Jenkins (born 1831), both born in Lauderdale County, Alabama. Following their marriage in Limestone County, Alabama, on December 11, 1846, they shared the home of Mahala's father, Moses Bonner (a wealthy man, worth $10,000 at the time), also in Limestone County; their son William Alonzo, always known as "Lon," was born there in 1850. Family tradition had it that they moved to Texas in 1851 when sur-

veyor and merchant Jonathan Jenkins was hired to lay out the townsite of Cleburne; records there do not support this proposition. More probably the family headed west because Jonathan's Tennessee-born older brother, William, was already there. A saddler by profession, William had come to Texas in 1845, bought 640 acres of land, and settled in Dallas County with his wife and three children; a fourth was born in April 1848, and there would eventually be ten. Later, Moses and Mary Bonner also joined them. Jonathan Jenkins and his wife settled in Dallas County and, it is claimed, established some of the earliest businesses in Dallas, including that city's first boarding house; their second child, Charles Harroway Jenkins, was born there May 17, 1852.[2]

About 1854 the Jonathan Jenkins family moved to Parker County, where he followed his profession as surveyor; he was also one of the county's early ranchers and stockmen. Over the next decade six more children were born, the last being Jesse, born August 10, 1863. Jonathan Jenkins is said to have served as a colonel in the Con-

**Jesse Jenkins (left) and his pal
Jim Langhorne at the 101 ranch, Dalhart. (Courtesy of the XIT Museum)**

federate army throughout the Civil War, returning home in broken health and dying
soon afterward.[3]

On January 27, 1867, his widow, Mahala Jenkins, was married by Justice of the
Peace Ben Davis to widower John Mitchell
"Mitch" Spillers, a forty-year-old farmer
and Methodist minister who lived on Duck
Creek in Dallas County. Spillers and his
first wife, Priscilla Ann (Little), born 1822,
had married in Illinois; they had eight children. The stepfather, the story goes, had
no tolerance for his wife's children. At
some point two of the girls were sent back
to Alabama to live with relatives; by 1870
Lon Jenkins, now twenty, was no longer
around, and Charles, eighteen years old,

had gone to study law in Dallas, leaving
Jesse Jenkins, age seven, to get along as best
he could with the rest of the Spillers brood.
It is a fair bet they gave him a rough ride.[4]

According to Jesse, Lon Jenkins joined a
group of buffalo hunters going to the Texas
Panhandle and eventually drifted west to
Mobeetie, where he worked making adobe
bricks and training racehorses—like gambling, a lifelong passion. He also "ran an
ice route, providing ice to saloonkeepers
which he obtained from the military facility at Fort Mobeetie [Elliott]. Usually without their permission." At one point Lon
also ran a saloon there, for on September
11, 1879, he and a man named William
Smith were charged with fighting in it;

———ᴄᴡᴼ———

Charles H. Jenkins, statesman.
(Courtesy of Frank Hilton)

———ᴄᴡᴼ———

Charles's wife, Annie (Smith) Jenkins.
(Courtesy of Wanda Carnell)

both were fined three dolla rs. On January 18, 1880, he was one of those summoned by Jucge Emanuel Dubbs to qualify for a jury commission at the first session of district court ever held in the Panhandle.[5]

About that time his brother joined him at Mobeetie, but it is impossible to be certain of the actual date: throughout his life Jesse Jenkins determinedly obfuscated the truth about his background and early years, muddying the waters so thoroughly that fact cannot easily be separated from fiction. The following claim, made when he was ar old man, is a good example:

When I was twelve years old I bought some land in east Dallas for $3 an acre. I ran a stable with a Jew and a mule dealer. That was west of the courthouse toward the river. Another boy and I started out

through the Indian Territory with a wagon, a good team, and a little shotgun. We camped one evening and wandered off down the creek. We saw some Indians and broke off in a run to the wagon. The Indians followed. I had a black pony that the Indian chief took a fancy to. He wanted to buy it but I refused everything he offered. He got mad and swore at me, saying that I was 'heap Texas ————.' . . . We sat up all night guarding the pony with the little gun but so frightened that if the Indians had given a whoop we would have torn up the wagon getting away.[6]

In another tale, he ran away from home at age eleven ("I guess the cotton patch run me off," he said) and went first to the home of his brother Charles in Dallas and then west. In yet another, he changes his age to fourteen; a still later history says he was *sent* to live with Charles. It may even be that he was simply kicked out by an exasperated stepfather, but whatever his age and whatever the year, it was without doubt to Charles that he went.[7]

Thanks to his considerable achievements as a lawyer, civic leader, and dedicated politician, there is a great deal on the record about the life of Charles Harroway Jenkins. As a boy he attended a private school in Dallas; in the fall of 1866, age fourteen, he was sent to Cedar Springs, where he studied the profession of surveyor, and in 1870 he read law at the offices of Kendall & Ault in Dallas. A year later, he took charge of the Dallas County surveyor's office. In September 1873, by which time he had been appointed city engineer of Dallas, he married former schoolmate Annie Elizabeth Smith, twenty; they would have three daughters: Willie, born 1874; Annie May, born 1876; and Roberta Jessie, born 1880.

While working as surveyor and engineer, Jenkins continued his law studies and was admitted to the bar in March 1874. After practicing in Dallas, he moved in 1877 to Brownwood, then just about to welcome the railroad. Jenkins served as alderman and mayor of that city and was prominent in all aspects of civic affairs; he also engaged in the newspaper business. A staunch Democrat, he was elected a member of the thirtieth legislature in 1907 and reelected in 1909, representing Brown County; among his colleagues were future speaker of the U.S. House of Representatives Sam Rayburn, and Sam Ealy Johnson, father of future president Lyndon B. Johnson. Famously absent-minded (he once chatted politely with a group of ladies until one of them exasperatedly interrupted, "Charlie Jenkins, you don't even

know your own sister!"), he also dabbled in poetry and is said to have invested in property in Mexico with a view to establishing a socialist agricultural commune for the Indians there.[8]

Jesse Jenkins made no effort at all to emulate Charles's shining example, but "spent most of his time around the race tracks where he was known as a fearless rider. He would take his lunch in the morning and leave his brother's [house] supposedly to go to school. Instead he went to the race tracks where he was much in demand." All that came to an abrupt end when some of the racehorse owners called on Charles Jenkins to get permission for Jesse to go to Chicago as their jockey.

Jesse also claimed that when he was about twelve or thirteen he went to Coleman County with Charles and worked breaking and riding horses. Coleman City, he said, was just being founded and had a picket saloon; at Camp Colorado Post there was "nothing much more than a good store." He was there when the Texas Rangers brought in a dead man named Bone Wilson in a wagon—"loaded in like a hog."[9]

Following the death of his stepfather (Spillers died July 4, 1878), Jesse either returned or was sent back by his brother to the farm in Dallas County, to live with his mother, who had reverted to her old name.[10]

Toward the beginning of 1881 (after perhaps bundling his mother off to live with Charles) Jesse went west to join Lon in Mobeetie. "When he first came in from buffalo camp, Lon [had] peddled vegetables at the fort. He built the government corrals, got 1700 government tents to cover his adobes when it rained. Used to get a wagon load of government ice and take it up to the saloon man in Mobeetie. I had a horse and buggy; went up [to the Fort] at night. I thought it was so the ice wouldn't melt but found it was because they could slip the ice out and officers not know it."[11]

At Mobeetie Jesse also earned five dollars a day delivering messages for Bert "Kicking" Clampitt, who with his partner Newt Locke co-owned a wagon yard and livery stable.

> He had a hundred horses that he rented on long-time terms. Sometimes a man would disappear with one of Clampett's [sic] teams, would travel over several states—Kansas, Missouri, Indian Territory—and then come trotting up some fine morning to pay Clampett [Clampitt] rental for a whole year. His teams always came back. Clampett held himself responsible for the delivery of all telegrams, be the distance what it might. Jesse Jenkins, then a boy of about fourteen, delivered them to cattlemen all over the Panhandle, no matter how hard they were to locate. He did not give up until he found his man."

Jenkins later described that work himself:

> In those days the only telegraph wire was the one at Fort Elliott. When the messages came for the cattlemen, they had to be delivered by a special messenger. I was just a kid then but Clampett would send me all over the country, hunting up men to give 'em a message. I was supposed to get on a horse and see that the man [got] his telegram, no matter where he was. . . . If a man got a wire, he might be as far off as Quanah but I found him anyway. Clampett got $100 a day for his messengers and gave us boys $10 a day. . . . Sometimes it took me two or three days to find an outfit."[12]

He spent two months at Mobeetie. "[It was an] awful good town. Seven companies [of soldiers with]in a mile of it; good payroll; good freighting; all those folks had to be fed and all that stuff had to be hauled in wagons. I hauled cottonwood at $14 a cord three miles; hauled three days and quit." Soon after Jesse's arrival, however, "Lon wanted to move over here [to Tascosa]. I moved his goods in a wagon while he came on ahead. . . . I nearly drowned my horses when I first came to the [Canadian] river. I drove off into the river and four or five cowboys came up and helped me. Pulled me out."

Jesse moved around a lot. "I never worked for anyone but for a month in my whole life," he once boasted. By the fall of 1881 he and Lon were firmly ensconced in Tascosa. His first job there "was to freight from Dodge. Then he staked some Mexicans [possibly Casimero Romero, who got into the freighting business about that time] to freight outfits and soon had a rather thriving business built up. He said that the saloon (in Hogtown) never did belong to him but to his brother Lon. He said Lon started to build a saloon and had to have help and Jess finished it for him."[13]

He was under no illusions about the place or the kind of men who lived there. "In 1881 Tascosa was at its worst," he said. "There were men here from everywhere, men who had done things in other places and had to run away. Some of them had killed folks. But they were the best men on earth. They were certainly good to me." And as they welcomed him, he made them welcome, whatever their sins: rustlers, horse thieves, tinhorn gamblers, and bandits of every stripe flocked to wet their whistles at Jesse Jenkins's honky-tonk.[14]

He wasn't educated or suave, and he wasn't interested in becoming either, but bit by little bit Jesse became Tascosa's man for all seasons. He stuck to what he knew he was good at, using booze, cards, girls, muscle, or money to manipulate things so they came out the way he wanted. He was the man behind Tom Harris when the latter planted "about 25 men on the LS ranch payroll where they would be in a better position to help secure a herd for Tom, and in the final wind-up, for Jess." During the cowboy strike of 1883 he was adviser, supporter, and even financier in the cowboys' attempt to bring the big ranches to heel, although smart enough to know they could never win an all-out war. At one point in the preparations for the strike, some of the hotter heads proposed bringing the big ranches down by killing all the horses they owned. Jenkins was appalled and "begged them not to do it. . . . You'd turn the whole world against you," he told them, and he was right. Fortunately, they took his advice; had things gone the other way there would almost certainly have been a full-scale range war.[15]

After the strike failed, the "barred" cowboys joined Tom Harris and with Jenkins's financial support moved across the Texas line into New Mexico, headquartering in the area around Endee and Liberty, where they formed the WA Cattle Company. Jesse quite literally had a lot of irons in the fire: "Eighteen fellows were in partnership with [him] and his brother in law Tom Harris in their cattle syndicate. Bob Wheatley, Tom Harris and Jenkins were [its] moving spirits. . . . Jim Gober called it the Get Even Cattle Company. The Tabletop and several other brands . . . were declared maverick brands by the court."[16]

As has already been remarked, Jenkins and "Tenderfoot Bob" Roberson of the LIT were also in thieving cahoots; how many others were involved can only be

guessed at. At one point Jordan McAllister of the LX told Jenkins he was going to inspect his herd for mavericked cattle. Jesse looked him straight in the eye and said, "You go get a slicker and put it over your window, because if you do this I'm going to be after you." McAllister decided not to bother.[17]

Of course, no proof exists—he would have seen to it—that Jesse knew that the midnight gunfight at Tascosa was about to happen and made a point of absenting himself from Tascosa by accompanying Tom Harris to Seymour. He always maintained he was sixty miles away when it happened, but then added slyly, "But I always had a few thoroughbreds standing by."[18]

During his visit to the Harris home, Jesse met Tom's sister Molly, and after what must have been a whirlwind romance they were married at Hallettsville on May 23, 1886. "I was a bad man when I married her," he said later. "I told her so. I told her I was a hyena with a lot of enemies, and might not last ten days. She was brave." She probably needed to be. "When Mrs. Jenkins came to Tascosa," a friend recalled, "she found out what kind of man Jenkins was. She was the worst cowed woman you ever saw. She wouldn't get outside the house."[19]

Jesse's new wife set out to make him respectable; he consented to letting her try. Molly had a skill that probably proved more than useful to Jenkins during her lifetime; Billy Jarrett, who later worked for Jenkins as a bookkeeper at Hartley, said Molly "could imitate any handwriting." Lon, he said, was a full-time gambler and "always kept a race horse or two and ran him in races that the boys at Tascosa would match once in a while. . . . Lon was easy to get along with. His wife was a niece of P. T. Barnum; used to be a snake girl in the cir-

Jesse and Molly (Harris) Jenkins at their Dalhart home. (Courtesy of Wanda Carnell)

cus; died in Tascosa when she was thirty two years old."[20]

Tough as he was, smart as he was, Jesse Jenkins knew when it was time to let go. And when the time came, he "moved from Tascosa to Hartley. He had a ranch on the Rita Blanca Creek which he had obtained when he traded his saloon to Berry Nations, an old XIT hand. Mr. Jenkins used to own the Marshall ranch below Tascosa. When he lived in Hartley he ran the livery stable and operated his ranch. . . . Many of Jenkins' friends were former foremen or cowboys for Col. [Albert] Boyce."

No doubt Jesse Jenkins planned to operate in Hartley pretty much as he had done in Tascosa, the power behind the "small men" up against the big ranchers, in this instance Al Boyce and the XIT. And by the same token, Boyce and the XIT were determined to make sure he did not get the chance to do so. Asked what caused the "long enmity between he and Al Boyce, Jenkins declared it came about because Mr. Boyce could not vote him. He said the XIT were quite interested in county politics and that he (Jenkins) had considerable influence with the Mexicans and the cowboys [and how they cast their votes]. He said this resulted in Boyce's becoming angry when he found he could not control Jenkins."[21]

Jenkins's technique, as he described it himself, was childishly simple: After the

Arrington-Willingham posse killed John Leverton, they arrested all the rest of the family and put them in jail in Tascosa. Jenkins offered to go their bond. "I didn't know them but I knew what kind of a dirty deal they had received and what would happen to them unless they had some friends, so I asked to go their bail." This action might at first seem to have been true generosity of spirit, but as always Jenkins was buying futures. A few years later, when there was an important election in Moore County, he was asked "to help one side of it. I went over to the Levertons and solicited their support. The old lady, who seemed to be the boss of the outfit, sat all of the eligible voters in a circle and told them to do whatever I said [because] I had befriended them at Tascosa when they were in real trouble." On another occasion, he claimed, he was paid two thousand dollars for his influence in moving the county seat of Dallam County from Texline to Dalhart. "He got the job done."[22]

Next, Dallam County wanted to organize, and again the XIT opposed the proposal and brought in lawyer and former state senator Avery L. Matlock to fight their corner. "But there was a group of 'small men' in Hartley County who were against anything the XIT's wanted, and they had a good deal of influence at the time," wrote Laura Hamner, carefully avoiding naming them. So when the motion that Dallam be organized was tabled and Judge Matlock rose to present his objections, County Judge Ruck Tanner (who could not even write his own name) told him to sit down. "Dallam County is organized," he said. And that was that.[23]

But in the end the XIT had its way. After a bitterly extended war of attrition between the two factions, and not one but two elections, the county seat was transferred from Hartley to Channing in 1903, by which time the only official in Dallam County who was not an XIT employee was the county judge. With nothing left to fight for, Jesse Jenkins sold his Hartley ranch and about 1905 bought another near Dalhart, where he "built Molly a three story home. It was a true museum piece and they lived in fine style." He had two big outfits, the 101 ranch and the Hip O, and "owned and leased as much as 100,000 acres of land, had from ten to twelve thousand head of cattle. . . . He established the Dalhart National Bank about 1906 and was its president for five years. He has never held public office but has taken an active interest in political affairs. 'I had too much sense to go into politics,' [he said]. 'Politics can be mean.'"

Jenkins was the first Dalhart rancher to ship cattle to Kansas City over the Rock Island line when it came in. He was also a member of the partnership that built Dalhart's DeSoto Hotel in 1909. The hotel, famous up and down the Fort Worth and Denver and Rock Island Railroads, contained sixty-one bedrooms plus kitchen, dining room, and lobby. From the time of its construction to its razing, roomers paid two or three dollars for rooms. The DeSoto was the scene of many glittering social affairs in Dalhart's early days, and many old settlers mourned to see it torn down.[24]

Jesse Jenkins's luck began to turn bad when he lost about seventeen thousand cattle in the big blizzard of 1918–19, and it worsened the following year. On August 31, 1920, Molly Jenkins died of cancer in Kansas City; she "had been in feeble health for a long time and . . . was twice taken to Baltimore and the costly radium was applied time and again . . . but to no avail. In all her sufferings she was patient, and thought rather of the welfare of others than herself." At fifty-seven years of age, Jesse perforce had to consider what to do with the rest of his life; in doing this he looked toward New Mexico.[25]

In 1889 his brother Lon had moved from Tascosa to Roswell, where he met Texas-born Lucy (Danner) Robbins, whose English husband, George Robbins, had abandoned her and their two children, Viola and Alex Jasper, before the latter's birth in 1886. Twenty years Lon's junior, Lucy was running a boarding house; they were married at Roswell in 1890, and almost immediately after the marriage he adopted Alex. According to family tradi-

tion, Viola, who remembered her father, chose to retain his name and "thought that someday he would come back for her. [Alex] was born after his father disappeared. Lon was the only father he ever knew and he loved him dearly."

Lon, his granddaughter said, "was a delightful man! Had several businesses. Had stocks with mineral companies and raised racing horses. . . . Traveled a lot to race tracks. He was very aristocratic, courteous and gentle with the most correct behavior." Like his brother, Lon was less than fortunate in his choice of women: descendants said Lucy turned out to be "a selfish domi-

Lon and Lucy (Danner) Jenkins at Corona,
New Mexico. (Courtesy of Wanda Carnell)

neering person but Lon loved her very much."[26]

It appears Lon was still getting some if not all of his income from gambling and that sometimes it was no more honest than it had been in Tascosa. In December 1893 he was one of a quartet of men playing cards in Felipe Frederick's saloon at Nogal, New Mexico, where he worked as a bartender. At the table were Lon, Frederick, Frank Bennett, and Noah Ellis, a onetime foreman of John Poe's ranch who was drinking and losing heavily. Someone told Ellis's brother Bill that Noah was being robbed, and Bill went into the saloon, watched the game for a few minutes, and then commenced beating both Jenkins and Frederick over the head with his six-gun. Lon Jenkins retreated behind the bar, where a sawed-off shotgun was kept, and when Bill Ellis walked up to the bar and pounded on it with his gun, demanding that Jenkins "Set 'em up, and be quick about it!" Lon reached beneath the bar, came up with the shotgun, and blew off the top of Ellis's head. As Noah Ellis ran for the door, Lon shouted, "Turn round, you sonofabitch, I don't want to shoot you in the back!" Ellis wisely ignored the invitation and escaped.

Lon was arrested by White Oaks deputy sheriff John Preston, who was on the spot. When a mob gathered, obviously intent on hanging Jenkins, Preston swore in a posse to defend him until Lincoln County sheriff George Curry, his deputy from Capitan, Sieb Grey, and jailer George Peppin arrived and took Lon to the jail in Lincoln, where he cooled his heels until the spring term of district court. At his trial the jury was instructed by the court to bring in a verdict of not guilty, and Lon was acquitted.[27]

Lon had never been in that kind of trouble, and he never was again. In 1908 he and Jess filed on a thirty-two-acre site southeast of Corona and developed it as the Red Cloud Mine; noting his departure from Roswell the following year, the local paper revealed an interesting fact about his business dealings in the city: "W. A. (Lon) Jenkins, at one time a partner of Pat Garrett in the machinery and hardware business in Roswell, and later a member of the sporting fraternity, is the secretary and general manager of a new mining company that is being organized to operate at the mining fields around Duran and Corona."

"Quartz miner" Lon (as he described himself in the 1910 census) and his wife, Lucy, each filed on 320-acre homesteads near Corona and in addition to mining activities ran a few cattle, but they devoted most of their energy to raising racehorses; they also bred Percherons (powerful draught horses of a gray or black breed originating from northern France), which at that time were fetching eleven hundred dollars a head at auction. They led a nomadic life, using their homesteads as security for mining claims and other ventures in White Oaks, Socorro, and even Arizona. By 1912 Lon had gained sufficient prominence to be appointed territorial delegate to the Northwest Mining Convention in Spokane, Washington. He was remembered as having "won and lost several fortunes." Sometimes he and Lucy would be "dressed to the hilt. Fancy suits and dresses, diamond stickpins and rings. . . . Several months later they would come to stay for awhile. The clothes and diamonds were gone. . . . Mom and my Grandmother coined the phrase 'Chicken one day, feathers the next' to describe Lon and Lucy's life."[28]

A year or so after Molly died, Jesse "fell for the younger of two sisters, gave her a

Red Cloud Mine, near Corona, New Mexico. Lucy and Lon Jenkins are on the left end
of the middle row; their son Alex is second from the right, middle row.
(Courtesy of Wanda Carnell)

$1000 diamond ring, took her and her mother on a trip to California; she sold the ring and he found out about it and dropped her; the older sister looked up the records and found out how much money Jess had; evidently thought he was old and would die and leave all to her; married him and made him a good wife." The lady thus described was schoolteacher Cleo Smith, daughter of a "rough neck" who came from "where they make 'em; used to live in Williamson County where cattlemen and sheepmen had trouble." On her wedding day, August 8, 1921, Cleo Smith was thirty-three years younger than her new husband.[29]

Soon after his marriage to Cleo, Jesse began selling off his Dalhart rangeland, retaining two thousand acres "for when the place comes back." While visiting his brother Lon in New Mexico in 1924, he bought ranchland in the Corona area, and he then moved there, bidding Texas a sour farewell: "A man ought to be put in the penitentiary for running cattle on those panhandle plains." Before he left, he arranged to turn the Dalhart ranch over to his widowed sister Molly; his offer of financial help and the use of the Dalhart property must have seemed like a blessing, but it turned out otherwise, for on Sunday, April 20, 1924, Molly was attacked and battered to death in one of the outbuildings.

"A shroud of mystery surrounds the brutal murder," shouted a newspaper report. "What was the motive? Was it murder? Robbery? What? Nobody knows. A widow, 67 years of age, harmless, respected, acquaintance in Dalhart and vicinity limited, not an enemy in the world, beaten down with a piece of water pipe two and a half feet long and an inch and a half in diameter, found in the stalks and hay in the barn stall at 6:30 Sunday evening by

[Florence Horton,] a neighbor girl who had gone over to spend the night with her. Apparently this is all that is known of the dark and bloody deed."

Although the Dalhart Sheriff's Department "pursued every semblance of a clue," and set up a dragnet that took in "every town and section of the Panhandle, eastern New Mexico and Western Oklahoma," although a dozen suspects were rounded up for investigation, and one local laborer "who had been doing odd jobs about the place was held and grilled all day Wednesday [April 23]," with no fingerprints on the murder weapon and no clues as to the identity of the assailant, the investigation got nowhere, and no arrests were ever made. The murder of Molly Bedingfield remains unsolved to the present day.[30]

In addition to raising cattle, Jesse also grew peach and apple trees, planted corn, and specialized in breeding high-priced Steel Dust thoroughbred quarter horses, many of which were shipped east to Long Island to be trained as polo ponies. Others he kept and raced at local meets; one time he and Lon went to Albuquerque, putting their racehorse between the shafts and hitching the buggy horse behind just before they got there. At the track they sneered at the competition, offering to bet their buggy horse could beat any horse present. Needless to say, the bets poured in, and needless to say, Jesse and Lon cleaned up.

But as the years passed, Cleo (whom Jesse always called "Little 'un") more and more dominated her husband's life, widening the rift she had created between him and his brother's family. She was "a very plain woman, and dressed the part. She always wore an ankle length shirt waist dress. They were gray or light blue pin stripe.

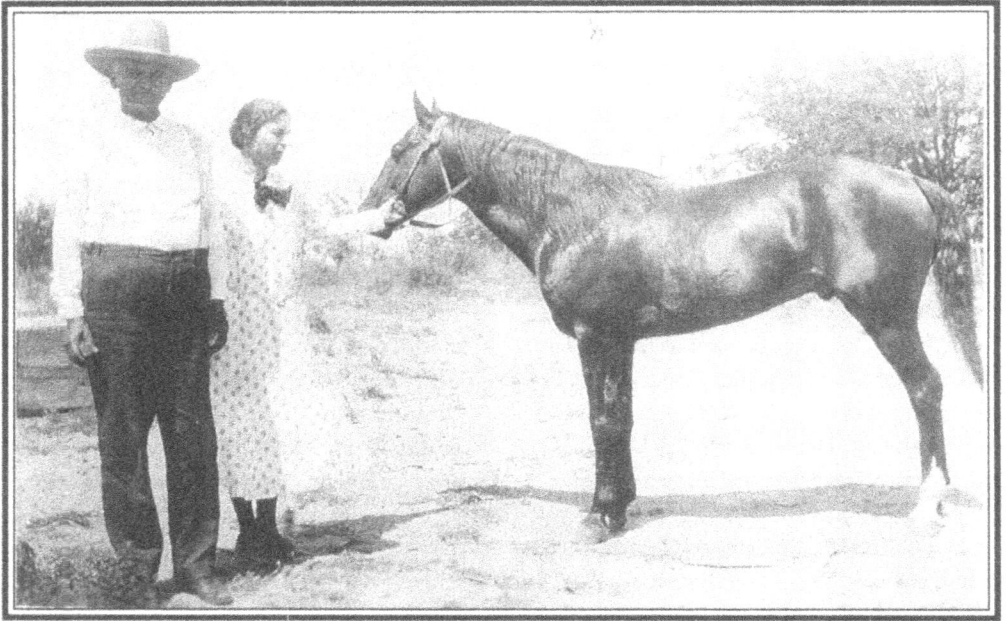

Jesse and Cleo Jenkins with their racehorse "Utellum." (Courtesy of Wanda Carnell)

She wore dark tan cotton hose. Her shoes were a laced oxford style with a two inch square heel, quite common to older women of that time. Her hair was brown, and always pulled back in a bun on her neck. She was very arrogant."[31]

In 1936 indefatigable researcher Laura Hamner determined to go to Corona and see if finally she could get the truth about Tascosa—about anything—out of Jesse Jenkins. Her account of the visit, a positively Kafkaesque study of hostility and paranoia, begins as she and a female friend named Winsome (no first name is ever mentioned) turn off the highway seven miles southwest of Corona. After bumping over the SP tracks and traveling miles and miles down a rutted, unmade road through what seemed like an endless valley "close-bound by mountains"—probably Bonito Canyon—they finally reached the ranch, "a

stone and stucco [building] of five or six rooms."

The door opened and a woman hurried out into the gentle sprinkle of rain that had started. We thought that hospitality was impelling her but her start of surprise and stammered "Go on in. I'll be back. I have to bring in my apples that are drying" dispelled this impression. . . . We went in. [In the unlit room] we saw a bed in the center of the main wall and on it an old man, eyes closed, apparently asleep. On the table by the door was an unabridged dictionary, a French-English dictionary, a red key-tag from some hotel, and a loaded revolver of unusually large proportions. . . . Suddenly I became conscious of bright black eyes staring at me out of a grim old face on the pillow. The man had been wide awake all the time. No welcome lay in that averted

[230]

face with its furtive gaze. [When the woman they had met outside reappeared] and I told her of my desire to talk to the old pioneer, her aspect changed. Her face grew tense. She gave no encouragement. "He will not talk," she said. "He has decided never to talk."

When Hamner offered to come back next day, Cleo told her that if she did, he would be gone when she returned. "At last," Hamner said, "I asked permission to go in and see if I could not interest him in what I had to say. Grudgingly she consented, but with the air of not answering for the consequences."

Sitting down by the bed, Hamner told Jenkins she wanted some information about early Panhandle history and that he alone could give it—he was the only living person who knew. "He snarled out a reply, evidently one given many times. He was not going to talk of the old days. The stories that he read were full of inaccuracies. He knew the straight of things but he would not give the lie to those who had talked and were now dead. He would keep what he knew so long as he lived."

Hamner talked of other things, trying to win the old man around.

They told me of the ranch—100,000 acres, 300 blooded horses, race stock, her herd of Shetlands which it amuses him to threaten to shoot, 4000 head of cattle, the remnant of his old immense herd, the garden, the orchard, the six other camps, all better than this though this is the one he prefers for a home. . . . His holdings are so large that he has to drive 1000 miles a week to look after his interests. She drives for him, keeps his books, and is his right hand. He does not want her to cook or dry fruit but go with him wherever he

wants to go. She always does what he wants without a protest although she told me in confidence that she hated book keeping, that her father had wanted her to study accounting but that after going to Clarendon College two years she had studied one year in the State University at Austin, taking an accounting course as part of her work, that she had her one last year's work at Norman, Oklahoma, and had gone to teaching in preference to business work.

When he was satisfied Hamner was "not going to crowd him upon territory that he wished for some reason to avoid," Jenkins loosened up enough to invite them to stay the night, although his wife was less than enthusiastic about the idea. "At last she said that he 'wanted it and what he wanted she wanted him to have.'" Supper was a weird meal at which Jenkins sat down, grabbed an ear of corn, smeared it with butter and started eating before the women were even seated. The sleeping arrangements were just as bizarre. The two visitors were given a flashlight and left to themselves. "No bath, no suggestion of one; a tumbled-up bed, warm from the bodies of both man and woman; no hangers for our clothes; scarcely enough chairs to place bags and garments on. . . . With only a murmured remark about the bed's being a mess, the hostess had left us to solve our problems unaided."

After a sleepless night Hamner and her friend washed their faces on the back porch in ice-cold water (it was mid-September) and dried themselves on the communal towel. Breakfast time was like supper: "Nothing passed to anyone. . . . We ate and talked without any attention from the people who were entertaining us." Their host and hostess remained at the table without either lifting a finger to help as the two women took their bags out to the car and drove off.

In spite of the hostile reception and the weird atmosphere she encountered, Hamner managed to get Jenkins to talk, but not about himself. He spoke freely about Frenchy McCormick or Charles Rudolph, Tobe Robinson or Bill Ruth, but when it came to his part in events in the Panhandle, he had nothing to say. The following year, when John McCarty talked to him at Dalhart, he was equally uncommunicative. Hamner tried again in November 1940 and January 1941; again, he gave her an avalanche of anecdotes and one-line descriptions of people he had known, but nothing with any meat on it. In 1942 Marion Armstrong's son Mel tried to get him to talk, but again Jenkins stuck to anecdotes. After making a final attempt at the Amarillo Hotel in 1942, John McCarty let his frustration show in his notes: "Time and again during the two hours

interview [he] returned to the big fight repeating information already in my possession."[32]

Jesse was nearly eighty now, drinking heavily and more and more isolated from other people. Following the death of both his brother and lifelong companion Lon Jenkins and Lon's wife, Lucy, in 1942, he and Cleo moved from Bonito Canyon to a small, run-down, three-room house a mile or two east of Gallinas, and there Jesse spent his last few years. Almost totally blind, suffering from colon cancer, cirrhosis of the liver, and general physical deterioration, he died in a hospital at Mountainair, New Mexico, on Saturday, July 26, 1947, and was buried alongside his first wife and his sister in a family plot in Dalhart cemetery. "He never owed a debt that he didn't pay," he told Laura Hamner a few years before he died. "Never said he'd do anything that he didn't do it," she noted. "Men knew that, too." It might have been his epitaph for himself.[33]

1887-1890

THE WRITING ON THE WALL

A T TASCOSA in the spring of 1887 railroad fever was the order of the day. Not only was the Fort Worth & Denver a mere two hundred miles away, but the Santa Fe's Southern Kansas spur was also driving into Texas from Woodward, about fifteen miles south of Fort Supply and was now at Carson City (later Panhandle), while a third railroad, the Chicago, Rock Island & Pacific, would in due course also transect the Panhandle. "The year 1887 will yet see Tascosa a railroad town," crowed Rudolph in the *Pioneer,* "and then her boom will discount all the little snide booms we have been hearing so much about."[1]

Although other accounts differ markedly, Rudolph claimed the overall cattle loss for the winter in the Panhandle had been less than 1 percent, and roundup was scheduled to begin May 15. Many of the major brands, notably the LS, not only shipped for sale but also directed herds north to replace stock lost during the Big Die. "The drive from here will aggregate many thousands, and [cattle] Inspector [L. C.] Pierce is at present given about all the work he wants," reported the *Pioneer.*[2]

Tascosa was enjoying perhaps its most prosperous year, and an April 30 special edition of the *Pioneer* celebrated that fact. As well as its imposing stone courthouse and jail, a church, and two schools, the town now boasted four mercantile houses, one of them co-owned by Dodge City entrepreneur Robert M. Wright. Porter & Clouthier of Springer, New Mexico, had opened the Springer Mercantile & Banking Company in a new building on Main Street. There were two hotels—the Exchange operated by Benjamin Bunce and "the other house" by O. S. Hitchcock— and two livery stables, one run by Tobe Robinson and John Wilkinson and one by Mickey McCormick. There were also three millinery shops, Shinebarger and Trescott's Dairy on the Rica, Scotty Wilson's meat market, Henry Kimball's blacksmith shop with a three-man woodwork department attached, three barbershops, a bakery, two law firms, and four saloons (with a fifth soon to come). Within another month or two Tascosa would also have a fine wagon bridge spanning the Canadian River. Begun on March 9 and completed in June, it gave travelers their first experience of ne-

———✺———

Henry Kimball and his wife in his Tascosa blacksmith shop.
(Courtesy of the Haley Memorial Library, Midland, Texas)

gotiating that treacherous crossing without so much as getting their feet wet.

An interesting coincidence—if indeed that is what it was—occurred on May 9 when W. M. D. Lee and his new foreman, Jim East, attended the commisioners court to claim repayment of taxes erroneously assessed the preceding year. A repayment of $215.47 in county warrants was made on the spot, plus a further $250.00 for damage caused by the road built through LS property. No one seems to have wondered why Lee troubled himself to press these seemingly insignificant claims or to have connected his presence with the fact that R. E. Montgomery, right-of-way and town lot agent of the FW&DC railroad, was also in town "rustling about."[3]

In light of later events it requires only a slight stretch of the imagination to picture Lee locking up Montgomery to discuss matters of mutual interest. The fact that

the work of the FW&DC's locating engineer, a man by the name of McCrickett—who would decide exactly where the rails crossed the Canadian River—was put on hold shortly after this suggests that if not at this point, it was certainly very soon afterward that Lee began his little war of revenge on Tascosa.[4]

Meanwhile, among those speculating in 640-acre lots around the site of rail-end "Amorillo City" as the impending organization of Potter County loomed were Jesse Jenkins, Marion Armstrong, M. A. Dunn, and others smart enough to see that a county seat town easily accessible to settlers on the southern plains and to the west as far as the Pecos might very rapidly develop into an important trading center, especially if the big ranches, which had never made any secret of their lack of affection for, not to say antipathy toward, Tascosa chose to support it.

On the Fourth of July, Charlie Rudolph rode down with Jesse Jenkins to what he called "the Amorilla country." Amorillo City, he reported, was "on the boom. We learn that they now have three stores there, two of groceries and one of general merchandise, one saloon, one beer stand, one eating house run by William Trescott. . . . Jenkins & Coan [Cone], of this place, will open a second saloon there by next Wednesday, of which Lee Coan will be in charge. Altogether the new town is making quite a promising start, not to claim the dignity of a town at all, and having sprung up from nothing in less than two weeks."[5]

The "town" Rudolph visited was not the future Amarillo, but a construction camp more generally known as Ragtown, built on a school section owned by Jesse Jenkins. It had "6 or 7 saloons, restaurants, 600 or 700 folks. There were always 50 to 100 men [working] on the railroad. They would go to a saloon and drink after work hours. Sometimes lay off and get drunk and more men would take their place. Restaurants and saloons did a big business. . . . Ragtown was the fastest town I ever saw."

During the seven or eight months it lasted, Ragtown made Jesse a serious amount of money; he was determined to make a great deal more by ensuring the land it stood on became the site of the new county seat. Meantime, he poured the booze into the Irish railroad workers and pocketed their pay while his brother Lon, who had the contract to supply them with beef, was also doing very nicely, because it seems a lot of the beef was being rustled to order.[6]

Just about that time—and surely not coincidentally—former LX range boss Bill Ruth arranged to buy a couple of cows on a regular basis from a man named Meek who

ranched in Bugbee Canyon. At that time John Arnot was living on Little Blue Creek, about halfway between Tascosa and the Meek place (he later married one of Meek's daughters, Martha), where Ruth would stay overnight before going on to the Meek ranch to butcher the cows and then haul them to town. These legitimate purchases were cover for a racket Ruth was running at the expense of his former employers; on his way into town "he would drive over to [a creek that was] a favorite watering place for cattle . . . , get his Winchester and shoot down two or three fat LX cows, skin them, load up the meat and proceed to Tascosa. Ruth ran very little risk of being caught up with as . . . at that time there was no law forcing anyone selling a beef to have the hide along to show ownership."[7]

Two small tragedies marred Tascosa's summer. The first was the death on June 14 of Josephine Wyness, wife of the popular LX bookkeeper. The former Josephine Elizabeth Terras of London, England, she was just twenty-six; she and James Wyness had been married a little over a year, and she had given birth to a twelve-pound baby boy on May 8; even sadder, her baby died of cholera on August 10. On the same day, Charlotte "Lottie" Barker, wife of constable Dave Barker, passed on, just twelve days after the birth of her own baby, also a boy. Barker and his family left Tascosa toward the end of September for Denver.[8]

In August 1887 the petition to organize Potter County was submitted and granted, and an election was ordered for August 30. Rudolph sneered at the proposition, although he must surely have realized, as doubtless did those who were investing in town lots there, that the county seat town that would inevitably follow would be a formidable rival for the railroad's favors.[9] At this juncture the commercial center of the Panhandle was yet to be decided. The Santa Fe Railroad's preferred option was Panhandle City; the FW&DC's was Washburn, where Montgomery owned the townsite. But with the "Amorillo" area looking more and more viable, Jesse Jenkins was not the only one betting on its future: a group of hard-headed businessmen from Colorado City, located in Mitchell County on the Texas & Pacific Railroad, were looking at it very closely indeed.

Their representative, Col. James T. Berry, an experienced townsite developer from Abilene, arrived in the Panhandle in April and selected a well-watered section of school land that fulfilled all the necessary requirements: his partners in this endeavor were Nacogdoches-born Col. Claiborne W. Merchant, a cattleman and ranch owner who had located and promoted Abilene in Taylor County in 1881, and James T. Holland, who had been mixed up in a shady New York counterfeit scam that ended with his killing a man.[10]

Other contenders were former Clay County attorney and judge William B. Plemons, who owned a section close to the headsprings of Amarillo Creek; Jesse Jenkins, who had Ragtown; and Frank Lester, a lawyer from Panhandle City said to be financed by Henry Sanborn. Berry made a deal with Plemons, who dropped out; as a result, only three locations were put forward: the Berry consortium's "Oneida," four miles east of Ragtown on Section 188; Frank Lester's "Plains City," on Section 156; and Jesse Jenkins's "Odessa"—the Ragtown site on Section 22.

Years later, Jenkins grudgingly admitted that "Amarillo literally stole the county seat from Rag Town. I offered my section as the county seat section and Berry and Mer-chant and their bunch offered the section where Old Amarillo was later located. It had to be voted on. The big voting boxes were the two ranches, the LXs and the Frying Pans. I thought I had the LXs sewed up so on election day I went over to the Frying Pans to vote them right. While I was gone, Berry and his bunch got in their work with the LXs."

In the robust manner in which such matters were handled in those days, Berry and his partners promised each man on the LX ranch a free business lot and a residence lot in the new town if they did the right thing. And it worked; all thirty-eight LX votes were cast for Oneida. At the Frying Pan, the vote went Oneida, seven; Odessa, five; Plains City, three. Oneida—it was renamed Amarillo just a few weeks later—had won hands down. Jesse Jenkins was not delighted. "While not one of them had any money except Berry, and he did not have much . . . the [LX] boys swallowed the offer and voted for the section belonging to that bunch but the cowboys didn't get nothing. That crowd all got pretty well off on that town."[11]

The birth of Amarillo, as it would become, spelled the death of Ragtown, whose inhabitants moved swiftly on to get their share of the opportunities waiting in the new metropolis. "Houses went up rapidly," Jim Gober recalled, "and a good many lived in tents with boarded-up sides for several months." Tascosa merchants Cone and Duran erected the first adobe building and freighted in a stock of general merchandise. Another mercantile firm, Carter & Morton, erected a frame building, as did a third called Smith & Walker. Garrett Johnson and Jack Ryan opened saloons. All were more than willing to tough out today's raw conditions for a shot at tomorrow's benefits.[12]

In September the FW&DC agreed to locate its depot on Berry's section 188, and construction began on large stock shipping yards to accommodate cattle for shipment east on the railroad, yet another nail in the coffin of the trail-driving tradition; by October, freight service was made available. A twenty-four-by-forty-foot frame building was constructed as a temporary courthouse on Lipscomb Street, and a dance was held there to celebrate its completion. Two days later, on November 27, Amarillo got its post office. It, and Potter County, were now a fact of life that would further downturn the waning fortunes of Tascosa.[13]

But nothing affected its fortunes as badly as the news that the FW&DC had decided to bypass the town completely, crossing the Canadian River instead at a new town called Cheyenne, to be built on LS land about four miles west of Tascosa. In short order the site was surveyed and platted and promotional leaflets and advertising bills distributed. At the beginning of December, in a "mammoth advertisement," FW&DC agent and promoter R. E. Montgomery offered town lots in the new location, which, the railroad claimed, "will command [the Panhandle's] entire trade that now goes to build up and has made Dodge City, Las Vegas, Springer and other cities in Kansas, Colorado and New Mexico, what they are."[14]

On December 15 an excursion train took would-be buyers from Clarendon to Cheyenne for a public sale of town lots by auction to the highest bidder; anyone who spent more than $150 had his fare refunded by the railroad. A promised two-story hotel was already under construction. A crowd said to have been in excess of three hundred attended (the *Pioneer* put it at less than two hundred), and sales in excess of twenty thousand dollars were claimed (Rudolph doubted the sum was even half that).

A number of Tascosans, among them C. B. Vivian, bought lots in the new town, but the *Pioneer* doubted they were the kind of men

who will be found on the ground, working day in and day out for the building up of a city. *The Pioneer* has never believed and still doubts that it ever was or that it is seriously intended by the railroad authorities to build or help build a town at the site of the incipient Cheyenne. Had they wished to build such a city, it is not reasonable that such a location would have been selected. They are not so silly as to choose a site subject to yearly overflow, and then make, or encourage in others, any vigorous sacrifices to the floods; they would scarcely think to ignore the law, the language of which is so conclusive, and leave this county seat, three miles from them, not even a station. They would hardly be guilty of the folly of antagonizing not merely the entire population of such a town as this, but the entire country, whose sense of justice will inevitably array it actively, and the tax-payers, who are not deceived as to the consequences that would shortly follow.

These are sufficient reasons on which to ground the belief that Cheyenne is not the product, even indirectly, of the avarice of a man, or of a company; but it is the direct outcome of a spleen that found its opportunity to dictate conditions there and to vent itself here.

Short of actually stating that Lee had deliberately sold Tascosa down (or in this instance, up) the river, Rudolph could hardly have been more frank. Certainly the

Cecil B. Vivian (detail from the photograph of a group of early Tascosans). (Courtesy of the Haley Memorial Library, Midland, Texas)

town wasn't taking it lying down; on another page he revealed that an application for a writ of mandamus, a judicial document ordering a person or company to perform a statutory duty, had been filed requiring the FW&DC to obey the terms of its charter and erect a depot at or within half a mile of the county seat. Morgan Jones, president of the railroad company, shrugged off the action by announcing that chief engineer Bissell already had orders to build a depot but was unable to proceed due to the fact that the owner of the land, W. M. D. Lee, had threatened to enjoin its erection because the right of way had not yet been settled.[15]

The impasse was settled toward the end of January 1888 when Jim Dobbs sold Jack Ryan and Ryan sold the town 320 acres he owned at the old Borrego *plazita*. After extended negotiations with Lee, the town fathers exchanged it for his land abutting the railroad that would accommodate an

FW&DC depot and side tracks. "So the agony is over," Rudolph announced. "We are a railroad town."

It was true, and yet of course it was not, because as part of the deal Lee stipulated that none of the land involved was to be sold to business firms, and no new houses would be built. Nevertheless, a wagon bridge was speedily installed to ferry passengers to and from the depot, and a flutter of speculators—Jesse Jenkins among them—bought tracts nearby in hope of a "new" Tascosa springing up beside the depot. It never happened, nor did the hoped-for improvement in the town's fortunes come about.[16]

In fact, the opposite: Lee's Parthian shot had inflicted a wound from which Tascosa would never recover. By the time the small, two-room depot was completed in May 1888, the FW&DC had completed its tracks through Texas; the only two towns shown on its map were Clarendon and Cheyenne. Ironically enough, Cheyenne went bust without ever booming; although an agent was kept there for a couple of years, the place never showed any real sign of flourishing. Rechristened Magenta Sidings, it never even got big enough to become a ghost town.

The last spike of the FW&DC was driven on March 14, 1888, and "Tascosa joined in the general celebration of the completion of the [rail]road, though the din of the jubilee was the town's requiem. The larger and more important of the construction camps along the railroad had become the nuclei for many plains towns. These new towns were more conveniently located to serve the ranches than Tascosa. Strangely, however, Tascosa furnished much of the supplies for the building of the towns which killed it."[17]

With nothing to cling to now but the

hope that the Chicago, Rock Island & Pacific would cross the Canadian at Tascosa, Rudolph's *Pioneer* continued to maintain the illusion that everything was in equilibrium: in June Commissioners Jim McMasters, Seth Mabry, Howson Wallace, and Ike Ryland entered into a contract with the Flint & Walling Company of Fort Worth to establish a system of waterworks for the town. In the November 1888 election Wallace was returned as county judge, Tobe Robinson as sheriff, and Alex Wilson as the town's unbudgeable justice of the peace.

It might have been seen as a ray of hope that the town's original founder, Casimero Romero, elected to return to Tascosa that spring. But over this and indeed the next couple of years, the hemorrhage of the town's residents to fresher fields continued. Lon Jenkins departed for a new start in Roswell. E. C. Godwin-Austen was survey-ing a townsite at Rivers, soon to be Channing. Isaiah Rinehart, partially paralyzed following a stroke, moved to the new town of Texline "because there is not local trade enough here now to give him his share." Rinehart's son Irwin left to manage the Cone & Duran branch store in Amarillo, and Jack Ryan's wife and children joined Jack, already there. Mickey McCormick sold the accoutrements of his livery stable to True & Wyness of Amarillo. And in what was perhaps the most significant departure of all, Jesse Jenkins sold out and moved up to Hartley County.[18]

Jenkins "had always had a strong following among the little men he championed, and when he moved from his ranch on the Punta de Agua to the new townsite of Hartley . . . a large number of men and their families followed. They filed on land in Hartley and Moore counties outside the

Early-day Channing. (Courtesy of the XIT Museum)

[239]

XIT spread and formed the nucleus of a strong nester settlement on the north plains," and with their departure leaving yet another large hole in the social fabric of the town. In 1888 Carson and Roberts Counties were organized, and with Ochiltree waiting in the wings, Tascosa's sphere of influence was being inexorably and massively reduced.[19]

At Amarillo the very opposite was the case: a large twenty-five-room frame hotel, The Champion, had been erected at the intersection of Third and Greene Streets; an enormous lumberyard stood near the depot On May 17, 1888, editor H. H. Brookes launched the town's first (weekly) newspaper, the *Amarillo Champion,* and later that same month a public sale of lots brought prospective buyers from as far afield as Fort Worth and Denver and generated about thirteen thousand dollars in sales. As Tascosa was discovering to its cost, railroads not only brought in new settlers, they also spirited them away.[20]

In December 1888 the Rock Island Line decided not to include Tascosa on its route, but instead to intersect the FW&DC on the border of Dallam and Hartley Counties. At this junction a town sprang up; taking its name from the two counties, Dalhart would by the turn of the century become the sort of Panhandle metropolis of which Rudolph had dreamed. And as if all that were not bad enough news, a year or so later Albert G. "Al" Boyce, who had become general manager of the XIT earlier that year, long galled by his failure to oust Jesse Jenkins and his cohorts and make Tascosa a "company town," announced plans to establish just such a town at Rivers, near the ranch's new headquarters in Hartley County.

The new town, which eventually became Channing, was as unlike Tascosa as any town could be. From the start, the deeply religious J. B. Farwell, Al Boyce, and the other XIT executives refused to tolerate lawless or immoral behavior. Indeed, so enlightened (or oppressive, depending on where you were sitting) was their regime that in October 1887 they had ruled that no card-playing and no gun-carrying were permitted on the ranch, and the following May they actually instituted a six-day week so the cowboys would not have to work Sundays. Within a few years many of the Tascosa businesses that had not defected to Amarillo relocated in Channing, which soon became the commercial center for its area.

Farther north, still more competition for Tascosa reared its unlovely head in the shape of Texline, to be "built up by a combined effort of the railroad company and the XIT interests, [and] as it is right at the line of Texas and New Mexico, close to No-Man's-Land and not far from the corners of Kansas and Colorado, it will be the biggest and the best and the fastest and the hardest and the busiest and the wildest and the roughest and the toughest town of this section," Rudolph noted. "They've already had to station the Texas rangers there—and when that's said, enough's said."[21]

Enough said indeed; for Tascosa, with the kind of competition it would inevitably get from Amarillo, Channing, Dalhart, and Texline, the writing was well and truly on the wall.

More wall writing, none of it optimistic, had already materialized: Charles Goodnight, convinced that the cattle business had "at last struck bed rock," persuaded Cornelia Adair (whose husband had died in 1885) that this was an appropriate moment to dissolve their partnership; he would leave the Palo Duro forever in

December. From Wyoming came news that the giant Swan Land & Cattle Company was in desperate trouble. Amid accusations that the herd books had been falsified, that the actual number of cattle was at least thirty thousand less than represented, and that the company had been cheated out of more than eight hundred thousand dollars, Alexander H. Swan was summarily dismissed. Nearer home, there were similar unexplained stock deficiencies at the English-owned Clarendon Land Investment & Agency; only fourteen thousand head could be found on the range instead of the twenty-five thousand that were supposed to be there; the fate of Swan and Clarendon heralded hard times to come.[22]

The cattle trade was in desperate trouble. In the wake of two murderous winters in 1885 and 1886, followed by a blistering drought in the summer of 1887, ranchers large and small, under pressure from banks and syndicates, had no option but to send their stock to market regardless of age or quality. Inevitably prices plummeted (from the 1882 high of $9.35 to $1.90 per hundred pounds), compounding the problem. Hit hardest by the downturn were the big syndicates, far too many of which were run by absentee owners who knew little or nothing about cattle and who conducted their business on an extravagant scale with multiple directors and highly paid managers working out of expensive office suites in Kansas City or even London. One by one, they followed each other into a financial quagmire. Dundee, the Scottish town that had been the citadel of investment in American ranching, watched dividends either going down or disappearing completely.

Between December 1886 and the same month a year later the capital value of eleven companies in which the town was

Charles Goodnight in later years.
(Author's Collection)

interested—Prairie, Swan, Texas, Matador, Hansford, Arkansas, Pastoral, Powder River, Western Land, Cattle Ranche, and Western Ranches—depreciated by £2,023,300, well over ten million dollars (something like a hundred million dollars in today's money). By 1888 the figure was £2,253,263—a drop of a further 10 percent. Even the mighty Capitol consortium took a beating. When the promised Capitol Building in Austin was completed at a cost of three and a quarter million dollars, it meant the land owned by the XIT had cost it over a dollar an acre, four times the going price for unwatered land—and further bad news for its English investors, none of whom had seen a dividend for years. Something had to give, and something did. The money men began looking for other, safer investments.[23]

Notable among the defectors—and they were many—was W. M. D. Lee. "I'm afraid we will see the grand rush of beeves [being dumped on the market] continued until none exist," he told a newspaper. "Every one seems to be trying to see who can get rid of his cattle first." None more so, he might have added, than himself; he had already invited his partner, Lucien Scott, to buy him out so he could invest in a brand-new project, the building of a deepwater port and docks at Velasco, Texas. Scott acquiesced, and the following February, 1888, Lee entered into an agreement with Austin and San Antonio moneymen to form a company (backed by a one-million-dollar investment) "for the purposes of constructing, owning and operating a deep water channel, from the waters of the Gulf of Mexico to the mainland at the mouth of the Brazos River."[24]

Within six months all the LS livestock in Montana were sold off and that ranch's employees transferred to Texas. In August the sale of Lee's prized Angus herd was advertised and completed. Throughout that year and the next, Lee continued to transfer his lands, cattle, and other rights to Scott; on November 29, 1890, Lee and his wife, Selina, signed the final deed that for "$1 and other various sums received" made Lucien Scott sole owner of the LS.[25]

By the time Scott began running the LS to suit himself, its tax—and other—disputes with Oldham County came to an end. Losses from rustling also dwindled; as bigger and bigger areas of the Panhandle plains were fenced in, the thieves took the easier option and preyed on the more accessible stock of the XIT, whose western line faced the last vast open spaces on the frontier, the length and breadth of New Mexico and, beyond it, Arizona. Jim East was replaced by Al

Popham, a tough old LS hand who frowned on the long-established practice of allowing herds to be driven across LS land on their way to Tascosa. Popham "believed a man had the right to protect his holdings as he saw fit. He did not intend to see LS grass trampled by any other than LS cattle, and broken fences were not to be tolerated." By thus denying other ranchers access to the shipping pens there, Popham hammered another nail into the coffin of Tascosa.[26]

Another side-effect of these changes was a sharp decrease in crime. "We find a generally law abiding and satisfactory state of affairs existing in this jurisdiction," the grand jury reported, "as is evidenced by the finding of but three true bills of indictment." But the old town still had a twitch or two in its system. In 1885 a "mustanger" from South Texas named Walter Harris Brown came in from Kansas. During that summer he and his outfit captured over 200 wild horses, which he sold for fifteen dollars a head. The following year, his luck ran out and he only caught about 30 head, but in 1888 things improved and he brought in 250.

The same year, brothers Bob and Tom Hightower, also mustangers, went south with "Mustang" Brown and together caught almost three hundred head. Working with them was a man named Bob Stewart, who was to receive a percentage of the animals caught as his remuneration, but when it became time to settle up, "the two Bobs disagreed as to terms. While Bob Hightower was gone from camp, Stewart cut out what horses he claimed was due him [but] just as he started away Bob Hightower rode up . . . , pulled his Winchester and commenced shooting at Stewart . . . only shooting close enough to scare him, running a blazer as the old saying was."

Not scared worth a damn, Stewart dismounted with his Winchester, knelt down, and calmly put a bullet through Hightower's shoulder. His brother, Tom, loaded the wounded man into the wagon and headed for help in Tascosa, a hundred miles away, where Bob died a few weeks later. "Mustang" Brown brought the Hightower horses in and sold them to a Kansas dealer; they may well have been the last large number of mustangs to be caught on the plains.[27]

The following year, Tascosa's last gunfight took place; it seems almost fitting that Jim East was one of the participants. Not long after his resignation as manager of the LS, East bought the Cattle Exchange saloon and the Equity Bar and amalgamated them under the latter name. For some reason he and Tom Clark, a one-legged gambler who operated in the saloon, "got into a dispute over the rent on a monte table and . . . Jim sent word to Clarke [sic] to 'come down and we will either bury the hatchet or fight it out.' Clark drew his gun as he entered the door and the fight started." In the *Pioneer*'s version of events, as East entered the saloon during the morning of Wednesday, May 7, 1890, Clark braced him and said, "Here's hopin' you'll land in Hell and that I'll be there to shovel the coal."

"East said, 'Here's back at you.'

"'Fuck you,' said Clark. 'Jim East, I'm not afraid of you.'"

Both men drew guns and several shots were fired "in tolerably rapid succession."

The Equity Bar consisted of two rooms about eighteen by twenty feet. In the center of the room nearest the street was a hexagonal column made of finished lumber cladding a cottonwood post that supported the roof. Dodging behind this post, East, who had not been hit, put down his six-

gun, picked up a Winchester, and slid out the back door. Clark, mortally wounded, lurched out the front door, where he encountered Texas Rangers "Grude" Britton and Tom Platt. They asked if anyone was hurt and demanded his weapon. "You may as well take it," said Clark. "I'll soon be a dead man."

He stepped back inside the saloon, reeled, and fell. Ed Donnelly and Al Morris carried him half a block to the Exchange Hotel, and Dr. Shelton was sent for. The good doctor took a while to arrive because he was busy taking care of a local gambler named Doc Cooley, who had remarked, "Ain't got nothin' I want!" when the shooting started and had run for the door, only to be hit in the backside by a stray shot.

Dr. Shelton did what he could for Clark, but the man had been shot through from side to side and died within ten or fifteen minutes. A postmortem revealed that seven shots had been fired and that one had passed through the fleshy part of Clark's left arm between shoulder and elbow, entered the body, then gone straight through.[28]

Jim East surrendered to Sheriff Tobe Robinson and was jailed until the coroner's verdict was received. Clark was buried the same day but not, according to one authority, in Boot Hill. The widow of Tom Smith, "who had bought several acres of land and moved several Hispanic families there, refused to permit it. She put a notice in *The Pioneer* that she would permit no more burials on Boothill."

As it happened, the grand jury was in session; the case was heard Friday, May 9. "The investigation showed that Clarke had missed two or three shots and apparently did not or could not shoot as well as he talked or thought he could." There was also

**Tascosa's Boot Hill with the original headstones, ca. 1925.
(Courtesy of the Haley Memorial Library, Midland, Texas)**

talk that East's bartender, Miles Roland, had killed Clark but in the end "it was determined that it was a dead fair fight."

Witnesses at the hearing testified that East, who was defended by attorneys Wallace and Woodman, had fired in self-defense, and he was acquitted. According to Harry Ingerton, however, "He didn't need to do that at all, but Clark was just as quarrelsome as Jim was, and drank just about as much. They were both drunk, as I understand it."

Interestingly, East's long biographical memoir makes no mention of the incident at all.[29]

The Clark-East fight was to prove the last exemplar of Tascosa's wild and woolly ways: it was becoming all too apparent now that its raggedy rows of adobes would never be transformed into the Queen City of the Plains that Charlie Rudolph had dreamed of. Like the western frontier, old Tascosa was disappearing. Mobeetie, too, was dying on its feet. In August 1890 the U.S. Army decided to close Fort Elliott. On

October 2 most of the garrison departed, and eighteen days later the fort was formally closed. Today nothing remains of it but a monument marking the site.

Change was coming into the Panhandle now at the speed of one of those clanking, panting "express trains" now plying forth and back across its once empty expanses. In October 1890 Deaf Smith County was organized, with Grenada as its county seat; four months later, in February 1891, it was the turn of Hartley County, with Hartley as its seat. Considerable resistance to both of these developments was offered by the XIT, but both were carried. The following November Castro County petitioned for organization unopposed, and a month later the election was held.

Just a decade after its own formation, Oldham County stood alone. Truly an island now, no longer on the trail to anywhere, "fenced in" by the big ranches and shut off from nearly all of its former customers, Tascosa controlled nothing but its own shabby Main Street.

Chapter 24

CHARLES FRANCIS RUDOLPH

"IT'S SAD TO DIE YOUNG."

IN THE LATE spring of 1886, twenty-seven-year-old newspaper publisher Charles Francis Rudolph, resident in Saint Jo, Montague County, Texas, decided to try fresh fields. His newspaper, the *St. Jo Gladiator,* originally a weekly, had in the three years following Rudolph's 1882 takeover become a successful and profitable daily. Young, ambitious, intelligent, and determined, Rudolph wanted more. Anticipating that when both the Fort Worth & Denver City Railroad, once again building west from Wichita Falls, where it had lain idle for three years, and the Kansas City & Southern, spearing southwest toward a junction with the FW&DC, reached the Texas Panhandle, they would open up many opportunities for prosperity and success, he decided he was going to be there when it happened.

The final routes of the two railroads had not yet been decided, but since there were only three frontier towns in the Panhandle, one of them must surely become a thriving railroad town. Rudolph made his choice, sold his paper to editor and publisher V. B. Jolly (who renamed it the *St. Jo Herald*), loaded his printing presses, his

personal belongings, and everything else he owned into three sturdy wagons, and set out with his wife and five-month-old son, Roy, for Tascosa, about 250 miles away.

Although he must have arrived just a few days after the murderous May 26 gunfight, Rudolph refused to let it deter him from embarking immediately on what would become, over the next four years, a one-man crusade to ensure, first, that the railroad would indeed come to Tascosa and, second, that when it arrived his adopted town would become—as he liked to describe it—"the Queen City of the Panhandle." One historian wrote: "He never missed a detail of surveying work or railroad gossip and never failed to hold out the promise of a big boom and much development." But no matter how much "razzoop" Rudolph put into it, pushing a recently coined replacement word for "boom" that never made it into the dictionaries, the growth he worked so hard for stubbornly refused to happen.[1]

Born February 3, 1859, in Marietta, Washington County, Ohio, Charles Francis Rudolph was the fourth of the six children of Israel Putnam and Catherine (Greene)

Rudolph. Charles Rudolph left home for Texas before reaching his majority. He had kept a handwritten journal (which he gave to his sister as a Christmas [possibly 1880] present and which is still in the family) of his travels by wagon and on horseback across Illinois, Missouri, Arkansas, Oklahoma, and into Texas near Sherman, then across the prairie to Gainesville, where he and his brother Nelson arrived in October 1877.[2]

Charles appears in the 1880 census for Montague County, Texas, as a single twenty-one-year-old schoolteacher boarding at the home of T. F. Morrow in Precinct Two, Saint Jo. Nelson was living in the adjoining house of J. M. Wiggins, listed as a farmer. Their sister, Mary Rudolph Herndon, and her husband, a doctor, came to Saint Jo in 1881, bringing their children and sister Myra. The following year, perhaps with financial support from his family, Rudolph bought and began publishing his weekly newspaper. On December 19, 1883, Nelson Rudolph was married to Mina Jones in Montague County; they would have at least five sons.[3]

By the time Charles Rudolph married Mary Jerusha McGregor at Gainesville, Cooke County, on December 9, 1884, he had also brought his father to live in Saint Jo. Charles and Mary Rudolph would have six children.[4]

One story about him suggests Rudolph may have been a tad rougher round the edges than his editorials suggest. It was court week in Tascosa, and

> when the court adjourned for the day, judge, jury, lawyers and clients roamed the town in company. They drank together, played monte, faro, roulette, poker or anything that suited the individual. As the hours advanced, one after another sloughed off of the crowd and went to

Charles and Mary Jerusha (McGregor) Rudolph, 1884. (Courtesy of Marsha Field Foster)

The Rudolph children: Roy, Frank, and Guy. (Courtesy of Marsha Field Foster)

bed. Always among the last was Temple Houston. . . . The only person who would "stay" with Houston on his bouts was the editor of the little paper in Tascosa. The two watched companion after companion slip away to bed while they were still "going good."

One night when the town was practically cleared, they decided to eat a snack. Sitting down to the table they asked for canned goods and crackers.

"Bring me some swimp," ordered the editor.

"It's not 'swimp,' it's 'shrimp,'" broke in Houston, ever meticulous in speech.

The round bore of a pistol came up over the table edge; Houston looked down into its steely depths and then into the steel of the eyes above it.

With portentous calm, the editor said, "By God, I say it's 'swimp.'"

"And by God, I say it's 'swimp,' too," quickly returned Houston, and the incident closed with a long toddy."[5]

From the beginning, the *Tascosa Pioneer* was always a true frontier newspaper, produced on an army press running off only one page at a time. Advertisements cost $1.00 per inch per month if contracted for a year, more if not. Brands were featured, with a cut of the animal, for $10.00 per annum, and additional brands, letters, blocks, or figures were $2.00 each (again, payable in advance). Announcements of candidacy for office during the November elections were: district offices, $15.00; county offices, $10.00; and precinct offices, $5.00. Legal notices and other ads cost fifteen cents a line; for double measure and for financial statements, charges were doubled. Never exactly inundated with business in that department, Rudolph probably balanced precariously on the razor's edge

between small profit and large loss throughout the life of the paper.

During his years as editor of the *Pioneer* he talked to everyone, attended every function, kept his finger on every development. He covered most, if not all, of the major events in and around it that influenced the growth and welfare of Tascosa: the "grass-lease fight," improvements to the mail service, the building of the Canadian River bridge, the "theatricals" held in the courthouse, the proceedings of the commissioners court, the twice-yearly roundups, the Christmas horse races, and the impeachment of Judge Frank Willis, and he contributed the big special edition published in April 1887 that puffed every business in town.

And always, over and over, he crowed the railroad, the railroad, the much-needed, long-awaited railroad. How confidently he anticipated its arrival, how triumphantly he announced it:

The completion of the Fort Worth & Denver City railway to this city on Tuesday evening inaugurates a new era in Tascosa's history. Henceforth the year 1887 becomes the year one in her calendar. No more of the frontier life, frontier ways, frontier denials and frontier prices. The old order of things was pleasant in its way and in parting with it we leave behind as much of the methodical quiet, the unassuming sociability and the easy financial status of everything, and in meeting the new arrangement we come upon more or less of the transitory people and things of false appearance and false values, of undue stimulation and systems not so frank and open. But we have made a forward step, and we will make others.[6]

Alas, it was not to be, and in 1891, after fifteen years, he simply gave up. Two years earlier, perhaps contemplating a move there, he had established printing facilities in Amarillo, and on New Year's Day, 1890, he began publishing a short-lived newspaper called the *Daily Northwest* there. In the same year he formed a two-year partnership with J. L. Caldwell, who subsequently published the *Amarillo Weekly News*. He closed down the *Tascosa Pioneer* on February 28, 1891, and bade the town farewell with a fulsome editorial, "the closing chapter in the history of the *Pioneer*. For five years it has gone forth proclaiming to the world that we had here a country and a town . . . but today we lay down the saber and give up the fight; and the *Pioneer* is an institution of the past, a back number, a remembrance, a reminiscence and a dream."

Nonetheless, some of the bitterness shows through. Elsewhere in the final issue Rudolph says "We quit the dump," or "Here it is finished," or "Here we quit you. Be a good boy and try to meet us in Heaven." Then his tone softens into regret. "Good by Panhandle. Good by Tascosa. Our briny tears fall upon the sands as we take a last and long farewell of thee, and crystallize there into large lumps of rock salt. It's sad to die young, but that's the way the good die."[7]

Many were the encomiums that followed his announcement of the paper's demise. In his former hometown, the *Saint Jo Herald* noted the "sad news that there would be no more *Pioneer*," adding, "its death has caused a vacancy on our exchange table, now draped in mourning, which may never be occupied again." Over in Mobeetie, the *Panhandle* was less sympathetic. "The *Tascosa Pioneer* has suspended publication. Tascosa has been gradually dying ever since the Denver railroad was built and now it is dead." Sympathies—some from newspapers as for-

gotten now as Tascosa itself—poured in: from the *Nocona Argus,* the *Fort Worth Daily Gazette,* the *Harrold Telephone,* the *Aurora Chronicle,* the *Bowie Cross Timbers,* the *Hall County Record,* the *Canyon Citizen,* the *Estacada Citizen,* the *Della Plain,* the *Quanah Tribune,* the *Cooke County Signal,* the *Clay County Chieftain,* and the *Mineral Wells Herald.* But sympathy wasn't what Rudolph was looking for. As he said himself, "Tascosa, old town, pleasant home, it's not without emotions of pleasure that we give you up. It's to go and make some lucre."[8]

The *Pioneer* office and printing materials were freighted to Channing, where Rudolph intended to "issue a paper in future on each Saturday. The initial number will appear on March 7 [1891]. A handsome patronage is already pledged and there need be no doubt about the permanency of town and paper. The name of the latter has not yet been determined upon, but it will be a 7-column folio, all home print, and will endeavour to keep up with the procession of live and enterprising southwestern journalism. This is its prospectus and this is enough. When it appears it can tell the story for itself. If you find you like it, read it, advertise in it, and subscribe for it. If you don't like it, let it alone."[9]

He published the promised weekly for a while but was discouraged by opposition to it from the XIT management (who didn't like his confrontational style any more than Mac Lee had). Much the same thing happened when he moved to Hartley, where he published the *Hartley County Citizen.* He continued publishing the *Amarillo Daily Northwest* until 1893, when he sold it to Frank Cates and A. R. Rankin, who renamed it the *Amarillo Northwestern.* In 1896 the Rudolphs moved to a ranch at Coldwater, the new county seat of Sherman County, where he ran cattle, opened a school, and also published the *Sherman County Banner.* Elected county clerk, he sold his newspaper plant to a man who started the *Stratford Star.* When Stratford became the county seat in 1901, Rudolph moved his family there to continue his duties.[10]

He left scant record of himself, and his descendants were—perhaps understandably—vague about the rest of his life, saying only that he had "died in the early 1930s." It was not quite the truth, and Jesse Jenkins, who knew where all the bodies were buried, took sour pleasure in correcting the record. "Editor Rudolph was a man who did not like to pay his bills," he said. "[He was] a damned smart crook. He altered deeds or land records and covered up for certain interests. He

was sent to the pen, finally dying there."[11] And sure enough, the record shows that in 1926 and 1927, while pursuing the profession of lawyer in Canyon, Texas, Rudolph was convicted on three counts of misappropriation of funds belonging to Joseph Williams, a Texhoma real estate speculator, and was sentenced to two years in jail.

Entering Huntsville Penitentiary as prisoner 57960 on December 5, 1927, Charles Francis Rudolph was sixty-eight years old, a gray-haired, ruddy-cheeked man with blue-grey eyes who stood five foot nine and weighed 162 pounds. Apparently a widower by this time, he was probably already terminally ill; he died in the penitentiary of cancer of the bladder and kidneys on June 8, 1929, just four months before he was due to be released. He is buried in El Reno, Oklahoma.[12]

∽
Chapter 25
∽

"HERE WE QUIT YOU"

I N 1890, realizing he would never break Jesse Jenkins's hold on Tascosa and make it the company town he wanted, Albert Boyce of the XIT proposed to his management board that the ranch purchase a town section in Hartley County on the FW&DC line and establish new headquarters there. The go-ahead was given, and with the enthusiastic cooperation of the railroad, the town of Rivers—it did not become Channing until the following year—was platted. In short order the XIT's storage buildings and warehouses at Tascosa were closed and their contents moved up to the new town, already a busy commercial center with two general stores, a livery stable, and two lumberyards.[1]

Channing became a "company town" with a vengeance. Unlike wide-open Tascosa, saloons and the oldest profession were not just discouraged in Channing but positively proscribed. The management of the XIT were not just antiwhoring, however; they were antiswearing, antidrinking, antigambling, antishooting, anti–wasting time, and very anti–not observing the Sabbath—in fact, J. B. Farwell sometimes went so far as to hold services and preach a ser-

mon to his employees. On one occasion some British bondholders visiting the ranch brought a case of whiskey with them; Boyce told them if the hired hands were not allowed to drink, neither were they, and if they didn't like it they could have his resignation on the spot. The Brits buckled under.

Virtue alone, however, was not going to ensure that Channing would become the

∽

XIT headquarters office at Channing about the time the Graham boys shot it up. (Courtesy of the XIT Museum)

county seat. Jesse Jenkins, doubtless seeking an opportunity to rectify the mistakes he had made at Amarillo, had sold his Tascosa saloon and filed on land on the fringes of the XIT near the FW&DC's end-of-track "ragtown," where he was soon joined by a group of the "little men" he had always supported and who in turn loyally supported him, among them Rucker Tanner, Dick Pincham, Dave Adkinson, Matt Atwood, Bill Wheeler, George Knighton, and Britt Roberts. They and others created a sizable and unwelcome "nester"—another word for "rustler" as far as the XIT was concerned—settlement there with enough voters to contest any unwelcome moves the big men might make.[2]

There had only been a hundred residents in Hartley County in 1880; by 1890 there were two and a half times that many. Forty-eight cattle or sheep ranches and farms, encompassing almost 180,000 acres, had been established, and more than 11,100 cattle and 3,200 sheep were counted in the area that year, more than enough to encourage Hartley County's residents, on January 9, 1891, to petition Oldham County for organization and ask that an election be held for the selection of a county seat. With Commissioners Al Popham and Ruck Tanner voting for, H. F. Mitchell and F. W. DeBoice against, County Judge J. L. Penry's casting vote decided the issue, and an election was called for Thursday, February 5, 1891.[3]

Boyce made no secret of the fact he expected Channing to become the county seat. The "little men"—notably Jesse Jenkins—were just as determined it would be Hartley. Boyce knew Jesse could make it happen: he controlled the votes not only of the "little men" but also of the Hispanic portion of the population. No use for Boyce to tell them Jenkins had his own

agenda; Jesse had already convinced them if the XIT got its way, they'd soon be forced out. And when election day came, and Hartley won, he made sure the right people took office, regardless of their qualifications. For example, "[Rucker] Tanner was elected to be County Judge of Hartley County. He would get up in the chair cowboy fashion. I went up and said 'Ruck, you can't be a judge if you don't know a damned thing about the law.' He says, 'Hell, what I don't know about the law, I've got a mule down the canyon that does.'"[4]

The election was pretty much a clean sweep for the nesters; Judge Tanner presided over a commissioners court consisting of Dick Pincham, W. C. Ferguson, George W. Knighton, and G. W. Lambert. Ben Lawson became county clerk, and J. M. "Tobe" Robinson was elected sheriff. With the law in their pocket, as it were, the boys went to stealing as if it was going out of style.

> There was a little company of them and they had a ranch on Rito Blanco [*sic*] right above the XITs. There was Ruck Tanner and Jess Jenkins and another fellow [Tom Graham] that got killed at Hartley. . . . It was a tough bunch. And when they'd arrest one of those for cow stealing, Jess would hire the lawyer and pick the jury. Judge Browning and Judge Plemons represented them. . . . Judge Plemons was a great criminal lawyer and if he couldn't get a clearance he'd have a hung jury to be carried over to the next term of court.[5]

Just how blatant the thieving became is perfectly illustrated in the short and happy rustling career of former LX range boss Bill Ruth. One of the more successful Panhandle rustlers in that he never got ar-

J. M. "Tobe" Robinson. (Courtesy of the Haley
Memorial Library, Midland, Texas)

He moved to Tascosa and in the fall of
1887, as we have seen, supplied Lon Jenkins with contraband beef to feed the railroad workers at Ragtown.[6]

Later, Jesse Jenkins said, Ruth

ran a butcher shop in Amarillo and used
to buy cattle from down on the Pecos.
The boys would sell to him for $10 or
more and he knew they were hot cattle
but he bought them just the same. I was a
partner of [Jim] Gober and knew when
they were getting ready to raid Ruth's
place. I went down and told Bill they were
coming tomorrow or next day and that he
better get rid of that hundred hides he
had. He said they were worth $2 apiece
and he wasn't going to lose that money so
he shipped them out that very night. He
got by with it but I wouldn't have dared
do it for a $1000.[7]

In 1888 Ruth filed on a section west of
Amarillo and bought some cattle. "By the
judicious use of the branding iron" he also
began acquiring strays—a stray, in his
judgment, being any animal capable of
walking as, for example, when two LX
cowhands gathered about fifty strays at the
various roundups in New Mexico and put
them into a Frying Pan branding pen, intending to return the following morning
and brand them. They returned next
morning to find the pen empty. Ruth,
whose section was nearby, "knew who put
the cattle in the pen so he turned them out,
knowing that they did not have time to
hunt them up and brand them, and that he
could . . . brand them at his own conven-
ience."

That fall, Ruth

rested or served time, Ruth—"very much
the same type of man as [W. C.] Moore
was, except the killer inclination which did
not enter into his makeup"—arrived in
Tascosa about 1881, "evidently on the
dodge for some law infringement," but of
course, as convention decreed, no one
asked questions.

Ruth (it seems to have been an open secret that his real name was Bill Thomas)
worked on the LX until 1884, then spent
about a year in New Mexico before returning to the LX (by then the American Pastoral Company) as a wagon boss; in 1886,
when Hollicott took over as general manager following the death of Jim Campbell
in an accident at Las Vegas, New Mexico,
he was promoted to range boss. Soon afterward he got married and "began to neg-
lect the ranch, finally losing his position."

and two others of his kind made a trip
into New Mexico and returned with

about 300 burros which they had stolen up in the Tucumcari country from the Mexicans. Bill told me he was going to take them down into Florida, where he could get $15.00 a head for them at the prominent watering places on the beach. When Bill returned from this trip he spent the winter in gathering and disposing of his cattle. In the spring of 1889 I traded Bill 30 head of horses for his place on the creek. On about the first of May he started out on the trail with about 75 horses, heading south; this was the last we ever heard of Bill except that a young fellow who used to work on the LX ranch with Bill and I wrote me two or three years later that he went to Florida with Bill, where he disposed of most of the horses and had been appointed city marshall [sic] of some Florida town.

In the early [18]90s Matt Atwood, a former LX wagon boss and a great friend of Ruth's, married [Sarah] the widow of Jesse Sheets . . . and also bought a half interest in the [Theodore] Briggs cattle located on the Rita Blanco creek west of Hartley and within the XIT pasture. After the wedding . . . Atwood moved on to the Briggs ranch and took active charge of the Flying N cattle.

When he first came to Tascosa, Atwood had boasted that his real name was Frank Jackson and that he had been a member of the Sam Bass gang; Arnot believed that Atwood and Bill Ruth were cousins.

On May 8, 1894, the XIT had Atwood arrested for the theft of a yearling. "One morning officers came to Matt Atwood's and arrested him for stealing a cow; the hide was hanging on his fence. Matt had not killed that cow; some one had framed him, did it in the night and then came [and arrested him] early the next day."

The case was transferred to Potter County for trial and . . . the result was a hung jury, 11 for conviction, 1 for acquittal. The case was continued to the next term of court and the defendant admitted to bail. When the case was called . . . , evidence was presented to the court that he had committed suicide in Florida . . . , and the case was closed. It has always been the opinion of we old timers who knew both men, that Matt went to where Ruth was and that Ruth in his position as city marshall concocted some sort of a plot to pass off some unknown body as that of Atwood [and] I think our supposition was a good guess.

Court records largely confirm these recollections: Atwood appeared before Judge Howson Wallace at the December term of court in Hartley County, charged that he "on or about 1 February 1894 did . . . unlawfully and fraudulently take from the possession of R. W. Barr one cattle." Maintaining that the defendant could not hope for a fair and impartial trial in this jurisdiction, his attorney asked for and was granted a change of venue to Potter County. There, in May 1895, his attorney pleaded that Atwood could not safely go to trial without the presence of witnesses who would testify that he had been in McClellan County prior to the alleged theft and that anyway, the cow was Atwood's own. These witnesses not being found, the case was continued to the following term of court. When it was called, Atwood failed to appear, and, one assumes, his bondsmen— one of whom was Charlie Rudolph— stumped up the $750 bail he had jumped.[8]

Meanwhile, Tascosa was dying of commercial malnutrition as Channing, Dalhart, and Texline siphoned off its trade to the north and Amarillo—the latter, after surviving some early setbacks, now well on its way to becoming one of Texas's busiest cattle shipping points—boomed to the south, with three newspapers, three churches, a new hotel, and even a college. But some things never changed: in the Oldham County election held on November 10, 1890, Scotty Wilson was yet again returned as justice of the peace for Precinct No. 1 and continued to dispense his own particular brand of "justice." On one occasion when he fined a man two hundred dollars for disturbing the peace, the outraged defendant threatened to take his case to a higher court. "Sit down, you sonofabitch!" shouted Scotty, "there is no higher court!"[9]

Nevertheless, inevitably, the old order changed. At the end of 1890, following the death of Henry Russell, his widow sold the Exchange Hotel to Oldham County's recently elected sheriff John King; later, A. L. Turner bought a half interest and took over the management. In February of the following year Turner also bought Tobe Robinson's saloon. Jim East sold his saloon and moved to Channing, where he bought lots to build houses; after striking up a partnership with Seth Mabry, Jim McMasters also relocated his store there. Dodge City tycoon Robert Wright bought out his partner Farnsworth and moved the store stock to El Reno. Cone and Duran abandoned their store on Main Street and moved to the new railroad town of Clayton.[10] And in the spring of 1891, when Hartley County held its first election, Tascosa's greatest—and last—champion threw in the towel. His final editorial was delivered in the grand manner. "HERE WE QUIT YOU," he announced.

It is useless to make a long to-do about it, or to magnify a thing of no great moment, but this, kind friends, is the closing chapter in the history of *The Pioneer*. . . . So we quit to seek a new field—it would be childish to hesitate about it longer. We surrender the whole question—we feel that we have all done our duty—and we go with a clear conscience, a heavy heart and a light pocketbook. Friends will be remembered for their friendship, and the years of pleasant association with place and people will never fade from memory. The warmest spot in our heart will long be for this little gem of a city on the turbid Canadian, sandy, sheltered, quaint Tascosa.[11]

And with that eloquent farewell, Charlie Rudolph packed his belongings and his printing press and moved to Channing to set up a new paper, the *Channing Register*. He soon discovered that, despite the XIT's strictures, the town was no more free from men accustomed to not just breaking, but positively shattering, the Ten Commandments than Tascosa had been.

In the late fall of 1891 the XIT's Al Boyce—who had known them in Williamson County—convinced Henry Kimball that Tom and Dave Graham, two cowboys Kimball had hired to break horses at his ranch on the Rita Blanca, were being a bit careless about whose calves they branded, and Kimball fired them. When the Graham boys found out who was responsible for their being let go, they rode into Channing intent on financing their immediate future by robbing the express office and, while they were at it, killing Boyce. After a drinking session during which they amused themselves by shooting at the bolt heads on the hitching rack outside the saloon, they headed for the XIT headquarters building, where Seth Mabry was sitting at a desk writing a letter.

Lurching into the office and either not realizing—or not caring—that Mabry was not Boyce, Dave Graham pulled out his gun and fired; the bullet missed, but the powder burned Mabry's face and hair. "Mabry was unarmed and this made him pretty mad," Jim East recalled, with nicely weighted understatement. Mabry ran out of the office and he and East grabbed Winchesters and went looking for the Graham boys, who had meantime broken into a store, stolen some clothes, and taken them to Kimball's blacksmith shop.

Someone had already wired Sheriff Tobe Robinson, who was at Hartley, to come down fast. Accompanied by Texas Ranger T. A. Owens, Robinson hitched a ride on the first freight train south, but when they got in Jim East realized the sheriff was drunk; he wasn't sure about the Ranger. The Grahams were now holed up in a pump house nearby.

"Come on!" Robinson said. "You and Mabry go to one end of the house and me and Owens will go to the other. If they run out at the front door, you and Mabry shoot them, and we will attend to the back door.

"He was standing within fifteen feet of the back door," East said. "Owens had a Winchester and Robinson a double-barreled shotgun and a six-gun. Just then Tom Graham came out and Robinson said to him: "Throw up your hands and surrender! I am sheriff of this county."

Tom said: "Go to Hell! I won't surrender to anybody." He jerked his six-shooter and shot Robinson in the groin. Robinson stood there like a gawk and had not fired a shot. As he fell he jerked his .41 caliber six-shooter and shot Graham, giving him

a scalp wound which did not knock him down. Owens stood there like a poor boy with the colic. . . . Just then we heard Dave and [a tramp named McKinley who had fallen in with the Grahams] start out the front door. . . . We ran to the front and shot Dave through the side and in the thigh as he ran off. McKinley did not make much resistance. Then I called my brother Bob . . . to take Robinson down to the hotel. We thought he was bleeding to death."

East and Mabry did what they could for Dave Graham, who was down and groaning with pain. They had figured the Ranger would take care of Tom Graham, but Owens hadn't fired a shot, allowing Tom to take shelter behind a windmill tower about fifty yards away. It was pretty much full dark now.

"Jim, are you out there?" Tom Graham called.

"Yes," East replied.

"Don't shoot any more, Jim," Graham pleaded. "My brains are all shot out and I want to surrender."

"All right," East said. "Leave your six-shooter there and come out with your hands up."

When Graham came out they took him to the hotel where Robinson had been taken and sent for the doctor. "When we got Tom into the light the blood [from his wound] was running down into his eyes," East remembered, "and he kept rubbing his hand through it and looking at it. He said: 'Ah, Hell! That's not brains. If I had known that, I wouldn't have surrendered.'"

There was no jail at Channing or at Hartley, so the Grahams were taken to Tascosa, where Dave died of his injuries. Tom

———— ⌘ ————

**Rivers Hotel, Channing, where the Graham boys and
Tobe Robinson were taken after the gunfight. (Courtesy of the XIT Museum)**

was tried and convicted, not for attempted murder but for robbing the Humphrey store, and sent to the penitentiary. "There was open season on shooting the sheriff in those days and it was not near as serious as stealing some shirts from a store," East said. "The only regret Mabry and I had was that we didn't finish Tom up. He was the worst of the two."[12]

For a year or two things looked good for the Jenkins camp up in Hartley County, but one by one Boyce leaned on the rustlers, and one by one they caved in. "I know a lot of cattle was stolen from the XIT," one eyewitness said:

There was an immense gang. No use talking. . . . Ruck Tabber [*sic*] was indicted. I saw him the day he left Hartley before daylight. He came to the 101 [Jenkins's

ranch] for breakfast on a cold, rainy day. He went to Cottonwood canyon in the Strip. Dick Pincham was indicted and [his case was] moved to Sherman County. The courts threw the case out. Jess Jenkins was indicted. He took his case to Claude and beat it. On the train coming back, Jenkins came up to Boyce with his six-shooter in his hand, twirling it lightly about his finger, saying "Well, Uncle Al, got your gun? I've got mine." Boyce said nothing, so Jenkins sat down and talked all the way to Channing.[13]

But whether the rustlers liked it or not, the casual crime and the kind of free-wheeling local government that had characterized the early days of Tascosa and Mobeetie were becoming a thing of the past. One of the first to experience this change of climate was Tobe Robinson, who "was re-elected to the office of Sheriff and Tax Collector for the years 1893–94 but he did not serve his second term as he was removed from office by the Commissioners Court during the last part of his first term. The reason assigned being some shortage in the county funds. J. M. Britton, a Texas Ranger who had been stationed at Amarillo was appointed to be Sheriff and Tax Collector for the ensuing two years. . . . Shortly after his removal from the sheriff's office, Tobe accompanied by his wife, whom he had married in Tascosa, left the country."[14]

Once more the facts are slightly different; they also properly fix the dates:

Britton rose to Sergeant and was serving in that capacity under Captain Bill McDonald when he was discharged at Quanah, March 17, 1894. While a Ranger he also served as sheriff of Hartley County in a dual role from January 4 to August 20, 1893, although he was carried simultaneously on the rolls of Company B as an active Ranger in a unique situation. Perhaps this was done at the discretion of Capt. McDonald, who may have preferred to have had a reliable man from his company in office rather than an officer whose ability had not been proven to him."[15]

In Jesse Jenkins's version of events, Robinson

got into trouble using some of the money belonging to the county. They brought Tobe to Amarillo and put him in jail because they didn't have any place anywhere else to keep him. Some of the boys came to the jail which was down in "Old Town" and cut the bricks out of the end of the jail and let all the prisoners get out.

James Magruder Britton.
(Courtesy of Robert W. Stephens)

When they had time to get away, Tobe went up to New Town, waked the sheriff and told him that if he didn't come down there and fix that hole, Tobe was going to leave for it was too cold with the wind pouring in. . . . The sheriff didn't make him go back. When they tried Tobe, the judge asked Tobe where the money was. He said that the saloons and the gambling boys had got most of it but that his wife had two or three hundred dollars of it. Nothing was ever done about it.

Once again the records support the recollections: the indictments alleged that on November 8, 1892, Robinson had converted the sum of $1,900 to his own use, and on December 29 of the same year "[he] had come into and was then in his custody and possession the sum of $1516.00 [which he] did then and there fraudulently take and convert the said money to his own use." His attorneys asked for and were granted a change of venue to Potter County, and Robinson was bailed for $750. When the case was heard in Amarillo during the June term of court, 1894, the lawyers brought in a cloud of witnesses ready to testify Robinson was "an honest, upright man and that he had not misapplied the money as charged" and presented a motion to quash the indictment because it "charges no offense in either court against the laws of the State of Texas [and also] fails to show the alleged offense was committed in Hartley County."[16]

Sideshows like this aside, Al Boyce was still determined to have Channing declared the county seat and didn't mind how much XIT money—or how much chicanery—was needed to bring about the desired result; the contest of wills that followed lasted for almost a decade. In one election, the XIT used its considerable influence to have the railroad move all its Hartley men to Clarendon to build a new bridge on voting day so the "little men" couldn't sew up their votes with free drinks in the Hartley saloons; on another occasion, Hartley supporters tampered with buggies at the livery stable (which it may be recalled belonged to Jesse Jenkins), blamed it on the railroad men, and then subpoenaed them so they would have to be in town on election day. But in 1903, following a final election that confirmed Channing as the county seat,

Tascosa Courthouse, ca. 1894. Two unidentified men are on the left; Scotty Wilson and Sheriff John King are on the right. (Courtesy of the Haley Memorial Library, Midland, Texas)

the Courthouse and all its records were transferred—quite literally moved en bloc—to Channing. And there they remained.[17]

It was a historical inevitability; in 1901 the Chicago, Rock Island and Mexico Railway, building southwest from Enid, Oklahoma, to Tucumcari, New Mexico, entered the county through Dalhart. With two rail connections now linking them to the outside world, Hartley County ranches shipped their cattle more easily than before, and as the railroads sold off land wholesale to beat government deadlines, settlers arrived in increasing numbers. About 1905 Jesse Jenkins cut his losses, quit fighting, and moved to Dalhart; a year or so later, as we have seen, he established the Dalhart National Bank and served as its president for five years. His two big cattle outfits, the 101 ranch and the Hip-O, owned or leased about a hundred thousand acres of land on which ranged ten to twelve thousand head of cattle. How many of them were the descendants of XIT mavericks no one will ever know.

Like a sandcastle on a beach, Tascosa was being washed into oblivion by each succeeding relentless wave of history that rolled across it. Then in September 1893 another wave, literal rather than metaphorical, engulfed it. For years Jesse Jenkins, John Cone, and other Hogtown residents had been concerned about the danger of a big flood. At that time the Canadian River made a sharp bend just a hundred yards below Main Street to run almost straight toward lower-lying Hogtown and the irrigated bottomland pastures nearby. As a preventive measure residents there decided to cut a deep ditch that would divert the course of the river. "They assembled teams

and workmen and got in one full week's work on this dry-land canal before McMasters [sic; McAllister] of the LS swore out an injunction that prevented them from continuing their work. The great scar had been made across the river bottom, however, and needed only a flood to change the course of the river."

After three days of torrential equinoctial rainstorms, Charlie Rudolph's "turbid Canadian" went on the rampage, rising high enough to take out a chunk of the railroad bridge at Cheyenne, which in turn smashed into the Tascosa wagon bridge, wrecking one complete span and severely damaging the rest of it, in the process washing away most of the buildings in Hogtown, including the old Cone & Edwards building and the deadfalls and shacks occupied by the gamblers and the saloon girls. The upper town fared only slightly better; when the floodwaters receded and the sun began to bake the mud dry, nearly twenty buildings were found to be damaged beyond repair, dirt roofs and adobe walls collapsed, awnings and porches fallen, wells polluted.[18]

With its lifeline to the rest of the world gone, repairing the bridge was clearly the most immediate priority facing the town, but the big ranches who had opposed its erection in the first place were immutably opposed to such an expensive proposition. And anyway, they argued, what was the point? Even if the bridge were rebuilt, the river—now something like three times as wide as it had been before the flood— would sooner or later sweep it away again. Tascosa was washed up, literally and figuratively, a ghost of its former self consisting only of its rock courthouse, a couple of stores, and a saloon. A few diehards, such as Scotty Wilson, Al Turner, and of course, Frenchy McCormick, hung on—primarily, one suspects, because they had no place else to go.[19]

The Old West itself was rapidly becoming the New, interlaced with railways, burgeoning with new farms and new cities. Settlers and farmers were pouring in, and one by one the big ranches began to flounder as these smaller stock-farming operations gobbled up the land. The first to go was the Frying Pan. In 1892 Glidden and Sanborn ended their partnership. Sanborn retained his town properties in Amarillo and 25,000 acres in Randall County; Glidden took the rest of the ranch, which was subsequently cut up into numerous pastures and leased out. About the same time the Hansford Land & Cattle Company also spiraled into disaster; Coburn cut his losses and sold the headquarters ranch, 7,280 acres of land, and five hundred of the best

blooded Herefords to Mart Cunningham, who had worked for the brand for many years. By 1915 the company had closed out its holdings, and Coburn disappeared from the ranching scene.[20]

Lucien Scott and his wife, Julia, ran the LS ranch until Scott's death in 1893, when his brother-in-law Charles Whitman took over as manager. In 1899 Julia Scott, far more interested in theosophy than ranching, deeded the operation—206,000 acres of land, fourteen thousand cattle, four hundred saddle horses, and thirty mules, not to mention a considerable mortgage debt—to Whitman. Learning that Jordan McAllister had recently sold his Colorado ranch and returned to Tascosa, Whitman offered "Mister Mac" his old job, and they set to work to solve the ranch's financial problems.[21]

Julia Scott. (Courtesy of the Panhandle-Plains Historical Museum, Canyon, Texas)

Charles Whitman. (Courtesy of the Panhandle-Plains Historical Museum, Canyon, Texas)

After two years, with the ranch virtually free from debt, McAllister resigned and moved to Channing, where he operated a livery stable and helped organize the Channing Mercantile and Banking Co. Later he went into partnership with Howson Wallace and built one of the finest purebred Hereford herds in the Panhandle. He died in Amarillo in September 1929. In the fall of 1896 Whitman began building new LS headquarters close to the FW&DC depot, to which supplies could be shipped in by the carload to be stored in the LS warehouse there. He also concentrated on further improving his herds, going so far as to purchase a purebred Hereford bull named Salisbury for the (then) unheard-of sum of twenty-five hundred dollars. He and his wife lived in Denver most of the time, but Whitman made frequent trips to the ranch. His death, on September 20, 1899, came as a considerable shock to the ranching industry, for Whitman had been the last of the line, the largest individual ranch holder in the Panhandle.

For a while, his wife, Pauline, and her brother Will Lingenbrink managed the operation; in 1902 Mrs. Whitman married a former sweetheart, Frederick H. Kreismann, and for a few years they made their home on the LS, leasing the western half of the ranch to the Landergin brothers. In 1905 they decided to sell all or part of the spread, but the Landergin lease presented difficulties that were not resolved until four years later, when W. H. Gray bought thirty sections in the eastern half of the ranch, the Landergins purchased the western portion they had leased, and Edward F. Swift of the Chicago meat company Swift & Co. bought the LS brand, the livestock, and the remainder of the land.[22]

The old LX, or the American Pastoral Company, continued in business until 1910, when it was divided into three by sales to Lee Bivins, Joseph Sneed, and R. B. Masterson, with Bivins acquiring the brand in 1915 and establishing headquarters in the former Tascosa courthouse. By 1912, badly hit by its 1886–87 losses and the departure of its general manager Murdo McKenzie in 1890, the Prairie Land & Cattle Co. had only two hundred thousand acres of land in the northern Panhandle. In 1913 the LIT properties were sold to Lee Bivins; the LE range, purchased in 1902, was sold to J. M. Shelton in May 1915. The following year the Prairie Land & Cattle Co., at one time the largest British investment company, had been liquidated.[23]

In one of the biggest financial disasters of them all, the Rocking Chair Ranche Company's business had gone from rack to ruin. When Baron Tweedsmouth and Lord Aberdeen arrived unannounced at the ranch to see for themselves how many cattle they owned, general manager John Drew contemptuously pulled the old "Indian agent" trick on them, driving the same herd of cattle around a hill and past them again and again, inflating the count each time. When the farce was over, the visitors departed, satisfied that all was in order. It was anything but. Following organization in 1890, open hostility erupted between nesters in the southern part of Collingsworth County and the Rockers in the north over the intended location of the county seat. Rustling from the ranch was so bad that the entire range had to be combed to fulfill an order for two carloads of yearlings. And while the world fell about his head, Archie Marjoribanks blithely continued to live the life of an English squire, drinking whiskey, smoking cigars, and hunting wolves with his pack of dogs.

By 1893 the stockholders were baying for blood, and a delegation consisting of Edward Marjoribanks and Earl Gordon was sent to Texas to investigate; what they found led them to bring proceedings against John Drew, but feelings were running so strongly against the British in general and two delegates in particular that they could not empanel a jury. Unable to convict him in court, the directors decided to fire Drew, but when they took their case before a justice of the peace, they failed again. Having made his point—that nobody could fire him until he was good and ready to be fired—Drew then got on his horse and rode away, leaving the ranch without a manager. In desperation, the company pre-vailed upon old Cap Arrington to take over and "smoke out" the rustlers, but it was too late: a count showed that instead of the fourteen thousand head listed in the company's books, there were just three hundred on the range. At an extraordinary general meeting held at 9 New Square in London on August 4, 1894, and a subsequent one held on August 20, it was decided to wind up the company. On December 22, 1896, the Rocking Chair's entire 152,320 acres were sold to the Continental Land & Cattle Company for $75,000 and became part of the Mill Iron ranch, which dissolved the Rocking Chair division and consigned the largest of all the British adventures in the cattle trade to history.[24]

Tascosa on the way out, 1898. The photo is said to have been taken by Charles Whitman. (Courtesy of the Panhandle-Plains Historical Museum, Canyon, Texas)

As with the Rocking Chair, so with the Capitol; there were no cheering stock-holders in the boardrooms now. Records of its annual general meetings present a vivid picture of the company's lingering but inevitable death. At its sixth annual general meeting, presided over by the Marquis of Tweeddale at London's City Terminus Hotel on June 4, 1891, share-holders learned that "after writing off all charges the net profit [for the year] amounted to £8,213 ($41,065). The value of the herd given in the balance sheet as £337,347 ($16,686,735) was "well within the mark." The company now had on its lands "two towns, one called Texline and the other Channing, and at both they had had satisfactory sales of town lots and building operations were now being actively carried on." But there were no dividends; nor would there ever again be any.[25]

Finally, at two further extraordinary general meetings held on April 19 and May 8, 1918, a special resolution was promulgated by which the company's operations would be wound up volun-tarily. "There has been no dividend on the shares for many years past," said *The Stock Exchange Year Book*. "At December 31, 1915, there was an excess expenditure over receipts of £320,306. It is the inten-tion to liquidate the company during the coming year."[26]

The beef bonanza was well and truly over. And with it went the last, faint hope that Tascosa might somehow survive. Only the diehard old-timers remained there now, and one by one, they, too, were slipping away. "Among those who Lee & Reynolds [had] employed to bring their cattle from El [Fort] Reno to the Panhandle were Uncle Billy Urion, Steve Conkle or Con-

klin and Jack Le[o]nard, all friends and companions of Scotty [Wilson] in many exciting Indian Adventures on the Western Plains. . . . Uncle Billy [born in New Jersey around 1839] died in 1890 or [18]91 and was buried in the Romero cemetery east of Tascosa. In the fall of 1910 Jack Leonard quit working on the ranch and went to trapping wolves."

Returning from a trip to Amarillo, he was camped on Tecovas Creek when a bliz-zard blew up; he wrapped a wagon sheet around himself and set out for the nearby C. T. Word (formerly Frying Pan) ranch. The next day cowboys found his wagon but no sign of Jack; a posse led by John Arnot and John Snider was raised at Amarillo to look for him. His body was found (he'd gone south instead of northeast) and taken to Tascosa. "When the train arrived . . . old Scotty was waiting, mounted on his old gray pony. With his long gray beard and whiskers he looked like a venerable patri-arch—he spoke to no one and as soon as the casket was placed in the hack he led the procession to the cemetery.[27]

Tascosa was now little more than a ghost town in the middle of nowhere. Until 1914 no highway crossed the county. Travel along its roads was greatly impeded by fences that could only be crossed after gates were opened. The completion of the Chicago, Rock Island & Gulf in 1909 brought about the birth of three new towns: Wildorado, Vega, and Adrian. But Tascosa "was [still] the county seat . . . , therefore the county officials remained at Tascosa until several years later when the Rock Island railroad extended their line from Sayre, Oklahoma, to Tucumcari, New Mexico. About 16 miles due south of Tas-cosa they started a town and called it Vega. This little railroad town . . . was the mercy shot that ended the last vestige of Tascosa's importance."[28]

By 1910 Vega was already the largest town in the county and had dreams of being even bigger if it could win the county seat. Tascosa, Vega's boosters pointed out, was far from the new center of population, and its facilities had diminished enormously since its glory days. In addition, it was north of the river, and there was no bridge across the Canadian, now two or three times its former width; people from the southern part of the county who needed to visit the county seat had to take their chances with high water and quicksand both going in and coming out; they often had to wait days before a suitable opportunity to cross presented itself. It was time for change, and it was not too long in coming.

On February 26, 1910, Jesse Giles presented to the commissioners court a petition bearing 119 names demanding an election for transferring the county seat to Vega. County Judge E. A. McKummon allowed the petition and ordered an election

for April 19. When the votes were counted, 101 were in favor of moving the county seat to Vega and 71 for it to remain at Tascosa. However, since Vega was not within the required number of miles of the geographical center of the county, state laws required that a two-thirds majority was needed before any change could be effected.

On April 25, six days after the election, Judge McKummon absented himself without explanation for more than an hour during the afternoon session of the commissioners court. Commissioner Jones proposed that "since the judge was absent more than one hour, a temporary chairman be elected to carry on business until it was finished or the judge returned." When the motion was seconded by Commissioners Peters and Landergin, the court continued its discussion of the recent highly unsatisfactory (from Vega's point of view) election. This ended with the commissioners' tabling a resolution stating that "whereas said proceedings and election were unauthorized by law, therefore be it

Scotty Wilson amid the ruins, 1915. (Courtesy of the Haley Memorial Library, Midland, Texas)

Tascosa, ca. 1915. Scotty Wilson outside what was left of the Howard & McMasters store. (Courtesy of the Amarillo Public Library)

Tascosa, ca. 1915. Al Morris's wagon horse "White Angel" outside Jack Cooper's saloon, site of the 1886 gunfight. (Courtesy of the Amarillo Public Library)

resolved by the Commissioner's Court of Oldham County that there has never been a legal location of the county seat." The county's original petition to the commissioners court of Wheeler County way back in November 1881 had "provided for the organization of Oldham County and the county seat located temporarily at Tascosa until a vote of the citizenry could be taken." Therefore, the commissioners argued "[that election is] hereby declared wholly void and of no effect." Then came the killer: "It is further declared that there has never been a legal election by the voters of Oldham County locating the county seat."[29]

On April 21, 1915, a new petition containing 109 names was presented by C. A. Wiseman, "praying for an order for an election to determine whether or not the county seat of Oldham County, Texas, shall be removed from Tascosa . . . to Vega," and Judge T. B. Jones ordered another election to be held May 22 for just that purpose. Indicative of how completely Tascosa had been abandoned by now was the fact that only 14 votes were cast there (as opposed to 91 in Vega, 30 in Adrian, and 24 in Wildorado). The final count was 134–45 in favor of moving the county seat, whereupon the judge declared county officers were "authorized and directed to remove all records of their respective offices from the court house in the town of Tascosa to the town of Vega in said County in accordance with the order . . . declaring the county seat be removed."

—⟨⟩—

Oldham County Courthouse abandoned, Tascosa, ca. 1915.
(Courtesy of the Panhandle-Plains Historical Museum, Canyon, Texas)

—⟨⟩—

Vega Courthouse, 2004. (Author's photograph)

Without even waiting for a courthouse to be built, the county seat was moved forthwith; on June 10 the first business there—a "special term"—was conducted in a Vega hotel. Eight days later, Amarillo architect O. G. Roquemore was commissioned to draw up plans for a two-story and basement brick and stone-trimmed courthouse and jail. On July 1 a $24,870 contract to build was let to W. M. Rice, and the first meeting held in the newly finished building took place on March 18, 1916.[30]

A lot of the documents recording its history never made it out of Tascosa; the officials who effected the move are said to have simply burned great piles of them as worthless. Not that it mattered anymore. In no time at all Tascosa was abandoned, to become the domain of pack rats, rattlesnakes, and its last, sad, lonely inhabitant—Frenchy McCormick.

CODA

FRENCHY MCCORMICK:

"SHE WAS A RING-TAILED TOOTER."

IN Elizabeth "Frenchy" McCormick, Tascosa had its own Scheherazade, and like that legendary weaver of dreams, no one was ever able to persuade her to tell the whole story. A little here, perhaps, a little more there, a detail mentioned, a hint dropped, but that was all. For all of the more than sixty years she lived in Tascosa, she declined to talk about her past, steadfastly maintaining the secret of her true identity and the reasons for its being secret. Only one man may have known the truth—her husband, Mickey McCormick—but if he did, he never revealed it either. As a result, a great deal of claptrap aimed at making her a "mystery woman" and a "legend" has come to be written about Frenchy. To be fair, she never made any such claim herself. Having spent most of her life as a saloon girl in Dodge City, Mobeetie, and God alone knows where else, she knew perfectly well what she was: tough, self-reliant, and stubborn, a woman with a life behind her that she didn't want to talk about.

A number of versions of that life have been constructed from the few facts she did let slip about her background; in one,

her father was a Mississippi steamboat captain who took her with him to Saint Louis following the death of her mother. There, teenage Elizabeth appeared on the burlesque stage and danced in the famous Benedict Bar, but when her disapproving father forbade her to ever again do such a thing, she got on a stagecoach and headed west, ending up at Dodge City. In another twist of the tale, she first ran away to Saint Louis from a Baton Rouge convent with a man who later deserted her; alone in the world, she drifted west to Dodge, where she acquired her saloon-girl nickname.

Alternatively, "Frenchy was Irish—and she had the dancing blue eyes and black hair to prove it." All these stories smack of the sort of romantic invention that surrounds the whole subject of prostitution; in real life, no young woman of Frenchy's professed class would have gone to a frontier town catering almost exclusively to male needs on the remote chance of finding legitimate employment. Far more likely she entered the oldest profession somewhere further east and/or went there with a man, who abandoned her. Either way, without means or protection, she would have had little or no choice in what followed; like so many before her, she traded her body to survive. Odds are, too, that if indeed this is so, it happened much earlier than the legend suggests. Largely it was the poor and the young who worked in the cribs and brothels. In one Kansas house, for example, six of twelve girls working there were between the ages of fifteen and nineteen.

In fact, prostitution was a major industry in every Kansas cattle town, and large sections of each were set aside to accommodate it: McCoy's Addition, a.k.a. "The Beer Garden" in Abilene; "Hide Park" in Newton; "Scragtown" in Ellsworth; and Delano in Wichita. In Dodge, the area was below what was called the "dead line"—infamously, the wrong side of the Santa Fe tracks. These unlovely suburbs of course made a considerable contribution to the revenue of their adopted cities through the fines regularly levied against their occupants for what was euphemistically referred to as "vagrancy."

Ironically, such "punishment" played a significant part in ensuring that the prostitutes continued practicing their trade. A breakdown of Wichita's system—which would not have been significantly different from that of Dodge—indicates that after "overheads" (bribes to cops and other payoffs, rent of rooms, clothing, liquor) the individual prostitute would be lucky to keep one-third of her weekly earnings.

In the larger cities there were upscale parlor houses—brothels by another name—operated by a "madam" and offering two or three drawing rooms, where while awaiting "clients" the girls lounged on sofas or sat on stools dressed in ball gowns as ornate as those seen in society,

Frenchy and Mickey McCormick. (Courtesy Cal Farley's Boys Ranch Museum)

[269]

the girls' manners often as refined. But there were precious few such places on the cow town frontier; in Abilene and Wichita and Dodge the girls, dressed in the typical dance hall dress—low-cut, short-skirted, spangled—would attract their customers into the saloon dance hall by leaning out of windows exposing their breasts or stand backlit in doorways showing off their legs. The "business" itself was often taken care of in a rented crib, usually a frame building with a door leading straight into a bedroom with a window fronting the street, a kitchen–living room to the rear, and a privy out back. It was a short-duration, quick-turnover transaction for which—depending how far down the line she had slid—the girl might expect to be paid between twenty-five cents and two dollars, with perhaps a percentage on the drinks she'd encouraged the man to order and a tip if he was a real sport.

To be a successful member of Dodge City's contingent of soiled doves—also referred to as nymphs du prairie, nymphs du pave, fair Dulcineas, girls of the night, girls of the period, fancies, calico queens, painted cats, scarlet ladies, demi-mondaines, or less glamorously, laundresses, saloon girls, or waitresses—a gal needed to be tough. Take, for example, a strapping young woman named Frankie Bell, just a while earlier slapped around by Wyatt Earp and fined twenty dollars for using language that offended him. In August 1877, after being hauled into court before Judge D. M. Frost, Frankie "made an oath . . . not to indulge in spirits fermenti until next Christmas." It's an odds-on bet she never made it—a saloon girl on the wagon was the frontier equivalent of a horse with three legs.[1]

Or take the case of another "girl of the period" identified only as Fannie, who was "peacefully ironing at the residence of Mrs. Curley when James [Cowan] entered (three-sheets-in-the-wind drunk) called Fannie a soldier ———, throwed her on the floor, elevated her paraphernalia, spanked her, and finally busted her a left hander in the right eye, accompanying the same with a kick in the stomach." Why poor Fannie was throwed, spanked, and busted history fails to relate, but chances are it was all in a day's work if you were a Dodge City saloon girl.[2]

On another occasion there was a "desperate fight" in a house on "Tin Pot Alley" between "two of the most fascinating doves of the roost. . . . Tufts of hair, calico, snuff and gravel flew like fur in a cat fight, and before we could distinguish how the battle waned a chunk of dislocated leg grazed our ear and a cheer from the small boys announced that a battle was lost and won. The crowd separated as the vanquished virgin was carried to her parlor by two 'soups.' A disjointed nose, two or three internal bruises, a chawed ear and a missing eye were the only scars we could see."[3]

From all of this it will be seen that, whatever else she might have been, Frenchy was neither a shrinking violet nor a prairie rose; the stories that she participated in saloon boxing matches and that she'd dance a jig while men threw money at her feet only more strongly confirm it.

Nonetheless, she was "a woman of a whole lot of education. . . . [She] had a whole lot of good old-fashioned common sense and a lot of culture," said Lucius Dills. "I never heard her mention one word that would have been out of place anywhere. After she and Micky married she didn't deal monte. She wasn't pretty but rather attractive, vivacious and smart."[4]

Since how she met Mickey McCormick is not on the record, we must perforce accept the legends, one of which is that as a service of his livery stable business, Mickey drove a lawyer from Tascosa to Mobeetie and, while there, sat in on a poker game or three. "There, at the gaming tables, Mickey always won when Frenchy was beside him. He called her his luck. When he left to return to Tascosa, he took Frenchy with him."[5]

In Louis Bousman's version, "She was from New Orleans originally, and from a good family of wealthy people. Mickey stole her from her people. She would never let them know where she was. She would never tell her maiden name and said that this failure to tell her people was the only thing that would keep her from going to Heaven."[6]

In yet another,

Old Mickey McCormick was with her a year or two. . . . They told him he would have to quit Frenchie or marry her, and he married her. I have seen her jig. They'd throw dollars out there on the floor and she'd pick up fifteen or twenty dollars dancing the jig. Oh, she was a ring-tailed tooter. . . . When Mickey left Fort Elliott . . . he started this livery stable up here [in Tascosa]. She'd come and sit along side of him in the livery stable and work along side of him in the saloon. But she never did stay with anybody [else]. They say she was a fine cook. Mickey was a poker playing fool.[7]

In one memoir, Jesse Jenkins seems to suggest that Mickey and Frenchy lived together at Mobeetie before they came to Tascosa. He said he "knew Mickey McCormick and his wife at Mobeetie in 1881. Mickey always had from $1000 to $2000 in his pocket and was one of the best little Irishmen in the world. . . . Frenchy was as straight as a string, a beautiful woman and one who watched over Mickey like a baby. [S]he was a powerful woman for her size and never failed to throw any women out of a room where her husband might be gambling. . . . She was very superstitious."[8]

On another occasion, however, he painted a slightly different portrait: "Most timid girl you ever saw," he claimed, "never dealt faro; never went in a saloon or gambling house unless Mickey was losing heavily then she'd go in and ask all the women to leave; she was superstitious; thought women brought Mickey bad luck; if they didn't get out it didn't take her long to make them understand she meant business."[9]

In the final analysis, whether Mickey McCormick met Frenchy while he was working at Mobeetie as a gambler or just visiting the town is largely irrelevant. What was important—to Mickey, anyway—was that he got lucky when she stood beside him at the table, and so he brought her with him and built her a two-room adobe house west of Tascosa Creek. Throughout the thirty years they spent together, Mickey never called her "Frenchy," nor did she call him "Mickey"—it was always Elizabeth and Mack. "Mack and I discussed the fact that we had lived somewhat on the seamy side," she said, doing her Scheherazade act later in life, "and then he took both my hands in his and we pledged to stick to each other and to the town of Tascosa." They were married on September 26, 1882; for the record, Frenchy (who gave her date of birth as August 11, 1852) said her name was Lizzie P. McGraw.[10]

Other than that he was born in Ireland on February 17, 1848, as little is known about Mickey McCormick's past as that of his wife. He "looked as little like a gambler as you ever saw and would be content to sit in a poker game and wait. He'd be perfectly willing to sit up all night and win twenty five or thirty dollars. If he got on a losing streak, he could lose less than anybody because he had one of the finest ways of staying out and had no curiosity, which is the principal element in successful gambling. If you haven't got hand enough to back yourself up, why, lay down."[11]

Whatever Mickey's capabilities were as the owner of a livery stable, his specialties as a gambler seem to have been patience and an air of *faux naïveté*. He

was one of those fellows that was perfectly willing to sit down all night and win twenty five or thirty dollars. . . . A fellow got in there [with him] and opened up a game, and the man that staked him said "Don't you allow any of these gamblers to play." Mickey walked in there smoking his little old Jane Gunter's pipe and took this fellow in, and the man [who staked him] came back and says "Where's your bank roll?" He says, "A damned little Irishman come in here a while ago and he took me in." The fellow says, "I told you not to gamble with any of these gamblers." He says, "He didn't look like a gambler." He was the slickest gambler in the Panhandle of Texas.[12]

But Mickey was not a pushover. On one occasion in Mobeetie he got into an argument during a poker game with John McCabe, a blustering Irish bully who was considered a dangerous man, having some time earlier killed Charles Goodnight's brother-in-law Granger Dyer. "Mickey held out a silk handkerchief and said, in a low tone, 'Catch hold, you cheap scoundrel, and shoot it out.' Mickey wouldn't let him take the money."[13]

Mickey's name appeared occasionally

in Rudolph's *Pioneer;* that of his wife did not. His profession, livery stable owner, and his avocation, gambler, were both perfectly acceptable in Tascosa society, but for all the years they lived there, Frenchy's former life—even though there is absolutely no indication that she continued her profession after marriage—kept her on the other side of that invisible, uncrossable line drawn down the center of the town's main street. As we have seen, Mary Snider, Marion Armstrong's sister, made it quite clear that "the respectable element of the town had nothing to do with Frenchy and the other girls of her class."[14]

Even Lena Dobbs echoed this peculiarly frontier town class distinction. She said she had seen Frenchy McCormick but would never associate with her, that Frenchy lived with Mickey several years before they were married. "Frenchy was pretty tough until they were married. I wouldn't have anything to do with her." She told how Frenchy would box with the men. She boxed with deputy sheriff Pierce in the saloon often. "She could whip me," Kid Dobbs said.[15]

Frank Mitchell's wife remembered Frenchy "especially for her goodness and kindness in carrying water to her folks when they had typhoid fever and other times because she had good well water and the other [family?] did not. Every time she went [past] the [other?] girl's homestead, she brought a bucket of the good water. Frenchy, as she was [known]; went to her husband's dance and gambling hall, but did not become one of the red light girls."[16]

Tascosa was already pretty much a shadow of its former self when, in the early years of the new century, Mickey Mc-Cormick contracted Bright's disease, a chronic inflammation of the kidneys. One day in October 1912 he collapsed and was taken to the hospital in Dalhart where he died. After Mickey was buried in the old Casimero Romero cemetery on the eastern end of town, Frenchy declared it was her intention to remain in Tascosa, near his grave, for the remainder of her life, and she did just that. Catholic organizations offered her a good job and a home at Saint Anthony's Hospital. When she turned them down, they offered her a permanent home at the Sisters of Charity, a Catholic institution in Fort Worth, but she again refused, saying she preferred to be near the grave of her husband.

After the county seat was moved to Vega in 1915, Tascosa quickly became a ghost town, and before long Frenchy McCormick was its only inhabitant. How she managed to feed and clothe herself remains something of a mystery; it's said the Oldham County authorities at Vega sent someone up to Tascosa once a week with food, coal for her stove, and kerosene. For almost a quarter of a century she lived alone in her tumbledown adobe shack refusing, despite the pleadings of well-meaning friends, to move away. It was not until January 1939, when she applied for a state pension, that the county decided she must be relocated in Channing. Finally Frenchy, eighty-seven years old, thin, unkempt, and increasingly feeble, relented. Even then, however, she exacted a promise from the authorities that when she died she would be brought back to Tascosa and buried alongside her husband.

She was "well and hearty up to her last illness," her caregivers said. "We took her to Amarillo . . . to see a movie. Everything was of great interest to her in the city. She visited the [Panhandle-Plains] museum in Canyon and the XIT rodeo in Dalhart. Every time she went somewhere it was

covered by the press, radio and newsreels." They all wanted to know the same thing: who was she? Two women from Louisiana thought they knew: she was their long-lost aunt Josephine Charlton, who had run away from home in Baton Rouge sixty or seventy years before. But despite their letters and their gifts and their offer of a home, Frenchy refused to confirm the story or reveal her true identity. "No one on earth knows who I am," she is reported to have said. "No one shall ever know."[17]

At 5:45 a.m. on Sunday morning, January 12, 1941, Elizabeth McCormick died in her sleep at the home of her friend Mrs. Lona Blackwell in Channing. She was buried the next day at Tascosa, as newspapers lamented the passing of "the last of

**Frenchy with Louis Bousman, 1934.
(From an unidentified newspaper photograph, courtesy of the Amarillo Public Library)**

the Girls of the Golden West." Much later, alumni of the "Boys Ranch" that had sprung up on the site of the old town raised money to erect a marble headstone.[13] The inscription reads:

FRENCHY
ELIZABETH McCORMICK
AUGUST 11, 1852
JANUARY 12, 1941

Today, the old Romero graveyard, accessed only by a rutted, unmade road, is ramshackle and overgrown; hardly anyone ever goes there anymore. Inch by inch, year by year, nature is inexorably reclaiming its own. Inch by inch, year by year, these last reminders of Tascosa's past are disappearing.

It was always a cruel land.

It still is.

Gravestones of Frenchy and Mickey McCormick, Romero cemetery. (Author's photograph)

NOTES

CHAPTER 1
1875-1876: LAST BUFFALO, FIRST SHEEP

1. A comprehensive biography is *Indians, Cattle, Ships, and Oil: The Story of W. M. D. Lee,* by Donald F. Schofield; the life of his partner is covered in *Albert Eugene Reynolds: Colorado's Mining King,* by Lee Scamehorn. The two works are not in complete agreement about the formation of the partnership or its dissolution.

2. W. S. Nye, *Carbine and Lance,* 166; Ida Ellen Rath, *The Rath Trail,* 99–100; G. Derek West, "The Battle of Adobe Walls—1874." *English Westerners Brand Book* 4, no. 2 (Jan. 1962): 1–12.

3. J. W. Mooar and James Winford Hunt, *Buffalo Days,* passim; Ty Cashion, *A Texas Frontier: The Clear Fork Country and Fort Griffin, 1849–1887,* 115.

4. Nye, *Carbine and Lance,* 169; Wayne Gard, *The Great Buffalo Hunt,* 131–32.

5. Nye, *Carbine and Lance,* 169–70; Rath, *Trail,* 102–4; J. Evetts Haley, Interview with J. W. Mooar, November 25, 1927, J. Evetts Haley Collection, Haley History Center, Midland, Texas (hereafter cited as HHC).

6. Schofield, *Indians, Cattle,* 22–26; Maj. C. E. Compton to AAG, Dept. of Missouri, July 16, 1874, Letters Received, Dept. of Missouri. Records of the Adjutant General's Office, Record Group 75, National Archives and Records Administration (hereafter cited as NARA).

7. Schofield, *Indians, Cattle,* 27; Haley, Interview with J. W. Mooar; J. Evetts Haley, Interview with J. D. McAllister, July 1, 1926, HHC.

8. James L. Haley, *The Buffalo War: The History of the Red River Indian Uprising of 1874,* 22–24; *Annual Report of the Commissioner of Indian Affairs, 1874,* 220.

9. Haley, Interview with J. D. McAllister.

10. Schofield, *Indians, Cattle,* 29–30.

11. *Dodge City Messenger,* reprinted in *Kansas State Record,* Topeka, July 15, 1874.

If Lee indeed sent a warning (although in the circumstances it seems highly unlikely), Leonard's remark that the hunters were "taken completely by surprise" suggests it was either not taken seriously or disregarded.

12. West, "Battle of Adobe Walls." Dixon had in fact lost his own "Big Fifty" just before the battle; he was shooting with a borrowed gun. Others were shooting at the same time, so when the Indian was hit, it was unclear whose bullet had killed him; postmortem recovery of the slug established it had been Dixon's. On-site calculations made in 1992 suggest the range may have been nearer twelve hundred yards. Dixon himself called it a "scratch" shot, that is, a fluke. Olive K. Dixon, *The Life of "Billy" Dixon, Plainsman, Scout, and Pioneer,* 180–81.

13. Michael D. Pierce, *The Most Promising Young Officer: A Life of Ranald Slidell Mackenzie*, 142–61.

14. *Record of Engagements with Hostile Indians within the Military Division of the Missouri from 1868 to 1882*, 41–46.

15. Carl Coke Rister, *Fort Griffin on the Texas Frontier*, 112ff.; Pierce, *Most Promising*, 150–61.

16. "Texas beyond History: The Red River War," College of Liberal Arts, University of Texas at Austin, http://www.texasbeyondhistory.net.

17. *Record of Engagements*, 46; Rister, *Fort Griffin* 124.

18. J. Evetts Haley, Interview with Richard "Dick" Bussell, July 19, 1926. HHC. Richard Bussell was born at Alton, Madison County, Illinois, on November 18, 1845. He began hunting buffalo in 1868; a decade later, he calculated he had killed nearly twenty thousand of them. He later farmed in Wheeler County and was married at age fifty-two in 1897. He died at Canadian, Texas, in 1935.

19. John Arnot, "My Recollections of Tascosa," Amarillo, Texas, March 1934, John L. McCarty Collection, Amarillo Public Library (hereafter cited as JLMC/APL).

20. Laura V. Hamner, *Short Grass and Longhorns*, 263.

Lee & Reynolds were bold, imaginative, and ambitious entrepreneurs. . . . They provided whatever goods and services were needed when there was a profit to be made in doing so. They operated saloons and billiard rooms in conjunction with sutler's stores. . . . They hauled their own goods as well as freight for the military. Later they transported supplies for Texas ranchers and for miners in the Colorado Rockies. . . . They grazed cattle on the open range in Indian Territory in order to supply, as private contractors, fresh beef to the Indian agency and to military posts. They operated slaughterhouses at Fort Supply and Fort Elliott. They transported U.S. mails and served as postmasters at Supply and Elliott. In 1879 they provided the cedar

poles with which the army linked Forts Supply and Elliott by telegraph. (Scamehorn, *Reynolds*, 9–10.)

21. Sallie B. Harris, *Hide Town in the Texas Panhandle*, 12–25.

22. E. R. Archambeau, "Pioneer Panhandle Settler Recalls Origin, Early Days, of Old Tascosa," *Amarillo Times*, February 28, 1946; Federal Census, San Miguel County, N.M., 1870; C. May Cohea, Interview with Mrs. Frank H. Mitchell, March 25, 1938, Library of Congress, Manuscript Division, WPA Federal Writers' Project Collection (hereafter cited as WPA).

23. J. Evetts Haley, Interview with James H. East, September 27, 1927, HHC (hereafter cited as Haley, "East"); Arnot, "My Recollections."

24. *Handbook of Texas Online*, "New Zealand Sheep Company"; Arnot, "My Recollections." Born in England on November 23, 1853, E. C. Godwin-Austen came to the United States by way of New Zealand in 1875 and settled first near Las Vegas, New Mexico, then Liberty. In 1880 he was working on the LS and later became foreman of the LX ranch. In 1896 he became manager of the XIT-owned Channing Hotel. He spent the years 1909–16 in Denver, then he returned to Channing, where he died on January 25, 1932. Federal Census. Hartley County, Texas, 1880; obituary, unidentified newspaper clipping marked "Channing, January 29, 1932," J. Evetts Haley Collection, HHC.

25. J. Evetts Haley, *Charles Goodnight: Cowman and Plainsman*, passim.

CHAPTER 2
HENRY HOYT: EL MEDICO COLORADO

1. Henry Hoyt, *A Frontier Doctor*, xxiii.

2. Ibid., 33, 181–82; Ted Yeatman, *Frank and Jesse James: The Story behind the Legend*, 186.

3. Hoyt, *Frontier Doctor*, 49–50.

4. Ibid., 63–64; *Sacramento Union*, September 19, 1879. In another account, Hoyt describes running into Calamity Jane in camp near Laramie. Dressed in soldier's uniform, she "was trying to get a mash on [that is, romantic with]

some of our party" and "made herself at home, and this was the only time I ever saw her."

5. Henry F. Hoyt, "Old Tascosa" to J. Evetts Haley, March 2, 1928, 2H 474, Earl Vandale Collection, 1813–1946, Center for American History, University of Texas, Austin (hereafter cited as CAH/UT).

6. Hoyt, *Frontier Doctor,* 75–78; Pauline Jaramillo, *Genealogical and Historical Data of the Jaramillo Family, 1598–1989,* 60.

7. Haley, "East"; Hoyt, "Old Tascosa."

8. Hoyt, *Frontier Doctor,* 92.

9. Hoyt, "Old Tascosa." For the full story of Jim Kenedy's life, see Chapter 6; Chuck Parsons, "James W. Kenedy: Cattleman, Texas Ranger, Gambler, and 'Fiend in Human Form.' *English Westerners Brand Book* 34, no. 1 (winter 2000).

10. Hoyt, *Frontier Doctor,* 95–98.

11. Ibid, 103–14.

12. Horse thief and gambler William Nicholson, alias "Slap Jack Bill, Pride of the Panhandle," was arrested at Las Vegas, New Mexico, on September 11, 1879, on suspicion of having been involved in a stagecoach robbery on August 30. Fellow suspects were Jordan L. Webb, Frank Cady, and John Piece, a.k.a. "Bull Shit Jack." Webb had been tried twice, but both times the jury failed to agree; at his third trial on February 11, 1881, the defense produced David Rudabaugh, who not only confessed to the crime but also stated categorically that Webb had not been involved. Webb was promptly acquitted, and after serving a year in the Santa Fe jail the others were also released. Howard Bryan, *Wildest of the Wild West,* 181–82; Hoyt, *Frontier Doctor,* 277.

CHAPTER 3
1876-1877: THE COMING OF THE LONGHORNS

1. Haley, *Charles Goodnight,* 276ff.

2. Ibid., 281–85.

3. The third child of John Brewer and Hannah (Sherman) Bugbee, Thomas Bugbee was born in Perry, Maine, in 1842 and died at Clarendon on October 19, 1925.

4. F. Stanley, *Rodeo Town: Canadian, Texas,* 83; *Dodge City Times,* September 8 and 15, 1877, and February 28, November 23 and 30, and December 14, 1878; John R. Cook, *The Border and the Buffalo,* 95.

Springer's ranch "was built on the blockhouse, stockade, Indian frontier plan," said Cook. "It faced south towards the river. A square pit six by six feet and six feet deep had been dug inside the building. Then from it, leading south, was a trench running outside fifty feet, where was dug a circular pit ten feet in diameter and five feet deep. This and the trench were then cribbed over and the dirt tamped down over it. The circular pit was portholed all around . . . [which] made the whole place so impregnable that a few cool, determined men could make it impossible for the allied tribes to take it without artillery." Stanley infers that the "relatives" from Delaware were impostors who simply helped themselves to Springer's money and possessions.

5. Haley, *Charles Goodnight,* 301–2. Like her husband, Cornelia Adair was of an autocratic nature. When her carriage became mired in quicksand during a crossing of the Canadian, "Scotty" Wilson, ever the gallant, pulled off his boots, waded out into the waist-high water, and rescued "Her Ladyship" by carrying her safely to the bank. To show her gratitude she gave him two bits. Arnot, "My Recollections."

6. John L. McCarty, *Maverick Town: The Story of Old Tascosa; Dodge City Times,* September 27, 1879. The son of the Rev. Reuben and Ann (Eddy) Torrey, Ellsworth Torrey was born September 27, 1829, in Eastford, Windham, Connecticut. On August 31, 1853, he was married there to nineteen-year-old Anna Maria White, and shortly thereafter they set up home near Boston; they had three children: Charles, born 1859; William, born 1861; and Elizabeth, born 1880. Following the sale of his ranch to W. M. D. Lee, Torrey settled in Providence, Rhode Island, longtime home of his mother's people, where he worked first as a bank clerk and for the last seventeen years of his life as clerk of the Clearing House there. "Quiet as to disposition

and never losing a day by illness from his post," he died on January 30, 1913; Anna Maria died September 11, 1928. *Providence Journal,* February 2, 1913.

7. For a full biography, see J. Evetts Haley, *George W. Littlefield, Texan* (Norman: University of Oklahoma Press, 1943).

8. Hamner, *Short Grass,* 89–90; McCarty, *Maverick Town,* 45–47; Warranty Deed, David T. Beals to Trustees for American Pastoral Co., Potter County Deed Records 3, 64, cited in Margaret Sheets, "The LX Ranch," *Panhandle-Plains Historical Review* 6 (1933): 45–64.

Not everyone loved Siringo.

We hired [him] at St Jo in [Montague County] Texas to help us through the Cross Timbers about 1877. He was to help . . . with the horse herd in getting through the timber. Wheat, one of our men, came loping back and said for me to get the horses to keep Siringo from stealing them. Then he went up the trail to Dodge and came back to the Panhandle with Bates and Beales [*sic*]. He was no cowhand, and there was not a damned thing to him anyway. He was always hard up and I still have a note from him for about a hundred and fifty dollars." (J. Evetts Haley, Interview with J. Phelps White, January 15, 1927, Roswell, N.M., HHC; hereafter cited as Haley, "White.")

A fine biography is Howard R. Lamar, *Charlie Siringo's West: An Interpretive Biography.*

9. Arnot, "My Recollections," 4–5. Arnot did not arrive in the Panhandle until 1884. Jim East, who was there in 1877, said Mitchell had "some sheep and a few goats [and] a Mexican wife whom the cowboys used to be always after. . . . A man named Judge Falby who had a Mexican wife was there with Mitchell. . . . He had some stock. Mitchell and Falby came there from New Mexico, I think from the Mora country." Haley, "East."

10. Haley, "East."

11. Roger Myers, "Murder in the Panhandle: The Killing of the Casner Brothers," *Jour-nal of the Western Outlaw-Lawman Association* 12, no. 1 (spring 2003): 27–36, 44; genealogical research by Elizabeth E. Freeman; *Dodge City Times,* April 28, 1877.

12. Clarence R. Wharton, L'Archevêque, passim. Most of the legends associated with l'Archevêque originated with Wharton's little twenty-one-page booklet. Where he got his information no one knows.

13. McCarty, *Maverick Town,* 20–21. It is tempting to wonder whether it was in Old, rather than New Mexico that l'Archevêque created such mayhem; on March 27, 1877, the *Dodge City Times* reported the Mexican government had offered a five-hundred-dollar reward for him.

14. Myers, "Murder"; *Dodge City Times,* March 24, 1877.

15. McCarty, *Maverick Town,* 22ff.; *Dodge City Times,* May 19, 1877.

16. *Dodge City Times,* May 19, 1877.

17. Ibid.; McCarty, *Maverick Town,* 32.

18. *Dodge City Times,* May 6 and July 7, 1877. Phelps White alleged Hall and McNab had committed other murders at this time.

I went over on the Big Blue in the winter of [18]77 just prowling around, and found five or six big mule wagons that had been burned. . . . We found out later that Hall and Frank McNabb [*sic*], who had been delivering cattle to Hunter & Evans for John Chisum, had run on to these wagons and a bunch of Mexican buffalo hunters. They killed the Mexicans in order to steal their work cattle and burned the bodies with their wagons. They spared only one person, some old Mexican told me later, who was a boy. They put him on a burro and he finally made his way to Chaperito. But by that time Hall and McNabb had got to Colorado and sold the cattle. Then they came back to New Mexico and got themselves killed, McNabb on the Bonito at the Spring Ranch during the Lincoln County War and Hall at the Rock Corral down the Pecos. (Haley, "White.")

19. *Dodge City Times,* May 6 and 19, 1877.

20. Myers, "Murder"; *Dodge City Times,* May 19, 1877.

21. Myers, "Murder"; *Dodge City Times,* May 26, 1877.

22. *Dodge City Times,* September 29, 1877. Frank McNab drifted west to Lincoln County and joined the Tunstall-McSween faction in the Lincoln County War; he was one of the sextet who ambushed and killed Sheriff William Brady and Deputy George Hindman at Lincoln on April 1, 1878. His luck ran out on April 29 when he and two others ran into a "posse" supporting the other side; in the ensuing gunfight McNab was killed. There is no record of the killing of anyone named Frank Hall.

23. Found guilty of "permitting irregularities in the sale of government property," Hotsenpiller was sentenced to four months' suspension from rank and confined to the post for his sins. He retired from the service on June 19, 1879 reportedly "on 3/4 pay on account of disabilities." His service record cannot be located. Witherell was suspended from rank and command on half pay for one year from January 31, 1878; amazingly, on March 20, 1879, he was promoted to the rank of captain. He retired from the service in 1898. Myers, "Murder"; *Ford County Globe,* February 12, 1878, and July 1, 1879; National Archives to the author, November 8, 2005; Francis B. Heitman, *Historical Register and Dictionary of the United States Army: From Its Organization, September 29, 1789, to March 2, 1903,* 1:544, 1052.

CHAPTER 4
CHARLES EMORY: SQUIRREL-EYE CHARLIE

1. Cook, *Border,* 139. It has not proven possible to establish whether John B. Greathouse was related to "Whiskey Jim" Greathouse; the one, perhaps understandably, is frequently mixed up with the other in many accounts of this period. A George Cornette (with a final *e*), age twenty, laborer, born in Texas of Alabama parents, appears in the 1870 census in Ellis County. Cook says only that he was "raised on the northern frontier of Texas, near Henrietta." A Charles Emery appears in the same census in Stephens County, but whether he is our man likewise cannot be confirmed. Federal Census, Oldham County, Tex., 1880; Ellis County, Tex., 1880; Stephens County, Tex., 1880.

2. Cook, *Border,* 145–47.

3. Rister, *Fort Griffin,* 172–73; Schofield, *Indians, Cattle,* 39–40; Naomi H. Kinkaid, "Rath City," *West Texas Historical Association Yearbook* 24 (Oct. 1948): 40ff.

4. Rister, *Fort Griffin,* 173; Rath, *Trail,* 145. Born in Ohio about 1850, William H. "Harvey" West, Rath's "business manager" and "trusted friend," had worked with Rath at his store (also a stage station) on the Walnut River "at the great bend of the Arkansas River, in Kansas" and accompanied him, with Dan Jones, on trading trips to the Indians. He worked for Conrad & Rath at Fort Griffin and later for Rath at Mobeetie, "knew all the hunters from Kansas, Colorado and many from Texas," and was "known by hearsay to every hunter in the south." He is last mentioned in Texas in the *Fort Griffin Echo,* May 24, 1879. "Mr W. H. West, who has been with Conrad and Rath at Fort Griffin for a long time, is now on his way to Dodge with a herd of cattle. He will arrive in June." Whether he ever did is uncertain; soon after this, he turned up in White Oaks, New Mexico, where he operated a livery stable and became involved in a counterfeiting operation; shortly thereafter he left for parts unknown. Federal Census, Lincoln County, New Mexico, 1880; Pat F. Garrett, *The Authentic Life of Billy the Kid: An Annotated Edition with Notes and Commentary,* ed. Frederick Nolan, 125–28.

5. *Fort Worth Democrat,* November 8, 1876.

6. Rister, *Fort Griffin,* 181; *Dodge City Times,* May 26, 1877.

7. Rex W. Strickland, ed., "The Recollections of W. S. Glenn, Buffalo Hunter," *Panhandle-Plains Historical Review* 23 (1949): 15–83; Rister, *Fort Griffin,* 184ff.; Miles Gilbert, Leo Remiger, and Sharon Cunningham, *Encyclopedia of Buffalo Hunters and Skinners,* vol. 1, *A–D* (Union City, Tenn.: Pioneer Press, 2003), 242–45. To

"persuade" him to reveal the whereabouts of the Comanche encampment, Mackenzie's troopers hanged Tafoya from a wagon tongue; it took three hoistings to get him to talk. J. Evetts Haley, *Fort Concho and the Texas Frontier*, 220.

8. Gilbert, Remiger, and Cunningham, *Encyclopedia* 1:151; Cook, *Border*, 241; *Dodge City Times*, June 2, 1877.

9. Strickland, "Glenn." It was probably not "Whiskey Jim" Greathouse (yet another player in the saga of Billy the Kid) but—since both Emory and Cornett were along—John B. Greathouse.

10. Earl Vandale and Hervey Chesley, Interview with Sam Baldwin, July 11, 1941, Vandale Collection, 2H470, CAH/UT.

11. Gilbert, Remiger, and Cunningham, *Encyclopedia* 1:246–47; Cook, *Border*, 259ff.; Philip J. Rasch, "Alias 'Whiskey Jim,'" *Panhandle-Plains Historical Review* 26 (1963): 103–14. Captain Nolan's column got hopelessly lost and dispersed in a desperate search for water. They finally reached safety, but not before four troopers, between twenty and thirty horses, and four to six mules had died of thirst. It is difficult to be more precise about the casualties because official reports, letters, newspaper accounts, and court-martial testimony offer different perspectives, and the men of Nolan's command were scattered. H. Bailey Carroll, "Nolan's 'Lost Nigger' Expedition of 1877," *Southwestern Historical Quarterly* 44 (July 1940): 55–75; Paul H. Carlson, *The Buffalo Soldier Tragedy of 1877*, passim.

12. Cook, *Border*, 275–83.

13. "Squirrel-Eye" Charlie is listed under his real name, Charles A. Arnim, in the 1880 census for Fayette County, Texas. Born November 3, 1861, probably in La Grange, Texas, he first appears as an eight-year-old schoolboy, the next to youngest of the six children of grocer Alex Arnim, forty-nine, and his wife, Marie (née Chaste), forty-three, living near La Grange. The oldest son, William, sixteen (later "Poker Tom" Emory), was a field hand; his brother Edward Alexander, fourteen, a clerk in the J. M. Harrison mercantile store in Flatonia. Charles Emory, or rather Arnim, died March 9, 1895. Alicia Mc-

Donald, Fayette County Heritage Museum and Archive, Flatonia, Texas, to the author, January 3, 2001; Wayne Ahr, College Station, Texas, to the author, July 20, 2002.

CHAPTER 5
1878: BILLY THE KID HITS TOWN

1. Philip J. Rasch, "Bad Days at Cimarron," *New York Westerners Brand Book* 18, no. 1 (1971): 12–13; Howard Bryan, *Robbers, Rogues, and Ruffians*, 18–23. Isaiah Rinehart (the name is often given as a variation of Reinhardt, which was probably the original spelling) came to Cimarron in 1864 to operate a new grist mill for Maxwell. He appears in the 1870 census as a thirty-year-old miller, born in Kentucky and living with his wife, Sarah, twenty-eight; and daughter, Elizabeth, eight, both born in Pennsylvania; and a son, Irwin J., four, born in Virginia. Sarah, born August 2, 1842, in Shrewsbury, Pennsylvania, contracted tuberculosis about 1871 and died May 24, 1874. Her "infant son," Melvin W., died on September 17 of the same year.

On September 1, 1877, the *Dodge City Times* reported: "The settlement, Tascosa, consists of thirty or forty families. Reinheart & Howard have established a store, and hundreds of thousands of sheep are being herded in the vicinity." That Rinehart was still in New Mexico late in 1877 is confirmed by his appearance at Cimarron on August 31 of that year in the matter of the sale of his "dwelling house . . . near the grist mill" for $250. There seems to be no truth in the allegation that he embezzled school funds (Rasch gives no source for the story); perhaps the embezzler was his successor, Sheriff Peter Burleson, who is said to have had gambling debts. Only Rinehart and his son, Irwin, appear in the 1880 census; what happened to his daughter Sarah is not known. He is said to have married again, but there is no record of any such event. In later years he had a stroke that left him partially paralyzed; he moved to Texline in the 1890s. Chuck Hornung, "The Forgotten Davy Crockett, Bad Boy of Cimarron, New

Mexico," *Quarterly of the National Association for Outlaw and Lawman History* 5, no. 13 (summer 1988): 8–15; *Cimarron News,* May 30 and September 19, 1874; records of the Colfax County Court and other research courtesy Chuck Hornung; Federal Census, Colfax County, N.M., 1870, courtesy Nancy Robertson; Federal Census, Oldham County, Tex., 1880; Dr. O. H. Lloyd, "Oldham County, Texas: An Authentic Historical Brief of Old Tascosa and Oldham County," Vandale Collection, 2J5, CAH/UT.

2. Arnot, "My Recollections." Arnot, who did not arrive in Tascosa until 1884, was repeating what he'd heard from others; McMasters did not arrive in the Panhandle until 1878.

3. McCarty, *Maverick Town,* 56; Cape Willingham, "History of the First Ranches," J. Evetts Haley Collection, HHC.

Howard became postmaster at Tascosa on June 24, 1878, but does not appear in the census for 1880. He is said to have died in 1883 and been buried on Boot Hill; his body was later taken to Kansas to be buried in a family plot. The latter statement may be so, but the former is not: on June 28, 1883, George Julius Howard was united in matrimony with Mary Ratcliff in Colfax County, New Mexico, by Justice of the Peace B. F. Houx. He was succeeded as Tascosa postmaster by Jim McMasters on March 10, 1884, so it might be inferred he either left Tascosa or died then or soon afterward. Arnot, "My Recollections"; Colfax County Marriage Book A, 33, courtesy Nancy Robertson; Federal Census, Oldham County, Tex., 1880.

4. *Pampa Daily News,* May 31, 1936, citing the *Herald* (Perryton, Tex.). John Dinan rented two rooms from Isaiah Rinehart for $7.50 a month in which he operated the second saloon in Tascosa. He then moved to Liberty, New Mexico, where in May 1887 he killed a cowboy named John Hill; about two years later he himself was killed by another cowboy he was trying to shoot. Arnot, "My Recollections."

5. Arnot, "My Recollections"; McCarty, *Maverick Town,* 72–73; Millie Jones Porter, *Memory Cups of Panhandle Pioneers,* 572.

6. Undated and unattributed document

"Boothill Cemetery, Tascosa," in JLMC/APL; *Amarillo Sunday News-Globe,* August 12, 1928.

7. Haley, "East"; a map of Boot Hill and a list of graves compiled by Jeanette Coaly are at www.rootsweb.com/txoldham/boothillcem; John Leverton is buried in the Leverton cemetery near Evans Canyon (see note 24, chapter 21). It might here be added that scattered through the judicial records in Tascosa beginning in May 1881 are many indictments for murder in which no perpetrator was named, no suspect ever arrested. In some, as in the case of one Pedro Tenorio, arrested in May 1881 for aggravated assault, no outcome is recorded; in others, such as the case of Estanislado Aries, an arrest for murder was made but no victim named. Bailed for ten thousand dollars, Aries took a change of venue to Wheeler County, where on August 1, 1882, he was sentenced to four years in prison. Whom he killed we will probably never know. John Arnot, "Leverton Brothers," Vandale Collection, 2H472, CAH/UT; *State of Texas* vs. *Pedro Tenorio,* May 3, 1881; *State of Texas* vs. *Estanislado Aries,* August 30, 1881, Oldham County, Judges State Docket Book (1) 1, 6, Oldham County District Clerk, Vega, Texas (hereafter cited as CDCV); Porter, *Memory Cups,* 519.

8. *Dodge City Times,* April 21, 1877–August 28, 1879.

9. John McCarty and Mel Armstrong, Interview with Garrett H. "Kid" Dobbs, Farmington, N.M., September 12, 1942, JLMC/APL (hereafter cited as McCarty and Armstrong, "Dobbs"). There actually were three interviews: in the morning and evening of September 12 and a third on October 20, 1942, with Pat Flynn and J. D. White on behalf of McCarty and Armstong. Much of the material repeats itself, so to avoid confusion they are referred to as one.

10. *Pampa Daily News,* May 31, 1936, citing the *Herald* (Perryton, Tex.).

11. The life of Billy the Kid and the events of the Lincoln County War have been featured in more than a thousand books, movies, plays, dime novels, and even a ballet. Kathleen Cham-

berlain, *Billy the Kid and the Lincoln County War: A Bibliography.*

One pithy observation of Charles Goodnight's suggests that had he been involved, the Lincoln County War might have had a different ending. "The Irishman who ran a store at Lincoln was the leader of the bunch against Chisum. This Irishman would give the thieves $5 a head for all they'd bring in. Then he would take the government contract for almost nothing and nobody could bid against him, since he didn't give anything for the cattle. Why Chisum didn't go up the hill and kill him is more than I can understand." Charles Goodnight to J. Evetts Haley, July 24, 1925, HHC.

12. Col. N. A. M. Dudley, Commanding, Fort Stanton, to AAAG, District of New Mexico, September 7, 1878, Consolidated File 1405, 1878, AGO, Microfilm M666, rolls 397–98, NARA.

13. Sallie Chisum, *Notebook,* Historical Society for Southeast New Mexico, Roswell.

14. McCarty and Armstrong, "Dobbs."

15. Hoyt, *Frontier Doctor,* 146–47; McCarty and Armstrong, "Dobbs."

16. McCarty and Armstrong, "Dobbs." For details of the later fracas, cf. chapter 7.

"[C. S.] McCarty came out from around Gonzales or Goliad. He was a handsome fellow. He would weigh about 175 or eight pounds, was pretty thick[set], was dark and had black hair and was a good cowman." J. Evetts Haley, Interview with Harry Ingerton, June 12, 1937, Amarillo, HHC (hereafter cited as Haley, "Ingerton").

17. Haley, "White."

18. McCarty and Armstrong, "Dobbs."

19. John L. McCarty, "Jess Jenkins, Ragtown Owner," *Amarillo Sunday Globe-News, Golden Anniversary Issue,* August 14, 1938.

20. McCarty and Armstrong, "Dobbs." Dobbs was quite wrong about Torrey's age; he was in his late forties at that time. The oft-repeated legend that his encounter with the Kid so unnerved Torrey that he sold up and skedaddled back to the safety of New England is just that; it was not until late November 1882, long

after the Kid's death, that Torrey sold his ranch and holdings to W. M. D. Lee.

21. Hoyt, *Frontier Doctor,* 148.

22. Mrs. Lige Roberts, "True Son of the Raven Handled a Gun at Tascosa Like Plainsman," *Amarillo News-Globe,* Sunday, April 6, 1941.

23. Hoyt, *Frontier Doctor,* 149–50.

24. Frederick Nolan, ed., *The Life and Death of John Henry Tunstall,* 249.

25. Hoyt, *Frontier Doctor,* 152–53.

26. "Tascosa's Lone 'Old Settler' Recalls the Wild Days in the Little Panhandle Cow Town," typed copy of a newspaper interview with "Frenchy" McCormick, credited to the *Kansas City Star,* n.d. [1930], JLMC/APL.

27. Hoyt, *Frontier Doctor,* 153–54.

28. Ibid., 155–56. "Dandy Dick" was probably a descendant of one of the racehorses brought to New Mexico in 1864 by Col. Emil Fritz, cofounder with Lawrence G. Murphy of the "House" (although by the time the Lincoln County War erupted, Fritz was dead). A record by his jockey, Hilario Gallegos, refers to one called "Dandy" raced by Fritz at Tucson. After the Civil War, Fritz took Gallegos east, and for five years he traveled to race meetings with the horses, visiting Saint Louis and Santa Fe before returning to Tucson. Hilario Gallegos, unpublished memoir, 1872, Hayden Biography Collection, Arizona State University, Tempe.

CHAPTER 6
JIM KENEDY: "HE WAS A WILD ONE."

1. Leon Claire Metz, *Border: The US-Mexico Line,* 130.

2. Genealogical research by Chuck Parsons; C. L. Douglas, *Cattle Kings of Tex.;* Federal Census, Cameron County, Tex., 1860; Nueces County, Tex., 1870; Hidalgo County, Tex., 1880.

3. *Ellsworth (KS) Reporter,* August 1, 1872; Harry E. Chrisman, *The Ladder of Rivers: The Story of I. P. (Print) Olive,* 117–23. Isom Prentice "Print" Olive (1840–1886) was born in Missouri but grew up in Williamson County, Texas. After serving in the Confederate army, he and

his brothers Tom, Ira, and Bob (in some accounts there are four brothers, with different names) built up a big ranch business. All three were hard men and not averse to killing. Print Olive himself faced two indictments for murder but won acquittal both times; Tom Olive was killed in a gunfight, and Bob shot a local rancher, Cal Nutt. In 1878 Print and Bob Olive relocated in Custer County, Nebraska, where they became embroiled in a dispute with two neighboring ranchers, Ketchum and Mitchell. After Bob Olive was killed in a gunfight on the Ketchum ranch, a lynch mob—reportedly led by Print Olive—hunted down Ketchum and Mitchell, hanged them, and then burned their bodies. Olive was convicted of manslaughter, but the case was dropped when witnesses failed to appear. Olive is said to have spent much of his personal fortune on bribes and legal fees to secure his release. He was shot and killed by one Joe Sparrow in a Trail City, Colorado, saloon on August 18, 1886. *Handbook of Texas Online,* "Olive, Isom Prentice."

4. Parsons, "Kenedy"; Records of the Adjutant General, Leander H. McNelly, Company Muster and Pay Roll records, Texas State Archives, Austin (hereafter cited as TSA).

5. Haley, "White"; J. Evetts Haley, Interview with J. Arthur Johnson, March 27, 1946, Midland, Tex., HHC; Hoyt, *Frontier Doctor,* 92.

6. Haley, "White"; Hoyt, *Frontier Doctor,* 95.

7. Robert DeArment, *Bat Masterson: The Man and the Legend,* 117–18.

8. *Dodge City Times,* October 5, 1878.

9. Ibid., October 12, 1878.

10. De Arment, *Bat Masterson,* 123.

11. Haley, "White."

12. *Ford County Globe,* October 29, 1878.

13. Ibid., December 17, 1878.

14. Stanley Vestal, *Queen of Cowtowns: Dodge City, 1872–1886,* 143; *Dodge City Times,* November 27, 1880; Tom Lea, *The King Ranch,* 1:366; Hoyt, *Frontier Doctor,* 95. In dismissing the possibility that King might have killed Wyatt Earp, who was said to be "engaged as a special messenger by Wells Fargo & Co. on a division of the railroad in New Mexico," the *Dodge City*

Times shot another hole in the latter's claims to fame: "Earp was never engaged in a difficulty with Kennedy [*sic*]. The latter was shot in the shoulder by a posse of officers at one time in pursuit of him. Earp was not of that party."

15. *Corpus Christi Caller,* January 4, 1885; Haley, "White."

16. *Corpus Christi Caller,* January 4, 1885.

CHAPTER 7
1879–1880: GROWING PAINS

1. Lloyd, "Oldham County"; John L. McCarty and Earl Vandale, Interview with Mrs. J. E. May, September 23, 1941, Vega, Tex., Vandale Collection, 2H481, CAH/UT; McCarty, *Maverick Town,* 59; Federal Census, Oldham County, Tex., 1880; Deaf Smith County, Tex., 1880.

Molly was wrong: Kimball did not open his blacksmith shop in town until 1880, following the sale of his claim to the LIT. On September 4, 1882, the commissioners court dissolved the marriage of Henry and Mary Kimball; that same day, he married Martina Valdez. Mrs. Kimball outlived her husband by many years and is said to have died in 1934 at Channing at age eighty-four. Oldham County District Court Minutes (1) 29; Oldham County Marriage License Record (1) 8, CDCV.

2. Arnot, "My Recollections." Of course, there were no "officers" in 1879.

3. Marion Armstrong, "East Tascosa," Vandale Collection, 2J5, CAH/UT. When Cone's partner, Shelton Edwards, ran out on him, "John Cone bore the brunt of all the debts." Porter, *Memory Cups,* 92.

4. McCarty, *Maverick Town,* 103; McCarty and Vandale, Interview with Mrs. J. E. May; Vandale and Chesley, Interview with Sam Baldwin. Soon after the shooting, Tom Henry, a twenty-one-year-old cowboy said to have had a "checkered career" in Texas, left for Las Vegas, New Mexico, reportedly to make a living stealing horses. On January 22, 1880, in George Close and Billy Patterson's dance hall on Railroad Avenue, he, John Dorsey, James West, and William Randall got into a fight with the town

marshal, Joe Carson, who had invited them to check their pistols. As the boys put nine bullets into Carson, Assistant Marshal "Mysterious" Dave Mather joined the fray. When the smoke cleared, Carson was dead, Randall was fatally wounded, and West was "lying in the street shot through the liver and yelling like a coyote." Dorsey and Tom Henry escaped but were captured two weeks later and thrown into the *juzgado*. In the early hours of Sunday, February 8, vigilantes took the prisoners from the jail and marched them to the notorious "Hanging Windmill" in the plaza, where Henry confessed his real name was Thomas Jefferson House. West would admit only that his real name was Lowe; later it was learned his first name was Anthony. Dorsey refused to say anything at all. Then, one account has it, as the final preparations were being made to hang them, Carson's widow cut loose with a rifle; in moments the shooting became general, and when it stopped all three men were dead. Shortly after this, Carson's widow eloped with "Hoodoo Brown," real name Hyman G. Neill. It was a short-lived romance; Neill was killed in late November or early December 1880 while gambling at Caddo, Indian Territory. Henry Hoyt was proud to have been one of the mob: "[Charles] Ilfelt [*sic*] and me both belonged to the vigilantes in Las Vegas and strung up six. Page B. Otero, also there, now of Los Angeles, says 'five.' Two the first and three the second time." Howard Bryan, *Wild West,* 130–36 153; *Las Vegas Daily Optic,* February 9, 1880; Hoyt, *Frontier Doctor,* 216–17; *Dodge City Times,* December 18, 1880; Henry Hoyt to James H. East, March 12, 1928, James East Collection, HHC.

5. Armstrong, "East Tascosa"; S. D. Myers, ed., *Pioneer Surveyor, Frontier Lawyer: The Personal Narrative of O. W. Williams, 1877–1902,* 89–92, 158–59. "Old man" Duran was thirty-five in 1880; he, his wife, Benicia, and their three children lived in Romero Canyon in Hartley County. He sold out to W. M. D. Lee in 1883 and went into business with John Cone (probably in what had been Jules Howard's store). To learn English he attended (along with the Russell, Armstrong, and Willingham children) the

first school in Oldham County, held in Rinehart's store; Jennie Mays Vivian was the teacher. Lloyd, "Oldham County"; Hamner, *Short Grass,* 167.

6. Hamner, *Short Grass,* 22–32; Ernest Cabe Jr., "A Sketch of the Life of James Hamilton Cator," *Panhandle-Plains Historical Review* 6 (1933); Schofield, *Indians, Cattle,* 141n6; Marion Armstrong, "W. M. D. Lee," Vandale Collection, 2J5, CAH/UT.

7. *Ford County Globe,* July 15, 1879; Harris, *Hide Town,* passim. Emanuel Dubbs was born at New Franklin, Ohio, on March 21, 1843, youngest of the six children of farmer Daniel and his wife, Elizabeth (Meckley) Dubbs. After serving in the 1st Ohio Infantry during the war, he moved to Indiana and entered the lumber business with his brother. In 1868 he married Angelina Freed: they would have four sons. In 1871, following the destruction of his sawmill by fire, he relocated to Newton, Kansas; he is said to have built the first house in Dodge City, where he hunted buffalo and also ran a buttermilk and beer farm. He was with the A. C. Myers group that built the Adobe Walls compound, but his claim to have participated in the famous fight is disputed. In 1878 the family moved to Sweetwater, where he served as county judge until 1888. In 1890 he moved to Clarendon, and six years later he became a minister. He died on April 23, 1932, and is buried there beside his wife (who died in 1911).

8. *Dodge City Times,* September 27, 1879.

9. Dulcie Sullivan, *The LS Brand: The Story of a Panhandle Ranch,* 27–29; *Handbook of Texas Online,* "McAllister, Jordan Edgar."

10. Armstrong, "Lee." In the Federal Census, Hartley County, Tex., 1880, Charles Sperling is thirty and his brother, Frank, twenty-eight.

11. Hamner, *Short Grass,* 166.

12. Arnot, "My Recollections." Steve Conkling got his nickname one night after he got drunk and decided to kill himself. The boys mixed him a "lethal" dose of flour and water and gave it to him. "Here goes Steve Nobody," Conkling said, went down to the railroad tracks, drank his "poison," and lay down to await

death. It didn't happen, of course, and he was known by that name for as long as he lived. Mc-Carty, *Maverick Town*, 168.

13. *Handbook of Texas Online*, "New Zealand Sheep Company."

14. Armstrong, "East Tascosa."

15. Harris, *Hide Town*, 26–27; Schofield, *Indians, Cattle*, 51; *Dodge City Times*, November 9 and 29, December 20 and 27, 1879; Jim McIntire, *Early Days in Texas: A Trip to Heaven and Hell*, 69, 138–39; Porter, *Memory Cups*, 70; Theodore D. Harris, *Black Frontiersman: The Memoirs of Henry O. Flipper*, 28–29. Born in Brown County, Ohio, in 1854 (he even lied about that), McIntire—at various removes an Indian fighter, buffalo hunter, Texas Ranger, saloonkeeper, gambler, and fugitive—was never a reliable reporter. His autobiography hardly mentions Tascosa, although he appears in the Oldham County census for 1880 as a "hotel keeper" and he gambled and raced horses there as late as December 1886, as other accounts confirm. He is known to have married, but no record of such a union has ever been located, nor are the place or manner of his death known. His account of these events is the only one that suggests Jim Courtright was involved.

16. McCarty and Armstrong, "Dobbs."

17. Ibid. Antonio Mexicana, fifty-five, was a freighter born in New Mexico. Living close to him in 1880 were three Chaves families: Jose, sixty-one, and his wife, Delphos, fifty-eight; Filemonte, twenty-eight, and wife, Maria, eighteen; and Melton, twenty-eight, with wife Mary, eighteen. There was no "Alicia Vorregos"; the nearest possibility appears to be Elisio, twenty-four, stockman, son of Ventura Borrego, although he did not live in Salinas. No Pablo Dierro or Guadalupe Circenos appears in the records. Federal Census, Oldham County, Tex., 1880.

18. Armstrong, "Lee."

19. *Pampa Daily News*, May 31, 1936; Schofield, *Indians, Cattle*, 52. Early the following year, Henry Russell and his wife leased the hotel to a man named Turner and moved to Deaf Smith County (not Las Vegas, New Mexico, as legend has it), where they opened and briefly ran a hotel; they returned to Tascosa after about six months and picked up where they had left off. Federal Census, Deaf Smith County, Tex., 1880.

CHAPTER 8
SELMAN AND LONG:
THE OUTLAW CONFEDERACY

1. J. Frank Dobie, *A Vaquero of the Brush Country*, 135–36.

2. F. Stanley, *The Texas Panhandle: From Cattlemen to Feed Lots, 1880–1970*, 65; *Kinsley [Kans.] Republican*, September 6, 1879; *Dodge City Times*, November 15, 1879.

3. *Dodge City Times*, February 1 and 15, 1879.

4. Full biographies of Selman and Larn are in Leon Claire Metz, *John Selman, Texas Gunfighter*, and Robert DeArment, *Bravo of the Brazos: John Larn of Fort Griffin, Texas*.

5. Frederick Nolan, *The West of Billy the Kid*, 179–80.

In 1887, W. A. Cone, wanted in a major embezzlement case in Harris County, was arrested in Tascosa by Texas Ranger Capt. Samuel McMurray; on November 8 he was handed over to the sheriff of Harris County at Quanah and taken to Houston. John Miller Morris, *A Private in the Texas Rangers*, 167–68.

6. Samuel R. Corbet to John Partridge Tunstall, October 1, 1878, cited in Nolan, *Lincoln County War*, 349; A. M. "Gus" Gildea to Maurice G. Fulton, December 14, 1929, Special Collections, University of Arizona, Tucson.

7. Wallace Collection, Indiana Historical Society, Indianapolis.

8. McIntire, *Early Days*, 136. The date McIntire gives (June 15, 1879) is suspect: Long was in Fort Stanton, New Mexico, on June 12–13 and was still in (or back in) the area on July 13 for the wedding of James Dolan. Nolan, *Lincoln County War*, 473.

9. Robert Barron, *Lieutenant Colonel N. A. M. Dudley Court of Inquiry, Fort Stanton, New Mexico, 1879*; Garrett, *Authentic Life*, 94; McCarty and Armstrong, "Dobbs."

On June 19, 1877, buffalo hunter James W. Grahame, who as "Comanche Jim" contributed occasional letters to the *Dallas Weekly Herald,* reported: "A young man named Harvey was recently shot by a buffalo hunter named Long. Harvey, after lingering a week the wounded man died, apparently without much suffering. The hunter, Long, although a poor man, honorably paid for the doctor's bill, an exceedingly heavy one, and all incidental expenses incurred from the effects of the shooting." *Dallas Weekly Herald,* July 21, 1877, cited in Chuck Parsons, "James W. Grahame—from Birmingham, England, to Fort Griffin," in Barry C. Johnson, ed., *Vignettes in Violence,* 15.

10. Barron, *Dudley,* 332ff.; Garrett, *Authentic Life,* 95; Nolan, *Billy the Kid,* 155ff.

11. McIntire, *Early Days,* 136.

12. Ibid.

13. Metz, *Selman,* 111; Haley, *Charles Goodnight,* 335.

14. Garrett, *Authentic Life,* 96. Upson's disinformation is all the more puzzling because the plaza of Trujillo is mentioned, in another context, on the same page.

15. Armstrong, "Lee."

16. McCarty and Armstrong, "Dobbs."

CHAPTER 9
1880: HUNTING BILLY THE KID

1. Orville H. Nelson, "The Story of the First Panhandle Stockmen's Association," unpublished ms., February 12, 1926, J. Evetts Haley Collection, Panhandle-Plains Historical Museum, Canyon, Texas.

2. Charles Goodnight to J. Evetts Haley, April 8, 1927, HHC.

3. There is no hard evidence that Garrett and the Kid were close friends, but since his sponsors—Joseph Lea, James Dolan, Warren Bristol, and John Chisum among them—viewed getting Garrett elected as "setting a thief to catch a thief," something more than acquaintanceship might be presumed, especially since Frank Coe stated flatly that Garrett "was a cow thief and everybody knew it." In Garrett's pursuit, capture, and killing of the Kid (aided especially by Mason, who later went to prison for rustling) there is ample indication that both were familiar with all the back trails and hideouts the Kid might use. Miguel Antonio Otero Jr., *The Real Billy the Kid, with New Light on the Lincoln County War,* 145–50.

4. McCarty and Armstrong, "Dobbs." "Frank Stewart" was an alias; his real name was John Green (1852–1935). Born in New York, he came west to Kansas after the death of his mother about 1867. He worked as a cowboy (some of the time at the LX) until 1887, when he was accused of rustling. After posting bond at Las Vegas, he disappeared, resurfacing in 1930 at Amarillo. About 1916 he settled in Raton, New Mexico, where he worked for the AT&SF Railroad. He died at age eighty-two in 1935, leaving a wife, Mollie, and a son.

5. Charles A. Siringo, *A Texas Cowboy, or, Fifteen Years on the Hurricane Deck of a Spanish Pony,* 85–86.

6. Haley, "East."

7. Cal Polk, "Life of C. W. Polk, Commenced January 25, 1896," author's collection, courtesy Mrs. Jessie Polk McVicar, Burneyville, Oklahoma, cited in James H. Earle, ed., *The Capture of Billy the Kid,* 18–19, 23–24.

8. John Francis Wallace [Frank Clifford]. "Deep Trails in the Old West," unpublished ms., author's collection, courtesy Michael E. Winter, Beebe, Arkansas.

9. Haley, "East."

10. McCarty and Armstrong, "Dobbs."

11. Haley, "East." East's comments about Mason might be considered further evidence supporting the proposition that he—and perhaps Garrett—had ridden with the Kid's gang.

12. Nolan, *Billy the Kid,* 271ff.

CHAPTER 10
"POKER TOM" EMORY:
RIDING UNDER A CONSUMED NAME

1. Haley, "East."

2. Earl Vandale, "Panhandle Pioneers: Interviews with J. R. Jenkins and W. H. Ingerton,"

1937, Vandale Collection, 2.325/D40c. CAH/UT.

3. Potter, Jack. "Tom Emery." Unpublished ms., n.d., JLMC/APL.

4. Haley, "East."

5. Morley, J. F., to James East, November 29, 1922. James H. East Collection, HHC.

6. Haley, "East."

7. Morley to East.

8. Haley, "East."

9. Polk, "Life."

10. Wallace, "Deep Trails."

11. Haley, "East."

12. Wallace, "Deep Trails." In August 1881, while Sheriff Cape Willingham was being tried for the murder of Fred Leigh, Emory appears to have served as a deputy sheriff of Oldham County, but for how long is not on record. Oldham County District Court Minutes (1) 10, August 31, 1881, CDCV.

13. Earl Vandale, Interview with Billy Jarrett, Dalhart, Texas, February 21, 1941, Vandale Collection, 2H481, CAH/UT; Potter, "Emery."

14. Jenkins said Emory's "real name was Bill Arnum and he came from Schulenburg, Texas. When he was dying, his brother Ed came from Flatonia and took Tom back to their old home. An application for a pardon was made, but Emory died before the papers reached the Governor." As noted, it was Charles Allen Culberson, who served from 1895 to 1900, to whom the request for a pardon was submitted; Oscar Branch Colquitt was governor 1910–15. John L. McCarty, "Jess Jenkins, Ragtown Owner," *Amarillo Sunday Globe-News, Golden Anniversary Issue*, August 14, 1938; Vandale, "Panhandle Pioneers."

15. Census records for 1870 show grocery store owner Alexander Arnim, forty-nine, and his wife, Marie, forty-three, living "between Buckner's Creek and the Hallettsville Road" near La Grange in Fayette County, Texas. They have six children: William, sixteen; Edward, fourteen; Theodore, twelve; Elizabeth, ten; Charles, eight; and Marie, two. Federal Census, Fayette County, Tex., 1870; Wayne Ahr, College Station, Texas, to author, July 20, 2002.

16. William Arnim, Convict Record Ledger, Prisoner 5339, TSA; John L. McCarty, Interview with Mr. J. R. Jenkins, September 16, 1937, Dalhart, Texas, Vandale Collection, 2H481, CAH/UT.

17. William Arnim, Judge L. W. Moore to Gov. C. A. Culberson, May 14, 1896, TSA; Dept. of State: Reasons for Executive Clemency File 4010, June 15, 1896, TSA.

18. Leon Claire Metz, *Pat Garrett: The Story of a Western Lawman*, 289; Kathy Carter and Alicia McDonald, Fayette County Heritage Museum and Archives, Flatonia, Texas, to the author, January 3, 2001.

CHAPTER 11
1880-1882: LAW AND (SOME) ORDER

1. Haley, "East."

2. McCarty, *Maverick Town*, 55.

3. Haley, "Ingerton."

4. Federal Census, Oldham County, Tex., 1880; Potter County, Tex., 1880; Wheeler County, Tex., 1880.

5. Haley, "East." This was not Tascosa's first attempt to organize: the Wheeler County Court rejected an August 16, 1880, petition signed by 88 persons that did not meet the requirements of the law (150 qualified voters were needed) and another unsuccessful attempt (turned down because the signatories were "not bonified [sic] residents of the county") on October 12 of the same year. Immediately prior to organization, the Wheeler County Court decreed "that the town of Tascosa, Oldham County, be the *temporary county seat until a vote of the citizens of Oldham County permanently locates a county seat*" (italics mine). This was the time bomb that ticked unheard for nearly thirty years before exploding in Tascosa's face. Wheeler County District Court Minute Book (1) 49, cited in Harris, *Hide Town*, 32; Porter, *Memory Cups*, 249–50.

6. John Arnot, "Tascosa Trail: John Arnot's Memoirs of the Old Cowtown," 16, Vandale Collection, 2H467, CAH/UT; Oldham County, Texas, Records of the Commissioners Court (1)

4–5 (May 9, 1881), CDCV. The "courthouse" was rented during the first year, then purchased outright for the sum of $710. When the deal went through, Jack Ryan paid $15 for a lot across the street and built another saloon; since it was paid for out of his profit on the sale, he called it the Equity Bar. It would become one of Tascosa's best-remembered and longest-surviving landmarks.

7. McCarty, *Maverick Town*, 60–61; Arnot, "Tascosa Trail," 23; *Dodge City Times,* December 18, 1880. Molly Russell indicated how the votes might have been swung: "On the day of the election, McMasters, [C. S.] McCarty and my mother served a free dinner. We fed lots of Mexicans that day. Mr. McMasters would bring the Mexicans in and seat them at the table, but he wouldn't eat with them." Lloyd, "Oldham County."

8. Haley, "White." Although his duties were similar to those of a county attorney, Woodman was in fact appointed legal adviser to the county commissioners; Jim McMasters became county judge, C. B. Vivian county clerk, Jules Howard treasurer, Juan Ortega assessor, and Marion Armstrong justice of the peace. It was not until February 15, 1881, with the creation of the 35th Judicial District (encompassing twenty-six Panhandle counties, with headquarters at Mobeetie, and referred to downstate as "the Jumbo District"), that a district judge, Frank Willis, and a district attorney, J. N. Browning, were appointed. When Browning stood down after a year, Temple Houston took his place.

9. J. Evetts Haley, Interview with H. Frank Mitchell, Amarillo, June 11, 1935, HHC (hereafter cited as Haley, "Mitchell"); John L. McCarty, Interview with Jess Jenkins, Dalhart, Texas, September 16, 1937, JLMC/APL.

Cecil Vivian was born in Louisville, Kentucky, on October 11, 1848; of Italian origin, the family came to America via France and England, where Vivian's father was born (his mother was from Virginia). According to family tradition, a steer tore off Vivian's arm while he was roping it; prior to his arrival in Tascosa

about 1880 he had been a surveyor. Licensed to practice law in Oldham County following an examination by Temple Houston, W. H. Woodman, and W. H. Grigsby in 1882, he moved in the late '80s to Amarillo, where he operated the Elmhurst Hotel. In May and June of 1891 his name appeared in Swisher County records, once as "acting judge"; four years later, he was back in Potter County, where he served briefly as deputy county clerk. By 1900 he was the Potter County tax assessor living in Amarillo with his wife and sons Homer, seventeen, and Roy, fifteen, and his daughter, Goldie, twelve. One contemporary said he abandoned his family and "went down the coast. There was a lawyer here [in Amarillo] that had a son-in-law and they all went down there and started a paper mill and he was a traveling salesman," but no hard evidence to support this assertion has been found. Cecil Vivian is said to have died at Amarillo in 1908, but his name does not appear in Potter County death records 1901–10; however, he was not enumerated in the 1910 census there. In that year his son Homer was foreman of a Roberts County ranch (coincidentally in the same precinct as rancher Manuel Brazil, who helped Pat Garrett capture Billy the Kid in 1880). In 1930 Jennie Vivian, a widow, was living in Albuquerque with her daughter Goldie (now Fletcher, divorced), a stenographer.

Lawrence and Helena Vivian to author, August 6, 2005; Haley, "Mitchell"; Jim Gober, *Cowboy Justice: Tale of a Texas Lawman,* 302; James East to J. Evetts Haley, February 22, 1928, HHC; Oldham County District Court Minutes (1) 48 (September 13, 1882), CDCV; Swisher County Commissioners Court dockets, July 1890–August 1891, 26, 36, County Clerk's Office, Tulia, Texas; Quincy Brown, Potter County District Clerk's Office, Amarillo, to author, August 24, 2005; Federal Census, Potter County, Tex., 1900; Roberts County, Tex., 1910; Bernalillo County, N.M., 1930; http://ftp.rootsweb.com/pub/usgenweb/tx/swisher/court/ctdocket.txt.

10. *Dodge City Times,* August 2, 1879.

11. Marion Armstrong, "Ysidro Serna,"
JLMC/APL.

12. John Arnot, "Thomas Wilson," Vandale
Collection, 2H471, CAH/UT.

13. *Dodge City Times,* February 12, 1881.

14. Haley, "East"; Arnot, "Wilson." The lake
later became and is still known as Skeleton Lake.

15. Armstrong, "Serna."

16. Lloyd, "Oldham County"; McCarty and
Armstrong, "Dobbs."

17. Henry Hoyt, letter to James H. East,
April 14, 1924, James H. East Collection, HHC.
In the 1880 census Ryan gave his nationality,
and that of his parents, as Swiss. This would
suggest he was from the Italian-speaking southern area of Switzerland known as Ticino. He
married Elsa Jane Kuney at Tascosa on September 12, 1882.

18. Vandale, Interview with Billy Jarrett.

19. Haley, "Ingerton."

20. Marion Armstrong, "Tascosa,"
JLMC/APL; J. H. Harshman, *Campfires and
Cattle Trails: Recollections of the Early West in the
Letters of J. H. Harshman,* 39.

21. McCarty, *Maverick Town,* 96. The grand
jury indictment dates the killing at March 15,
1880; the fact that Lizzie is shown alone, keeping house, in the 1880 census tends to confirm
it. Howard was tried and found not guilty of
murder on August 31, 1881, by a jury led by
Theodore Briggs. There were strong feelings
about the renaming of what had been called the
Graveyard, which "was not called Boot Hill
until a man who styled himself the town's leading humorist, but whom fellow townsmen considered a stupid clown, began to promote the
idea. . . . Right-minded people were appalled at
the unseemly suggestion, but the name caught
on." Federal Census, Oldham County, Tex.,
1880; *State of Texas* vs. *G. J. Howard,* Indictment
No. 11, Oldham County District Court
Records, CDCV; Sullivan, *LS Brand,* 62.

22. *Dodge City Times,* September 8, 1881.

23. McCarty, *Maverick Town,* 101; Marion
Armstrong, "J. N. Browning," JLMC/APL.

24. *Dodge City Times,* September 9, 1881.
The name appears variously—even in official

records—as McCullough, McCullar, McCuller,
and so on. I have used what seems the likeliest
correct spelling.

25. Oldham County, Texas, Records of the
Commissioners Court (1) 14–15 (October 17,
1881). Asa Shinn Mercer (1830–1917) started
at least four newspapers in Texas. In 1883 he
moved to Wyoming to publish another, the
Northwestern Livestock Journal; out of his experiences during and after the Johnson County
War, he wrote *The Banditti of the Plains, or, the
Cattlemen's Invasion of Wyoming in 1892.* Sup-
pressed, the book became famous—perhaps in-
famous—but Mercer seems not to have much
profited from it and died largely forgotten.

26. Stanley, *Texas Panhandle,* 102–4; Van-
dale, "Panhandle Pioneers"; research at Corona,
New Mexico, by Lanita Rasak.
Jenkins's relationship with Phoebe Miller
caused them to be indicted (probably in the
wake of the Edmunds Act) for adultery; the case
against Jenkins was not prosecuted, and Dutch
Phoebe was found not guilty. *State of Texas* vs.
Jesse Jenkins and Phoebe Miller, Oldham County
District Court Judges State Docket Book (1) 26
(April 5, 1883), CDCV.

27. Charles Goodnight, Undated material
No. 11, J. Evetts Haley Collection, HHC.

28. Oldham County, Records of the Commissioners Court (1) 12–13 (October 17, 1881).

29. Armstrong, "Tascosa."

30. Polk, "Life."

31. Marion Armstrong, "Henry Brown, Lincoln County War Number One," JLMC/APL.

32. Oldham County, Records of the Commisioners Court (1) 10 (September 21, 1881);
Armstrong, "Brown."

33. Frederick Nolan, *Bad Blood: The Life and
Times of the Horrell Brothers,* 105–31.

34. Arnot, "My Recollections."

35. Oldham County Marriage License
Record (1) 4, CDCV; Haley, "East." Not all the
weddings were so Arcadian. Scotty Wilson was
called on to marry "a young cowboy who was of
a spare and light build. The bride on the contrary was of considerable heft and wide abeam.
After the ceremony 'Scotty,' according to his

wont, gave a few words of admonition and advice to the groom and finished up by saying 'Weel, me lad, go on and fly your kite high, for ye've plenty of tail to hold it down with." Arnot, "My Recollections."

36. McCarty, *Maverick Town*, 186–87; Cases #1–3, report of the Grand Jury, Oldham County District Court Minutes (1) 4–9, CDCV.

37. Garrett H. Dobbs and Mary Helen "Lena' Atkins, daughter of Virginia-born former Quantrill raider and buffalo hunter John Atkins and his native New Mexican wife, Maria, were married on September 18, 1881, by Judge Jim McMasters. The wedding (said to have been Tascosa's first) may also have been "encouraged" by Wilson. Oldham County Marriage License Record (1) 1, CDCV.

38. J. Evetts Haley, Interview with Lucius Dills, Roswell, N.M., August 5, 1937, HHC.

CHAPTER 12
"OUTLAW BILL" MOORE:
LOS MUERTOS NO HABLAN

1. Hamner, *Short Grass*, 91; Walter Prescott Webb, *The Texas Rangers: A Century of Frontier Defense*, 322.

2. John Arnot, "Some Smooth Rustlers," Vandale Collection, 2H472, CAH/UT.

3. N. Howard (Jack) Thorp as told to Neil McCullough Clark, *Pardner of the Wind*, 153–54; Hamner, *Short Grass*, 96; Laura V. Hamner, Interview with Jesse Jenkins, November 11, 1940, JLMC/APL. Jenkins told another story about Moore: "One time when the river was up and the LX outfit was camped across from Tascosa, [LX cook Keg] Bill came into town. He was afraid to go back across the river (and drunk, too). W. C. Moore swam the river, put Bill on a horse, and about every fifty yards gave Bill a lick with his rope. But Bill did not go back on Moore for that, said Moore was just doing it for his own good."

4. Thorp as told to Clark, *Pardner*, 155.

5. Federal Census, Potter County, Tex., 1880; Haley, "East"; Arnot, "Smooth Rustlers." East said Miller (Müller) Scott was a former

buffalo hunter who came to the Panhandle from central West Texas with a herd a little after September 1880.

6. Hamner, *Short Grass*, 97.

7. Haley, "Ingerton."

8. Charles A. Siringo, *The Lone Star Cowboy, Being Fifty Years' Experience in the Saddle as Cowboy, Detective, and New Mexico Ranger*, 79.

9. John C. McCubbin, *The McCubbin Papers: An Account of the Early History of Reedley and Vicinity*, 39–45. Wright's wound proved not to be life-threatening—in fact, he lived to the ripe old age of ninety-six. Two months after the shooting, he published a rambling account of it in which he and Moore exchanged words; then, as Wright turned away, "I heard him set his pistol. My first thought was to get hold of the pistol, and turning quick to my left, as I faced him he fired." Badly wounded, he grabbed Moore's pistol, and as they struggled, four more shots were fired, the last of which took off one of Moore's fingers. Another, less friendly paper mocked his self-serving account, commenting that local opinion "was unanimous in feeling that Clayborne Wright got what was coming to him." *Visalia Weekly Delta*, May 25, 1871; *Fresno Weekly Expositor*, May 31, 1871.

10. Federal Census, Merced County, Calif., 1870.

11. Carl Hallberg, Wyoming State Archives, to the author, April 8, 2002.

12. Haley, "East."

13. Haley, "Ingerton."

14. Haley, "East."

15. Seymour V. Connor, "Early Ranching Operations in the Panhandle: A Report on the Agricultural Schedules of the 1880 Census," *Panhandle-Plains Historical Review* 27 (1954).

16. Frank H. Slaven, *William C. Moore: Good Guy or Outlaw Bill?* 68.

17. *Dodge City Times*, October 6, 1881; *Warrensburg Standard*, December 1, 1881.

18. *Dodge City Times*, February 2, 1882; Slaven, *Moore*, 77.

19. Haley, "East."

20. *Dodge City Times*, June 8, 1882.

21. Philip J. Rasch, "Murder in American Valley," *English Westerners Brand Book* 7, no. 3 (April 1965): 2–7; Howard Bryan, *True Tales of the American Southwest: Pioneer Recollections of Frontier Adventures*, 139–48; Slaven, *Moore*, 71ff.

22. Victor Westphall, *Thomas Benton Catron and His Era*, 152ff.

23. W. C. Moore, Oath of Commission, September 12, 1882; Muster Roll, New Mexico Volunteer Militia, n.d. [1882]. Valencia County, Adjutant General Collection, Box 10831, New Mexico State Records Center and Archive, Santa Fe; Frederick Nolan, "Boss Rustler: The Life and Crimes of John Kinney," *True West* 43, no. 9 (Sept. 1996): 14–21, and 43, no. 10 (Oct. 1996): 12–19; *Santa Fe Daily New Mexican*, December 14, 1882.

24. *Albuquerque Daily Democrat*, May 7, 1883; Rasch, "Murder."

25. *Albuquerque Morning Journal*, May 24, 1883; *Santa Fe Daily New Mexican*, May 15, 1883.

26. *Albuquerque Morning Journal*, May 17 and 18, 1883.

27. Rasch, "Murder."

28. *Albuquerque Morning Journal*, June 6, 1883; Westphall, *Catron*, 158; Thorp and Clark, *Pardner*, 156; J. Evetts Haley, "Jim East—Trail Hand and Cowboy," *Panhandle-Plains Historical Review* 4 (1931): 39–61. Or did "Outlaw Bill" go back to his old stomping grounds? Late in the night of November 30, 1887, a William Moore, operating a "road house" near Fort Laramie, attacked and badly beat Charlotte "Lottie" Smith, who had earlier been involved in an altercation (fueled by cards and whiskey) in which one Pat Kavanaugh got stabbed. Moore pursued the woman to her residence and attacked her, claiming she had killed Kavanaugh. When her companions tried to intervene, Moore pulled a gun and said, "I'll kill her, and I'll blow the brains out of the first sonofabitch who dares to interfere." Smith was finally taken to her room, where a physician declared her recovery would be "little short of a miracle."

Moore's friends were "at a loss to account

for his despicable action." He was "well and not unfavorably known in this city," according to the local paper. On December 9 the *Cheyenne Leader* reported that Moore had arrived at the county seat to "avoid placing the officials to any inconvenience in arresting him in case that proceeding should follow." It did; on December 12 he was arraigned in court before Laramie County prosecuting attorney W. R. Stoll and pleaded not guilty. The witnesses against him included Lottie Smith (miracles do happen), her doctor, L. Brechemin (Brickman?), and Ida (Mrs. Moore) Mitchell. On February 11, 1888, Moore changed his plea to guilty as charged and was fined one hundred dollars and ten dollars in costs and sentenced to six months in the county jail. Released August 28, 1888, he disappeared from the record. *Cheyenne Daily Leader*, December 8, 9, 11, and 16, 1887; February 12 and 15, 1888; Laramie County Prison Calendar, 1888/Criminal Case 173, *Territory of Wyoming vs. William Moore*, Wyoming State Archives, Cheyenne.

CHAPTER 13
1882: THE BEEF BONANZA

1. Although Glidden is always credited with the invention of barbed wire, strictly speaking he was its developer. While attending an Illinois county fair in 1873 with two neighbors, Isaac Ellwood and Jacob Haish, he saw an exhibit of a type of barbed wire invented by Henry M. Rose. After tinkering with Rose's idea, Glidden took out a patent on his own "improved" version on October 27, 1873. He was not alone, however: Haish also filed for a patent, challenging the priority of Glidden's application. The courts ruled in Glidden's favor, and in 1874 he began manufacturing barbed wire. He formed a partnership the following year with Ellwood, then sold his half interest to the Washburn & Moen Manufacturing Company of Worcester, Massachusetts, for sixty thousand dollars and a royalty deal. The new owners bought up all competing patents and developed machinery needed to mass-produce the wire. Production

soared from 2.84 million pounds in 1876 to more than 80 million pounds four years later. Henry D. McCallum and Frances T. McCallum, *The Wire That Fenced the West*, passim.

2. Haley, "East."

3. Hamner, *Short Grass*, 211–13; *Dodge City Times*, March 9, 1882.

4. Haley, *Charles Goodnight*, 321–22.

5. Sullivan, *LS Brand*, 78–79. "Severe storms drove stock from Kansas, Colorado, the Cimarron country and as far away as Nebraska and on south to the Pecos River in New Mexico. . . . In one instance cattle wearing the LS brand were discovered as far south as the Rio Grande." That cattle drifted such distances is borne out by Jim East, who recalled, "We had to go as far south as the head of the Colorado River and over to Chisum's ranch on the Pecos after drift cattle. . . . I have cut cattle on the Pease River that came from the Platte in Nebraska. . . . It probably took two seasons for them to get that far. . . . I believe the heaviest winter drift was in the Fall of '80 . . . there were thousands upon thousands of cattle in that country that had drifted from the far North, as there were no fences from Montana to the Rio Grande." Haley, "East."

6. Sullivan, *LS Brand*, 32.

7. Hamner, *Short Grass*, 168–69; Schofield, *Indians, Cattle*, 59 and 159n25. On October 27, 1881, emphasizing the seriousness of Lee's intent, the *Dodge City Times* noted that "two carloads of blooded polled Angus stock was delivered on Monday to Lee & Reynolds. This is the largest importation ever made of this class of stock to America and the first importation to Dodge City." The cattle had cost about twenty-five thousand dollars. Shipped at one hundred dollars a head from Liverpool to Quebec, they were quarantined for ninety days then forwarded to Pleasant Hill, Missouri. "The breeding of fine blooded stock is becoming a rage with western stockmen and in a few years the best bloods and the finest herds will be found on the western prairies."

8. Hamner, *Short Grass*, 168–69; Haley, "East," 53; Laura V. Hamner, "Jess Jenkins," Jan-

uary 3, 1941, Vandale Collection, 2H475, CAH/UT. Jesse Jenkins also said that "once [when Russell was driving a bull team for Lee & Reynolds], a Mexican stood on the tongue of the wagon and Monchy told him to get off. The Mexican refused, Monchy lifted his gun and shot him off. They halted the train, buried the Mexican by the side of the road, and went on." For six years following Reynolds's purchase of the LE, Russell was its ranch foreman and Charles Reynolds, the owner's brother, its local manager. It was an uncomfortable arrangement, and in 1889 Russell resigned. In 1893 he was appointed caretaker of Reynolds's Gold Cup mine and adjacent properties in Gunnison County, Colorado. Scamehorn, *Reynolds*, 69, 141.

9. Sullivan, *LS Brand*, 36–37.

10. Ibid., 40–41.

11. W. G. Kerr, *Scottish Capital on the American Credit Frontier*, 17; *Dodge City Times*, March 18, 1880.

12. Clare Sewell Read and Albert Pell, "Reports for Commissioners and Inspectors," *Parliamentary Papers*, House of Commons, Agricultural Interests Commission, vol. 18 (1880), no. 856, cited in E. R. Archambeau, "British Contribution to the Opening Up of the West," *English Westerners Tally Sheet* 14, no. 2 (Jan.–Feb. 1968): 2–6, and no. 3 (Mar.–Apr. 1968): 1–4.

13. *Dodge City Times*, July 28, 1881; *Handbook of Texas Online*, "Quarter Circle T Ranch." The bonanza was big news: on July 20, 1882, the *Dodge City Times* reported that D. H. Barry had "sold his ranch in the Panhandle, Texas, consisting of a range of forty miles and between 10,000 and 11,000 head of cattle and 90 horses to the London Cattle Ranch & Land Co. for $225,000," and the following month the paper noted that H. H. "Hank" Creswell had "sold his 30,000 cattle to E. F. Wilson and W. R. Green for $850,000. Included in the purchase are 100,000 acres of land, 30,000 of which Mr. Creswell has title to and 70,000 [which] a patent has been applied for." *Dodge City Times*, August 28, 1882.

14. *Dodge City Times*, July 6, 1882; John

Arnot, "The Hall Brothers and the Prairie Cattle Co.," Vandale Collection, 2H472, CAH/UT. The lightning bolt "set Johnson's undershirt on fire and his gold shirt stud, which was set with a diamond, was melted and the diamond was never found. His hat was torn to pieces and mine had all the plush burned off of the top. I was not seriously hurt, but G. B. Withers [a brother] lost one eye in the same stroke that killed Johnson." Mark Withers in J. Marvin Hunter, *The Trail Drivers of Texas*, 103.

15. *The Times* (London), January 26, 1883.

16. Lester Fields Sheffy, *The Francklyn Land & Cattle Company: A Panhandle Enterprise, 1882–1957*, passim; Hamner, *Short Grass*, 228ff.

17. *Investors Guardian* (London), March 24, 1883.

18. Porter, *Memory Cups*, 529; *Times*, April 7, 1883.

19. *Investors Guardian*, October 3, 1885. A marquess is a nobleman ranked above an earl but below a duke; marquis is a similar title used in European countries also, ranking above a count but below a duke.

20. *Times*, August 28, 1883.

21. "Wyoming Tales and Trails," at www.wyomingtalesandtrails.com/swan.html.

22. Haley, "Ingerton"; Arnot, "Tascosa Trail." By "an awful good trail driver" we may presume Ingerton meant an unusually honest one.

23. Nelson, "Stockmen's Association."

24. Haley, "East."

25. Glenn Shirley, *Temple Houston: Lawyer with a Gun*, 96–97.

26. Arnot, "Tascosa Trail"; Haley, *Charles Goodnight*, 376.

27. John L. McCarty and Laura V. Hamner, "Jess Jenkins, King of Hogtown," JLMC/APL.

28. On March 23, 1882, citing the *Mobeetie Panhandle*, the *Dodge City Times* reported that J. A. Hullum had "recently" sold Alfred Rowe "his outfit, consisting of 1500 cattle, 230 head of stock horses and 58 saddle horses for the neat little sum of $40,000. Mr. Rowe also purchased within the past few days the cattle, horses and ranch outfit of Charles Wills of the Wills & Dor-

rance range on Salt Fork, paying therefore $56,000."

29. Charles Goodnight to J. Evetts Haley, April 11 and September 2, 1927, HHC; Nelson, "Stockmen's Association."

CHAPTER 14
CAPE WILLINGHAM:
"TOUGH, FAIR, AND RESPECTED."

1. Genealogical research by Jane R. Newton, Forsyth, Georgia; John Arnot, "Early Panhandle Sheriffs," Vandale Collection, 2H472, CAH/UT (for the record, Lee's army was never in Georgia, only Longstreet's corps); Federal Census, Lincoln County, Ga. 1850; Forsyth County, Ga., Deed Record Book (o) 1–340 (February 10, 1858), Monroe County, Ga., Farmer Isaac Willingham, forty, owned real estate valued at three thousand dollars and personal estate worth fifteen thousand dollars, a substantial sum in those days; in the 1860 census the entry for his thirty-four-year-old wife, Martha "Mary" (Garrett) Willingham, carries the annotation "Blind from sickness." Their children at this time, all Georgia-born, were Nancy Jane, sixteen; William Newton, fourteen; Georgia Crawford, male, twelve; M. E., male, ten; C. B. T., male, eight; and Mary L., six. Federal Census, Mitchell County, Ga., 1860.

2. *Handbook of Texas Online*, "Willingham, Caleb Berg"; J. Evetts Haley, Interview with Charles Goodnight, August 21, 1929, HHC. Having served in Company F, 6th Regiment (Camilla Guards), from May to September 1861, Isaac Willingham enlisted on April 8, 1862, at Camilla "for three years or the War" in Capt. W. J. Lawton's Company C, 2nd Regiment of Georgia Cavalry. He served to the end of the war and was one of the prisoners, estimated to number between seventy-two hundred and eight thousand, who were surrendered on May 10, 1865, by Maj. Gen. Samuel Jones, CSA, commanding the District of Florida, to Brig. Gen. Edward M. McCook, USA, and paroled at Albany, Georgia. It seems unlikely that Cape could have joined the 2nd Georgia

Cavalry (although William, one of his older
brothers, did); he was only thirteen when the
war ended. A Caleb Willingham enlisted as a
corporal in Capt. J. S. Freeman's company in
July 1863 in Meriwether County, but in view of
his father's service record this can hardly have
been Cape. There is no record at Camilla of his
ever having been a peace officer. Muster Roll of
Company F, 6th Regiment, Georgia Volunteer
Infantry; Isaac Willingham, Service Record,
NARA; Susan D. Taylor, Probate Judge,
Camilla, Georgia, to author, September 14,
2004.

3. John L. McCarty, "Jenkins." Upon what
facts Jenkins based this accusation it is impossible to guess, but he was not alone; another old
Tascosan also hinted at a shady past. "Cape had
wore out one or two names when he got [to Tascosa, and he] had a water bucket full of lead in
him." J. Evetts Haley, Interview with D. J.
"Dick" Miller, June 23, 1937, Lovington, N.M.,
HHC. No corroboration of this allegation has
been found.

4. Willingham, "First Ranches." In the 1880
census Willingham's age is shown as twenty-six;
his wife, Mary, twenty-three, was born in Texas
about 1857. Her father was Texan and her
mother was from Iowa. Their children were
Drew, seven, born in Texas; Homer, three; and
Ada, one, both born in Colorado. Federal Census, Oldham County, Tex., 1880.

5. Charles A. Siringo, *Riata and Spurs,*
57–59; *Dodge City Times,* September 21, 1878;
DeArment, *Bat Masterson,* 166–70.

6. Hervey E. Chesley, *Adventuring with the
Old Timers: Trails Traveled—Tales Told,* ed. Byron
Price, 51.

7. Willingham, "First Ranches"; McCarty
and Armstrong, "Dobbs." Could this "good old
clever" Californian have been Tascosa's first
mail carrier, "Dad" Barnes?

8. G. W. Arrington, "Organization of Pan-
handle Counties," unpublished manuscript,
Lestor B. Wood Collection, HHC; Hamner,
Short Grass, 165; Arnot, "Panhandle Sheriffs";
Haley, *Charles Goodnight,* 360; Haley,
"Ingerton."

9. Willingham, "First Ranches"; Hamner,
Short Grass, 133–34.

10. Hamner, *Short Grass,* 135.

11. Arnot, "Panhandle Sheriffs."

12. *Handbook of Texas Online,* "Turkey Track
Ranch."

13. *Handbook of Texas Online,* "Grass-Lease
Fight"; Haley, *Charles Goodnight,* 381–401.

14. Arnot, "Leverton Brothers."

15. Arnot, "Panhandle Sheriffs"; Hamner,
Short Grass, 138.

16. Hamner, *Short Grass,* 131.

17. Ibid., 138; Goodnight, Undated material,
No. 11.

18. Willingham, "First Ranches."

19. Death Certificate, January 21, 1925,
State of Arizona, Office of Vital Records,
Phoenix. Willingham's wife gives her name not
as Mary but Margareth (or Margarette) Mays;
her sister was the Jennie Mays who married C.
B. Vivian. The annals of Georgia are replete
with accounts of the lives of many substantial
Willingham families, including those of a Caleb
Willingham (see note 2, this chapter) who was
killed at Gettysburg. William J. Northen, ed.,
Men of Mark in Georgia, vols. 5 and 6.

CHAPTER 15
1883: THE GREAT COWBOY STRIKE

1. J. Evetts Haley, Interview with Lucius
Dills, Roswell, N.M., June 12, 1935, HHC;
Shirley, *Temple Houston,* 76–77. Perhaps it was
on this occasion that Houston had to swim the
Canadian to get to court "and came near
drowning. When he was under the third time
the cowboys tossed him a rope which he
grabbed. They were some thirty minutes getting the water out of him and reviving him.
When he came out of it he said, 'The dam
Mississippi wouldn't make a ramrod for
the Canadian!'" Vandale, "Panhandle
Pioneers."

2. McCarty and Armstrong, "Dobbs."

3. Haley, Interview with Lucius Dills, June
12, 1935.

4. J. Evetts Haley, Interview with Louis P.

Bousman, Waurika, Okla., October 23, 1934, HHC (hereafter cited as Haley, "Bousman").

5. Haley, Interview with Lucius Dills, June 12, 1935. "Featherlegs" was a fairly common name for someone who wore long, lacy leggings that fluttered in the wind and made her look, as Jim East put it, "like one of these old Shanghai chickens." Here, however, Carrie "Feather-legs" Gauntz may have been maligned; when she was indicted for complicity in the murder of Mc-Cullough, Houston abandoned the case against her for lack of evidence. Oldham County District Court Minutes (1) Case #15 (Sept. 5 and 13, 1881), CDCV.

6. *State of Texas* vs. *Frank Largus alias Mexican Frank*, Oldham County District Court Records, Case #14 (Sept. 12, 1882), CDCV; Haley, Interview with Lucius Dills, June 12, 1935. On one trip to Tascosa, the attorneys' carriage turned over as they were crossing the Canadian. Browning and Houston, who were strong swimmers, were helping Willis across the swirling torrent, while Woodman carried the Panhandle's only copy of the 1879 Texas statutes. When the current tore it from his grasp, Woodman cried out, "Save the statutes of Texas!" Willis replied, "Let the law go, Woodman, and save the district court!" In the end, both survived.

7. Oldham County, Records of the Commissioners Court (1) 25 (October 27, 1882). Convicted on September 14, 1882, Frank Largus was twenty years old, with a height of five feet six and one-half inches and a weight of 145 pounds. On arrival at Rusk Penitentiary on October 26, he had seven dollars in his pocket. His complexion was described as "Mexican" (hardly surprising, since Mexico was his birthplace), and he had a scar on his upper lip and a tattoo on his left arm. On December 10, 1883, he escaped from jail, but he was recaptured four days later. On February 3, 1896, with eight years of his twenty-two-year sentence still to serve, he was pardoned by Governor C. A. Culberson and restored to full citizenship. Convict Record Ledger, Prisoner 1051, Frank Largus, TSA.

8. *State of Texas* vs. *Charles Donnelly*, no. 18, Charge of Court, April 6, 1883, Oldham County District Court Records, CDCV; Lucius Dills to John L. McCarty, December 10, 1942, Vandale Collection, 2H484, CAH/UT. Temple Houston served as district attorney only until November 4, 1884, when he was elected to succeed Avery L. Matlock as senator from the 56th District of Texas; he had little further contact with Tascosa. Deciding not to seek a third term in the legislature in 1888, he became attorney for the Atchison, Topeka & Santa Fe Railroad and moved to Canadian. In 1893 he removed to Woodward, Oklahoma, where he died on August 5, 1905, from a brain hemorrhage. Shirley, *Temple Houston,* passim.

9. Haley, "East." During his ten-year administration, Indiana-born Frank Willis oversaw the organization of Hall and Childress Counties and became involved in the bitter controversy over the use by cattlemen of state-owned land without payment, which became known as the "grass-lease fight." Impeached by the attorney general of Texas, he won his acquittal with a speech in his own defense and was subsequently hailed as a hero by Wheeler County citizens. He later practiced law in Canadian and became general attorney for the Panhandle and Santa Fe Railroad. He died August 4, 1894.

10. Ibid.; Vandale, "Panhandle Pioneers." "Wild Bill" was probably Texas-born Willie Riggs, who appears, age twenty-two, divorced with a one-year-old son, whose name is given as I. B. J. McGahy, in the 1880 census for Mobeetie. Whether the marriage to Resoner was for real is another matter. Federal Census, Wheeler County, Tex., 1880.

11. Gober, *Cowboy Justice*, 54; Vandale, "Panhandle Pioneers"; Vandale, Interview with Billy Jarrett; Oldham County District Court Minutes (1) Cases #15–31 (Sept. 5, 1882), and Report of the Grand Jury (April 7, 1883), CDCV; Anne M. Butler, *Daughters of Joy, Sisters of Misery: Prostitutes in the American West, 1865–90*, passim; C. May Cohea, Interview with Mary A. Snider, n.d., WPA.

12. Arnot, "Tascosa Trail."

13. *Dodge City Times,* March 15, 1883.

14. Arnot, "Tascosa Trail." At the time Norwood was indicted, the spring roundup was well under way, and it was soon close enough to town for the cowboys to ride in. "Among [them] were a number of 'Norwood's' friends. Late one night some of these fellows began a terrific shooting in 'Hogtown,' a row the sheriff and his deputy quickly set out to investigate. Finding no dead, certain fruit of so much shooting, and getting no information from witnesses, the sheriff decided he had been tricked and hurried back to the jail. Here he found a number of picks and crowbars, a side of the jail torn out, and the cell empty. 'Norwood' was never seen again in the Tascosa country, and his case was soon dismissed from the docket." On June 10, 1883, Sheriff Jim East issued a one-hundred-dollar "reward card" for Ed Norwood, who had escaped from the Tascosa jail on June 6. He was described as being "about 24 years old, fair complexion, light brown hair, very little beard, grayish-blue eyes, about 5'11" and weighs 160 lbs." He was never apprehended. Arnot, "Tascosa Trail"; reward card in James H. East Collection, HHC.

15. John Arnot, "The First and Only Cowboy Strike," Vandale Collection, 2H472, CAH/UT. Contrary to popular belief, the Panhandle strike was not the only one, nor even the first. There had been a strike in Kansas on the Comanche Pool ranch owned by Hunter & Evans just three months earlier, and there was another in Colorado in 1886. Sullivan, *LS Brand,* 68–69; Clifford P. Westermeier, *Trailing the Cowboy,* 130.

16. Jot Gunter to A. L. Matlock, March 15, 1883, Gunter and Munson Collection, Texas Tech University Library, Lubbock. Gunter took extreme measures to protect himself: "A blacksmith shop about a hundred yards south of the T-Anchor headquarters was mined in anticipation of attack by the striking cowboys. A bomb of scrap iron was placed in the shop, beneath the dirt floor with a keg of gunpowder under it and a fuse leading to the headquarters building." Fortunately for all concerned, the expected attack never took place. Mrs. C. May Cohea,

"Related by S. P. Merry," n.d., Amarillo, Texas, District #16, *Panhandle Pioneers,* WPA.

17. Some of the signatures are between difficult to read and illegible; the list of names is not definitive.

18. McCarty, *Maverick Town,* 110–11.

19. McCarty and Armstrong, "Dobbs."

20. Schofield, *Indians, Cattle,* 64.

21. *Fort Collins (CO) Courier,* April 12, 1883.

22. *Fort Worth Texas Live Stock Journal,* April 21, 1883.

23. *Trinidad (CO) Weekly Advertiser,* April 25, 1883.

24. *Dodge City Times,* May 10, 1883.

25. McCarty and Armstrong, "Dobbs."

26. Arnot, "Tascosa Trail," 23; Lucius Dills, "Life and Times of the Author," Vandale Collection, 2H464, CAH/UT. Lucius Nelson Dills, first of the nine children of John Harmon and Julia Ellen (Desha) Dills, was born at Cynthiana, Kentucky, on July 7, 1858. Three brothers and a sister died in childhood. Two years after he matriculated at Prof. Newton F. Smith's Select School in 1873, the family moved to Sherman, where in 1877 Lucius joined the law office of Silas Hare and Henry O. Head. He was admitted to the bar by Judge Joseph Bledsoe at McKinney, Collin County, on his twenty-first birthday, leaving Sherman on March 2, 1882, for the Panhandle, settling first in Mobeetie and then Tascosa. When he stood for district attorney in the fall of 1884, he was—he claimed—"eliminated" by Charles Goodnight, "the recipient and beneficiary of more obsequiously lying propaganda and laudation than any individual ever to have lived in the watershed of Red River." In May 1885 he moved to Lincoln County, where he ran a store at Nogal and worked as a cowboy. In March 1888 he entered into a law partnership with Moses Wiley but found the road too rocky and instead went to work for Pat Garrett in Roswell. In 1890 he opened a law office there "and made a meager living." In 1891 he and Joseph D. Lea launched the *Roswell Record,* still published to this day. Later that year he returned to Sherman to practice law and married Joe Lea's sister Gertrude on April 24, 1892. Returning to Roswell, he sold

his interest in the newspaper in 1898, abandoned the law, and became a surveyor. In the spring of 1904 he was appointed city engineer, a post he held for four years before returning to private practice. In that position he created the ground plans and superintended the erection of the Masonic Temple and, in the fall of 1911, the Chaves County Courthouse. After a brief stint as editor of the (short-lived) *Roswell Morning News,* he was appointed surveyor general of New Mexico, and he held that office for eight years. After some years of ill health, he was appointed to a post in the state highways department. He died at Roswell on December 1, 1944. Dills, "Life and Times"; Haley, Interview with Lucius Dills, June 12, 1935.

27. McCarty and Hamner, "King of Hogtown."

CHAPTER 16
TOM HARRIS:
"I'M TIRED OF THIS, PUT ME AWAY."

1. Federal Census, Hartley County, Tex., 1880; James R. Gober, "A Contention between Capitol and Labor," unpublished ms., 1932, Harold Bugbee Papers.

2. J. Evetts Haley, Interview with J. Dave Lard, June 26, 1937, Hot Springs, N.M., HHC.

3. G. B. Harris, pension application, August 30, 1913, TSA; Federal Census, Lavaca County, Tex., 1870; *Shiner (TX) Gazette,* July 7, 1955, and August 14, 1975.

4. Federal Census, Lavaca County, Tex., 1860; Paul C. Boethel, *On the Headwaters of the Lavaca and the Navidad,* 93.

5. Harris, pension application.

6. Federal Census, Lavaca County, Tex., 1870; *Hallettsville Tribune,* August 5, 1952.

7. Federal Census, Lavaca County, Tex., 1880; Lavaca County, Texas, District Court Records, Civil Case No. 2343, *Thos. B. Harris et al.* vs. *G. Buckner Harris et al.* In his 1913 pension application, Buck Harris, who "always kept a fiddle on his mantle and played it from time to time," declared himself "indigent." He died at his daughter Sally's home on February 22, 1918.

Harris, pension application; *Shiner Gazette,*
February 28, 1918, and February 8, 1979.

8. *Tascosa Pioneer,* December 15, 1886; Federal Census, Fayette County, Tex., 1880; Haley, "Ingerton"; Fayette County Marriage Records (4), 198.

9. Report of Commissioners H. H. Russell, M. M. Dillard, and S. J. Dickey, February 11, 1887, Lavaca County, Texas, District Court Records, Civil Case 2343. Just two years later, Kate, Susie, and Sally Harris opened the Harris Sisters' Dress and Millinery Shop in Shiner, the first business ever established there by ladies. Dorothy Blohm Goerte, *After Half Moon: A History of Shiner, Texas, 1887–1975,* 14.

10. John Arnot, "New Mexico Ranches," Vandale Collection, 2H472, CAH/UT; Lester Fields Sheffy, "Sam Isaacs," *Panhandle-Plains Historical Review* 19 (1946); *Tascosa Pioneer,* August 27, 1887. It sounds from its location very much as if Harris's ranch was the one where Bill Gatlin was captured by Pat Garrett and Jim East in 1884.

11. Gober, "Contention"; Haley, "Mitchell."

12. Haley, Interview with Dave Lard; Haley, "Ingerton"; Shirley, *Temple Houston,* 115. The last source infers that Harris's death occurred before the 1886 gunfight; this is clearly incorrect.

13. Sharon Wright, Director, River Valley Pioneer Museum, Canadian, Texas, to author, September 16, 2004. By the time of Harris's death, several members of his family in Lavaca County, including his father, had added an extra *s* to their names. It is probably safe to assume that Tom's wife, Clara, followed the family example.

14. Arnot, "Panhandle Sheriffs." Thomas T. McGee was born on September 13, 1849, in what is now West Virginia. After working as a cowboy for a time in Colorado, in 1884 he accompanied Creswell's CC Bar herd to its new location in Ochiltree County, and he worked later on the Moody-Andrews PO ranch. In December 1883 he registered his own Quarter Circle C brand at Mobeetie. About 1886 he bought William Young's interest in the PO ranch and became its foreman. When the county was organized in 1887, McGee was elected sheriff of

Hemphill County. On June 5, 1889, he married eighteen-year-old Mary Blandy Taylor at the home of her uncle, George T. Lynn, in Kansas City. With his deputy sheriff, Vastine Stickley, as a partner, McGee operated a wagon yard and livery stable in Canadian until 1893; it was there Tom Harris committed suicide.

Spare a thought for Mary McGee, a sad lady whose first unnamed baby died the day it was born, April 6, 1890; whose son, Talbott, died three days after his birth on September 29, 1892; and who lost her husband just three years later. She even had difficulty in settling his estate, since he did most of his banking in Kansas City. She served as a nurse's aide in England during World War I and remained there until her death on July 24, 1943. Her ashes were returned to Canadian for burial beside her husband.

Vastine Stickley, McGee's partner, was born in Shenandoah County, Virginia, on February 14, 1849. After serving an apprenticeship as carriage maker, in 1878 he came to Texas, where he worked as a wagon boss for the T-Anchor. In 1887 he helped organize Canadian and Hemphill Counties. On August 9, 1892, he married Sue E. Burnette (born in Hamburg, Iowa, on February 7, 1873) at Mobeetie. He died at Canadian on January 3, 1929. *Handbook of Texas Online*, "McGee, Thomas T."; Wheeler County website: "Marriages: 1892," and Canadian cemetery records, dated 1967; Stanley, *Rodeo Town*, 374.

15. Stanley, *Rodeo Town*, 193; *Canadian Record*, January 21, 1897.

16. *Handbook of Texas Online*, "Isaacs, George W."

17. Glenn Shirley, *Gunfight at Ingalls: Death of an Outlaw Town*, 109–11.

18. Stanley, *Rodeo Town*, 193.

19. *Canadian Record*, January 21, 1897.

20. Ibid., January 28, 1897; Stanley, *Rodeo Town*, 196–99. Harbolt was

> a small, wiry built man, straight as an arrow, coal black hair, dark complexion and dark, keen eyes. He . . . was born in Sherman,

Texas, but when very young his parents removed to Cook [*sic*] county, where they resided on a farm and where young Harbolt grew to manhood. He is now thirty-two years old. He was married at Ardmore, I.T. several years ago and his wife and two small children are at present living on a farm in D county, O.T. His father is dead and his mother lives in California. He accepts his conviction philosophically, but asserts his entire innocence of the crime for which he is to remain behind prison bars the balance of his life.

The fact that Harbolt's name does not appear in any Texas prison record would seem to confirm that he never served time for his crimes. *Canadian Record*, February 19, 1897; Donaly Brice, Texas State Archives, to author, December 3, 2004.

21. Arnot, "Panhandle Sheriffs." After eight months in the Hardeman County jail, George Isaacs entered Rusk Penitentiary as prisoner 15531 on August 11, 1897. Alabama-born, he was thirty-nine years old, married, five feet, seven inches tall, with blue eyes, gray hair, and a dark complexion. The Conduct Register confirms he escaped on September 30, 1899, by means of a forged pardon signed four days earlier by Governor Joseph Draper Sayers. Convict Record Ledger, TSA.

22. *Handbook of Texas Online*, "Isaacs Brothers."

CHAPTER 17
1884: RUSTLERS VS. RANGERS

1. Oldham County, Records of Commissioners Court (1) 44 (May 12, 1884). The LX sale, which comprised 187,141 acres of land and "between 36,000 and 45,000 head of cattle by roundup and actual count," at $32 per head, was effected by two deeds dated August 1, 1884—one for £91,427 ($457,135) and the other for £11,608 ($58,040). A by-product of the transaction was that nineteen-year-old John Arnot, related to one of the new owners, got a

job on the LX and arrived in Tascosa from Scotland a few months later. Sheets, "LX Ranch," 45ff.; Hamner, *Short Grass,* 105; Arnot, "Tascosa Trail."

2. McCarty, *Maverick Town,* 123–24; Gober, *Cowboy Justice,* 49–50.

3. McCarty, *Maverick Town,* 124; McCarty and Armstrong, "Dobbs."

4. Arnot, "My Recollections"; Haley, "East"; McCarty and Armstrong, "Dobbs."

5. J. Evetts Haley, Interview with J. E. McAllister, Channing, Tex., November 7, 1927, HHC.

6. Haley, "East."

7. McCarty and Armstrong, "Dobbs."

8. McCarty, *Maverick Town,* 135.

9. McCarty and Armstrong, "Dobbs."

10. Haley, "East."

11. Arnot, "My Recollections."

12. Haley, "East"; *State of Texas* vs. *J. R. Jenkins,* No. 109; *J. E. Thompson,* No. 110; *Lee Blackmore,* No. 120; and *A. N. Fitzgerald,* Nos. 124 and 127, February 3, 1884 (not all are dated), Oldham County District Court Records, CDCV. Jenkins's cases—he was implicated in the deaths of both of the Martinez boys—were continued; he was cleared of both charges at the October term of court, during which nine felony cases were tried and all the defendants found not guilty. The cases against J. L. Stroope, also charged on two counts, were abandoned for lack of evidence. Cases #108, 109, 114, and 119, Oldham County District Court Minutes (1) 113, 138 (February 2 and October 15, 1885), CDCV.

13. Endee was a scratch-ankle settlement named for ranchers John and George Day, who moved there about 1882 and whose brand was ND. It was in the area known as "Little Texas," about three miles west of the Texas line and thirty miles east of Liberty and Fort Bascom in San Miguel (now Quay) County. Robert Julyan, *The Place Names of New Mexico,* 124.

14. Sullivan, *LS Brand,* 97.

15. McCarty and Armstrong, "Dobbs."

16. Sullivan, *LS Brand,* 101–3. Brophy recovered and was appointed officer of the 1888 election for Tascosa's Precinct No. 2; in 1892 he served as a district court bailiff. He later became a lawman in Union County, New Mexico, surviving an 1895 gunfight with outlaws during which two horses were shot out from under his fellow possemen. In 1905 and 1906 he served first as constable then as town marshal of Clayton (where he prevented a lynching). He was also a member of the New Mexico Mounted Police, a fledgling force that came into existence in 1905 and never consisted of more than eight officers. Born October 24, 1864, in Oconto, Wisconsin, John James Brophy died of food poisoning on June 4, 1916, on a ranch in Cimarron County, Oklahoma. During the last months of his life John (whose firstborn had died in infancy) was in a deep depression over the tragic death of his oldest and favorite son during a hunting accident with his younger son. Oldham County, Records of Commissioners Court (1) 173–77 (May 25, 1888); District Court Minutes (1) 434 (October 1892), CDCV; Reynolds, *Trouble in New Mexico,* 257–58; biographical details courtesy Chuck Hornung.

17. "Tascosa Directory," typed copy dated July 26, 1939, from an original owned by Mrs. J. E. May, Vega, Texas, JLMC/APL, also in Lestor B. Wood Collection, HHC. In 1883, while retaining his Hogtown "hotel," John Cone formed a partnership with Dolores Duran after the latter sold his ranch on Romero Canyon to W. M. D. Lee of the LS, and they opened a general store directly opposite Russell's Exchange Hotel. Arnot, "My Recollections."

18. Isaac P. Ryland, "Untold Tales," *Panhandle-Plains Historical Review* 9 (1936): 61–66. Croft had previously been a hospital steward at Fort Elliott; he came to the United States from England in 1876 when he was twenty-one. In 1882 he was granted American citizenship at Tascosa. Oldham County District Court Minutes (1) 23 (May 4, 1882), CDCV.

19. Haley, "Mitchell." On another occasion a Mexican was haled before Scotty Wilson for stealing a burro. "Well, you Goddamned sonofabitch, I'm going to fine you twenty five dollars, and weel ye know ye deserve it!" roared His

Honor. "Stealing ass in Tascosa when so much of it may be had here for nothing!" Arnot, "My Recollections."

20. E. C. Godwin-Austen to J. Evetts Haley, August 4, 1925, HHC.

21. Arnot, "Smooth Rustlers." Following the death of Gus Johnson, Coburn appointed Thomas L. Coffee as range manager. When Coburn discovered Coffee was running his own cattle on Hansford land and tried to fire him, some of the other hands—it's fairly easy to guess which—would not let him do it. This defiance, it is suggested, led Coburn to hire Cape Willingham as not just his range manager but also his bodyguard. *Handbook of Texas Online*, "Coburn, James M."

22. Arnot, "Smooth Rustlers"; Hamner, *Short Grass*, 79; Haley, Interview with Lucius Dills, June 12, 1935; Haley, Interview with D. J. "Dick" Miller. Apart from the fact that his real name was William T. Hughes, "Tenderfoot Bob" Roberson (Robertson, Robinson) remains something of a mystery. He changed his name after killing a man at Huntsville. He told Lucius Dills it was an unintentional murder, although since it certainly doesn't sound like one, perhaps he meant "justifiable":

> "The Baptists were having a great big meeting," Dills said, "and they were right by the side of a big waterhole to baptize them. . . . There was one big blab-mouthed fool in the bunch and he said, by God, he didn't believe there was ever a virtuous woman born, and Bob hit him on the chin and knocked him in the water and when he came up he kicked him in the top of the head and kicked him back under the water and he never come up any more. Of course, he skipped. That was right in Walker County, right in sight of the penitentiary."

When Dills contacted him, the district attorney there set aside the indictment, saying, "I'll take pleasure in having that damned thing dismissed. I was present when that thing occurred, and if he hadn't have done it, some of the bal-

ance of us would." After the LIT sold out, Roberson was "put in as manager of the Prairie Cattle Company." Later, according to Dills, he "sold out his brand of cattle . . . and the last I heard of him he was up somewhere either right in the end of Oklahoma or in the extreme northeast corner of the state." It has not proven possible to establish the date of Roberson's death.

23. Metz, *Pat Garrett*, 142.

24. J. Evetts Haley, Interview with John Meadows, Alamogordo, N.M., June 13, 1936, HHC.

25. McCarty and Armstrong, "Dobbs"; Haley, "East."

26. Pat F. Garrett to W. H. King, May 19, 1884, Ireland Papers, June–December 1884, TSA. Garrett spells the name "Rasor," but it appears in other contexts as Reasoner, Reasor, and Reason; the man's own signature gives it as Resoner. The name R. A. Griffin is also on the roster; whether this was Roy Griffin, an LX hand who was one of the signatories of the strike manifesto, is not clear; he seems never to have served as a Ranger.

27. McCarty and Armstrong, "Dobbs"; Pat F. Garrett to Gov. John Ireland, April 28, 1884, Ireland Papers, June–December 1884, TSA.

28. McCarty and Armstrong, "Dobbs"; Haley, Interview with John Meadows.

29. Sullivan, *LS Brand*, 88; McCarty, *Maverick Town*, 131–32.

30. Oldham County, Records of the Commissioners Court (1) 55 (August 22, 1884) and (1) 58–59 (October 10, 1884).

31. McCarty, *Maverick Town*, 133. Nearly every account of Tascosa has this story in one form or another.

32. Oldham County District Court Minutes (1) 87ff. (August 1884), CDCV; McCarty and Armstrong, "Dobbs." According to Dobbs, Harris had been "the first man Mason arrested after Governor Hogg [sic] passed a law against carrying guns."

33. McCarty and Armstrong, "Dobbs"; Haley, "East." On a trip to Dodge City late in 1884, Jim East met a young woman named Net-

tie Bouldin, and after what must have been a whirlwind romance they were married on December 6 of that year. Nettie was "big and buxom, and [East] took her buggy riding and got married before they got back. . . . It was a two or three hours courtship. But she made him a good wife." The record reads: "James H. East of Tuscosa [sic], Texas aged 29 and Miss Nettie S. Bouldin of Clay Center, Kansas aged 20 applied 6 Dec 1884. Married 6 Dec 1884 at Dodge City, Kan. by R. G. Cook, JP." Cook was the magistrate who acquitted Jim Kenedy of the murder of Dora Hand. Ford County Marriages Book A (February 19, 1874–December 21, 1886), 157, Ford County District Court Clerk's Office, Dodge City; Haley, "Ingerton."

34. Haley, "East." "Tom Harris offered $5 for one of Bill Gatlin's pictures. Dobbs got it out of Sally Emory's album and they posted it all over the country." Of course, Dobbs meant Jim East, not Harris. McCarty and Armstrong, "Dobbs."

Jesse Jenkins said Pierce was "the best officer he ever saw, left-handed, a boxer who frequently knocked rough ones down and walked off and left them. He was tall, slim and a nice dresser." Vandale, "Panhandle Pioneers."

35. *Globe Live-Stock Journal* (Dodge City), March 31, 1885; Metz, *Pat Garrett*, 145.

36. Haley, Interview with John Meadows.

37. Haley, "East."

38. Vandale, Interview with Billy Jarrett.

CHAPTER 18
BILL GATLIN: BAD CLEAR THROUGH

1. *Cheyenne (WY) Sun*, July 22, 1887; Hervey E. Chesley Jr., "Bogan," and "The Assassination of Mr. Snell," Hamilton County Interviews, People and Places: Gazetteer of Hamilton County, Texas, at http://freepages.genealogy. rootsweb.com/~gazetteer2000 (hereafter cited as HCI).

2. *Cheyenne Daily Leader*, July 22, 1887.

3. Petition for the pardon of David Kemp, n.d. [1887], TSA.

4. H. E. Chesley Jr., "When Dave Kemp Killed Smith," HCI. Kemp and Bogan were

both charged with murder on May 10, 1881, but no further details have survived. *State of Texas vs. Daniel Bogan*, Case No. 674, and *State of Texas vs. David Kemp*, Case No. 662, Hamilton County District Court Records, County Clerk's Office, Hamilton, Texas.

No records for this period exist in Coryell County. Research by Frank Sprague, Hamilton County Historical Commission, Hamilton, Texas.

5. H. E. Chesley Jr., letter to Dee Harkey, May 25, 1945, HCI. "Uncle Sid Ross said he attended the trial at Gatesville, and that David Kemp told him, he didn't know there was such a thing as an appeal. That when they tried a man down on the [Leon] river, they just hung him, and there was no appeal. Mr. Jack Moon, who ran the hotel at Gatesville, told me of Kemp's jumping out of the upper story window of the court house. . . . broke his ankles, and was captured by citizens who through [sic] down on him with rifles." H. E. Chesley Jr., "Old Man Snow," HCI.

6. "David Kemp, age 21 . . . convicted April 2, 1883, murder, sentenced to 25 years from Erath County . . . received into Huntsville, April 6, 1883," Convict Record Ledger, Huntsville, Texas, Book 1998–038/151, p. 171, TSA.

7. Armstrong, "Lee."

8. *Cheyenne Daily Sun*, July 22, 1887; William McLeod Raine, *Guns of the Frontier*, 124–28. Daniel B. Bogan, born in Alabama, was twenty in 1880. He is shown as the son of (twice?) widowed D. B. Pierce, forty-eight, also an Alabaman, as are sisters Emma Oldham, sixteen; and Minnie Pierce, thirteen. Federal Census, Hamilton County, Tex., 1880.

9. "The first night out a thunder storm came up and the cattle stampeded and we ran them all night. I held between 400 and 500 and Billie Gatling [Billy Gatlin] held about 600 until after daylight, when several of the boys helped us bring them back to camp." T. J. Burkett Sr., Waelder, Texas, "On the Fort Worth and Dodge City Trail," in Hunter, *Trail Drivers*, 927. The reference to Gatlin's possible culinary career is in Haley, "Ingerton." One wonders whether In-

gerton misremembered Tom Harris as Gatlin and his backer not as Sheets but Jesse Jenkins.

10. John Arnot, "Bill Gatlin," Vandale Collection, 2H471, CAH/UT; Murray L. Carroll, "As an Outlaw and Escape Artist Dan Bogan Was the Real McCoy," *Journal of the Western Outlaw-Lawman Association* 2, no. 1 (spring–summer 1992): 10–15, 28. In all likelihood Hall/Nichols was the cowboy who signed himself G. F. Nickell at the time of the cowboy strike.

11. Raine, *Guns of the Frontier,* 124–28; T. A. Larson, *History of Wyoming,* passim; "Lusk Photos," at http://www.wyomingtalesandtrails.com /lusk.html. In Raine's version, the name of the victim is given as Charles Miley, alias Red Bell, who "admitted while drunk he was one of the rustlers. Trumbull [Trumble] arrested him and tied his wrists, dragging him around until he was bleeding. Owens stepped in with a shotgun and told Trumbull to go home and sleep it off. He himself took Red Bell to jail. Next day as Trumbull was releasing Miley, he asked him if he had any hard feelings. Miley held out his wrists and said, 'Do you suppose I'm a friend of a man who'd do that?'"

Charlie Trumble was sentenced to hang. An appeal was lodged arguing that the conviction was fatally flawed because even though the prosecution had proved there was a dead body on the floor of Whittaker's saloon, and that Trumble had shot that man, they had not proved the body was that of Charles Miley, also referred to during the trial as the Prisoner, Gilliand, Red Bill, Gunny Sack Bill, and Pete Gilmore. The Territorial Supreme Court rejected this argument; no matter what name the deceased had been using, Trumble had undeniably killed him. They did, however, agree the judge's instruction as to malice had been defective. At his new trial, Trumble pleaded guilty to manslaughter and was sentenced to six years' imprisonment with three years' credit for time served. *Cheyenne Daily Leader,* June 19, 1887.

12. *Lusk Herald,* January 21, 1887.

13. Laramie County Commissioners Journal (C) 352 (January 4, 1887), Wyoming State

Archives, Cheyenne. John Owens was born in Marshall, Texas, on August 11, 1843. It was said that the only man who ever made him back down was Wild Bill Hickok; it was also said that he had been involved in twenty-four killings, although no authority is cited for either claim. While he was a lawman at Lusk he also operated a saloon known as the House of Blazes at Newcastle, Wyoming. He killed his gambling-house partner, a man named Davis, "in the infant days of the town" and "was one of the chief factors in keeping Newcastle free of crime during the [18]80s." In 1892 he was elected sheriff of Weston County; defeated for a following term, he served as a deputy, then won reelection in 1904. In 1894 he married Addie Owens, a forty-year-old saloon girl. In 1906, after prisoner Logan Blizzard escaped his custody by leaping from a train, Owens took up his trail in dead of winter and tracked him to a shack in Nebraska, where he killed him. While acting as a guard at Cambria, Weston County, Owens killed another man named Davis, no relation to the first one. In 1923 he formed a relationship with a destitute woman known only as Serena and last worked as a guard at the State Industrial Institute at Worland; he died at that place on his eighty-fourth birthday, August 11, 1927. *Sheridan Post-Enterprise,* August 26, 1927; James A. Browning, *Violence Was No Stranger,* 2:79–80.

14. Hervey E. Chesley Jr., Interview with F. C. Williams, n.d. [early 1930s], HCI; *Lusk Herald,* July 29, 1887. Felix Cadmus "Uncle Cad" Williams (1861–1951) was a deputy sheriff in Hamilton County in 1884–85 and served later as county clerk.

15. *Cheyenne Daily Sun,* February 11, 1887.

16. *Lusk Herald,* January 21, 1887; *Cheyenne Daily Sun,* January 23, 1887.

17. *Lusk Herald,* January 21, 1887; *Cheyenne Democratic Leader,* January 18, 1887.

18. *Cheyenne Daily Sun,* February 5 and 11, 1887.

19. Laramie County Sheriff Prison Calendar (1) 29, Wyoming State Archives; *Cheyenne Daily Sun,* February 6, 1887. Philip Watson was also

arraigned and entered a plea of not guilty. *Cheyenne Democratic Leader,* June 4, 1887.

20. Carroll, "Real McCoy," 13.

21. *Cheyenne Daily Leader,* July 22, 1887; *Cheyenne Daily Sun,* July 22, 1887; *Lusk Herald,* July 29, 1887.

22. *Cheyenne Daily Sun,* August 9, 1887; ibid., September 3, 1887.

23. *Cheyenne Daily Sun,* September 3, 1887.

24. Ibid., September 4, 1887; Territory of Wyoming, Court Docket 3, p. 137, Wyoming State Archives.

25. Armstrong, "Lee."

26. *Cheyenne Daily Leader,* July 17 and 19, 1887.

27. "The lately constructed upper tier of cells were apparently so formidable . . . , and as it was alleged to contain all the latest improvements, nobody appeared to seriously think that escape from it was possible." *Cheyenne Daily Leader,* October 5, 1887.

28. *Cheyenne Daily Sun,* October 5, 1887.

29. Carroll, "Real McCoy," 14–15; *Cheyenne Daily Sun,* October 9, 1887.

30. Siringo claimed to have got his information from Woodruff at Hot Springs in 1915, but Woodruff died in 1902. In addition, his ranch was at McMillan (Lakewood), not Portales Springs, although that doesn't mean Bogan didn't visit it. Tom Hall and four others were arrested as accessories and sent for trial January 3, 1888. On January 28 the county attorney entered a *nolle prosequi,* and all were discharged. Great scorn was heaped on the heads of the detectives who had been regaled with "confessions" of gunfights with lawmen and ruthless murders of black men and generally "treated as tenderfeet and mercilessly guyed" by the boys. Charles A. Siringo, *A Cowboy Detective: A True Story of Twenty-Two Years with a World-Famous Detective Agency,* 51–65; Siringo, *Riata and Spurs,* 201–3; *Cheyenne Daily Leader,* December 29, 1887.

31. Dee Harkey, *Mean as Hell.* Harkey's book was so inaccurate that he was successfully sued twice and forced to publish a statement that the book was fiction. The publisher was also sued successfully and lost all rights to the book,

the copyright of which was thrown into the public domain. It is said that after Harkey died, his daughter burned about twenty unpublished chapters in her backyard.

32. Dennis McCown, "'. . . despite big losses . . .': The Last Shooting of the Old West," *Quarterly of the National Association for Outlaw and Lawman History* 24, no. 4 (Oct.–Dec. 2000), 9–16; Bill O'Neal, "They Called Him Mr. Kemp," *True West,* April 1991, 31–32, 37; Robert K. DeArment, "Dave Kemp (1862–1935)," in *Deadly Dozen: Twelve Forgotten Gunfighters of the Old West.*

33. Kemp was born March 1, 1862, in Coleman, Texas, the son of William A. (1834–1903) and Mary Jane (Snow) Kemp; there were six other children. Kemp Sr. appears to have remarried: the 1880 census shows Tennessee-born Sarah Kemp, thirty-five, as head of household (her husband, who on different occasions gave Tennessee, Alabama, and North Carolina as his birthplace, was in the local jail at the time). As we have seen, Dave Kemp was involved in various acts of violence in Hamilton County, Texas, in his teens and was sent to the penitentiary in 1883 for the murder of "Doll" Smith. Prison records show he was married at that time (he had become engaged to one of Dan Bogan's sisters in 1881), but by the time his conditional pardon was granted on January 17, 1887, by Governor John Ireland (for "reasons on file in the office of the Secretary of State"), the marriage had been either dissolved or abandoned. Research by Dennis McCown, Austin, Texas; Texas Department of State File 538, *State of Texas* vs. *David Kemp,* "Reasons for Executive Clemency," January 1, 1887, TSA; Dennis McCown, "Broken Heart, Broken Dreams," *Quarterly of the National Association for Outlaw and Lawman History* 27, no. 4 (Oct.–Dec. 2003): 5–13; Federal Census, Hamilton County, Tex., 1880.

34. J. A. Eidson to Gov. L. S. Ross, September 2, 1890, Texas Department of State File 538, TSA.

35. *Eddy Argus,* December 13 and 20, 1890, and November 10, 1893, cited in Jed Howard,

Phenix and the Wolf: The Saloon Battles of Eddy and the Dave Kemp Saga, 3, 44; McCown, "'. . . despite big losses,'" 10.

36. F. Stanley, *The Seven Rivers (New Mexico) Story,* passim; *Pecos Valley Argus,* October 25 and November 7, 1895, and May 8, 1896, cited in Howard, *Phenix.* James Leslie Dow was born at Clinton, DeWitt County, Texas, on April 30, 1860. He married Mary A. Neatherlin January 10, 1884, and they had four sons, two of whom died in infancy. They moved to New Mexico, where Dow became a deputy sheriff and stock detective. In the spring of 1890 he killed Zack Light at Seven Rivers, was tried for murder, and was acquitted. He became the bitter enemy of Oliver Lee and Bill McNew when he tried to prove they were stealing cattle and were also involved in the January 1896 murder of Col. Albert Fountain and his son.

37. *Eddy Current,* October 16 and 23, 1897, and April 2, 1898; *Pecos Valley Argus,* November 19, 1897, all cited in Howard, *Phenix;* A. C. Campbell ms., T. A. Campbell Collection, Wyoming State Historical Publications Division, Cheyenne. Campbell found out that the reward for Bogan/McCoy had been withdrawn and so informed Stewart, at which point the sheriff completely lost interest.

38. *Laramie Sentinel,* December 1889; Raine, *Guns of the Frontier,* 128; *Cheyenne State Leader,* November 7, 1931, all cited in DeArment, *Deadly Dozen,* 167, 230; Arnot, "Gatlin."

39. McCown, "'. . . despite big losses,'" 12.

CHAPTER 19
1886: "ILL MET BY MOONLIGHT"

1 Arnot, "My Recollections."

2 McCarty and Armstrong, "Dobbs."

3 Haley, "Bousman."

4 Gober, *Cowboy Justice,* 57; Federal Census, Oldham County, Tex., 1880; Haley, "Ingerton." Theodore Briggs, born in Illinois in 1835, enlisted at San Francisco, California, as a private in Company B, 1st Regiment of California Cavalry Volunteers, on December 21, 1861. He was shot through the right shoulder and right

lung and also lanced under the right arm in the "first" Battle of Adobe Walls on November 25, 1864. Loaded into a wagon with eleven other wounded (only two soldiers were killed), Briggs survived the fifteen-day trip back to Fort Bascom. Mustered out of the army at Fort Union on February 3, 1865, on June 25 he married Yñesa Montoya at Sapello, New Mexico; they lived first at Las Tecoletenas near Las Vegas, then moved to Tascosa with their daughter, Perfillia, born September 27, 1867. A carpenter and cabinet-maker by trade (despite the disablement of his right arm and side), he fashioned many of the coffins in which gunfight victims were buried. Yñesa Briggs died in 1897; Briggs married Emma L. Mitchell on January 4, 1900, and died December 11, 1903. Federal Census, San Miguel County, N.M., 1870; Darlis A. Miller, *The California Column in New Mexico,* 21; Theodore Briggs, pension file, Department of the Interior, Bureau of Pensions, NARA; Oldham County Marriage License Record (1) 31, CDCV.

5. Oldham County District Court Judges State Docket Book (1), *State of Texas* vs. *L. A. Woodruff,* Case #62, August 13, 1884, CDCV; J. Evetts Haley, "Wheeler County, Tex., District Court Records, Minutes of District Court, Book 2, 125," Handwritten notes, Haley Collection, HHC; Porter, *Memory Cups,* 526; McCarty, *Maverick Town,* 141ff.

6. McCarty and Armstrong, "Dobbs."

7. Gober, *Cowboy Justice,* 55–57.

8. Gober, *Cowboy Justice,* 80. At the March 1886 term of court the grand jury of Baylor County determined that on July 21, 1885, Harris "did fraudulently take from the possession of John Rainbolt ten head of horses . . . and to appropriate it to the use and benefit of him the said Thomas Harris." The case was heard in the 39th District Court before Judge J. V. Cockrill on March 11. There does not appear to have been a jury hearing; on September 6, 1886, the case was dismissed upon motion of the state's attorney, indicating that Charles Jenkins convinced the court there was no case to answer. Baylor County District Court Records, *State of*

Texas vs. *Thomas Harris,* Case No. 273. County Clerk's Office, Seymour, Tex.

9. McCarty and Armstrong, "Dobbs."

10. Sullivan, *LS Brand,* 89.

11. McCarty and Armstrong, "Dobbs"; Haley, "Bousman."

12. Sullivan, *LS Brand,* 97–100. It should perhaps be emphasized that neither Chilton nor Valley were ever "Rangers." Valley, who had been raised in Missouri, was from a Catholic family. When he left home his mother gave him a Bible. He "could preach a good sermon. When the boys at the line camp were all tired out he would read out of this Bible and get up and put on a sermon just for the fun of it." McCarty and Armstrong, "Dobbs."

13. McCarty and Armstrong, "Dobbs."

14. Gober, "Contention."

15. Lester F. Sheffy, Interview with John Lang, October 13, 1936, L. F. Sheffy Memorial Collection, Cornette Library, West Texas A&M University, Canyon, cited in Schofield, *Indians, Cattle,* 165. The librarian was unable to locate the actual interview when requested.

16. McCarty, *Maverick Town,* 145ff.

17. Haley, "East." Jesse Sheets was born in Van Zandt County, Texas, in 1853. As a boy he was engaged as a jockey with Stanfield and Hickey, famous racehorse owners. He married Sarah R. Anderson at La Junta, Colorado, in 1874 and moved to Mobeetie in 1877. After an unsuccessful venture in the cattle business there, he brought his family to Tascosa in November 1885 and opened a restaurant, intending to move to Oregon in the fall of 1886. His children were Martha, Ella, David, Henry, and William, who was exactly one year old on the day his father was buried. E. M. McDonald, letters to John L. McCarty, August 25 and November 1, 1928, JLMC/APL.

18. McCarty, *Maverick Town,* 145ff. Pierce "was a man absolutely without fear. A Virginian by birth he had come to the West on account of lung trouble which finally got the better of him and he died at Tascosa about 1889." In fact, Pierce's mother was from Virginia and his father was Scottish; Pierce was born in Kentucky

about 1857. Arnot, "Panhandle Sheriffs"; Federal Census, Oldham County, Tex., 1880.

19. Haley, "East."

20. Haley, "Bousman."

21. Arnot, "Tascosa Trail"; Sheffy, "Lang"; McCarty and Armstrong, "Dobbs."

22. Sebastian "Boss" Neff, diary for his grandson, January 1–August 25, 1939, unpublished ms., JLMC/APL; McCarty, *Maverick Town,* 151. At about 4:00 a.m. that night, Sheets's twenty-five-year-old wife, Sarah, "took her one-year-old baby Billie in search of Father herself. The March wind was very chilly. She came to some Cord-Wood that Father had corded at the back of his restaurant. Some men were lined up with their guns across the Cord-Wood. They took their guns down while she passed. She found my Father dead, near Ed King, Frank Valley and Fred Chilton. She fainted and fell over King. She and the baby were both bloody. . . . When she fell among those dead men she almost broke her cheek bone." McDonald, letters to McCarty.

23. Haley, "Bousman." All other accounts agree that Woodruff remained at the Briggs place, too ill to be moved.

24. Mel Armstrong, Interview with J. R. Jenkins, Amarillo, Texas, August 29, 1942. JLMC/APL; McCarty and Armstrong, "Dobbs." Jesse Jenkins said flatly "that Valley, King and Chilton were Pat Garrett's hired men and were laying for him and his partner [Harris] when the fight took place. They were over at Chalk Hollow on the other side of Amarillo having come up from South Texas. . . . He said that John Lang ran, that Jim East ran, and that Louis Bousman had nothing to do with the killing but that his gun was most certainly used." Vandale, "Panhandle Pioneers."

25. Haley, "Mitchell."

26. Godwin-Austen to Haley. Temple Houston appeared as defense attorney for John Lang at Mobeetie and assisted District Attorney Woodman in the prosecution of Bousman, who was defended by Charles Jenkins.

27. Sullivan, *LS Brand,* 113–14; McCarty, *Maverick Town,* 154–55; McCarty and Arm-

strong, "Dobbs." Louisiana-born Duncan "Dunk" Cage was a Harvard or Yale graduate; he had at one time been private secretary to the governor of Louisiana. "He was a fine man but bad at borrowing money and gambling it away. Spoke German, French and Spanish, but you could take him on the hill from the ranch, turn him around three times and he couldn't find his way back." Cage and his brother Hays quit the LS in 1886 and returned to Louisiana. John Bouldin to J. Evetts Haley, March 8, 1937, Haley Collection, HHC; Sullivan, *LS Brand*, 135.

28. Haley, "East."

29. McCarty, *Maverick Town,* 154.

30. *Amarillo Sunday News-Globe,* August 12, 1928.

CHAPTER 20
THE ANIMAL AND THE CATFISH KID:
"US FELLOWS HAVE TO STICK TOGETHER."

1. Fred Post, "Reminiscences of Louis Bousman, 1934," unpublished ms. and undated newspaper clipping of an interview in the *Amarillo News-Globe,* JLMC/APL.

2. Ethel V. Elder, Interview with Louis P. Bousman, June 17, 1936, Waurika, Okla., Indian Pioneer Papers, Oklahoma Historical Society, vol. 104, 127–30.

3. Haley, "Reminiscences of L. P. Bousman," Waurika, Okla., October 23, 1934; Kenneth R. Bailey, West Virginia Historical Society, Charleston, to author, March 27, 2002; Haley, "Bousman."

As well as his wife, Anna, twenty-nine, born in Pennsylvania, there are three children: Phillip, seven; Louis, three; and Mary, one year old. Federal Census, Lafayette County, Mo., 1860.

4. Haley, "Bousman"; Dan L. Thrapp, *Encyclopedia of Frontier Biography,* 1:146; *Barber County (KS) Mail,* May 29, 1879. Bousman claimed that after he, Phelps White, and other cowboys chased Cheyennes who had broken out of Fort Reno, he was hired as a scout and went by train to South Dakota to join Custer in the pursuit of "Sittin' Bull and his whole outfit."

The scouts located the Indians and Custer started down a little swag where "the teepees were standing there thick as my fingers." When the fighting started, Bousman saw "there was only one way to get out . . . , jumped down, got an Indian's blanket from one that had been killed, and threw it around me, and I rode right down amongst the Indians and . . . was the only one to get away. [Then] I went on to the Panhandle and went to work for Littlefield again. This was in the fall of 1877." It was actually in September 1878 that Dull Knife and some three hundred northern Cheyennes left the reservation; the proposition that Bousman scouted for Custer *after* that event is ridiculous.

5. Ethel V. Elder, Interview with Mrs. Sarah Eldora Cruce Bousman, June 17, 1937, Waurika, Okla., Indian Pioneer Papers, vol. 16, 38–43, Oklahoma Historical Society; Charles Robinson III, *The Frontier World of Fort Griffin: The Life and Death of a Western Town,* 73–74, 77; Cashion, *Texas Frontier,* 196. On page 106 Cashion also notes the death in an 1868 fight near Fort Griffin of a Comanche war chief, an African American named Cato. Kate, daughter of John and Betsy (Helm) Rutledge, was born in the Cherokee Nation on December 24, 1845. She married Tom Cruce in Lampasas, Lampasas County, Texas, about 1859 and married George Gamel (ca. 1847–ca. 1880) sometime around 1865. Kate Rutledge Cruce Gamel Bousman died March 1915 in Newport, Jack County, Texas, at age sixty-nine. George Gamel's brother John William also had a "wife" up in the Nations; apparently having an Indian woman was a ploy used by cattlemen to ensure the Indians did not raid their herds. George may have been involved seriously in the Mason County War; a note in the *Galveston Daily News,* February 12, 1878, records: "*Lampasas Dispatch* Feb 7 . . . George Gamel was arrested in Mason county last week, accused of being one of the party that broke into our jail in May, 1876, and released Scott Cooley and John Ringo."

6. Elder, Interview with Mrs. Sarah Eldora Cruce Bousman.

7. Norma Karter, genealogical research, In-

dian Pioneer Papers, Oklahoma Historical Society, Oklahoma City; Haley, "Bousman."

8. Haley, "Ingerton"; J. Evetts Haley, Interview with John Arnot, June 14, 1937, Amarillo, Texas, HHC.

9. *State of Texas* vs. *Charles Emory*, Cause No. 165; *Charles Emory* vs. *State of Texas*, Cause No. 192; and *State of Texas* vs. *John Gough*, Cause No. 164, Oldham County District Court Records, May 11–12, 1886, CDCV; Oldham County, Records of the Commissioners Court (1) 105–7 (June 14, 1886).

10. *State of Texas* vs. *Charles Emory*, Cause No. 165, Donley County District Court records, July 13, 1886, District and County Clerk's Office, Clarendon, Texas (hereafter cited as DCCC).

11. *Tascosa Pioneer*, July 3, 1886. One witness, a niece of the founder of Clarendon, contended that Woodruff did appear. "There was a big killing in Tascosa and the trial was held in Clarendon and this was the biggest court we ever had. Dr. Shelton of Tascosa brought one of the men who was shot through the bowels. [President] Garfield was not shot half as badly as this fellow." J. Evetts Haley, Interview with E. E. Carhart, June 20, 1926, HHC.

Albert Gentry, who became Donley County's first sheriff in 1882, spent his formative years "in the exalted life of diplomatic Washington and the luxuries of a Tennessee plantation." At age sixteen he ran away from school to join the Confederate army; after the war he spent four years at Washington University. Legend has it that he had a run-in with Wild Bill Hickok in Abilene, Kansas, when the latter "called for Gentry to dance to his music, firing shots near his feet to test his nerve. Gentry endured the poor jest stoically, without flinching or responding. When Hickock [*sic*] came forward to express admiration, Al pulled his own gun, threw down on Wild Bill, and called in a menacing voice for Hickock to dance or die. Covered unexpectedly by Gentry's gun, Wild Bill Hickock, the Prince of Pistoleers, gamely danced away to everyone's bemused satisfaction." Morris, *Private in the Texas Rangers*,

241. There is no mention of Gentry in the most authoritative biography of Hickok: Joseph G. Rosa, *They Called Him Wild Bill*.

12. Gober, "Contention."

13. Sworn statement of Charles Emory, Donley County District Court Records, June 24, 1886, DCCC.

14. State Docket No. 1, Donley County District Court records, 33, 39, 41, DCCC; Haley, "Handwritten notes."

15. State Docket No. 1, Donley County District Court records, 33, DCCC; *Tascosa Pioneer*, April 20, 1887.

16. Shirley, *Temple Houston*, 124. John Gottlieb Lang was born at Galena, Illinios, January 15, 1862; his father operated a lead mine. In 1874 the family moved to Coffeyville, Kansas, where they opened a butcher shop; while working there John accidentally amputated the top of his right thumb. At age fifteen he found work as a sheepherder, and in 1882 he found his way to Dodge City; the following year, Lang signed on at the LS ranch. Subsequent to events in Tascosa, he may have served briefly as town marshal of Amarillo. By 1890 he had rejoined his family, who had moved to Oregon in 1883 and settled in Haines; he took part in the 1896 Alaska gold rush, enlisted in Company E, Oregon Volunteers, during the Spanish-American War. In 1910 he married Ella Stilts (born June 7, 1866; died June 5, 1931). He served as mayor of Haines and later as Baker County's Democratic representative in both the regular and special sessions of the Oregon House of Representatives in 1933. He became the owner of the Western Union gold mine at Rock Creek and operated it for some thirty years. In 1938 he revisited Tascosa and gave his version of the fight to a couple of newspapers. John G. Lang died at Baker, Oregon, on April 4, 1942. Biographical details courtesy Miles Gilbert Jr. and Jim Gordon, Glorieta, New Mexico. "Pioneer Cowboy Recalls Bloody Feud at Tascosa," *Dalhart Texan*, July 30 1938; Brude Gerdes, "Ghosts of Comrades Again Walk among Cottonwoods as Survivor Recalls Bloody Tascosa Affair," unidentified newspaper clipping, n.d., both in

JLMC/APL; Obituary, *Baker (OR) Record Courier.* April 9, 1942; Haines, Oregon, family records at www.rootsweb.com/~orbaker/data-base/baker/aqwg298.htm#7081.

17. McCarty, Interview with Mr. J. R. Jenkins.

18. Shirley, *Temple Houston,* 124; District Court Minute Book II, 392–93, DCCC; Haley, "Handwritten notes." Bousman claimed, "Goodnight had come to me before the trial . . . and said, 'Don't you move your case. Set steady in the boat. They can't have a jury here without my men from the JA's, and you won't be stuck.'" Haley, "Bousman."

19. Haley, "East." Bousman said, "Sally Emory told some lies on me. A sporting woman named Jo Rice put a crimp in [her]. She was a nice kind woman, and she came to Clarendon, set there in jail, and talked to me, and said, 'Anytime Sally Emory starts a lie against you, I'll put her behind the bars so far the dogs won't even bark at her.'" Haley, "Bousman."

20. Godwin-Austen to Haley.

21. Statements of James Thurber, P. L. Shelton, Isaiah Rinehart, and Dave Barker, June 22, 1887, Oldham County District Court Records, CDCV. John Cone had moved uptown in 1883 and opened a store on Main Street in partnership with Dolores Duran, "a red-headed Mexican," according to Jim East, "[who] settled on [what became known as Dolores Canyon] the first creek east of Mitchell canyon. He was a blacksmith, and the Mexicans called him *Huero Herrero. Herrero* means iron-worker and *Huero,* sandy complexioned. The red-headed Mexicans come from the Maya tribe in Old Mexico, so this creek was named after [Duran] in 1877. The cowboys got to calling it El Dorado and then Wildorado, which is a villainous corruption of El Dorado, or anything else." Dolores Duran died at Tascosa on May 21, 1888, of "congestion of the bowels." He was forty-two years old. Haley, "East"; *Tascosa Pioneer,* May 26, 1888.

22. Statements of Jesse Jenkins, Lee Cone, and J. M. Robinson, June 22, 1887, Oldham County District Court Records, CDCV. David Henry Barker was born in Lafayette County, Missouri, on Christmas Day 1852. In 1874 he married fifteen-year-old Charlotte "Lottie" Durkin, an Indian captive he had rescued. She had been tattooed on her forehead and arms by her captors. Barker ran a meat market and served as a deputy sheriff at Fort Griffin and then about 1883 moved to Mobeetie. After he left Tascosa he settled in Colfax County, New Mexico, where in 1888 he killed Charles Gardner while trying to arrest him for murdering Alexander Weir at the Long Canyon Mining Camp. Barker was killed by James T. Gibbons at Catskill, New Mexico, on November 22, 1890, after killing Gibbons's dog. Gibbons was found guilty, fined four hundred dollars, and jailed until he paid the fine. Robinson, *Frontier World,* 133, 187, 191–92; Bill Reynolds, *Trouble in New Mexico: The Outlaws, Gunmen, Desperados, Murderers, and Lawmen for Fifty Turbulent Years,* vol. 1, *The A's & B's,* 117; DeArment, *Bravo of the Brazos,* 158; Porter, *Memory Cups,* 185; James R. Hewitt to the author, 2003.

23. "Findings of the jury of inquest, June 22, 1887," Oldham County District Court Records, CDCV.

24. *Tascosa Pioneer,* June 25, 1887; "Findings of the jury of inquest"; Statement of E. B. Hagins, June 22, 1887, Oldham County District Court Records, CDCV.

25. Haley, "East." East stipulated in telling this story that it not be published until after his death. This is its first appearance.

26. McCarty, Interview with Mr. J. R. Jenkins; Haley, "Ingerton."

27. John B. Gough, Convict Record Ledger, TSA.

28. Elder, Interview with Sarah Eldora Cruce Bousman.

29. *Waurika (OK) News Democrat,* Friday, January 9, 1942. One possible clue: Molly Russell May recalled that the posse that was sent from Tascosa to help Pat Garrett catch Billy the Kid "took one man along who could smell water," but she could not recall his name: could this be why they called Louis Bousman "The Animal"? McCarty and Vandale, Interview with Mrs. J. E. May.

30. Gober, "Contention"; Territory of New

Mexico, Eddy County, Statements of Thomas M. Waller, Executor, and W. R. Owen, Probate Clerk, Leonard Albert Woodruff Probate Records, 1902–5, Eddy County Clerk's Office, Carlsbad, New Mexico.

CHAPTER 21
1886–1890: WHEN TROUBLES COME . . .

1. Gober, *Cowboy Justice,* 76–77.
2. Haley, "Ingerton."
3. Neff, diary.
4. Sullivan, *LS Brand,* 119.
5. Haley, "East"; Ryland, "Untold Tales"; Sullivan, *LS Brand,* 120.
6. Oldham County, Records of the Commissioners Court (1) 48–50 (June 5, 1884), 63 (February 4, 1885), and 68–70 (February 9, 1885), CDCV.
7. *Tascosa Pioneer,* June 12, 1886.
8. Ibid., July 3, 1886. Not everyone loved having preachers around. On one occasion in a saloon "a man came in with a paper to take up a subscription for the parson. A gambler at our table said 'Is the God damn son of a bitch leaving town?' They said yes. The gambler said put him down for $35. . . . I guess [he] felt like the preacher was hurting his business." McCarty and Armstrong, "Dobbs."
9. The Spanish San Diego is Saint Didacus, the great friar of the fifteenth century. November 12 is his day.
10. *Tascosa Pioneer,* July 31, 1886.
11. Oldham County, Records of the Commissioners Court (1) 96, 98–100 (March 17 and May 10, 1886), CDCV.
12. McCarty and Armstrong, "Dobbs."
13. *Tascosa Pioneer,* July 10, 1886.
14. Oldham County, Records of the Commissioners Court (1) 118 (October 30, 1886), CDCV.
15. Schofield, *Indians, Cattle,* 81. In what seems a much likelier version, Jim East remembered this transaction as having been the other way around. "We exchanged land on the Rito Blanco [*sic*] with the Capitol Company for land that was south of the river and east of them. We got land at the ratio of one and one-half acres to an acre in exchange. . . . It was a good trade for us. We got our cattle out in the fall of 1886 and the XIT did not fully stock that country until about the spring of 1887." Haley, "East."
16. Oldham County, Records of the Commissioners Court (1) 120 (November 8, 1886), CDCV. The "new" LS ranch on Alamosa Creek was to be built by local stonemason "Uncle Tom" Nolan. Unfortunately, he fell out of a wagon and was run over by one of the wheels; brought into town and taken to the Tascosa House, he was nursed by Scotty Wilson for twelve days before he died on Friday, September 3. This was the same Tom Nolan summoned as a witness in the trial of Charlie Emory. *Tascosa Pioneer,* September 8, 1886.
17. Sullivan, *LS Brand,* 139; Oldham County, Records of the Commissioners Court (1) 108–9 (July 5, 1886), CDCV. On May 30 Jim East sold his saloon, its stock, fixtures, furniture, billiard tables, and license to John Hollicott and John Ryan for thirty-five hundred dollars cash. James H. East Collection, HHC.
18. *Fort Worth Gazette,* December 2, 1885; Sheffy, *Francklyn Land & Cattle Co.,* 7; *Handbook of Texas Online,* "Grass-Lease Fight"; Haley, *Charles Goodnight,* 381ff. "English born and Virginia educated, Woodman came to the Panhandle from Henrietta. . . . Some called him the 'Lone Wolf of the Yellow House,'" said Jim Gober. He had

a very remarkable memory and had on his tongue's end the volume, page and style of case and the controlling question decided in each case. He never used an office brief or any kind of reference memoranda, yet his accuracy was not questioned. He did not practice civil law. . . . His nativity and his early career were matters for conjecture. . . . He was ever affable and courteous to all, regardless of their station in life, and was generous to a fault. He wore his black streaming hair down to his shoulders, and each day it was trimmed and groomed by his barber. His dress was faultless. His power before juries was phenomenal and he figured in every important criminal trial, generally for the defense, that took place on the Plains during his meteoric career. He . . . later moved to Washburn, in Armstrong County, where he died.

The stone over his grave says simply, "W. H. Woodman. Pioneer Attorney, 1837 to 1891. Erected by Amarillo Bar Association, 1929." Gober, *Cowboy Justice*, 298–99; J. L. Penry in Arnot, "Tascosa Trail."

19. *Tascosa Pioneer*, September 1, 1886; Sheffy, *Francklyn Land & Cattle Co.*, 7; *Handbook of Texas Online*, "Francklyn Land and Cattle Co."

20. *Tascosa Pioneer*, September 15, 1886.

21. In November 1885, while a gang of XIT men were plowing fireguards on the north line of the pasture, their cook "let the fire get away from him at their camp. . . . The wind was blowing from the west and headed the fire right down the south side of the Beaver. The next night the wind changed and blew a gale from the north. The grass was very rank and dry and burned about as fast as a horse could run. This fire swept the ground clean from the Beaver to the drift fence and from the New Mexico line 100 miles east." John Arnot, "Prairie Fires," Vandale Collection, 2H471, CAH, UT.

22. McCarty, *Maverick Town*, 238; Arnot, "Leverton Brothers." The Levertons had bought their cattle from former LIT wagon boss Mel Davis. How he got them explains perfectly the rustlers' modus operandi: "While [working for the LIT on the South Plains, Davis] picked up eighteen head of cattle supposed to belong to some [New] Mexicans. Bringing them up on the Canadian he branded them MEL. . . . Bob Robertson [sic], the LIT boss, found out what had happened and discharged him. Using those few head of cattle for a nucleus of a herd, [Davis] formed a partnership with two or three other cowboys to steal and brand all mavericks and stray cattle they could find. In three years this bunch of cattle increased so well that Lever-

ton Brothers bought them [and the brand], paying $2500." Arnot, "Leverton Brothers."

23. Arnot, "Leverton Brothers." Just seven months after the death of John Leverton, Texas Rangers arrested his brother George along with another nester, George Meeks, on charges of "unlawful assembly." Meeks's brother Ike was charged with "carrying a pistol," and another man, William Dawson, was hauled in for "bribing [a] witness." Again, this was interpreted as harassment; the Big Die of the preceding winter had left even the syndicates anxious to recover their losses, and—since there were only so many mavericks to go around—the competition for them had become pretty fierce. One way of easing the pressure was simply to put the nesters in jail on whatever trumped-up charges could be mustered. These events and some of the other underhanded methods used to discredit the nesters are discussed in Morris, *Private in the Texas Rangers*, 92–97.

24. *Tascosa Pioneer*, December 8 and 15, 1886. In spite of the tragedy, the Leverton family stayed on, and a tight little community formed around them. In 1900 the census showed George W. Leverton, born March 1854 in Arkansas; wife, Cora, born May 1862 in Norway; and six children born between 1886 and 1899. A small cemetery was located near the Leverton house in Evans Canyon. In it are buried John Leverton, Mrs. William R. Leverton, Casinda Leverton, Mary A. Leverton, and Billy Green. This may have been the William Green who was a twenty-four-year-old cowboy on the LX ranch in 1880.

Two or three years later, Robert Archibald Spurlock (born March 1852 in Arkansas) and his wife, Elizabeth Phoebe (a sister of the Levertons, born January 1859), settled in adjacent Martin's Canyon. They had fourteen children; in 1900 those with them were five children born in Arkansas, 1875–1885, and six more born in Texas between 1887 and 1900, the last an unnamed baby. The first school in Moore County was held in a room of George Leverton's house; the teacher was Lula Gammany. During the 1894–95 term, using timbers from the washed-out FW&DC railroad bridge at Tascosa, the Spurlocks, Levertons, and Foremans built one of the first rural schoolhouses in Moore County. In 1906 the Levertons moved to Arizona, and the Spurlocks followed them in 1917. Wes Merritt, "Panhandle Creeks and Canyons," at www.PanhandleNation.com; Federal Census, Oldham County, Tex., 1880; Potter County, Tex., 1880; Moore County, Tex., 1900.

25. McCarty and Armstrong, "Dobbs." Garrett Hunt Dobbs, one of the eight children of W. M. and Elizabeth (Creech) Dobbs, was born in Panola County, Texas, on March 24, 1857. The father died at Franklin, Tennessee (November 1864), when, shot through both legs, he refused to let doctors amputate. "Kid" Dobbs grew up on the family farm near Paris, worked on a gristmill, drove bull teams, hunted buffalo, and became a cowboy. In 1878 he signed on with the LX, then he worked sheep, rode awhile for the XIT, and sold meat at Amarillo. He married Mary Helen "Lena" Atkins (born February 4, 1865, at Santa Fe, New Mexico, the only child of buffalo hunter John Atkins of Missouri and Chrysanthia Revella of Santa Fe) at Tascosa on September 18, 1881; they would have ten children. In 1893 they left Tascosa and lived for twenty years near Cheyenne, Oklahoma. In 1911 they moved to Las Cruces, New Mexico, and in 1932 Dobbs became blind; he died at Farmington, New Mexico, on October 6, 1948, and his wife died three years later on November 13, 1951.

26. Charles Goodnight, undated material, Interview No. 14, Haley Collection, HHC. George Washington Arrington, real name John C. Orrick Jr., was born in Greensboro, Alabama, on December 23, 1844, the son of John and Mariah (Arrington) Orrick. On April 13, 1861, he enlisted as a private in the 5th Alabama Infantry, and he served under Longstreet, J. E. B. Stuart, and Wade Hampton at First and Second Manassas (Bull Run), Seven Pines, Richmond, Sharpsburg (where he was wounded), Harpers Ferry, Antietam, and Shepherdstown. Reported first missing in action, then killed at Funkstown,

Maryland, he had in fact been captured and sent to Fort McHenry, but he escaped from the train en route. He then served with the 43rd Virginia Cavalry ("Mosby's Rangers") until it was disbanded on April 21, 1865, and he was paroled. "I enlisted in the Confederate army the day after Sumter was fired upon, aged 16–3 mo. And after serving 4 years and 16 days I had to make a living and have never looked in a school book since . . . ," he told Laura Hamner.

He then joined Emperor Maximilian's army in Mexico, returning to Greensboro after two years. On June 13, 1867, he killed a black businessman named Alex Webb and fled to Honduras. When he returned to the United States, he changed his name to that of his mother's family and headed for Texas, working for the Houston and Texas Central Railway and later at a commission house in Galveston. In 1875 he enlisted in Company E of the newly organized Frontier Battalion of Texas Rangers. After two years he was promoted to the rank of captain of Company C, and in July 1878 he was ordered to Fort Griffin to restore peace in the wake of vigilante activities. In September 1879 Arrington established Camp Roberts, the first Ranger camp to be established so deep into West Texas, near what is now Crosbyton. By now he was known universally as "Cap."

In June 1882 Arrington resigned his commission in order to run for the office of sheriff of Wheeler County. On October 18, 1883, he married twenty-one-year-old Sarah C. "Sally" Burnette of Atchison County, Kansas, at Westboro, Missouri. They became the parents of three sons and six daughters; the first son, Gilbert, died in infancy. Arrington served as sheriff of Wheeler County for eight years, during which time he established his own ranch near Canadian. In 1893 he became manager of the Rocking Chair ranch, but he resumed management of his own spread three years later. He died there on March 31, 1923. His wife remained active in the Canadian Woman's Christian Temperance Union and Baptist Church until her death on June 1, 1945. Mrs. G. W. Arrington to J. Evetts Haley, July 18, 1926, Haley Collection, HHC; G. W. Arrington to L. V. Hamner, Canadian, Tex., September 10, 1916, Vandale Collection, 2H471, CAH/UT; Jerry Sinise, *George Washington Arrington*; *Handbook of Texas Online,* "Arrington, George Washington," passim.

27. *Tascosa Pioneer,* December 29, 1886. Both men insisted they would "stand trial if indicted, and if not indicted, demand trial." The case against Arrington was heard at Clarendon in July 1887; although his actions in the Leverton arrest had been at best questionable, he was acquitted on grounds of self-defense. Willingham's case was heard at the same term of Oldham County District Court that tried the Catfish Kid in September 1887. After the jury was sworn in, the district attorney stated that he had no evidence to offer; a verdict was called for and the defendant was acquitted. Many of the old-timers saw all this as a travesty of justice; Kid Dobbs, who was on the jury, claimed "the whole thing was railroaded and the jury didn't have a thing to do with the decision." *Tascosa Pioneer,* April 20, 1887; Morris, *Private in the Texas Rangers,* 96–97; McCarty and Armstrong, "Dobbs."

28. *Tascosa Pioneer,* December 15 and 29, 1886, January 5 and 26, and February 9, 1887. On September 5, 1882, Molly Russell married a William A. Wilson, said to have been "one of [Senator] Dorsey's [Star Route] lieutenants and he slipped out of the room one night while she was asleep and she never heard of him again. They had been married about three months." Others said her husband was a Texas Ranger. Jim May, who was born in Illinois April 14, 1853 died at Vega, Texas, on November 26, 1935 Molly passed away there March 15, 1939. There were five children from the marriage. McCarty and Armstrong, "Dobbs"; McCarty and Vandale, Interview with Mrs. J. E. May; Oldham County Marriage License Record (1) 6, 12, CDCV; Federal Census, Hartley County, Tex., 1880; tombstone, Memorial Park Cemetery, Vega, Texas.

29. *Tascosa Pioneer,* January 12, 1887; *Dodge City Daily Globe,* January 11, 1887. Rudolph

may have been whistling past the graveyard. On the night in question a blizzard driven by a fifty-eight-mile-per-hour wind raged for two days and three nights, and area cattlemen lost thousands of head of stock. One rancher, it was reported, recovered 80 out of 22,000 head as a result of the storm. John Hollicott of the LX said his men skinned 250 cattle per mile for thirty miles along one section of the drift fence. Gober, *Cowboy Justice,* 292; McCarty, *Maverick Town,* 165.

30. John Clay, *My Life on the Range,* passim.

31. *Tascosa Pioneer,* February 23, March 2, and July 30, 1887.

32. Sullivan, *LS Brand,* 133–34; McCarty, *Maverick Town,* 224–25.

CHAPTER 22
JESSE JENKINS:
"HE NEVER OWED A DEBT THAT HE DIDN'T PAY."

1. "Families United," in June Tyree, comp., *Tales from Corona and More: History and Families,* 177ff.

2. Federal Census, Limestone County, Ala., 1850; Limestone County Marriage Book (1832–62), 522; research by Charlotte K. Borden. Records at Cleburne indicate the surveyor of record was B. Chambers and a street named after him commemorates that fact. Lois Cochran, Records Coordinator, City of Cleburne, to author, September 9, 2004.

3. Parker County records show that "J. E. Jenkins" paid taxes on "1 Negro, 2 Horses and 22 Cattle" (but no land) for the years 1856, 1857, and 1859; in 1858 a "J. E. Jenkins" is shown owning three hundred acres of land. Frank W. Johnson, *A History of Texas and Texans,* vol. 4, *1870–71;* Stanley, *Texas Panhandle,* 102–4; *Handbook of Texas Online,* "Jenkins, Charles H."; Federal Census, Dallas County, Tex., 1850; Parker County Tax Rolls, 1856–59, Dallas Public Library; genealogical research by Jean Shanelec, Ellsworth, Kansas, courtesy Wanda Carnell.

If his father immediately left for the Civil War and did not return until it was over, Jesse could not have been born in 1863, so 1861 is the likelier date. But if, as seems probable, his brother Lon is the thirty-year-old adobe maker "A. Jinkens," living with his wife, Sarah, in Mobeetie in 1880, then Jonathan Jenkins's Civil War service either began later or was interrupted. In another version of his life, Colonel Jenkins is said to have died of pneumonia contracted "while on a guard against Indians." William Leroy Jenkins, who served as the second sheriff of Dallas County, died November 6, 1871, aged fifty-eight. Vandale, Interview with Billy Jarrett; Federal Census, Dallas County, Tex., 1870 and 1880; Wheeler County, Tex., 1880; Tyree, *Tales from Corona,* 177; *Memorial and Biographical History of Dallas County, Texas,* 995.

4. Abram L. Spillers, in *Memorial and Biographical History of Dallas County,* 952–53; Tyree, *Tales from Corona,* 177; Federal Census, Dallas County, Tex., 1870. Charles Jenkins was enumerated in the household of twenty-nine-year-old John F. Ault, Georgia-born lawyer in Dallas; Lon's whereabouts at that time are as yet undocumented.

5. Federal Census, Wheeler County, Tex., 1880; Tyree, *Tales from Corona,* 177; Harris, *Hide Town,* 39, 46. Lon Jenkins had appeared earlier in the legal calendar when (probably during or after a high-stakes card game that ended in a fight) gambler Jack Greathouse charged him with assault with intent to murder and Nettie Jenkins with using "obscene, vulgar and indelicate language." At the suggestion of the attorneys, Lon's case was indefinitely postponed; Nettie pleaded guilty and paid a three-dollar fine. Porter, *Memory Cups,* 38.

6. Laura V. Hamner, "Notes from interview with Jess Jenkins," October 1, 1936, Vandale Collection, 2H475, CAH/UT.

7. Vandale, "Panhandle Pioneers."

8. Jenkins became an associate judge in the Court of Civil Appeals in 1910 and served in the Texas Legislature between 1906 and 1930; in his later years he wrote a weekly column about the history of Brownwood in the local newspaper. His wife, Annie, died in 1909. Charles Jenk-

ins died February 23, 1931. *Handbook of Texas Online,* "Jenkins, Charles H."; *Brownwood Bulletin,* February 24 and 25, 1931; James C. White, *The Promised Land: A History of Brown County,* 104–6; Lorene Bishop, "Brownwood's Model Citizen," *Brownwood Bulletin,* September 15, 2002; Susan J. Orton (a great-granddaughter), "Charles H. Jenkins (1852–1931), A Biographical Sketch," manuscript courtesy Wanda Carnell.

9. Vandale, "Panhandle Pioneers." Military use of Camp Colorado ceased at the end of the Civil War; it was used by local militia until about 1874. Napoleon Bonaparte "Bone" Wilson, a.k.a. S. Watson, had on June 25, 1877, killed Erath County sheriff James Martin, who tried to arrest him for horse theft. Receiving information of the wanted man's whereabouts, on September 22 Sgt. Thomas M. Sparks led a party of Texas Rangers to Silver Creek in Coleman County, where they laid in wait for Wilson and his father, out hunting buffalo. When Wilson rode in slightly ahead of his father, "seven Winchesters were pointed at him and he was commanded to hold up his hands, which he refused to do, but made for his gun." The Rangers shot down his horse, whereupon Wilson got behind it for cover. Unfortunately—for him—the horse was not dead; when it jumped to its feet and ran away, Wilson got behind his father's horse, and while attempting to fire at the Rangers was shot and killed. "His body was properly identified by the coroner and decently buried in the Stephenville cemetery." *Austin Daily Democratic Statesman,* September 27, 1877; *Weatherford Exponent,* September 29, 1877; Webb, *Texas Rangers,* 340–41.

10. Federal Census, Dallas County, Tex., 1880.

11. Hamner, "Jess Jenkins," Amarillo Hotel, July 1942, John L. McCarty Papers, Southwest Collection, Texas Tech University, Lubbock; Tyree, *Tales from Corona,* 177. Her stepson places Mahala Bonner Jenkins Spillers in Brownwood in 1892. She remained there until she died in November 1912; she is buried next to her son in that city's Greenleaf Cemetery. Spillers, in *History of Dallas County.*

12. Hamner, *Short Grass,* 124; Hamner, "Jess Jenkins," January 3, 1941.

13. Hamner, "Jess Jenkins," July 1942; Mel Armstrong, Interview with J. R. Jenkins, Vandale Collection, September 1, 1942, CAH/UT; Vandale, "Panhandle Pioneers."

14. Hamner, "Jess Jenkins," July 1942.

15. Haley, "East"; McCarty and Hamner, "King of Hogtown"; Hamner, "Jess Jenkins," January 3, 1941. Jesse Jenkins was always on the edge of trouble. On April 7, 1883, he was arraigned on a charge of assault with intent to murder one William Diefen, or Dufer, and fined twenty-five dollars and costs. No other details have survived.

16. Armstrong, Interview with J. R. Jenkins.

17. Hamner, "Jess Jenkins," July 1942; Vandale, "Panhandle Pioneers."

18. "The Jenkins Family," in Tyree, *Tales from Corona.*

19. Hamner, "Jess Jenkins," July 1942; Lavaca County Marriage Records (Vol. E), 255; Mrs. J. W. Howard to Winnie D. Hale, February 1941, John L. McCarty Papers, Texas Tech University Library, Lubbock.

20. Vandale, Interview with Billy Jarrett. If Lon Jenkins's wife was the "Sarah E. Jinkens" of the 1880 Wheeler County census, then she died in 1883. There is no record of her death in Mobeetie or Tascosa. Whether she was also the Nettie Jenkins featured in note 5 of this chapter it is impossible to say.

21. John L. McCarty, Interview with Jess Jenkins and Bob Bonner, Amarillo Hotel, August 28, 1942, JLMC/APL. Albert Gallatin Boyce was born near Austin, Texas, on May 8, 1842. He served in the 32nd Texas (Woods') Cavalry and was wounded at the Battle of Chickamauga; paroled, he walked home to Round Rock, where he reenlisted, fighting in what may have been the last battle of the Civil War at Palmito Ranch, Texas, five weeks after the surrender. After the war he began rounding up wild cattle, and in 1867–68 he drove a herd to California. On December 20, 1870, he married Annie Elizabeth Harris; they had six children. He began his career with the XIT in 1885,

when he was trail boss of a herd being driven to the Buffalo Springs division, among the first to arrive at the ranch. He became general manager of the XIT in June 1887 and remained in that position for eighteen years, during which time he made his own fortune. He was a strong supporter of the Farwell credo forbidding cowboys to gamble or carry six-shooters and insisting on the strict observance of Sundays. Boyce retired from the XIT in 1905 and moved to Amarillo, where he helped organize the Amarillo National Bank. Later he organized the Midway Bank and Trust Company at Dalhart and was its president until his death. On January 13, 1912, Boyce was assassinated in the lobby of the Metropolitan Hotel in Fort Worth by John Beal Sneed, an Amarillo rancher whose wife, Lena, had eloped with Boyce's son Al. Sneed was arrested and tried for the killing, but the jury acquitted him; later, on the night of September 14, 1912, Sneed murdered Al Boyce in Amarillo. The killings ignited a Texas-style blood feud that lasted for several years. *Dallas Morning News,* January 14 and February 8, 1912; Hunter, *Trail Drivers,* 672–73; J. Evetts Haley, *The XIT Ranch of Texas and the Early Days of the Llano Estacado* 102, 217; *Handbook of Texas Online,* "Boyce, Albert Gallatin."

22. Armstrong, Mel. Interview with J. R. Jenkins.

23. Hamner, *Short Grass,* 246.

24. Tyree, *Tales from Corona;* Vandale, "Panhandle Pioneers"; Lillie Mae Hunter, *The Book of Years: A History of Dallam and Hartley Counties;* "Jess Jenkins," *The Cattleman* 34, no. 4 (Sept. 1947).

25. *Dalhart Texan,* January 9, 1920.

26. *Tascosa Pioneer,* July 13, 1889; Wanda Carnell, "Notes from Interview with Ruth Jenkins Gray, Granddaughter to Lon Jenkins," unpublished ms, n.d., reproduced courtesy of the author.

Lon Jenkins's move to Roswell may have been prompted by financial difficulties; in October 1888 he was sued in Oldham County for two promissory notes, one to T. W. McGuire for $466.59 and the other to B. H. White for

$525.66. When Lon failed to appear, judgment was given for the plaintiffs; whether they ever got paid is another matter. Oldham County District Court Minutes (1) 314–15 (October 1, 1888), Cases #40–41, CDCV.

27. George Curry, *George Curry, 1861–1947*, ed. H. B. Hening, 77–78. Another version of the story lists this as Nogal's third shooting and says the bartender (that is, Lon Jenkins) "hit Ellis over the head with a billiard cue. Ellis went to the ranch and told his brother Bill Ellis about it. Bill Ellis came to town and . . . told the bartender he was going to shoot him. Bill Ellis pulled his six-shooter and the bartender put his shotgun over the bar and shot Bill's head off." Herbert L. Traylor and Louise Coe Runnels, *The Saga of the Sierra Blanca*, 65. No record of this or any such case can be found in either Lincoln County Civil and Criminal Docket Book #14592, 1873–1896, or Criminal Docket Book B, #14594, 1893–1895. Lucille A. Martinez, Archivist, New Mexico State Records Center and Archive, Santa Fe, to author, November 11, 2004.

28. Nolan, *Billy the Kid*, 234–36; *Roswell Register-Tribune*, September 17, 1909; *Tales of Corona*, 184–86; Lanita Rasak, Interview with Wanda Duke, 2001, author's collection; Wanda Carnell, "Memories of the Jenkins Family," manuscript, author's collection.

29. Laura V. Hamner and Annie Teague, "Interviews Concerning Old Tascosa," February 1941, Vandale Collection, 2H480, CAH/UT; *Dalhart Texan*, August 12, 1921; Haley, Interview with D. J. "Dick" Miller.

30. Carnell, "Memories"; Federal Census, Lauderdale County, Ala., 1900; Brown County, Tex., 1910; *Dalhart Texan*, April 25, 1924.

31. "Jenkins Family," in *Tales of Corona*; Lanita Rasak, Interview with Geraldine Perkins, 2001, author's collection; Carnell, "Memories." Steel Dust was, of course, the most famous of all Texas quarter horses; Jesse was obviously breeding from that champion's bloodline.

32. Carnell, "Memories"; Laura V. Hamner, "Notes from interview with Jess Jenkins," October 1, 1936, and "Visit to the Hip O Ranch,"

Vandale Collection, 2H475, CAH/UT; Mel Armstrong, "Interview," Amarillo, September 1, 1942; McCarty, Interview with Jess Jenkins and Bob Bonner.

33. Hamner, "Jess Jenkins," July 1942. The exact date of Lon Jenkins's death cannot be established because it appears no death certificate was ever filed. Cleo Jenkins passed away in Amarillo on March 17, 1980; before she died she instituted a college scholarship to be given annually in her name to a high school senior living in Dallam or Hartley County. Note that it was not in Jesse's name, but in hers. Revenge is bitter. New Mexico Office of Vital Records, Santa Fe, to author, November 19, 2004; *Dalhart Texan*, March 19, 1980.

CHAPTER 23
1887–1890: THE WRITING ON THE WALL

1. *Tascosa Pioneer*, March 2, 1887.
2. *Tascosa Pioneer*, May 14, 1887. The actual wording is "the cattle loss for the winter was far below even one percent. From two to five head lost out of a stock of twenty to thirty thousand is getting off well." This seems out of all accord with the statements of the LX's John Hollicott and others; cf. note 29, chapter 21.
3. Oldham County, Records of the Commissioners Court (1) 133–37 (May 9, 1887). On Tuesday, May 17, XIT superintendent Berry Nations accidentally shot Steve Arnold, one of his cowboys, through the stomach at the Buffalo Springs ranch. Nations rode down to Tascosa to get Dr. Shelton, but by the time they arrived, Arnold had died.
4. *Tascosa Pioneer*, May 21 and 28, 1887.
5. *Tascosa Pioneer*, June 11, July 9 and 16, 1887.
6. McCarty, "Jess Jenkins, Ragtown Owner"; *Tascosa Pioneer*, May 28, 1887.
7. Arnot, "Smooth Rustlers."
8. *Tascosa Pioneer*, June 18, August 13, and September 24, 1887. Josephine Wyness's death may have been hastened by the shooting at the XIT (note 3, this chapter); she had given birth on May 8, "but owing to the absence of Dr.

Shelton from Tascosa she lacked proper care and medical attention, and finally passed to her reward." Arnot, "My Recollections."

9. Oldham County, Records of the Commissioners Court (1) 146–51 (August 8, 1887); *Tascosa Pioneer,* June 18 and July 30, 1887.

10. Holland is said to have gone to New York to "outwit" some confidence men who had defrauded one of his friends. His plan, which involved counterfeit money, went awry, and in the brawl that followed he killed one man and wounded another. He was tried and acquitted, but the costs of his defense left him broke. James D. Hamlin, *Flamboyant Judge,* 18–19.

11. Laura V. Hamner, "Notes from an Interview with Jesse Jenkins," Corona, N.M., September 11, 1936, Vandale Collection, 2H475, CAH, UT; *Tascosa Pioneer,* September 3, 1887.

12. Gober, *Cowboy Justice,* 104; *Tascosa Pioneer,* September 3, 1887.

13. *Tascosa Pioneer,* September 10 and November 26, 1887; Gober, *Cowboy Justice,* 108, 296.

14. *Tascosa Pioneer,* December 3, 1887; McCarty, *Maverick Town,* 226.

15. *Tascosa Pioneer,* December 3, 1887. Just six days after this item appeared, May Rudolph was delivered of a second son, Guy Francis.

16. *Tascosa Pioneer,* January 28 and February 4, 1888.

17. Arnot, "My Recollections."

18. *Tascosa Pioneer,* June 1888 to May 1889, passim; Oldham County, Records of the Commissioners Court (1) 186 (November 19, 1888). In 1882, after a blizzard wiped out half his sheep, Romero sold the remainder and—possibly with seed funds provided by Jesse Jenkins—began freighting between Tascosa and Dodge City. After winning a two-year contract with Wright & Farnsworth in 1883, he moved to Dodge, where his adopted son Ynocencio was already in school, and bought and operated the Saint James Hotel. In November 1884, while he was absent freighting, his home was destroyed by fire; several hundred dollars' worth of jewelry and gold were found melted in the ruins. He remained in the freighting business until 1887,

when he returned to Tascosa, opened a butcher shop, and began hauling barbed wire and supplies for the XIT ranch. In 1896 he bought a ranch at Bard, near present-day Endee, New Mexico, and sold his Tascosa properties to Al Morris a year later. He died at age seventy-nine in 1912. Federal Census, Mora County, N.M., 1870; *Dodge City Times,* November 6, 1884; *Amarillo Sunday News-Globe, Golden Anniversary Issue,* August 14, 1938; *Amarillo Daily News,* July 16, 27, and 28, 1953; *Amarillo Times,* February 28, 1946.

19. McCarty, *Maverick Town,* 234.

20. *Tascosa Pioneer,* May 26 and June 2, 1888; Gober, *Cowboy Justice,* 110. Even Rudolph—although he made little mention of it—was coppering his bets by publishing another newspaper in Amarillo.

21. *Tascosa Pioneer,* October 15, 1887; May 26 and October 20, 1888.

22. Haley, *Charles Goodnight,* 332–33; *Tascosa Pioneer,* July 9, 1887; "Wyoming Tales and Trails," at www.wyomingtalesandtrails.com/swan.html.

23. Kerr, *Scottish Capital,* 45.

24. *Fort Worth Gazette,* October 13, 1887; Schofield, *Indians, Cattle,* 92.

25. Schofield, *Indians, Cattle,* 97, 104. Lee's deepwater project was completed successfully in December 1891; he next turned his attention to chartering tugs and barges and was involved in the development of harbors at Calcasieu and Sabine Passes. From 1906 to 1925 he was in the oil exploration business. In 1923, as his first wife, the former Selina Whitley, had died in 1900, Lee married Leila Schumacher, forty-three, of Fayetteville, Arkansas. He died of kidney failure on January 6, 1925. Schofield, *Indians, Cattle,* passim.

26. Sullivan, *LS Brand,* 148. Popham married Elizabeth Florence Russell on November 16, 1890, but the marriage did not last. According to Jesse Jenkins, not a sentimental man, Al "would never let anyone touch a single thing she left in the house. He kept thinking she'd come back and he wanted her to find things just as she'd left them." But she never did. Oldham

County Marriage License Record (1) 22, CDCV; Hamner, "Jess Jenkins," January 3, 1941.

27. Oldham County District Court Minutes (1), Report of the grand jury, November 11, 1889, CDCV; John Arnot, "The Horse," Vandale Collection, 2H471, CAH/UT.

28. McCarty and Armstrong, "Dobbs"; *Tascosa Pioneer*, May 10, 1890; Vandale, Interview with Billy Jarrett. There were three Texas Ranger Britton brothers: James Magruder "Grude" (1863–1910), Edward S. (1866–1948), and Joseph Calvin (1874–1920). "Grude" Britton enlisted in Capt. Sam McMurray's Company B at Quanah, Hardeman County, on June 15, 1887, and was discharged there seven years later; during his service he replaced Tobe Robinson as sheriff of Hartley County following the latter's arrest (see chapter 25). Tom Platt, also of Company B, entered the service September 1, 1881, and served until February 28, 1891. He apparently enlisted again at Austin in 1899, but records of him after that date are sketchy. Robert W. Stephens, *Texas Ranger Sketches*, 26–32; James Magruder Britton, Adjutant General Service Records, Frontier Battalion, Box 401-177, TSA.

29. McCarty and Armstrong, "Dobbs"; Haley, "East"; Haley, "Ingerton"; Oldham County District Court, Case #347 (May 9, 1890), Judges State Docket Book (1) 98, CDCV. Whether the cessation of burials on Boot Hill came about thus (a Bill Smith is buried there) is uncertain; more likely it was because of the appearance in the *Pioneer* on July 30, 1887, of a notice by Isaiah Rinehart (who owned the property) warning "all parties against burying in future within five hundred and twenty yards north of my southwest corner, and within ninety yards west of my west line." W. C. Collins averred that Clark "came from Denton; [was] a one-legged cowpuncher, tough hombre, looked like half Mexican, worked on LS; was running for county clerk and was killed in Jim East's saloon. Jim said he did it. I don't know. Four or five were shooting, political feud; nobody liked Jim East." Other hints suggest that perhaps the shooting was not quite so straightforward as has been represented; at the same term of court that heard East's case, Matt Atwood was fined twenty-five dollars and costs for "carrying arms," and cowboy, bartender, and roughneck Tom Higgins was indicted for assault with intent to murder, but there was not enough evidence to sustain the charge. Hamner and Teague, "Interviews Concerning Old Tascosa"; Oldham County District Court Minutes (1) 369–70 (May 5, 1890), CDCV.

CHAPTER 24
CHARLES FRANCIS RUDOLPH: "IT'S SAD TO DIE YOUNG."

1. McCarty, *Maverick Town*, 213–14.

2. Marsha Field Foster to author, August 13, 2002.

3. Ibid.; Federal Census, Montague County, Tex., 1880.

4. Marriage Record, December 9, 1884, Cooke County Clerk's Office, Gainesville, Texas.

5. Hamner, *Short Grass*, 99–100.

6. *Tascosa Pioneer*, clipping, n.d., Panhandle-Plains Historical Museum Collections, Canyon, Texas. Just before Christmas 1887, May Rudolph's father, A. W. McGregor, and family arrived in Tascosa, and he took a lease on the Exchange Hotel, which he sold in May 1888, when he left to run the new hotel in Amarillo. *Tascosa Pioneer*, December 24, 1887, and May 26, 1888.

7. *Tascosa Pioneer*, February 28, 1891.

8. Undated clippings from the newspapers listed, n.d., Panhandle-Plains Historical Museum Collections, Canyon, Texas.

9. *Tascosa Pioneer*, clipping, n.d., Panhandle-Plains Historical Museum Collections, Canyon, Texas. Probably from the final issue, February 28, 1891.

10. E. R. Archambeau, ed., "Old Tascosa: Selected News Items from the *Tascosa Pioneer*, 1886–1888," *Panhandle-Plains Historical Review* 39 (1966): 182–83.

11. Ibid.; Vandale, "Panhandle Pioneers."

12. Charles F. Rudolph, Convict Record Ledger and Conduct Register, Prisoner 57960, TSA.

CHAPTER 25
"HERE WE QUIT YOU"

1. The town was named for George Channing Rivers, paymaster of the Fort Worth & Denver City Railroad; when it was learned a Texas town already bore that name, they used his middle name instead.

2. Hamner, *Short Grass,* 247; McCarty, *Maverick Town,* 234–35.

3. United States Agricultural Census, Hartley County, Tex., 1890; Oldham County, Records of the Commissioners Court (1) 270–77 (January 8 and February 9, 1891).

4. Haley, "Mitchell."

5. Ibid. "Ruck Turner and Dick Ponchon [*sic*] established the VIX ranch on the Rito Blanco [*sic*] a few miles west of Tascosa and used it as a base for mavericking during the years 1888 to 1890. Mat[t] Atwood also had a ranch on the Rito Blanco. He, according to Haley, was the champion mavericker of the Panhandle." Dobie, *Vaquero,* 146.

6. Arnot, "Smooth Rustlers." Arnot coyly avoided naming Ruth's customer, but since it is a matter of record Lon Jenkins had the contract to feed the workers, it seems safe to assume it was he.

7. Hamner, "Jess Jenkins," January 3, 1941.

8. "Stealing by John Shrader" in John L. McCarty, Interview with John Collins, October 9, 1941, JLMC/APL; Vandale, Interview with Billy Jarrett; Arnot, "Smooth Rustlers"; *State of Texas* vs. *Mat Atwood,* Case #46, May 8, 1894, and *State of Texas* vs. *Mat Atwood,* Case #125, May 16, 1895, Potter County District Clerk's Office, Amarillo, Texas.

Who knows if Atwood's claim was true? Frank Jackson, born in Llano County in 1856, was the only one to escape unhurt from the Round Rock robbery in which Sam Bass died; no one knows what happened to him. Atwood married Sarah Sheets on December 1, 1889. After he disappeared, she moved to Roswell,

where she died on November 6, 1902, as Sarah R. Dunne. One contemporary said Atwood went to Louisiana, where he committed suicide. Or did he, as others believed, fake his own death and live to a ripe old age? As late as 1927 efforts were being made to get murder charges against Jackson in Williamson County dropped. Oldham County Marriage License Record (1) 19, CDCV; E. M. [Martha Sheets] McDonald to John L. McCarty, November 1, 1928, JLMC/APL; Hamner and Teague, "Interviews Concerning Old Tascosa"; Thrapp, *Encyclopedia,* 2: 715–16.

9. Oldham County, Records of the Commissioners Court (1) 258 (November 10, 1890); Haley, "Ingerton"; Haley, *XIT Ranch,* 202. Hence, perhaps, Rudolph's urbane observation in the *Pioneer* of October 13, 1888, that His Honor had "presided with his usual grace and dignity."

10. *Tascosa Pioneer,* 1890–91, passim. James McMasters died at Channing on June 5, 1899. Willingham, "First Ranches."

11. *Tascosa Pioneer,* February 28, 1891.

12. Haley, "East."

13. McCarty, "Stealing by John Shrader." An undated clipping from the *Tascosa Pioneer* states that "Pincham was arrested by Sheriff J. M. Robinson on papers sent him by Sheriff Houchins of Lavaca County charging theft of horses thirteen years ago. The [Rangers] had nothing to do with it, and Pincham gave bond." There is no record of any file on Jesse Jenkins in the Armstrong County District Court at Claude, Texas. *Tascosa Pioneer,* n.d., Panhandle-Plains Historical Museum Collections, Canyon, Texas; Joe Reck, Armstrong County and District Clerk, to author, September 22, 2004.

14. Arnot, "Panhandle Sheriffs."

15. Robert W. Stephens, *Texas Ranger Sketches,* 30, courtesy Chuck Parsons.

16. Vandale, "Panhandle Pioneers"; *State of Texas* vs. *J. M. Robinson,* Case #32, May 16, 1893, and *State of Texas* vs. *J. M. Robinson,* Cases #110 and 113, June 26, 1894, Potter County District Clerk's Office, Amarillo, Texas. Tobe Robinson, "a tall, slender, blond fellow," hailed from Atlanta; he arrived in Dodge City in 1872

and found work as a skinner for J. Wright Mooar. In spite of his being universally called "Tobe," his initials on official documents are always J. M. Among the hunters who stayed on at Adobe Walls after the battle to guard the merchandise and supplies, Robinson and a man named George Huffman were caught in a thicket by a war party; when they made a run for it, Huffman was killed, but Robinson escaped. The following year, he became a partner in the Fletcher and Donley stage station, a rest stop on the Dodge-Mobeetie route about nineteen miles southeast of Canadian. By 1883 he had sold his partnership and moved to Tascosa, where he ran a livery stable with Joe Krause and occasionally raced horses. He later worked for the LS ranch, and in November 1886 he was elected sheriff of Oldham County, serving two terms before selling his livery stable and moving to Hartley.

On March 4, 1891, Robinson married Mary Anderson, better known to the saloon fraternity as "Santa Fe Moll." What kind of love match this was can only be guessed at: according to Jesse Jenkins, Moll was "a big fat woman 50 or 60 years old." After Robinson's trial, the couple left the Panhandle, in one story going to Bisbee, Arizona, and in another, to Colorado. "They hadn't lived [there] but a few months when early one morning they quarrelled and Tobe started walking off to town. Santa Fe Moll picked up a Winchester rifle and shot Tobe in the back, killing him instantly, for which she was sentenced to prison at Santa Fe for a long term of years." Gard, *Great Buffalo Hunt,* 180; Vandale, "Panhandle Pioneers"; Gober, "Contention"; Oldham County Marriage License Record (1) 25, CDCV.

According to extant records, no J. M. or Tobias or Tobe Robinson died in Arizona between 1891 and 1920. Nor was any Mary or Mollie Anderson or Robinson (or any woman at all, come to that) admitted to the Santa Fe penitentiary on a charge of murder between 1891 and 1900. Without a location it is impossible to check Colorado records. Arizona Department of Vital Records, *Deaths 1891–1920;* New Mexico State Penitentiary records researched by John Tanner.

17. John L. McCarty, "Interview with Mel Armstrong," n.d., JLMC/APL.

18. McCarty, *Maverick Town,* 250.

19. Ibid., 250–51.

20. Hamner, *Short Grass,* 138–40; *Handbook of Texas Online,* "Coburn, James M."

21. Sullivan, *LS Brand,* 149–56.

22. Ibid., 159–68; Hamner, *Short Grass,* 224–27.

23. *Handbook of Texas Online,* "LX Ranch."

24. Records of EGM, August 4 and 20, 1894, Ref. BT31/3135/18063, Public Record Office, Kew, London; Hamner, *Short Grass,* 80–87; *Handbook of Texas Online,* "Rocking Chair Ranch."

25. The downfall of the Capitol Syndicate is chronicled in great detail in the *Times* (London), June 5, 1891; December 17, 1895; September 23, 1897; October 18, 1902; and October 14, 1904. See also Capitol Freehold Land & Investment Co. Notice of Debenture Issue, October 10, 1907, Ref. BT31/14803/21322, Public Record Office, Kew, London.

26. Records of EGM, April 19 and May 8, 1918, Ref. BT31/14803/21322, Public Record Office, Kew, London; *The Stock Exchange Year-Book for 1918,* 759–80.

27. Arnot, "My Recollections." Jack Lenard, memorialized on his gravestone as "One of Custer's Gallant Scouts," died November 27, 1909. Arnot says Scotty Wilson died in 1912 and "was laid to rest close to his two old friends."

28. Gober, "Contention."

29. Oldham County District Court Minutes (1) 67–68 (April 25, 1910), CDCV.

30. Ibid., 68–97 (May 28, 1915); Oldham County, Records of the Commissioners Court (2) 344–97 (April 21, 1915–March 18, 1916), CDCV.

CODA: FRENCHY MCCORMICK: "SHE WAS A RING-TAILED TOOTER."

1. Butler, *Daughters of Joy,* 15, 59–60; *Dodge City Times,* July 21 and August 18, 1877. With respect to the stories that Frenchy was a saloon girl in Dodge City (which, like everything else

said and written about her, she neither denied nor confirmed), it should perhaps be noted that there is no documentary evidence of her ever having lived there. She might as easily have come to Mobeetie not from Dodge but from Fort Griffin, which witnessed the departure in that direction of most of its "floating population" early in 1880. Cashion, *Texas Frontier,* 263; Rister, *Fort Griffin,* 198–99.

2. *Dodge City Times,* March 24, 1877.

3. *Ford County Globe,* January 21, 1879.

4. Haley, Interview with Lucius Dills, August 5, 1937; ibid., June 12, 1935.

5. McCarty, *Maverick Town,* 187.

6. Haley, "Bousman."

7. Haley, "Mitchell."

8. McCarty, "Jess Jenkins, Ragtown Owner."

9. Hamner, "Jess Jenkins," November 11, 1940, Vandale Collection, 2H474, CAH/UT.

10. Oldham County Marriage License Record (1) 14, CDCV.

11. Haley, Interview with Lucius Dills, June 12, 1935.

12. Ibid., August 5, 1937.

13. Hamner, "Notes from interview with Jess Jenkins," October 1, 1936.

14. Cohea, Interview with Mary Snider.

15. McCarty and Armstrong, "Dobbs."

16. Cohea, Interview with Mrs. Frank Mitchell.

17. "Her 32 Years of Separation from Husband Are Over: Death Ends Long Wait for Belle of Old Tascosa," clipping from *Amarillo Star-Telegram,* n.d. [1941], JLMC/APL; Cohea, Interview with Mrs. Frank Mitchell.

18. McCarty, *Maverick Town,* 187.

BIBLIOGRAPHY

PUBLISHED MATERIAL

Annual Report of the Commissioner of Indian Affairs, 1874. Washington, D.C.: Government Printing Office, 1874.

Anonymous. "Jess Jenkins." *The Cattleman,* 34 (September, 1947): 4.

Archambeau, E. R. "Pioneer Panhandle Settler Recalls Origin, Early Days, of Old Tascosa." *Amarillo Times,* February 28, 1946.

————, ed. "Old Tascosa: Selected News Items from the *Tascosa Pioneer, 1886–1888.*" *Panhandle-Plains Historical Review* 39 (1966) 1–183.

————. "British Contribution to the Opening Up of the West." *English Westerners Tally Sheet* 14, no. 2 (Jan.–Feb. 1968): 2–6, and no. 3 (Mar.–Apr. 1968): 1–4.

Barron, Robert. *Lieutenant Colonel N. A. M. Dudley Court of Inquiry, Fort Stanton, New Mexico, 1879.* Lincoln County War Series, 4 vols. El Paso: n.p., 1955.

Boethel, Paul C. *On the Headwaters of the Lavaca and the Navidad.* Austin: n.p., 1967.

Browning, James A. *Violence Was No Stranger,* Vol 2. Douglasville, Ga.: n.p., 2002.

Bryan, Howard. *Wildest of the Wild West.* Santa Fe: Clear Light Publishers, 1988.

————. *Robbers, Rogues and Ruffians.* Santa Fe: Clear Light Publishers, 1991.

————. *True Tales of the American Southwest: Pioneer Recollections of Frontier Adventures.* Santa Fe: Clear Light Publishers, 1998.

Butler, Anne. *Daughters of Joy, Sisters of Misery: Prostitutes in the American West, 1865–90.* Urbana: University of Illinois Press, 1985.

Cabe, Ernest, Jr. "A Sketch of the Life of James Hamilton Cator." *Panhandle-Plains Historical Review* 6 (1933).

Carlson, Paul H. *The Buffalo Soldier Tragedy of 1877.* College Station: Texas A&M University Press, 2003.

————. *Deep Time and the Texas High Plains.* Lubbock: Texas Tech University Press, 2005.

Carroll, H. Bailey. "Nolan's 'Lost Nigger' Expedition of 1877." *Southwestern Historical Quarterly* 44 (July 1940): 55–75.

Carroll, Murray L. "As an Outlaw and Escape Artist Dan Bogan Was the Real McCoy." *Journal of the Western Outlaw-Lawman Association* 2, 1 (spring–summer 1992): 10–15, 28.

Cashion, Ty. *A Texas Frontier: The Clear Fork Country and Fort Griffin, 1849–1887.* Norman: University of Oklahoma Press, 1996.

Chamberlain, Kathleen. *Billy the Kid and the Lincoln County War: A Bibliography.* Albuquerque: University of New Mexico Press, 1997.

Chesley, Hervey E. *Adventuring with the Old Timers: Trails Traveled—Tales Told.* Ed. Byron

Price. Midland, Tex.: Nita Stewart Haley Memorial Library, 1979.

Chrisman, Harry E. *The Ladder of Rivers: The Story of I. P. (Print) Olive.* Athens: Ohio University Press, 1950.

Clay, John. *My Life on the Range.* Chicago: n.p., 1924.

Cook, John R. *The Border and the Buffalo.* Austin: State House Press, 1989.

Connor, Seymour V. "Early Ranching Operations in the Panhandle: A Report on the Agricultural Schedules of the 1880 Census." *Panhandle-Plains Historical Review* 27 (1954).

Curry, George. *George Curry, 1861–1947.* Ed. H. B. Hening. Albuquerque: University of New Mexico Press, 1958.

DeArment, Robert. *Bat Masterson: The Man and the Legend.* Norman: University of Oklahoma Press, 1979.

———. *Bravo of the Brazos: John Larn of Fort Griffin, Texas.* Norman: University of Oklahoma Press, 2002.

———. *Deadly Dozen: Twelve Forgotten Gunfighters of the Old West.* Norman: University of Oklahoma Press, 2003.

Devereaux, Jan. "Jagville." *Quarterly of the National Association for Outlaw and Lawman History* 28, no. 1 (Jan.–Mar. 2004): 3–17.

Dixon, Olive K. *The Life of "Billy" Dixon, Plainsman, Scout & Pioneer.* Dallas: Southwest Press, 1927.

Dobie, J. Frank. *A Vaquero of the Brush Country.* Dallas: Southwest Press, 1929.

Douglas, C. L. *Cattle Kings of Texas.* Fort Worth: Branch Smith, 1968.

Earle, James H., ed. *The Capture of Billy the Kid.* College Station: Creative Publishing, 1988.

Freeman, G. D. *Midnight and Noonday, or, the Incidental History of Southern Kansas and the Indian Territory, 1871–1890.* Ed. Richard L. Lane. Norman: University of Oklahoma Press, 1984.

Gard, Wayne. *The Great Buffalo Hunt.* New York: Alfred A. Knopf. 1959.

Garrett, Pat F. *The Authentic Life of Billy the Kid: An Annotated Edition with Notes and Com-mentary.* Ed. Frederick Nolan. Norman: University of Oklahoma Press, 2000.

Gilbert, Miles, Leo Remiger, and Sharon Cunningham, comp. *Encyclopedia of Buffalo Hunters and Skinners,* vol. 1, A-D. Union City, Tenn.: Pioneer Press, 2003, 242–45.

Gober, Jim. *Cowboy Justice: Tale of a Texas Lawman.* Lubbock: Texas Tech University Press, 1997.

Goerte, Dorothy Blohm. *After Half Moon: A History of Shiner, Texas, 1887–1975.* La Grange, Tex.: Fayette Publishing Co., 1976.

Gressley, Gene M. *Bankers and Cattlemen.* New York: Alfred A. Knopf, 1966.

Haley, J. Evetts. "Jim East—Trail Hand and Cowboy." *Panhandle-Plains Historical Review* 4 (1931): 39–61.

———. *George W. Littlefield, Texan.* Norman: University of Oklahoma Press, 1943.

———. *Charles Goodnight: Cowman and Plainsman.* Norman: University of Oklahoma Press, 1949.

———. *Fort Concho and the Texas Frontier.* San Angelo: *San Angelo Standard Times,* 1952.

———. *The XIT Ranch of Texas and the Early Days of the Llano Estacado.* Norman: University of Oklahoma Press, 1953.

Haley, James L. *The Buffalo War: The History of the Red River Indian Uprising of 1874.* Norman: University of Oklahoma Press, 1976.

Hamlin, James D. *The Flamboyant Judge.* Canyon, Tex.: Palo Duro Press, 1972.

Hamner, Laura V. *Short Grass & Longhorns.* Norman: University of Oklahoma Press, 1943.

Harkey, Dee. *Mean as Hell.* Albuquerque: University of New Mexico Press, 1948.

Harris, Sallie B. *Hide Town in the Texas Panhandle.* Hereford, Tex.: Pioneer Book Publishers, 1968.

Harris, Theodore D. *Black Frontiersman: The Memoirs of Henry O. Flipper.* Fort Worth: Texas Christian University Press, 1997.

Heitman, Francis B. *Historical Register and Dictionary of the United States Army: From Its Organization, September 29, 1789, to March 2,*

1903. Vol. 1. Urbana: University of Illinois Press, 1965.

Hornung, Chuck. "The Forgotten Davy Crockett, Bad Boy of Cimarron, New Mexico." *Quarterly of the National Association for Outlaw and Lawman History* 5, no. 13 (summer 1988): 8–15.

Howard, Jed. *Phenix and the Wolf: The Saloon Battles of Eddy and the Dave Kemp Saga.* Carlsbad: Southeastern New Mexico Historical Society, 1992.

Hoyt, Henry F. *A Frontier Doctor.* Chicago: Lakeside Press, 1979.

Hunter, J. Marvin. *The Trail Drivers of Texas.* Austin: University of Texas Press, 1985.

Hunter, Lillie Mae. *The Book of Years: A History of Dallam and Hartley Counties.* Hereford, Tex.: Pioneer Book Publishers, 1969.

Jaramillo, Pauline. *Genealogical and Historical Data of the Jaramillo Family, 1598–1989.* N.p.: n.p., 1989.

Johnson, Frank W. *A History of Texas and Texans.* Vol. 4, 1870–71. Chicago and New York: The American Historical Society, 1914.

Julyan, Robert. *The Place Names of New Mexico.* Albuquerque: University of New Mexico Press, 1996.

Kerr, W. G. *Scottish Capital on the American Credit Frontier.* Austin: Texas State Historical Association, 1976.

Kinkaid, Naomi H. "Rath City." *West Texas Historical Yearbook* 24 (Oct. 1948: 40 ff.

Lamar, Howard R. *Charlie Siringo's West: An Interpretive Biography.* Albuquerque: University of New Mexico Press, 2005.

Larson, T. A. *History of Wyoming.* Lincoln: University of Nebraska Press, 1965.

Lea, Tom. *The King Ranch.* 2 vols. Boston: Little Brown & Co. 1957.

McCallum, Henry D., and Frances T. McCallum. *The Wire That Fenced the West.* Norman: University of Oklahoma Press, 1965.

McCarty, John L. "Jess Jenkins, Ragtown Owner." *Amarillo Sunday Globe-News, Golden Anniversary Issue,* August 14, 1938.

———. *Maverick Town: The Story of Old Tascosa.*
Norman: University of Oklahoma Press, 1946.

McCown, Dennis. "'. . . despite big losses . . .': The Last Shooting of the Old West." *Quarterly of the National Association for Outlaw and Lawman History* 24, no. 4 (Oct.–Dec. 2000): 9–16.

———. "Broken Heart, Broken Dreams." *Quarterly of the National Association for Outlaw and Lawman History* 27, no. 4 (Oct.–Dec. 2003): 5–13.

McCubbin, John C. *The McCubbin Papers: An Account of the Early History of Reedley and Vicinity.* Reedley, Calif.: Reedley Historical Society, 1988.

McIntire, Jim. *Early Days in Texas: A Trip to Heaven and Hell.* Norman: University of Oklahoma Press, 1991.

Memorial and Biographical History of Dallas County, Texas. Chicago: Lewis Publishing Co., 1892.

Metz, Leon Claire. *John Selman, Texas Gunfighter.* New York: Hastings House, 1966.

———. *Pat Garrett: The Story of a Western Lawman.* Norman: University of Oklahoma Press, 1974.

———. *Border: The US-Mexico Line.* El Paso, Texas: Mangan Books, 1989.

Miller, Darlis A. *The California Column in New Mexico.* Albuquerque: University of New Mexico Press, 1982.

Mooar, J. W., and James Winford Hunt. *Buffalo Days.* Austin: State House Press, 2005.

Morris, John Miller. *El Llano Estacado.* Austin: Texas State Historical Association, 1997.

———. *A Private in the Texas Rangers.* College Station: Texas A&M University Press, 2001.

Myers, Roger. "Murder in the Panhandle: The Killing of the Casner Brothers." *Journal of the Western Outlaw-Lawman Association* 12, no. 1 (spring 2003): 27–36, 44.

Myers, S. D., ed. *Pioneer Surveyor, Frontier Lawyer: The Personal Narrative of O. W. Williams, 1877–1902.* El Paso: Texas Western College Press, 1966.

Nolan, Frederick, ed. *The Life and Death of John Henry Tunstall.* Ed. Frederick Nolan. Albuquerque: University of New Mexico Press, 1965.

———. *The Lincoln County War: A Documentary History*. Norman: University of Oklahoma Press, 1992.

———. *Bad Blood: The Life and Times of the Horrell Brothers*. Stillwater, Okla.: Barbed Wire Press, 1995.

——— "Boss Rustler: The Life and Crimes of John Kinney." *True West* 43, no. 9 (Sept. 1995): 14–21, and no. 10 (Oct. 1996): 12–19.

———. *The West of Billy the Kid*. Norman: University of Oklahoma Press, 1998.

Northen, William J., ed. *Men of Mark in Georgia*. Vols. 5 and 6. Atlanta: A. B. Caldwell, 1912.

Nye, W. S. *Carbine and Lance*. Norman: University of Oklahoma Press, 1937.

O'Neal, Bill. "They Called Him Mr. Kemp." *True West*, April 1991, 31–32, 37.

Otero, Miguel Antonio, Jr. *The Real Billy the Kid, With New Light on the Lincoln County War*. New York: Rufus Rockwell Wilson, 1936.

Parsons, Chuck. "James W. Kenedy: Cattleman, Texas Ranger, Gambler and 'Fiend in Human Form.'" *English Westerners Brand Book* 34, no. 1 (winter 2000).

———. "James W. Grahame—From Birmingham, England, to Fort Griffin." In Barry C. Johnson, ed. *Vignettes in Violence*. Pp. x, 1–30. London: The English Westerners Society, 2005.

Pierce, Michael D. *The Most Promising Young Officer: A Life of Ranald Slidell Mackenzie*. Norman: University of Oklahoma Press, 1993.

Porter, Millie Jones. *Memory Cups of Panhandle Pioneers*. Clarendon, Tex.: Clarendon Press, 1945.

Raine, William McLeod. *Guns of the Frontier*. Boston: Houghton Mifflin Co., 1940.

Rasch, Philip J. "Alias 'Whiskey Jim'" *Panhandle-Plains Historical Review* 26 (1963): 102–14.

———. "Bad Days at Cimarron." *New York Westerners Brand Book* 18, no. 1 (1971): 12–13.

———. "Murder in American Valley." *English*

Westerners Brand Book 7, no. 3 (April 1965): 2–7.

Rasch, Philip J., Joseph E. Buckbee, and Karl K. Klein. "Man of Many Parts." *English Westerners Brand Book* 5, no. 2 (Jan. 1963): 9–12.

Rath, Ida Ellen. *The Rath Trail*. Dodge City: McCormick Armstrong Co. 1961.

Rathjen, Frederick W. *The Texas Panhandle Frontier*. Austin: University of Texas Press, 1973; rev. ed., Lubbock: Texas Tech University Press, 1998.

Record of Engagements with Hostile Indians within the Military Division of the Missouri from 1868 to 1882. Washington, D.C.: Government Printing Office, 1882.

Reynolds, Bill. *Trouble in New Mexico: The Outlaws, Gunmen, Desperados, Murderers and Lawmen for Fifty Turbulent Years*, Vol. 1, *The A's & B's*. Bakersfield: n.p., 1994.

Rister, Carl Coke. *Fort Griffin on the Texas Frontier*. Norman: University of Oklahoma Press, 1956.

Roberts, Mrs. Lige. "True Son of the Raven Handled a Gun at Tascosa Like Plainsman." *Amarillo News-Globe*, April 6, 1941.

Robinson III, Charles. *The Frontier World of Fort Griffin: The Life and Death of a Western Town*. Spokane: Arthur H. Clark, 1992.

Rosa, Joseph G. *They Called Him Wild Bill*. Norman: University of Oklahoma Press, 1964.

Ryland, Isaac P. "Untold Tales." *Panhandle-Plains Historical Review* 9 (1936): 61–66.

Scamehorn, Lee. *Albert Eugene Reynolds: Colorado's Mining King*. Norman: University of Oklahoma Press, 1995.

Schofield, Donald F. *Indians, Cattle, Ships & Oil: The Story of W. M. D. Lee*. Austin: University of Texas Press, 1985.

Sheets, Margaret. "The LX Ranch." *Panhandle-Plains Historical Review* 6 (1933).

Sheffy, Lester Fields. "Sam Isaacs." *Panhandle-Plains Historical Review* 19 (1946).

———. *The Francklyn Land & Cattle Company: A Panhandle Enterprise, 1882–1957*. Austin: University of Texas Press, 1963.

Shirley, Glenn. *Temple Houston, Lawyer with a Gun.* Norman: University of Oklahoma Press, 1980.

———. *Gunfight at Ingalls: Death of an Outlaw Town.* Stillwater, Okla.: Barbed Wire Press, 1990.

Sinise, Jerry. *George Washington Arrington.* Burnet, Tex.: Eakin Press, 1979.

Siringo, Charles A. *A Cowboy Detective: A True Story of Twenty-Two Years with a World-Famous Detective Agency.* Chicago: W. B. Conkey, 1912.

———. *The Lone Star Cowboy, Being Fifty Years' Experience in the Saddle as Cowboy, Detective and New Mexico Ranger.* Santa Fe: n.p., 1919.

———. *Riata and Spurs.* Rev. ed. Boston: Houghton Mifflin, 1931.

———. *A Texas Cowboy or, Fifteen Years on the Hurricane Deck of a Spanish Pony.* New York: William Sloane Associates, 1950. Reprint, New York: Signet Books, 1951.

Slaven, Frank H. *William C. Moore: Good Guy or Outlaw Bill?* Mesa, Ariz.: n.p., 1996.

Stanley, F. *Rodeo Town: Canadian, Texas.* Denver: World Press, 1933.

———. *The Seven Rivers (New Mexico) Story.* Pep, Tex.: n.p., 1963.

———. *The Texas Panhandle: From Cattlemen to Feed Lots 1880–1970.* N.p.: n.p., 1971.

Stephens, Robert W. *Texas Ranger Sketches.* N.p.: n.p., 1972.

The Stock Exchange Year-Book for 1918. London: T. Skinner, 1918.

Strickland, Rex W., ed. "The Recollections of W. S. Glenn, Buffalo Hunter." *Panhandle-Plains Historical Review* 23 (1949).

Sullivan, Dulcie. *The LS Brand: The Story of a Panhandle Ranch.* Austin: University of Texas Press, 1968.

Thorp, N. Howard (Jack), and Neil McCullough Clark. *Pardner of the Wind.* Caldwell, Idaho: Caxton Printers, 1945.

Thrapp, Dan L. *Encyclopedia of Frontier Biography.* 3 vols. Spokane: Arthur H. Clark, " 1990.

Traylor, Herbert L., and Louise Coe Runnels.

The Saga of the Sierra Blanca. Roswell N.M.: Old-Time Publications, 1968.

Tyree, June, comp. *Tales from Corona and More: History and Families.* Corona, N.M.: n.p., n.d.

Vestal, Stanley. *Queen of Cowtowns, Dodge City 1872–1886.* New York: Harper & Bros., 1952.

Webb, Walter Prescott. *The Texas Rangers: A Century of Frontier Defense.* Boston: Houghton Mifflin, 1935.

West, G. Derek. "The Battle of Adobe Walls—1874." *English Westerners Brand Book* 4, no. 2 (Jan. 1962).

Westermeier, Clifford P. *Trailing the Cowboy.* Caldwell, Idaho: Caxton Printers, 1955,

Westphall, Victor. *Thomas Benton Catron and His Era.* Tucson: University of Arizona Press, 1973.

White, James C. *The Promised Land: A History of Brown County.* Brownwood, Tex.: Starnes Printing Co., 1982.

Wharton, Clarence R. *L'Archéveque.* Houston: Anson Jones Press, 1941.

Yeatman, Ted. *Frank and Jesse James: The Story Behind the Legend.* Nashville: Cumberland House, 2000.

Zeigler, Robert E. "The Cowboy Strike of 1883," *West Texas Historical Association Year Book* 47 (1971): 32–46.

UNPUBLISHED MATERIAL

Haley History Center, Midland, Texas

J. Evetts Haley Collection

J. Evetts Haley Interviews

John Arnot, June 14, 1937, Amarillo, Texas.

Louis P. Bousman, October 23, 1934, Waurika, Okla.

Richard "Dick" Bussell, July 19, 1926., Canadian, Tex.

E. E. Carhart, June 20, 1926.

Lucius Dills, June 12, 1935; August 5, 1937, Roswell, N.M.

James H. East, September 27, 1927, Douglas, Ariz.

Charles Goodnight, August 21, 1929.

Harry Ingerton, June 12, 1937, Amarillo, Texas.

J. Arthur Johnson, March 27, 1946, Midland, Tex.

J. Dave Lard, June 26, 1937, Hot Springs N.M.

J. E. McAllister, July 1, 1926; November 7, 1927, Channing, Tex.

John Meadows, June 13, 1936, Alamogordo, N.M.

D. J. "Dick" Miller, June 23, 1937, Lovington, N.M.

H. Frank Mitchell, June 11, 1935, Amarillo, Tex.

J. W. Mooar, November 25, 1927, Snyder, Tex.

J. Phelps White, January 15, 1927, Roswell, N.M.

Letters

Arrington, Mrs. G. W., to J. Evetts Haley, July 18, 1926.

Bouldin, John, to J. Evetts Haley, March 8, 1937.

East, James, to J. Evetts Haley, February 22, 1928.

Godwin-Austen, E. C., to J. Evetts Haley, August 4, 1925.

Goodnight, Charles, to J. Evetts Haley, July 24, 1925; April 8, April 11, September 2, 1927.

Goodnight, Charles. Undated material No. 11.

Goodnight, Charles. Undated material, Interview No. 14.

Manuscripts

Arrington, G. W. "Organization of Panhandle Counties." Lestor B. Wood Collection.

Bugbee, Helen Frances. "The Story of Thomas Sherman Bugbee and Mary Catherine Dunn." *Panhandle Notes* 1.

Haley, J. Evetts. "Wheeler County, TX. District Court Records. Minutes of District Court, Book 2, p. 125." Handwritten notes.

Willingham, Cape. "History of the First Ranches." *Panhandle Notes* 2, no. 239.

James East Collection

Hoyt, Henry, to James H. East, April 14, 1924; March 12, 1928.

Morley, J. F., to James East, November 29, 1922.

Amarillo Public Library, Amarillo, Texas

John L. McCarty Collection

Armstrong, Marion. "Henry Brown, Lincoln County War Number One."

———. "J. N. Browning."

———. "Ysidro Serna."

———. "Tascosa."

Armstrong, Mel. "Interview with Mr. J. R. Jenkins," Amarillo, Texas, August 29, 1942.

Arnot, John. "My Recollections of Tascosa." Amarillo, Texas, March, 1934.

Gerdes, Bruce. "Ghosts of Comrades Again Walk Among Cottonwoods As Survivor Recalls Bloody Tascosa Affair." Unidentified newspaper clipping, n.d. [1938].

Gober, James R. "A Contention between Capitol and Labor." Unpublished manuscript, 1932. Harold Bugbee Papers.

Hamner, Laura V. Interview with Jesse Jenkins. November 11, 1940.

———. "Jess Jenkins." Amarillo Hotel, July 1942.

"Her 32 Years of Separation from Husband Are Over. Death Ends Long Wait for Belle of Old Tascosa." Clipping from *Amarillo Star-Telegram*, n.d. [1941].

McCarty, John L. Interview with Jess Jenkins. September 16, 1937. Dalhart, Tex.

———. Interview with John Collins. October 9, 1941.

———. Interview with Jess Jenkins and Bob Bonner. August 28, 1942. Amarillo Hotel.

McCarty, John, and Mel Armstrong, "Interview with Garrett H. 'Kid' Dobbs." September 12, 1942. Farmington, N.M.

McCarty, John L., and Laura V. Hamner. "Jess Jenkins, King of Hogtown."

McDonald, E. M., to John L. McCarty, August 25 and November 1, 1928.

Neff, Sebastian "Boss." Diary for his grandson, January 1–August 25, 1939. Manuscript.

Post, Fred. "Reminiscences of Louis Bousman, 1934." Manuscript and undated newspaper clipping of an interview in the *Amarillo News-Globe*.

Potter, Jack. "Tom Emery." Manuscript. N.d.

"Tascosa Directory." Typed copy dated July 26, 1939, from an original owned by Mrs. J. E. May, Vega, Texas.

"Tascosa's Lone 'Old Settler' Recalls the Wild Days in the Little Panhandle Cow Town." Typed copy of a newspaper interview with "Frenchy" McCormick, credited to the *Kansas City Star*, n.d. [1930].

Timmons, Herbert, and Carolyn Timmons. "Life in Tascosa Not All Gun-Play." Unidentified newspaper interview with Mrs. Jim May, n.d.

Center for American History, University of Texas, Austin

Earl Vandale Collection, 1813–1946
Armstrong, Marion. "East Tascosa."
———. "Interview with J. R. Jenkins," September 1, 1942.
———. "W. M. D. Lee."
Arnot, John. "Bill Gatlin."
———. "Early Panhandle Sheriffs."
———. "The First and Only Cowboy Strike."
———. "The Hall Brothers and the Prairie Cattle Co."
———. "The Horse."
———. "Leverton Brothers."
———. "New Mexico Ranches."
———. "Prairie Fires."
———. "Some Smooth Rustlers."
———. "Tascosa Trail: John Arnot's Memoirs of the Old Cowtown."
———. "Thomas Wilson."
Arrington, G. W. to L. V. Hamner, Canadian, TX. September 10, 1916.
Dills, Lucius, to John L. McCarty, December 10, 1942.
———. "Life and Times of the Author."
Hamner, Laura V. "Notes from interview with Jess Jenkins." October 1, 1936.
———. "Jess Jenkins," January 3, 1941.
———. "Notes from an Interview with Jesse Jenkins," September 11, 1936. Corona, N.M.
———. "Visit to the Hip O Ranch." N.d.
Hamner, Laura V., and Annie Teague. "Interviews concerning Old Tascosa," February 1941.

Hoyt, Henry F., to J. Evetts Haley, March 2, 1928. "Old Tascosa."
Lloyd, Dr. O. H. "Oldham County, Texas: An Authentic Historical Brief of Old Tascosa and Oldham County."
McCarty, John L. Interview with Mr. J. R. Jenkins. September 16, 1937. Dalhart, Tex.
McCarty, John L., and Earl Vandale. Interview with Mrs. J. E. May. September 23, 1941. Vega, Tex.
Vandale, Earl. Interview with Billy Jarrett. February 21, 1941. Dalhart, Tex.
———. *Panhandle Pioneers,* Interviews with J. R. Jenkins and W. H. Ingerton, 1937.
Vandale, Earl, and Hervey Chesley, Interview with Sam Baldwin, July 11, 1941.

Oklahoma Historical Society, Oklahoma City

Elder, Ethel V. Interview with Louis P. Bousman, June 17, 1936, Waurika, Okla., Indian Pioneer Papers, vol. 104, 127–30.
———. Interview with Sarah Eldora Cruce Bousman, June 17, 1937, Waurika, Okla., Indian Pioneer Papers, Vol. 16, 38–43.

Jim Gordon Museum, Glorieta, New Mexico

"John Gottlieb Lang." Biographical material. N.d.

Texas Tech University, Lubbock, Texas

John L. McCarty Papers, Southwest Collection
Hamner, Laura V. "Jess Jenkins," Amarillo Hotel, July 1942.

Wyoming State Historical Publications Division, Cheyenne

Campbell, A. C. Manuscript. T. A. Campbell Collection.

Author's Collection

Carnell, Wanda. "Notes from Interview with Ruth Jenkins Gray, Granddaughter to Lon Jenkins." Manuscript. N.d.

————. "Memories of the Jenkins Family." Manuscript. N.d.

Martinez, Lucille A. Archivist, New Mexico State Records Center and Archive. Letter to author, November 11, 2004.

Orton, Susan J. "Charles H. Jenkins (1852–1931), A Biographical Sketch." Courtesy Wanda Carnell.

Rasak, Lanita. Interview with Wanda Duke. 2001.

————. Interview with Geraldine Perkins. 2001.

Wright, Sharon. Director, River Valley Pioneer Museum, Canadian, Texas. Letter to author, September 16, 2004.

DOCUMENTARY RECORDS

Amarillo, Texas, Potter County District Clerk's Office

Death records, 1900–1910.

State of Texas vs. *J. M. Robinson*, Case No. 32, May 16, 1893.

State of Texas vs. *J. M. Robinson*, Case Nos. 110 and 113, June 26, 1894.

State of Texas vs. *Mat Atwood*, Case #46, May 8, 1894

State of Texas vs. *Mat Atwood*, Case #125, May 16, 1895.

Arizona Department of Vital Records

Deaths, 1891–1920.

Carlsbad, New Mexico, Eddy County Clerk's Office

Woodruff, Leonard Albert. Probate Records, 1902–1905.

Clarendon, Texas, Donley County, District and County Clerk's Office

District Court records.

District Court Minute Book II (2).

Dodge City, Kansas, Ford County District Clerk's Office

Marriages Book A (February 19, 1874–December 21, 1886).

Forsyth, Georgia, Monroe County Clerk's Office

Deed Record Book (O) 1–340 (February 10, 1858).

Gainesville, Texas, Cooke County Clerk's Office

Marriage Records, December 9, 1884.

Hallettsville, Texas, Lavaca County Clerk's Office

District Court Records, Civil Case No. 2343.

Marriage Records (Vol. E).

Hamilton, Texas, Hamilton County Clerk's Office

District Court Records, *State of Texas* vs. *Daniel Bogan*, Case No. 674, and *State of Texas* vs. *David Kemp*, Case No. 662.

La Grange, Fayette County, Texas.

Marriage Records (Vol. 4).

Athens, Limestone County, Alabama.

Marriage Book (1832–62).

Raton, New Mexico, Colfax County County Clerk's Office

Marriage Book (A).

Tucson, Arizona, State of Arizona, Office of Vital Records

Deaths, 1891–1920.

Death certificate, Caleb B. Willingham.

Seymour, Texas, Baylor County Clerk's Office

District Court Records, *State of Texas* vs. *Thomas Harris*, Case No. 273.

Texas State Archives, Austin

Arnim, William

Convict Record Ledger, Prisoner 5339.

Judge L. W. Moore to Gov. C. A. Culberson, May 14, 1896.

Dept. of State: Reasons for Executive Clemency File 4010, June 15, 1896.

Britton, James Magruder. Adjutant General Service Records, Frontier Battalion, Box 401–177.

Garrett, Pat F.

Garrett, Pat. F., to Gov. John Ireland, April 28 and to W. H. King, May 19, 1884, Ireland Papers, June–December, 1884.

Gough, John B.

Convict Record Ledger, Prisoner 2936.
Conduct Register, Prisoner 2936.

Harris, G. B.

Pension application, August 30, 1913.

Isaacs, George

Convict Record Ledger, Prisoner 15531.
Conduct Register, Prisoner 15531.

Kemp, David

Petition "To His Excellency the Hon. John Ireland, Governor of the State of Texas." N.d. [1887].

Eidson, J. A., to Gov. L. S. Ross, September 2, 1890. Texas Department of State, File 538.

Texas State Penitentiaries: Certificate of Prison Conduct, January 13, 1887.

Convict Record Ledger, Huntsville, Texas, Book 1998–038/151.

Texas Department of State, File 538, *State of Texas* vs. *David Kemp*, "Reasons for Executive Clemency," January 1, 1887.

Kenedy, James W.

Records of the Adjutant General, Leander H. McNelly, Company Muster and Pay Roll records.

Largus, Frank

Convict Record Ledger, Prisoner 1051.

Rudolph, Charles F.

Convict Record Ledger, Prisoner 57960.
Conduct Register, Prisoner 57960.

Tulia, Texas, Swisher County Clerk's Office

County Commissioners Court dockets, July 1890–August 1891.

Vega, Texas, Oldham County and District Clerk's Office

District Court Minute Book (1).
Judges State Docket Book (1).
Marriage License Record (1).
Records of the Commissioners Court (1 and 2).

Wyoming State Archives, Cheyenne

Laramie County Commissioners Journal (C) 352 (January 4, 1887).

Laramie County Prison Calendar, 1888/Criminal Case 173. *Territory of Wyoming* vs. *William Moore.*

Laramie County Sheriff Prison Calendar (1) 29.

Territory of Wyoming, Court Docket 3, 137.

Miscellaneous Archival Material

Ahr, Wayne, College Station, Texas, to author, July 20, 2002.

Bailey, Kenneth R., West Virginia Historical Society, Charleston, Va., to author, March 27, 2002.

Brice, Donaly, Texas State Archives, to author, December 3, 2004.

Briggs, Theodore, Pension File, Dept. of the Interior, Bureau of Pensions, National Archives and Records Administration, Washington, D.C.

Brown, Quincy, Potter County District Clerk's Office, to author, August 24, 2005.

Capitol Freehold & Land Investment Co., Records of Extraordinary General Meetings, April 19 and May 8, 1918. Ref. BT31/14803/21322. EGM. August 4 and 20, 1894. Ref. BT31/3135/18063. Public Record Office, Kew, London.

———. Notice of Debenture Issue, October 10, 1907, Ref. BT31/14803/21322.

Carter, Kathy, and Alicia McDonald, Fayette County Heritage Museum and Archive, Flatonia, Texas, to the author, January 3, 2001.

Chisum, Sallie, *Notebook.* Historical Society for Southeast New Mexico, Roswell.

Cochran, Lois, Records Coordinator, City of Cleburne, Texas, to author September 9, 2004.

Cohea, Mrs. C. May. "Interview with Mary A. Snider," n.d. Library of Congress, Manuscript Division, WPA Federal Writers' Project Collection.

———. "Related by S. P. Merry." N.d. Amarillo, Texas, District #16, *Panhandle Pioneers*.

———. Interview with Mrs. Frank H. Mitchell. March 25, 1938. Library of Congress, Manuscript Division, WPA Federal Writers' Project Collection.

Compton, Maj. C. E., to Acting Adjutant General. Dept. of Missouri, July 16, 1874. Letters Received, Dept. of Missouri. Records of the Adjutant General's Office, Record Group 75. National Archives and Records Administration, Washington, D.C.

Dudley, Col. N. A. M., Commanding, Fort Stanton, to Acting Assistant Adjutant General, District of New Mexico, September 7, 1878. Consolidated File 1405, 1878, Adjutant General's Office, Microfilm M666, rolls 397–98. National Archives and Records Administration, Washington, D.C.

Gallegos, Hilario. Memoir. 1872. Hayden Biography Collection, Arizona State University, Tempe.

Gildea, A. M. "Gus," to Maurice G. Fulton, December 14, 1929. Special Collections, University of Arizona, Tucson.

Gunter, Jot, to A. L. Matlock. March 15, 1883. Gunter and Munson Collection, Texas Tech University Library, Lubbock.

Hewitt, James R. to author, 2003.

Howard, Mrs. J. W., to Winnie D. Hale. February 1941. John L. McCarty Papers, Texas Tech University Library, Lubbock.

Moore, W. C. Oath of Commission, September 12, 1882. Muster Roll, New Mexico Volunteer Militia, Valencia County, Adjutant General Collection, Box 10831, New Mexico State Records Center and Archive, Santa Fe.

Muster Roll of Company F, 6th Regiment. Georgia Volunteer Infantry.

Nelson, Orville H. "The Story of the First Panhandle Stockmen's Association," February 12, 1926, J. Evetts Haley Collection, Panhandle-Plains Historical Museum, Canyon, Texas.

New Mexico Office of Vital Records, Santa Fe, to author, November 19, 2004.

Polk, Cal. "Life of C. W. Polk, Commenced January 25, 1896." Author's collection, courtesy Mrs. Jessie Polk McVicar, Burneyville, Okla.

Reck, Joe, Armstrong County and District Clerk, to author, September 22, 2004.

Taylor, Susan D. Probate Judge, Camilla, Ga. to author, September 14, 2004.

Vivian, Lawrence and Helena, to author, August 6, 2005.

Wallace, John Francis [Frank Clifford]. "Deep Trails in the Old West." Author's collection, courtesy Michael E. Winter, Beebe, Ark.

Wallace Collection, Indiana Historical Society, Indianapolis.

Willingham, Isaac. Service Record. National Archives and Records Administration, Washington, D.C.

U. S. Bureau of the Census

Bernalillo County, N.M., 1930.

Brown County, Tex., 1910.

Cameron County, Tex., 1860.

Colfax County, N.M., 1870.

Dallas County, Tex., 1850, 1870, 1880.

Deaf Smith County, Tex., 1880.

Ellis County, Tex., 1870, 1880.

Fayette County, Tex., 1870, 1880.

Hamilton County, Tex., 1870, 1880.

Hartley County Tex., 1880, 1890.

Hidalgo County, Tex., 1880.

Lafayette County, Mo., 1860.

Lauderdale County, Ala., 1900.

Lavaca County, Tex., 1860, 1870, 1880.

Limestone County, Ala., 1850.

Lincoln County, Ga., 1850.

Lincoln County, N.M., 1880.

Merced County, Cal., 1870.

Mitchell County, Ga., 1860.

Monroe County, Ga., 1870.

Montague County, Tex., 1880.

Moore County, Tex., 1900.

Mora County, N.M., 1870.
Nueces County, Tex., 1870.
Oldham County, Tex., 1880.
Potter County, Tex., 1880, 1900, 1910, 1920.
Roberts County, Tex., 1910.
San Miguel County, N.M., 1870.
Shackelford County, Tex., 1880.
Stephens County, Tex., 1880.
Washington County, Ill., 1870.
Wheeler County, Tex., 1880.

*United States Agricultural Census,
Hartley County, 1890.*

Newspapers

Albuquerque [NM] Daily Democrat
Albuquerque Morning Journal
Amarillo [TX] Sunday News-Globe
Amarillo Times
Austin [TX] Daily Democratic Statesman
Baker [OR] Record Courier
Barber County [KS] Mail
Brownwood [TX] Bulletin
Canadian [TX] Record
Cheyenne [WY] Daily Leader
Cheyenne Daily Sun
Cheyenne Democratic Leader
Cheyenne State Leader
Cheyenne Sun
Cimarron [NM] News
Corpus Christi [TX] Caller
Dalhart Texan
Dallas Morning News
Dallas Weekly Herald
Dodge City [KS] Daily Globe
Dodge City Globe Live-Stock Journal
Dodge City Messenger
Dodge City Times
Eddy [NM] Argus
Eddy Current
Ellsworth [KS] Reporter
Ellsworth [KS] Reporter
Ford County [KS] Globe
Fort Collins [CO] Courier
Fort Griffin [TX] Echo
Fort Worth [TX] Democrat
Fort Worth [TX] Gazette

Fort Worth Texas Live Stock Journal
Fresno [CA] Weekly Expositor
Hallettsville [TX] Tribune
Investors Guardian [London]
Kansas State Record
Kinsley [KS] Republican
Laramie [WY] Sentinel
Las Vegas [NM] Sentinel
Lusk [WY] Herald
Mobeetie [TX] Panhandle
Pampa [TX] Daily News
Pecos Valley [NM] Argus
Perryton [TX] Herald
Providence Journal
Roswell [NM] Register-Tribune
Sacramento Union
Santa Fe Daily New Mexican
Sheridan [WY] Post-Enterprise
Shiner [TX] Gazette
Tascosa Pioneer
Times [London]
Trinidad [CO] Weekly Advertiser
Visalia [CA] Weekly Delta
Warrensburg [MO] Standard
Waurika [OK] News-Democrat
Weatherford [TX] Exponent

Internet Resources

Handbook of Texas Online
"Amarillo, Texas."
"Arrington, George Washington."
"Beals, David Thomas."
"Browning, James Nathan."
"Boyce, Albert Gallatin."
"Cator, James Hamilton."
"Channing, Texas."
"Coburn, James M."
"Dubbs, Emanuel."
"Francklyn Land and Cattle Co."
"Frying Pan Ranch."
"Grass-Lease Fight."
"Isaacs Brothers."
"Isaacs, George W."
"Jenkins, Charles H."
"Kenedy, Mifflin."
"Lee, William McDole."

"LS Ranch."

"LX Ranch."

"Mabry, William S."

"McAllister, Jordan Edgar."

"McGee, Thomas T."

"New Zealand Sheep Company"

"Olive, Isom Prentice."

"Prairie Cattle Company."

"Quarter Circle T Ranch."

"Rocking Chair Ranch."

"Sanborn, Henry Bradley."

"Torrey, Ellsworth."

"Turkey Track Ranch."

"Vidal, Adrian J."

"Willingham, Caleb Berg."

"Willis, Frank."

Websites

http://freepages.genealogy.rootsweb.com/~gazet
teer2000/

http://ftp.rootsweb.com/pub/usgenweb/tx/
swisher/court/ctdocket.txt

http://www.PanhandleNation.com

http://www.rootsweb.com/txoldham/boothillcem

http://www.rootsweb.com/~orbaker/database/
baker/aqwg298.htm#7081

http://www.texasbeyondhistory.net

http://www.wyomingtalesandtrails.com

INDEX

Page numbers in *italics* refer to illustrations.

———— ⚭ ————

McCormick, George, 150

McCormick, "Mickey," 50, 99, 140–141, 233, 259, 268–274, *269*, *274*

McCoy, William ("Bill"). *See* Gatlin, Bill

McCoy's Addition, (Abilene, Kansas), 269. *See also* Beer Garden

McCracken, John, 70

McCrickett, Mr., 217, 234

McCullough, Henry, 100, 138–140, 141, 289n24, 295n5

McCulloch, John, 39

McCure, Hugh B., 15–17

McDonald, Bill, 257

McDonald, Ella Sheets, 41, *189*, 305n17

McFadden, T. M., 30

McGahy, I. B. J., 295n9

McGee, Mary Blandy Taylor, 298n14

McGee, Talbott, 298n14

McGee, Tom, *151*, 152–154, *153*, 297–298n14

McGinnis, Chief Justice, 178

McGraw, Lizzie P. *See* McCormick, "Frenchy"

McGregor, A. W., 317n6

McGregor, Mary Jerusha ("May"). *See* Rudolph, Mary Jerusha (McGregor)

McGuire, T. W., 314n26

McIntire, James ("Jim"), 67, 74–75, 114–116, 234, 285n15, 285n8

McKaney & Hamburg, 33

McKenzie, Dan, 153

McKenzie, Murdo, 261

McKinley (tramp), 255

McKunmon, E. A., 264

McMasters, James ("Jim Mac"), 40, *40*, 41, 59, 69, 89, 93, 98, 103, 104, 138, *161*, *162*, *168*, *170*, 208, 239, 254, 259, 281n2, 281n3, 288n7, 288n8, 290n37

McMasters & Mabry store, 160

McMillan, New Mexico, 204

McMurray, Samuel, 285n5, 317n28

McNab, Frank, 29, 31, 278n18, 279n22

McNalty, Richard E., 62, 64, 112

McNelly, Leander H., 53–54

McNew, Bill, 304n36

McNulty, Richard E. *See* McNalty, Richard E.

McSween, Alexander, 45–46, 75, 279n22

McSween, Susan, 75

Meade City, Kansas, 55, 130

Meadows, Jim, 156, 165–166, *167*, 171

Meckley, Elizabeth. *See* Dubbs, Elizabeth (Meckley)

Mecosta County, Michigan, 58

Medicine Lodge, Kansas, 154

Medicine Lodge Treaty, 4

Meek (ranched in Bugbee Canyon), 235

Meek, Martha. *See* Arnot, Martha Meek

Meeks, George, 310n23

Meeks, Ike, 310n23

Mercer, Asa Shinn, 100, 289n25

Merchant, Clairborne W., 236

Methodist religion, 97

Mescalero Apaches, 16, 34, 45-46, 79

"Mexican Joe." *See* Camps, "Mexican Joe"

Mexicana, Antonio, 69–70, 285n17

Miami, Texas, 135

Middleton, John, 49

Mier, Mexico, 52

Miles, Nelson A., 6–7

Miley, Charles, 302n11

Miller, Benjamin, 150

Miller, Dutch Phoebe, 101, 141, 289n26

Miller, Jim, 144

Miller, L. D., 199–200

Milligan, Bill, 35

Mill Iron ranch, 262

Mineral Wells Herald, 248

Mitchell, Bob, 103–104

Mitchell, Emma L. *See* Briggs, Emma L. Mitchell

Mitchell, Frank, 208, 215, 272

Mitchell, Georgia Byrum, 215

Mitchell, H. F., 251

Mitchell, Ida (Mrs. Moore), 291n28

Mitchell, Jim, 26, 278n9

Mitchell Canyon, 26

Mitchell County, Texas, 236

Mitchell County, Georgia, 128

Mitchell (lynched rancher), 283n3

Mitchison County, Texas, 122

Mobeetie, Texas, 32, 40, 41, 50, 66–68, *67*, 71, 93, 94, *95*, 100, 105, 123, 125, 130–132, 135, 137, 140, 164, 169, 199, *200*, 201, 203, 209, 212–213, 220–222, 244, 248, 256, 268, 271

Mobeetie Mollie, 44

Monroe, Tom, 96, 164
Monroe County, Georgia, 128–129
Mont, A. L. ("Long John"). *See* Long, John
Montague County, Texas, 137, 208, 245–246
Montgomery, R. E., 234, 236–237
Montoya, Mariano, 11, 159
Montoya, Pascual, 159
Mooar, John Wesley, 3
Mooar, J. Wright, 2, 4, 319n16
Moody, Robert, 78
Moody-Andrews ranch, 298n14
Moon, Jack, 301n
Moonlight, Thomas, 180
Moore, Anna Mary, 112
Moore, Clempson. *See* Moore, William C. ("Bill")
Moore, Harriet, 110
Moore, Jenny F. Wright, 109, 111, 112
Moore, Jim, 170–171
Moore, L. W., 91
Moore, William C. ("Bill" "Outlaw Bill"), 19,
    43, 47, 80, 88, 107–116, *108*, 132, 252,
    290n3, 290n5, 291n28
Moore County, Texas, 93, 225, 239
Moore Creek, Texas, 62
Mora County, New Mexico, 9, 10
Morgan, Ed, 42
Morgan, Mrs. William, 180
Morley, J. F., 88–89
Morley, Michigan, 58
Morris, Al, 243, *265*, 316n18
Morris, J. A., 144
Morris, J. N., 43
Morris Chapel, 203
Morrison, Alexander L., Sr., 114–115
Morrison, J. N., 62
Morrison, Tom W., 62
Morrow, Charley, 43
Morrow, T. F., 246
Moulton, Texas, 91
Mountainair, New Mexico, 232
Mulberry, Texas, 118
Murfreesboro, Tennessee, 129
Murphy, Dr. John Henry, 13–14
Murphy & Co., L. G. ("The House"), 45, 72,
    75, 282n28
Myers, Alexander Charles ("Charley"), 2, 4, 5,
    284n7

Nacogdoches, Texas, 236
Nashville, Tennessee, 26
Nations, Berry, 224, 315n3
National Hotel (Cimarron, New Mexico), 39
Native Americans, 1. *See also specific tribes*
Navajos, 16, 159
Nay, Bill, 35
Neatherlin, Mary A. *See* Dow, Mary A.
    Neatherlin
Nebo, Charlie. *See* Neebow, Charlie
Neebow, Charlie, 46
Neff, Sebastian ("Boss"), 191, 206–207, 305n22
Neil, Doc, 35
Neill, Hyman G. ("Hoodoo Brown"), 284n4
Neis, Tony, 115
Nelson, Judge Orville H., 78, 286n1
Newcombe, "Bitter Creek," 153
Newell, Johnny, 46
New Hampshire Academy, 25
New Orleans, Louisiana, 26, 65, 181, 271
Newton, Kansas, 269
New York & Texas Land Company, 122, 212
New York City, New York, 119, 122
New Zealand Sheep Company, 11, 65
Nichols, Tom, 175, 180, 303n30
Nicholson, William. *See* Nickel, William
Nickel, William ("Slap Jack Bill, Pride of the
    Panhandle"), 19, 277n12
Nickell, G. F., 144, 302n10
Nigger Hill, Texas, 35
Nobility Ranch, 123, 164
Nocona Argus, 248
Nogal, New Mexico, 79, 227
Nolan, Agapito, 29
Nolan, Nicholas, 35, 36, 68–69, 280n11
Nolan, Thomas ("Uncle Tom"), 199, 309n16
Nolan County, Texas, 181
Nolan expedition, 33, 60, 68
Norman, Oklahoma, 231
North Abington, Massachusetts, 25
Northfield, Minnesota, xv, 13
North Fork (Red River), 60, 95, 131
North Palo Duro Creek, Texas, 62, 183
North Star restaurant (Tascosa), 189
Northwestern Livestock Journal, 289n25
Northwest Mining Convention, 227
Norton, A. B., 66–68

www.ingramcontent.com/pod-product-compliance
Lightning Source LLC
Chambersburg PA
CBHW08032427C326
41927CB00014B/3088